Chinese Communicating Interculturally

Li Mengyu
Michael H. Prosser

Chinese Communicating Interculturally

North American edition of:

Communicating Interculturally
Higher Education Press, Beijing, P.R.C.

Higher
Education
Press

Dignity Press
World Dignity University Press

This edition published by:
World Dignity University Press,
an imprint of Dignity Press
16 Northview Court
Lake Oswego, OR 97035, USA
www.dignitypress.org

Design and copyediting: Uli Spalthoff
Front cover images: Toronto Skyline, by Andreas Meck
Great Wall of China, by Bjoern Kriewald

Printed on paper from environmentally managed forestry:
http://www.lightningsource.com/chainofcustody

Book website: www.dignitypress.org/communicating-interculturally
ISBN 978-1-937570-28-6

Contents

List of Guest Essays and Authors

Chapter Seven: Contemporary Youth

Chapter Eight: Cultural Media

Chapter Nine: Intercultural Communication in Business, Training and Education

Chapter Ten: Intercultural Theories and Research

MA Thesis Abstracts in Chapter 10 (Shanghai International Studies University)

Preface to the North American Edition

Professor Li Mengyu of Ocean University of China and I cooperated very well as intercultural authors in developing an intercultural communication textbook for Chinese university students, entitled *Communicating Interculturally*, which was published in 2012 by Higher Education Press in Beijing. We have been very pleased at the long and very gracious foreword composed by Professor Jia Yuxin of the Harbin Institute of Technology and long time President of the China Association for Intercultural Communication.

Although there are now many English language books on intercultural communication also published in English by various Chinese university presses, *Communicating Interculturally* is the first book on the topic specifically for Chinese university students. An important contribution has been made by Professor Li's rich experience as a native Chinese expert on intercultural communication as seen in many of the examples which she provides in the book. Her scholarly opportunities in the West, especially the United States and the United Kingdom, have given her a strong understanding both of Chinese and Western theories, concepts, and practical examples for the Chinese students' greater understanding of various aspects of intercultural communication. Additionally, joint intercultural scholarly co-

operation is very important in the academic field of intercultlural communication, and we are pleased to have had this precious opportunity to be joint authors on this project, with her as the first author.It has been my pleasure to be her American coauthor.

When we first proposed the title to Higher Education Press, *Chinese Communicating Interculturally*, it became clear that since the book was for Chinese univerity students, the word *Chinese* in the title for a Chinese readership seemed unnecessary. However, for the North American edition it is reasonable to add back the word *Chinese*, so that potential readers will be aware that the book is not specifically a book for American, but still as a book oriented toward Chinese students, of considerable potential interest to American readers in illustrating the nature of Chinese communicating interculturally.

Since this is an American edition, we have also agreed to remove the Chinese introduction by Professor Li, and the Chinese references at the end of chapters and at the end of the book's References section.

Shortly before the book was published by Higher Education Press, I offered complementary prepublication online versions of the book on a communication list serve, and about 50 persons requested a copy.Thus we hope that for those Western readers and also Chinese living in the West interested in intercultural communication from a mixed Chinese/Western perspective, will find this book to be very valuable and instructive. Both of us are using the book in our classes in Chinese universities, with good results, and some students indicating that not only is the book helping them to understand cultural communication more broadly, and with Chinese characteristics, but that the sophisticated vocabulary in the book is very good for their increased usage of words that are common in English and good background for taking GRE, and English language exams.

We are especially grateful to Dr. Uli Spalthoff of Dignity Press and Sun Yunpeng of Higher Education Press for their cooperation in making this joint Dignity Press/Higher Education Press volume available.

Your comments are welcome to Li Mengyu (limengyu1968@163.com) and Michael H. Prosser (prossermichael@gmail.com).

Michael H. Prosser, Ph.D.,
Distinguished Professor,
College of International Studies,
Yangzhou University, Yangzhou, China,
autumn 2013

September 1, 2013

Foreword

My colleagues and I never wavered in our conviction that you are always creating wonders. It is really gratifying to let the readers—teachers and students—know that scholarly and sophisticated soundness in the *Dialogue* will find a practical resonance with them. The *Dialogue* is truly what is called for by 21st century as a response to the challenge of intercultural communication predisposed by globalization. I really enjoy reading and re-reading this coauthored book. I consider it my honor to write the foreword.

I have been reading or to be exact, learning intercultural dialogues from this book. It is really rewarding. It is not only original in content but also in form. I believe what Marshall McLuhan stated "The medium is the message," and the form of the creation is itself really the message as the Platonic Dialogue is the source of ethical enquiries and philosophical explorations. The theory behind the content is updated as it is based on the synthesis of well-established etic and emic approaches and sociopsychological, interpretive, and critical approaches and what is more, the project is embedded in the perspective of cultural globalization.

I remember the author's first book that laid the foundation for intercultural study in America is also called dialogue, *The Cultural Dialogue*. I used that book as a rich resource in 1987 when I taught intercultural communication in the United States. The dialogue in this book just like the Cultural Dialogue sparkles with wit, is the heritage of ancient Greek philosophy. You really sound like a philosopher before anything else, always full of wit and penetrating ideas. The Dialogue is at the same time serious and light hearted and the serious side of the Dialogue is imbued with authoritative knowledge while the light-hearted side always shines with humor and induces students' interesting responses with a grain of humor, too.

The two authors, Michael Prosser and Li Mengyu, who come together to make this intercultural communication book possible are from very different cultural background and research traditions. I believe this intercultural cooperation, added by the authentic stories of personal experience of the "imaginary" students across the globe renders this book unique and truly international, intercultural, and multicultural. Now let me briefly introduce the coauthors here so that by the end of the book the readers will have a complete understanding of who they are and why they are important to the readers.

I first met Li Mengyu of Ocean University of China at the 2007 China Association for Intercultural Communication eighth Conference which my colleagues and I hosted at Harbin Institute of Technology. Later, we met again at the Beijing Foreign Studies University ninth Conference in 2009, as well as at Kumamoto Gakuin University in Japan during September, 2009, and still later in Guangzhou for the International Association for Intercultural Communication Conference in 2010. After our first meeting, she was a visiting scholar at the University of Louisville in Kentucky, where she worked with the outstanding IAICS* leader, Professor Robert St. Clair with whom I have also worked closely. Now, as author or coauthor of several books on comparative literature, she teaches intercultural communication and foreign literature at Ocean University of China and frequently has attended conferences on intercultural and international communication in China, and recently at communication conferences in Japan and Singapore.

Professor Michael Prosser and I met for the first time when he was a keynoter at the 2001 CAFIC** Conference in Xi'an, and subsequently again at the 2003, 2005, and 2007 CAFIC conferences where he continued to serve as a keynoter. Also, he was a keynoter at the HIT Conference on Language and Culture in 2004. In the 2009 CAFIC conference, as the CAFIC President, I had the pleasure to present him a special recognition award on behalf of CAFIC for his promotions

---

* Int. Association for Intercultural Communication Studies

** China Association for Intercultural Communication

and contributions to the academic study of intercultural communication in China. In May, 2010, Michael Prosser gave a week of lectures at HIT and as his host I was present at each lecture as well as had the opportunity to introduce each lecture and then comment on it after it was completed. Not only was he a founder of this study in North America, having chaired the first three conferences to create intercultural communication as a field of study, but he was also a critically important voice for its development in China as well. I have had a long time leadership role in both of these professional associations. Thus, it gives me considerable pride to write the foreword for Professors Li Mengyu and Michael Prosser's exceptional intercultural communication text book for Chinese university students, *Chinese Communicating Interculturally*. It might be seen as the Chinese equivalent of the always popular American text in intercultural communication, *Intercultural Communication: A Reader* co-edited by Larry Samovar and Richard Porter in their more than ten editions. While both coauthors have worked closely together in true intercultural cooperation and have integrated the entire text, each has additionally made specific contributions to the text and her/his individual influence is seen in separate chapters and particular essays that each author has written. We have the best of both approaches: an integrated text with intercultural coauthorship and unique contributions to the text. I still remember that Gudykunst in his book *Theorizing about Intercultural Communication* suggested that scholars in Asia create theories in the Asian perspective so that a complete picture will be drawn of what intercultural communication is all about. Now

I am very happy to see that the two authors of this book are making a successful endeavor towards this end.

Professor Hui-ching Chang of the University of Illinois at Chicago writes: "Thanks for sharing your very exciting book with me! It looks like a very good integration of theory and practice, especially effective in inducing students' interest through very thoughtful yet light-hearted dialogue. I am sure it will be well received by students and instructors in intercultural communication!" My HIT colleague, Professor Song Li, President of AICIS, has written: "Thanks for sharing your manuscript with me. As I said earlier the book is a valuable contribution for both academic and the more practically oriented readers. Here's my congratulations again on your completion of the book!"

Professor Aliaa Khidr, MD, PhD of the University of Virginia, and a contributor about the youth in Egypt to Chapter Seven *Contemporary Youth*, has written: "Thank You for this unique opportunity to be part of a true 'across the globe' project. The writing exercise made me personally realize how passionate I am about Egypt and how lucky I was to have lived among such great people. I know that everyone in this book has the same passion and I am looking forward to enjoy seeing each country through their words. I am also very proud of Ali [her twelve-year old son] who shared with us his own thoughts about Egyptian youth. I realize more than ever that whatever our thoughts "as older adults" may be regarding the leadership role of our youth, Tunisian, Egyptian and other Middle Eastern youth have revolutionized them forever!"

In 2009, Peter Zhang Long wrote his Master's thesis in intercultural communication at the Shanghai International Studies University with a longitudinal study on the contributions of Professor Prosser: "Investigations into the Influence of an Intercultural Communication Founder and His Contemporary Scholars," and he received comments from a number of scholars in intercultural and international communication.

Jia Wenshan, PhD, Professor at Chapman University in California, writes: "(1) Michael has continued and expanded Robert Oliver's tradition by writing, lecturing, editing and mentorship. (2) Michael is a visionary with a broad and inclusive and forward-looking intellectual vision on humanity and human communication across cultures. He lives his life, lecturing, researching and teaching by this vision. (3) Michael has mentored a new generation of leading intercultural scholars. My academic life has been significantly influenced by Michael's mentorship. The three English books which I wrote and co-edited on China are possible because of Michael's vision and boldness of action. (4) Michael has also played a central role in the development of IC in China in the past ten years by giving keynote speeches and mentorship of graduate students and other professors including Steve Kulich."

D. Ray Heisey, PhD, Professor Emeritus at Kent State University, comments: "His [Prosser's] Intercommunication book was a landmark in the field as it covered all the important areas of international communication. He covered all of the areas that now have developed into their own fields of specialty and he did this by assembling some of the best scholars in the field. His *Cultural Dialogue* book was an outstanding early textbook for those teachers and scholars in the intercultural area. His focus on the dialogue dimension of the field has continued and expanded for a proper understanding of intercultural communication whether at the interpersonal level or the rhetorical level or the political level." Professor Yun Young Kim, PhD of the University of Oklahoma notes: "When I entered the field of intercultural communication after completing my PhD degree in 1976, Professor Prosser was one of the most prominent figures in the field. All of us are truly indebted to Professor Prosser and his colleagues, whose visionary efforts laid the intellectual and organizational foundation for the field of intercultural communication." Carley H. Dodd, PhD, Professor at Abilene Christian University in Texas, states: "The *Cultural Dialogue* made a huge impact on my early writing, where several articles in the book highly influenced aspects of three chapters in one of my textbooks. I cannot begin to tell you how grateful I am for this contribution, which helped the entire field develop and begin to grow." Professor Emeritus of Syracuse University and the East-West Center at the University of Hawaii, Paul B. Pedersen, PhD comments: "Michael's contribution has been especially strong in networking and developing a professional identity for intercultural communication in the field of communication."

Michael Prosser served as the chair of one of the first doctorates awarded in intercultural communication in the United States to William J. Starosta, PhD, Professor at Howard University in Washington, DC, who writes: "The *Intercommunication* book [1973] was more interdisciplinary than almost any book of its day. It was early, it forced us to look

closely at definitions, and it gave us a platform to see intercultural communication more rhetorically than is done today. Everything we did was worthy of note. We were at the dawn of a discipline. I was the first PhD; Prosser was the first PhD mentor in intercultural [communication]. We were definitional."

His coauthor of *Diplomatic Discourse: International Conflict at the United Nations*, Ray T. Donahue, PhD, Professor at Nagoya Gakuin University in Japan, comments: "The intercultural communication field (IC) can be viewed as having four historical threads: (1) Cultural anthropology (i.e., Edward T. Hall's work); (2) Communication studies, particularly interpersonal communication and rhetorical studies; (3) IC training rooted in group counseling methods (e.g. the T-group method and role play) for intercultural and international relations; (4) Academic coursework in intercultural/international communication. The first three threads were almost simultaneous and together led to the fourth thread of academic coursework, largely in departments of communication or communication studies. Michael H. Prosser made important contributions to the later three threads."

When Steve J. Kulich's and Michael Prosser's book, *Intercultural Perspectives on Chinese Communication*, was published in 2007, Professor Guan Shijie of Peking University, writing in the "Foreword," emphasized: "It is quite illuminating for some scholars to suggest that the ultimate goal of China's IC [intercultural communication] research is to reach harmony: harmony, therefore, becomes one of the special features of China's IC perspective. Professors Kulich and Prosser have committed themselves to the education and research of IC in China for years; and with their initiatives, Shanghai International Studies University has established its SISU Intercultural Institute. They have made positive contributions in promoting China's IC studies with their unique perspectives and connections with Western scholars, and are widely applauded among the Chinese IC scholars."

It is certainly of particular interest to Chinese teachers and students of intercultural communication that at the kind invitation of Professor Li Mengyu, Michael Prosser, who has also coedited or coauthored intercultural research previously with Indian scholars Nemi C. Jain and K.S. Sitaram, and more recently with Zhang Shengyong of Dezhou University, has agreed to coauthor *Chinese Communicating Interculturally* with her.

This textbook has several prominent features.

(1)   Each chapter and the concluding epilogue include a dialogue between an imaginary group of intercultural communication students, an imaginary young Professor Zhang, whose gender we never know in the dialogues, and with the real and much older Michael Prosser himself. Some of the comments above note his networking and interest in cultural dialogue. As Professor Hui-ching Chang comments, these dialogues are both serious and light hearted. There is considerable humor in the dialogues, and at the same time, serious teaching is also taking place as Professor Zhang and Michael Prosser speak authoritatively. Often, also, the imaginary students, who actually represent a cross section of the 2,200 Chinese students that Michael Prosser has taught in China, speak authoritatively with a wide array of topics covered in the different chapters. Some students are nationalistic, some are typically humorous,

some are frivolous, and still others are very serious about their own goals and intercultural development. As Cooper Wakefield at the University of Kansas has suggested: "I think you nailed the Chinese classroom feel and responses from students. Very clever."

(2)   There are more than 30 guest essays, some written by professors in the US; one written by an international banker from Portugal; another written by a professional intercultural trainer from Canada; one written by an American cinema teacher, another by a Chinese teacher on the media, one by a British blogger on language; some by Chinese graduate students studying abroad or recent graduates; and several international writers discussing contemporary youth in different countries or their own intercultural business problems. There are very interesting case studies at the end of each chapter, some theoretical and some very practical. Chapter Three: "Creating Our Own Cultural Stories" includes both cultural stories by the book's coauthors, and also how Chinese and one young Russian see their own cultural backgrounds, and in Chapter Seven: "Contemporary Youth," there are essays not only by Professors Li Mengyu about Chinese youth and Michael Prosser about American youth, but also authoritative essays about youth in Latin America, Egypt, Africa, Belgium, Japan, and Russia, which provide the basis for cross-cultural analysis.

(3)   Each chapter not only includes the introductory dialogue, but substantial academic content on the theme, with both traditional and innovative ideas. Each chapter has a case study, a summary, a dozen thoughtful questions for discussion, intended to make the students understand the nature and development of their

own critical thinking, and additional resources. There are extensive citations throughout the text and a rich reference list. Student readers are considered to be sophisticated enough to understand both the theoretical and practical aspects of the book.

(4) Unlike most of the imported intercultural texts from overseas available in China, this text specifically incorporates Confucian and intercultural communication with Chinese characteristics. That is, this is not a textbook written by authors in the US or elsewhere where a number of references are made to Chinese communication, but it clearly is about Chinese intercultural communication and written specifically for Chinese students who are studying it. No recently coauthored intercultural textbook for Chinese students focuses so specifically on the Chinese situation as does *Chinee Communicating Interculturally.* This gives great benefit to teachers and students in China.

(5) Each chapter has some especially interesting concepts developed that both include traditional understanding of intercultural communication and new thoughts to stimulate the students' broader interests in the study, theories, and practice of intercultural communication. As Deng Xiaoping suggested, one tests theory by real practice, and this text certainly does that.

Now I would like to share with the readers my comments on each chapter.

In Chapter One, Culture, I was enthralled by the well-organized integration of theory and practice, especially by the Platonic Dialogues, which throw the students into an intercultural space. I appreciate the authors' rationale: learning through experiencing and on the basis of the students' and the teachers' personal intercultural experience, which is embedded in the discourse of the Dialogue; authoritative knowledge and theory including intercultural essays, and critical work on case studies and discussions are provided. I like the way the teacher deals with the concept of culture and cultural identity, the most important aspects of intercultural communication. The teacher skillfully gets the imaginary students from different cultural backgrounds actively involved in sharing with each other their interesting and intriguing cultural stories. In this way, the students are expected to learn about what culture is all about. What is also worth mentioning is that they are at the same time introduced to the 21st century in which they are living and by so doing, the students get to know the defining features of globalization, which are best characterized by buzzwords such as multiculturalism and cultural diversity. I like the thoughtful dialogue which is sparkled with wit and shining with humor as it is fun and amusing and induces the students' interest and humorous response. The First Chapter is the first step of the intercultural journey of learning to be human in the direction of global citizenship. Here, in the first step, students may be found to be tentative learners. However, by and by, and by the time they travel to the end of the journey, the Tenth Chapter, they will find themselves confident intercultural communicators.

In Chapter Two, Communication and Intercultural Communication, there is a very well-organized dialogue of virtue in Platonic terms. It is a dialogue of virtue between the

East and the West respectively represented by Greek philosophers such as Socrates, Plato, and Aristotle in the West and Confucius in the East. We are happy to find that the philosophers of both sides shared the same ethical and moral concern that constitutes the core of humanity. It is this universal ethics and moral value that constitutes the core of inter-human or intercultural communication and will make a peaceful and harmonious globe possible. I especially like the authors' emphasis on turning the students into critical thinkers. This is something that is absent in the traditional Chinese education classrooms and should be introduced into the tertiary education. It should be a crucial characteristic of Higher Education in China. I argue that such a development of criticality will lead to critical reflection and the building of capacity for critical awareness of self and otherness in the course of intercultural communication.

In Chapter Three, Creating Our Own Cultural Stories, you are creating wonders again here, my dear buddy. You are a wizard. It is one of the chapters that I like best as from this chapter I have learned what I wished to learn and what I have learned has special meaning to the age of globalization. The identity issue has become more crucial than ever before in this dynamic globalization age, not only because we are often puzzled about who we are but also because everyone of us is being engaged in a ceaseless, unending process of creative self-transformation. I wonder how you could have managed to get so many people from so many different cultures — local, regional, organizational, ethnic, religious, national, and global — to tell their own stories to show who they were, who they are, and who they are yet to become. You are trying to let the people

from different cultures voice out for themselves the global reality: "It is now not so much physical boundaries … that define a community or nation's 'national limits.' Increasingly we must think in terms of communications and transport networks and of the symbolic boundaries of language and culture … as providing the crucial and permeable boundaries of our age" (Morlehy & Robins, 1995). In this light, due to communication and other mediated forms of communication, intercultural communication can be described as a process of intercultural identification in which a person is regarded as an open system evolving throughout life (Bertalanffy, 1968, Ruben & J. Kim, 1975). To live, survive, and develop in this accelerated globalization age, we constantly ask ourselves from time to time who we are and who we may yet to become in relation to others and the global society. I tentatively conclude my learning from this chapter with the following points: (1) We should take a critical view of the "taken-for-granted" concept of culture and cultural identity prevalent in our traditional discourse of intercultural study; (2) In the dynamic and ever-changing globe, every person will remain as culturally distinct, yet interculturally incorporated and globally hybridized. As to what extent people are culturally distinct and globally hybridized, it differs from person to person depending on how creatively they adapt to the dynamic global environment and how open-minded and morally inclusive they are, and (3) Intercultural identification is a process in which everyone of us is involved towards the direction of learning to refine self, adopt a self-other reciprocal orientation, and learning to be human. So, you see, after all, you are getting the students involved in learning to be human. That is, "to engage oneself in a ceaseless, unending process of creative self-transformation" (Tu Weiming, 1998).

Chapter Four, Perceptions, Beliefs, World Views and Values, is a good continuation of the discussion of criticality dealt with in the previous chapter. However, the dialogue starts the discussion of cultural matters such as perception and values with a comparative study of philosophy. The contemporary philosophy in the West is represented by Descartes who moved from subjective certainty to objective certainty, using god-given power of reason and thus leading the mind away from bodily senses, that is, bodily experience while the philosophy in the East is represented by Confucius and Lao Zi, who, unlike Descartes upholding dualism, took the stance that knowledge about the world and self is grounded in human bodily experiences, especially those of the senses. Thus experientialism rather than objectivism, harmony rather than dualism, serve as the defining feature of the Eastern philosophy. However, the authors of this book seem to be saying what is needed today is the innovative combination of these two philosophies. This is a very good start for the discussion of cultural value systems which is the core of human behavior.

In Chapter Five, Cultural Patterns and Cross-Cultural Value Orientations, we find a great storyteller again. It is the vivid and moving true-to-life stories from both the teacher and the students that show us the cultural differences in terms of values, social and cultural norms and conventions, and behavior underpinned by the norms and conventions. Indirectness and directness, for example, are illustrated and expounded in such an interesting way. And the

interesting and humorous cultural stories are naturally followed by insightful knowledge and theories that explain why we behave the way we do.

Chapter Six, Verbal and Nonverbal Communication demonstrates that grasping another language is crucial in intercultural communication. When people travel in a different country or around the world the first thing they encounter are language differences, as the language differences throw them into bewildering and embarrassing moments. Then people tend to think that learning another language may solve all the problems. However, seldom do they realize the importance of nonverbal language. Seldom do they realize that where languages differ, the values, social conventions and social identity differ. As this chapter demonstrates, communicating with people from different cultures is far beyond mastering another language. It shows that language is not merely a symbolic process. It is a social process. However, symbols have meaning only in relation to social, cultural, and intercultural context. Symbols represent, grow out of the dynamic interaction of these parameters. So, the authors successfully inform the students that to understand issues of meaning, identity, and how they influence and are influenced by social, cultural, ethnic, and as well as many other variables, we need to gain insights into the dynamic social, cultural and intercultural processes out of which they grow. Fortunately, the authors successfully create a sociolinguistic and intercultural space in which the students automatically enter into face-to-face interaction both verbally and non-verbally and learn to make appropriate interpretations in different contexts.

In Chapter Seven, Contemporary Youth, you give us a special treat. A special treat in every sense of the word. You invited young people from different cultures to the class to disclose or "act out" who they are or their self-identity. "Some of them are nationalistic, some are typically humorous, some are frivolous, and still others are very serious about their own goals and intercultural development." (M. Prosser: 6) How did you come up with this idea? I will follow your suit in my teaching. So, facts speak louder. By so doing, you don't have to go to the trouble of going all the way through to elaborate theoretically on the differences of cultural identity and values that form the core of identity. I like these young people and their self-identity performance. I like the young Mike. Great! I feel young again. How good it is to be a young guy and to be an intercultural young guy like you. It is very good to understand the broader world in the various essays by authors from several countries and regions.

In Chapter Eight, Cultural Media, we find ourselves traveling around the world again. We just sit in the classroom and enjoy ourselves in sharing with our professors a big variety of communication including different kinds of mediated forms of communication such as books, newspapers, magazines, recordings, movies, radio, television, and the Internet representing almost all cultures in the world. In so doing, what is unknown and unfamiliar in the world is being turned into our new friends. I truly wonder how the authors could be so well-informed and so open-minded. Just imagining Professor Michael knows Han Han, the current Chinese critic and writer. Michael deserves the name of a man of the world. As the authors introduce in this chapter, "mass communication is the process by which ... a message is created and transmitted to a large audience, and the source is typically a professional communicator or a complex organization." To me, the "source" it seems, are the authors of this book If we believe that the medium is the message, then the authors of this book are the message. Thanks to the authors, with your effort, the students and me as well, are getting acquainted with the world famous books, newspapers, magazines, recordings, movies, and so on and in this way, with the world.

In Chapter Nine, Intercultural Communication in Business, Training and Education, the authors spotlight and highlight the role and importance of intercultural communication in the world of international business and trade, and introduce authoritative essays and theories on intercultural training. It is an important subject and necessary as there are few books now related to this topic in China. We must remember that it is global economy that shapes what is known today as globalization. The world market is becoming more and more complex and it is high time we did something to be able to take the pulse of the international business and intercultural trade. Fortunately, the authors provide us with interesting stories from personal intercultural experience to demonstrate the ups and downs people in the business world have been undergoing and how they could possibly manage to avoid touching the tiger's tail.

Chapter Ten, Intercultural Theories and Research, moves beyond what has been covered in the previous chapters by emphasizing the nature of actual intercultural theories and research methodology, using specific facts and examples as illustrations. However, a small space like this chapter is poorly adequate to deal with such a big and complex issue. Fortunately, the authors provide an excellent overview of the major theories currently in use and examine how these theories support the foundations of research in this area. The authors seem to propose an integration of different theories and approaches in their incorporating culture into intercultural communication study. These theories prevalent to date are compatible with each other thus allow for the possibility of integration. I believe the integration of different theories and approaches, especially etic and emic, subjectivistic and objectivistic theories and approaches will enhance our ability to understand intercultural communication. I remember in his early works, William B. Gudykunst stated, "There is nothing more practical than theories." The insightful ideas implied in this statement have far-reaching significance and may always push us in the direction of learning and creating theories so as to enhance our intercultural knowledge and practice. Actual thesis abstracts are very helpful.

The final imaginary epilogue dialogue, "Think Globally and Act Locally," reminds us that we should relativize self and value others, globalize self from within the local and above all, we should learn and unlearn, practice acculturation and deculturation and it is through so doing we can learn to be human before anything else. With that we can grow up interculturally, acquire intercultural personhood, and become global citizens. Let's re-learn what Michael said to heart, "I am neither a citizen of Athens, nor of Greece, but of the world." and "I am neither a citizen of Beijing, Shanghai, Guangzhou, nor Xi'an, nor of China, but of the world!"

In conclusion, we are now coming to the end of our journey of intercultural learning.

We were tentative learners at the very beginning of the journey, and now, when we are nearing to its end, we are proud to say that we have become confident intercultural communicators and explorers.

We all owe this to Professor Prosser and Li Mengyu. We really feel indebted to them. Without their updated knowledge, conscientious teaching, and their intercultural personhood, we can hardly come to where we are today. Before we say goodbye to them, let's remember: the challenge of globalization will always push every one of us in the direction of greater learning, self-refinement, self-other reciprocal orientation, and intercultural or global citizenship.

Jia Yuxin
Harbin Institute of Technology

To the Reader

Welcome to *Chinese Communicating Interculturally,* a textbook written specifically for you as Chinese readers. Before you start learning about the topic, you might ask two questions: "What is it?" "Why should we study it?"

In today's highly interdependent world, individuals, organizations, and nations can no longer live alone. We now live in a global age when all the inhabitants of the earth are interconnected. It is a thrilling experience as well as a great challenge for us to understand people whose cultural backgrounds, identities, perceptions of the world, and verbal and nonverbal messages are different from our own. This is what the book is mainly about, and it will offer us rich theoretical knowledge, various personal experiences, and useful skills as well as instructive research methods related to intercultural communication.

The reason that intercultural communication is a thrilling experience lies in the fact that different people, organizations, and countries can benefit greatly by sharing common interests and appreciating differences in the meantime. However, due to various intercultural barriers, such as misunderstanding, problems in language stereotyping, prejudice, racism, and ethnocentrism, intercultural communication turns out to be a challenging venture that

provides the reasons why we want you to read the book and learn intensively about intercultural communication. In a practical way, your lives are certain to become more and more intercultural as you live in the global society. J. Shen, writing in *China Youth Daily* (2010) calls the post-90s generation "The weathercock of times in transition."

Evelin Lindner (2010) calls for "the creation of a new field, the field of global interhuman communication to complement the field of intercultural communication" because as she says, "humans are naturally cultural ... At a minimum, in an increasingly interconnected world, it is unwise to stay uninformed about the larger world." Thus a major goal in studying intercultural communication is to prepare yourselves for participation in a globalizing culture, but also one with more and more cultural diversity. Paulo Freire, the indigenous educator for Brazilian peasants states: "The ontological vocation of being human is to be fully human, fully human and alive, fully human, alive and aware, and fully human, alive, aware, and creative." It is our goal to improve your own cultural competence and creativity as you must out of necessity become increasingly multicultural individuals, if possible as critical thinkers culturally, and eventually as world citizens. We gratefully acknowledge Socrates' significant statement: "I am neither a citizen of Athens, nor of Greece, but of the world." Through this class, we hope that you will eventually be able to say: "I am neither a citizen of Beijing (Guangzhou, Shanghai, Xi'an), nor of China, but of the world."

In this textbook for you Chinese university students in intercultural communication classes or for any others interested in the topic, there are ten chapters. Each chapter includes the following aspects: an imaginary dialogue with a class of intercultural communication students, an imaginary Chinese teacher Professor Zhang, and Michael Prosser; the academic content of the chapter; a case study; a summary; questions for discussion; and suggested additional readings. The book concludes with references, and the coauthors' biographies. Li Mengyu has taken the initial responsibility for the final proof reading of the whole book, the Chinese Introduction and Chapters 4–6, plus several brief identified essays and Michael Prosser has taken the initial responsibility for Chapters 1–3, 7–10, the dialogues for each chapter, questions for discussion, and other brief identified essays. This procedure has allowed us to work in a complementary fashion, but additionally with sole authorship for some aspects of the book. Both authors take full responsibility for integrating the entire book.

In the chapter dialogues which are imaginary and thus an illusion, Professor Zhang (though imaginary) and Michael (a real coauthor) nevertheless speak authoritatively, as do often the imaginary students as the semester proceeds. Lively classes, with students as critical thinkers, however, should challenge their instructors as happens in these dialogues, and should share not only serious learning, but also joint humor between the faculty members and the students. We see this occurring in these classes.

We are especially grateful to those who have written invited brief essays for the book. Li Mengyu wishes to thank Professor Michael Prosser, Emeritus Professor at the University of Virginia and at Shanghai International Studies University, her coauthor as well as good friend; Professors Jia Yuxin and Song Li at the Harbin Institute of Technology; and her colleagues and students at Ocean University of China. Particularly, she wishes to thank her husband professor Wen Fengqiao and son Wen Haiqi (Kevin) for their love and support. Michael Prosser wishes to thank his former Shanghai International Studies University colleagues: Steve J. Kulich, David Henry, Zhang Hongling, Cooper Wakefield, Ron Lustig, Cherry Chi, Kathy Zhou, Zhang Rui, Zhong Min, and Zhang Shengyong, and his 2200+ Chinese students at Yangzhou University, Beijing Language and Culture University, Shanghai International Studies University, and Ocean University of China, a number of whom have become close and long-term friends. Besides, those who have established their own "opening up" policies by traveling with him to many Chinese cities, Nick Deng, Sean Chen, David Xu, Tony Wei Tong, David Li, Charles Cheng, and Jacky Zhang have all become more internationally oriented since their travels with Michael.

Special thanks are due to his Chinese web-master, Wing Mars, who established Michael's website in 2003 while he was a university student and has maintained it since that time, with a new Wordpress international web version in 2011, as it has expanded to more than 200 essays and many photos, including also Sylvia's and Laura Gosten's articles about him and Peter Zhang Long's MA thesis about him.

Li Mengyu,
Ocean University of China, Qingdao
limengyu1968@163.com

Michael H. Prosser,
Charlottesville, Virginia
prossermichael@gmail.com
International blog: wwwmichaelprosser.com

Chapter ONE

Culture

1.1 Dialogue

These Chinese students are among those in an **imaginary Chinese university intercultural communication class. Professor Zhang is also an imaginary Chinese teacher. Michael is real and a coauthor of** *Chinese Communicating Interculturally.* **As Chinese students often take English names, the females in the class have adopted the following names:** Amelia, Angel, Ava, Catherine, Cherry, Cindy, Coco, Echo, Eva, Fiona, Gloria, Grace, Ivy, Jade, Jasmine, Jenny, Joy, Maria, Michelle, Robin, Ruby, Sara, Sophia, identical twins—Spring and Summer, Tulip, Vivian, and Yolanda. The males have taken the following English names: Ali, Ben, Forest, Jason, Lucky, Mike, Peter, Sunny, Tiger, Tony, and True Nation.

Please note

The comments made by these imaginary students are reasonably consistent with real statements often made in previous Chinese university classrooms taught by Michael Prosser at three different Chinese universities or in conversations with him outside of the classroom situation. They are meant to be illustrative and cannot be generalized to all Chinese students. Comments ascribed to the imaginary Professor Zhang are only illustrative of those which might be made by some Chinese professors in an intercultural communication classroom, but are authoritative as are those of Michael. The statements of a number of students are reasonably authoritative as well often in the dialogues. All of the English student names appearing in the imaginary dialogues are actual English names of students in Michael Prosser's real classes at Chinese universities.

Culture

Professor Zhang:	Good morning, boys and girls. This class is "Intercultural Communication," and the text for the class is *Communicating Interculturally*. Active class participation is important. I am Professor Zhang, and this is my visiting co-teacher, Professor Michael Prosser. I have studied in America, and have been a teacher at this university for several years. Before you were born, students, Professor Prosser wrote a book entitled *The Cultural Dialogue*. Professor Prosser, would you like to introduce yourself?
Professor Prosser:	*Ni men hao*, ladies and gentlemen! In China, I am regularly called Michael (*Mikai*). You can all call me Michael. I have taught at several universities in the United States, as well as in Canada and Swaziland and for several years in Chinese universities. Some of my Spanish friends call me Migueleito! "Little Michael!" It's just a pun. As you can see, I am quite tall and big.

Class laughter

Jason:	Professor Zhang and we look small compared to you. Did you play basketball?
Michael:	I played it very badly. In my first game in high school, I hit the basket at the wrong end of the court! Then the other boys called me "Wrong Way Michael!"

Class laughter

Michael:	Class, I would like to ask you some questions. Don't be too shy to respond. Ok? What color are your eyes?

Silence

Ava:	Black of course!
Michael:	Really? I see some people in the class with brown eyes. You all learned as children that you had black eyes. This is a cultural stereotype. I have a mirror here. Pass it around and see if you have black or brown eyes.

Class laughter

Ivy:	I have brown eyes. I never knew that.
Ruby:	I have brown eyes too. Teacher, what color are your eyes?
Michael:	I think that they are blue. One of my children has blue eyes, another has green eyes, and the third has brown eyes. I wonder how we can explain that genetically.
Cindy:	Perhaps there are three different mothers?

Laughter

Michael:	Here is a second question. What color is your skin?

Class members:	Our Chinese skin is yellow. We come from the Yellow River, you know.
Gloria:	We are children of the Dragon.
Michael:	I don't see anyone here with yellow skin. Look at this student's shirt. It's yellow. Do you look like that?
Jason:	No. Perhaps we are brown?

Class laughter

Michael:	Here's another question. How many foreigners are there in this room?
Sophia:	Just one, you.
Michael:	Oh my! I see many foreigners in the room, Professor Zhang and all of you! You see, it's a matter of cultural perspective as you are all foreigners to me. You can see that we have many stereotypes about ourselves and others. For example, in the US, many people have positive stereotypes about Chinese students being so bright in science and math. Are you so bright?

Class laughter

Professor Zhang:	Now boys and girls, let's have a brief introduction from each of you so that we can get started talking seriously about intercultural communication. Please state your English name and where you come from, with a very brief statement about yourself or your interests.

Silence

Professor Zhang:	Please pay attention, class. The class period is short. Introduce yourselves.
Ali:	I am Ali, a Muslim boy from Xi'an. Allah is great and Mohammed is his prophet. Peace be upon him. We have a grand mosque in Xi'an.
Michael:	Salaam, Ali. You have identified your religious and cultural background. This is good self-disclosure. And you are brave, being the first to introduce yourself.
Tulip:	I am Tulip, just an ordinary Chinese girl from Wuxi, but I like flowers, especially tulips. We have lots of tulips in the spring and that is why I took this name.
Michael:	You also have the giant golden statue of Buddha there.
Angel:	My boyfriend says I look like a little angel. That's why I took this name. I am from Kunming, China's spring city. He and I are head over heels in love.
Forest:	I am Forest, after Forrest Gump. As his mom said, "Life is like a box of chocolates; you never know what you are going to get."

Culture

Laughter

True Nation: I am a proud Chinese from Beijing. That's why I took this name. I like the American pop music and anime from Japan. I don't mean I don't like you, Michael Professor, but I don't really know you yet except that you are a bit funny. Han Han is my hero.

Michael: An interesting English name! Actually I could be called Professor Michael if you wish, but my name is not Michael Professor. You can call me Michael. How are you?

True Nation: Ok, Michael. I am fine, thank you, and you? Glad to meet you.

Tiger: Well, my name is Tiger from the movie, *Crouching Tiger, Hidden Dragon*. I am from Hong Kong.

Michael: Then perhaps instead of Tiger, I should call you Crouching Tiger?

Laughter

Coco: I picked the name Coco after a famous actress. Also, I like hot chocolate and coca cola. I am from Nantong.

Michael: Ah! Not so far from Shanghai?

Tony: I am Tony from Xiamen, and a proud CPC member. My grandfather, father, and uncle were all party members too. I joined the Party in middle school. I am the head of the Youth League for my university major. My given Chinese name is Yonghong, meaning "forever red."

Echo: Hello. My name is Echo. Hello.

Michael: Hello. My name is Echo. Hello.

Laughter

Echo: Well. I hear that all the time. I am from near Chengdu, where the May 12, 2008 earthquake hit us very hard. Many people died, but we are survivors. Premier Wen Jiabao came and encouraged us. We called him Grandpa Wen.

Professor Zhang: Yes, that was a hard time there. Perhaps some of you donated some money to help the earthquake victims.

Michelle: I spent a year in America, in Seattle, Washington. I am from Wuhan. I like poetry, drama, debate, and writing. People call me a "third culture kid" because I lived in a country different than where my parents lived and where my passport is from.

Chinese and American Flags

Spring: Yes, Michelle wrote a book in Chinese about her life in America. It has been very popular. We are glad that she is back in China. My name is Spring, and this is my identical twin sister, Summer. We wore matching clothes until we came to the university. We grew up together in Ru Gao. Have you been there, Michael?

Michael: Yes, it is the city of longevity, and I have been to the Longevity Park which honors people who have lived to be 100. Since I am three quarters of being 100, perhaps I could live there too?

Robin: Oh you are too old to still be teaching! You should enjoy your rocking chair!

Grace: You can call me Grace. I am a Christian from Huabai. My favorite song is *Amazing Grace*. I also like Mariah Carey's song *A Hero Born in You*. *Avatar* is an outstanding movie and very spiritual.

Jade: I like green jade, and that's why I took this name. I am from Nanjing.

Lucky: I took the name Lucky when I got admitted to this university. I am also from Wuhan, the center of China and the center of the world. My English song is Michael Jackson's "*Beat it*"! My favorite TV series is *Lost*, but I like *The Simpsons* and *South Park* too. My favorite movies are *Titanic*, *The Terminator*, *Rocky*, *Pearl*

Culture

Harbor, Forrest Gump, Finding Nemo, 2012, Finding Private Ryan, Brokeback Mountain, Hurt Locker, The Aliens, all of the Harry Potter movies and *Avatar. Avatar* was really awesome. All of my friends and I loved it!

Jasmine: I am from the loveliest city of Hangzhou, with China's biggest West Lake. I love the smell of jasmine in the spring time there. Oh, I really like the songs *Yesterday, There's a Hero Born in You,* and *Country Roads.* I will be happy to get home to see my parents and friends.

Michael: The ancient Greek philosopher, Aristotle, in his book *The Nicomachean Ethics,* talks about all the ways that we become happy, and two of the top ones are families and friends, plus a good community, good education, good health, sufficient wealth, good patriotism, and perhaps at the end of one's life dying gloriously on the battle field for one's country.

Lucky: I am happy and in my life. I have had all of the things that Aristotle talks about except wealth. I am patriotic too. But I haven't died gloriously on the battle field for China. Thanks to the god.

Laughter

Professor Zhang: No doubt you all know that there are 56 West Lakes in China, like the 56 nationalities in China. The smallest West Lake is in Yangzhou, Slender or Slim West Lake, the home of President Jiang Zemin. Lawrence Robert Kuhn wrote a book about him which he published in 2004, *The Man Who Changed China: The Life and Legacy of Jiang Zemin.* It is in English and also in Chinese.

Michael: Yangzhou is also supposed to have the most beautiful women in China. You all remember the Chinese proverb: "Best to be born in Suzhou, best to live in Hangzhou, and best to eat in Guangzhou."

Gloria: Oh! My name is Gloria. I am from Yangzhou! Do you think that I am beautiful? My name represents the glory of China, particularly at the Beijing Olympics. I was a volunteer in the Olympics, and I was very proud to be a part of this glorious and harmonious event. Two thousand and eight drummers on August 8, 2008 at 8 PM. The number 8 is our lucky number. Did you see the Olympics, Michael? Perhaps you saw me volunteering. I wanted to volunteer for the World Expo, but I was too busy then.

True Nation: That's great that you could volunteer, Gloria.

Professor Zhang: Today, let's just hear from two more people as our time is running out for introductions.

Yolanda: I am from near Urumchi, a long way from home. I am a Muslim, like Ali. I have three brothers and one sister. My family has horses, sheep and two camels. I love my parents and my community and want to help them. Chinese is my second language and English is my third language. I feel very different as a Uighur than my Han classmates and I am rather frightened of foreigners. You are the first actual foreigner that I have met, Michael. I have seen foreigners on TV but never in person. You seem nice in person.

Michael: Yolanda, your love for your parents is an aspect of the Confucian value of filial piety. Are your brothers and sister your siblings or cousins? Lots of Chinese young people call their cousins brothers and sisters, as you know. As an only child myself, I never had any cousins.

Yolanda: No, they are my real brothers and sister. Do you have children or grandchildren?

Michael: Yes, three children and nine grandchildren.

Sunny: Wow! I am Sunny, an only child. My father is an English teacher and he started teaching me English when I was three. I passed the Cambridge test for my age with a high score. I am proud to speak both Chinese and English. Now, I am learning French too.

Mike: I guess I am the last one. I come from a small village in Anhui Province and my parents are farmers. They don't read or write Chinese. I have a real sister. I didn't have an English name before I came to this class and I asked Tiger what name I should choose. He said, "Why not take the name Mike?" But then I didn't know, Michael, about your name. Does it offend you if I have almost the same name as yours? Should I change my name?

Michael: No problem, Mike. When I was little, I was called Mickey, then later, Mike, and sometimes Michael. When I was 36, I decided to be a Michael from then on. And now, it is curious, as my Chinese name is Mikai, or like Mike again. Perhaps, Mike, this shows our culturally similar characteristics even though we are from different cultures.

Professor Zhang: Thank you class. These are good introductions and lots of humor too. Now, what have we learned today about our class topic, intercultural communication?

Catherine: Excuse me, Professor, but I don't think we have learned anything about the course topic of intercultural communication.

Professor Zhang: Think about it class. Today, you have met a foreign teacher whose thinking about several topics is quite different from ours, but expressed in a friendly way and even

Culture

also a bit funny too. We have had an interesting intercultural dialogue; and there is a lot of cultural diversity in this class. We have learned different perceptions about some of our own cultural beliefs, attitudes, and values plus probably some different characteristics even in the Chinese culture. We have found out about different meanings of your English names. You know that your own Chinese given names often have very special and sometimes auspicious meanings. We know that some of you girls have chosen sweet or flowery English names and some of the boys have selected much more powerful names; we have heard some students speaking modestly and others who seem nationalistic, proud for China.

Michael: We have started providing some personal self-disclosure, and thinking about our own cultural histories which are often the basis for better intercultural understanding.

Professor Zhang: You have seen Professor Michael challenging some stereotypes that we have about ourselves. He has also been giving us some proverbs and providing us some useful historical, geographical, cultural, or literary information. You have been reminded about the nature of our own language, Chinese, and Michael's understanding of his monolingualism. You have started to be aware of cross-cultural similarities and differences, and your personal intercultural communication competence. For example, as a younger Chinese professor, I tend to be more formal and Michael, an older American professor, appears to be more informal. This is of cross-cultural interest to us. Is it an isolated example or more generalizable? Believe it or not, class, we have really begun to have a first understanding of intercultural communication in your own lives. Now let's proceed to a better understanding of what it means for us. Shall we?

1.2   Culture

1.2.1   Definitions and the Nature of Culture

Let us first understand the nature of **culture**, and then explore levels of **cultural communication**. One of our first goals is to learn about human social discourse through a cultural perspective, thus **cultural dialogue**. Is there any one without culture? The world renowned cellist, Yo Yo Ma calls three major ingredients of every society: politics, economics and culture (2010: March 6). Igor Klyukanov notes that culture stemming from the Latin word cultura, is a system of symbolic resources, shared by a group of people, whether it is based on nationality, ethnicity, gender, sexual orientation or physical ability or disability; thus **intercultural communication** includes groups of people with different systems of symbolic resources coming into contact and communicating with each other (2005: 8–9). The anthropologist Clifford Geertz says that without humans there would be no culture, but **without culture there would be no humans**. In this way, he suggests that as humans we have created culture and therefore have created ourselves as cultural beings. He defines **culture as the accumulated totality of cultural patterns, organized systems of significant symbols**, not just an ornament of human existence, but its principal basis and its essential condition of being human (1973: 44–51). Geertz further identifies culture as those webs of significance which we humans have spun, spider-like, for ouselves. As humans, he believes that we are symbol-making, symbol-using, laughing, lying self-completing animals and tool-makers who can make tools that make tools. Thus, Geertz says that culture is an ordered system of meanings and symbols, through which social interaction takes place

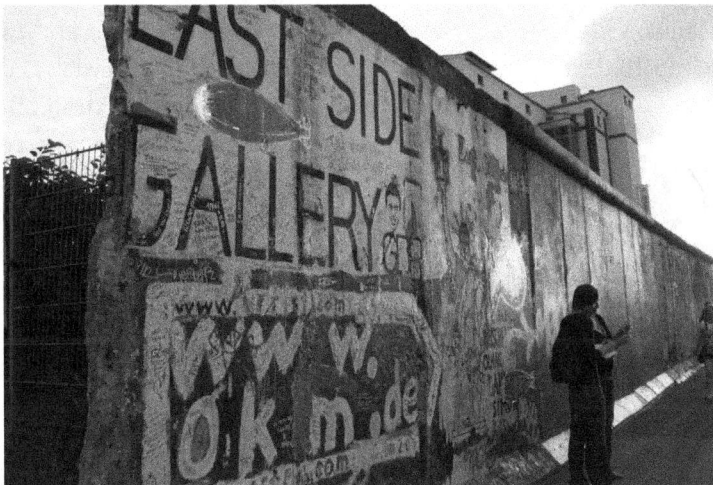

Berlin Wall

Culture

in the development of a social structure. To become human is to become an individual, even in a collective society, and to become individuals, we must all do so through the cultural milieu in which we live, mature, and exist. Culture shapes us as members of a society, in a specific community, and individually. And we shape culture too (144–145).

Culture is passed down vertically through generations, and horizontally by spreading the cultural patterns outward, sometimes benignly and sometimes forcefully. Sometimes, horizontal cultural tendencies are imperialistic, as during the colonial periods of the Americans, British, French, Germans, Italians and Portuguese. Often this horizontal spreading of culture happens both through internal and external migration, such as the great "*mingong*" migration of Chinese rural residents to urban areas within China, which was 560 million in 2005, or 43% of China's total population and with a labor surplus in the rural areas of 150 to 170 million in 2009 (State Commission for Population and Family Planning, 2007: January 18; Steven, 2010: January 12). In the top 10 developing cities in

The Piano in Strauss's House

China in 2009, there were more than 98 million residents all of whom expand Chinese culture vertically and horizontally (*Global Times*, 2009: November 30). The Chinese overseas disapora, in Indonesia, Thailand, Malaysia, Singapore, the United States, Myanmar, Canada, Peru, Vietnam, the Philippines, and Russia in that order alone constitutes approximately 38 million residents, plus 15 more countries with sizable Chinese communities, thus promoting the Chinese culture in a widespread horizontal fashion (Jacques, 2010: 417).

Our grandparents are a part of our culture, and have passed down language, customs, beliefs, attitudes, and values to their children and grandchildren. In a sense, they are the historians or archivists of culture. In an oral culture, where people do not read or write their language, they are, as the philosopher Bertrand Russell says, a part of a system where culture is like a memory chain that links the past to the present and to the future (1959). The American poet, e. e. cummings, has this interesting line, "The woman named tomorrow sits with a hairpin in her teeth and turns and says, 'My grandmother yesterday is dead. Well what of it? Let the dead be dead." Buddhists, however, believe that there is no precise yesterday, as it becomes today, and no precise tomorrow, as it also becomes today. Nonetheless, it is tragic that in many areas of Africa, because of the ravages of HIV/AIDS, many parents have died, leaving only the grandparents to pass down their culture to their grandchildren, thus breaking the links in the memory chain of culture and denying much of a future for the grandchildren. At the same time that grandparents are a part too of our culture, we can also see that their cultural period was quite different than that of their grandchildren. Consider the city of Ru Gao, with many citizens who lived to 100. How different their lives were as children and young adults than those living there now as children and young adults. It is in fact a great cultural distance between the centanarians' early lives and those of current Chinese youth and an example of intercultural communication over time, as the anthropologist Margaret Mead suggests.

1.2.2 Cultural Survival

Cultural survival is perhaps the most important value that cultures promote. Most people would want their own culture to survive, even if great change seems needed to make their lives better. Harold L. Nieburg proposes that all cultures go through continuous cycles: "The cycle develops because there is a relentless tendency to refresh old culture forms by variation and invention on the one hand, and on the other hand, to work jealously to preserve old forms" (1973: 76–81). **A key question in understanding our culture is to ask**, "Who are we? How do we fit in our culture? What are our cultural stories? Who were our parents when they were our age? Who were our grandparents when they were our age? What about our own village, city, or province? What is our country's own future like?" The anthropologist, Margaret Mead, has stated that most cultures must include at least three generations in order to survive into the future: grandparents, parents, and children. She discussed three different aspects of culture, the **postfigurative** society, hierarchically rooted changelessly in past traditions and a culture of the past; the

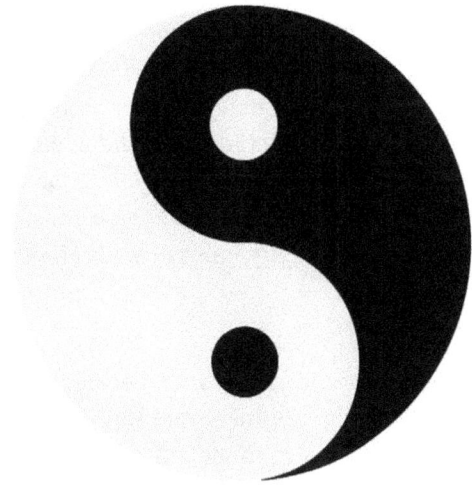

Yin-yang Figure

cofigurative society, where the cultural models are the beliefs, attitudes, values and customs of one's own contemporary generation, or perhaps two generations with just the presence of parents and children, essentially a culture of the present; and **prefigurative** culture, with the development of new unknown cultural forms and patterns, or the culture of the future (1970: 1–17; 25–26; 48–50). Particularly Mead expressed her speculations about new emerging cultural forms:

> *As I see it, children today face a future that is so deeply unknown that it cannot be handled, as we are currently attempting to do, as a generation change with configuration, within a stable, elder-controlled and parentally modeled culture in which many postfigurative elements are incorporated.... For the figure of migration in space (geographical migration), I think we must substitute*

Culture

a new figure, migration in time ... Even very recently, the elders could say, "I have been young, and you have never been old." But, today's young people can reply, "You have never been old in the world I have been young, and you can never be ... This break between generations is wholly new; it is planetary and universal (1970: 48–50).

Greek Temple

Writing at the same time period, Daniel Bell argued that **culture is paramount**, and the most dynamic component of civilization, as people develop reality in their minds through the cultural behavioral customs and rituals which have been passed down to them. At the same time, "the idea of change and novelty overshadows the dimensions of actual change ... our culture has an unprecedented mission. It is an official, ceaseless searching for a new sensibility" (1970: 17). Charles A. Reich has argued that it is culture, and not necessarily politics that provides the true revolutionary spirit for change in a society. He has proposed that in the perspective of culture, there is not often so much resistance to generally expressive symbols and forms, as cultural abstractions offer us a reasonably low risk, flexible and universal forum, allowing the development of new values or rituals for a very wide audience (1971: 311).

1.2.3 Objective and Subjective Culture

When we consider **objective** and **subjective culture, we can ask**, can we touch it? If so, we can call it *objective culture*—comparing artifacts and the technologies that produced them, such as tools, habitations, transports, paintings, newspapers, magazines, and books, for example. If we visit the Forbidden City, the Temple of Heaven, the Summer Palace, the Birds Nest or the Aquatic Center in Beijing or the Pearl of the Orient in Shanghai, or the pavilions and the objects inside at the Shanghai 2010 World Expo, we can recognize that these are aspects of objective culture. **Or, we can ask**, is it untouchable or even invisible to the eye? Then we are speaking of *subjective culture*, which Charles Osgood, William H. May, and Murray S. Miron called the study of **human cognitive processes** which may be linguistic, such as meanings, beliefs, or values, and the linguistic structures which express them, or non-linguistic such as perceptual styles of different cultures, motivational patterns and skills (1975: 335).

Ritual, a major concept in culture, has both objective and subjective elements. For example, in the western world, three groups of people tend to wear gowns officially: judicial officers such as judges and sometimes lawyers, academics for special ceremonies, or clergy. In each case there are also subjective examples of the meanings or perceptions behind the rituals, such as law, knowledge, or religious beliefs. Nationally, each country has a decorated piece of cloth which we call a flag, an aspect of objective culture, but the meaning, patriotism and nationalistic fervor behind the flag represent subjective culture. In this case, the reality of the piece of cloth becomes the perceived reality of the flag's importance. When residents of one country are angry at the leaders of another country, often the leaders of the second country are burned in effigy, the flag is burned, and buildings such as embassies or stores from that country are destroyed, boycotted, or protested.

Reasoning or **logic** forms a major aspect of **subjective culture**. Karl Pribram in his book *Conflicting Patterns of Thought*, identifies four major thought or reasoning patterns of thought: **universalistic reasoning** or **deductive logic**, often utilized by those speaking the romance languages, such as French, Spanish, Italian, or Portuguese in which "reason is credited with the power to know the truth with the aid of given general concepts"; **nominalistic, inductive, empirical or hypothetical reasoning**, and often called **grounded theory**, which is distrustful of "pure reason" without first finding relevant examples or evidence to back up generalized assumptions and hypotheses; **intuitive reasoning**, frequently attributed to Asian societies, which stresses the organic whole and its parts, and relies on arguments from analogy and ancient authority such as Confucius; and **dialectical reasoning** , resembling universalistic reasoning, in that it is systemic and deductive, but it assumes either/or and antagonistic forces found in Marxist

ideology or Marxism/Leninism [with Chinese characteristics] (Pribram,1949).

Western Romanized writing or Chinese, Japanese, or Korean ideographic characters or calligraphy, which is the basis of East Asian art, are examples of **objective culture**, but the intention behind the writing or art is a part of **subjective culture**. When one writes his or her name, or finds it in print, we have an example of objective culture, but the meaning behind the name is an aspect of subjective culture. For example, the written name, "Michael Prosser," implies a whole list of subjective meanings: the given name "Michael" (and there are many different cultural variations), is usually a male, named after the Judao/Christian Archangel Michael in this precise case, with a potentially Welsh family background, a son of his parents, a father of his children, and the grandfather of his nine grandchildren. Teaching in China, he often just used the name "Michael." Nonetheless, the name "Michael H. Prosser" is for his professional writing and for official documents. One son's given name is "Leo Michael," named after the middle name of a maternal grandfather, and his father's given name. **Names** are part of **subjective culture** (Prosser, 1985: 209–210).

In Chinese culture, as is well known, the first question often asked when meeting a stranger is "May I know your name, please?" There are "the old 100" family names ("baixing") based on the Northern Song Dynasty *Surnames of a Hundred Families* by *Bai Jia Xing*. Most Chinese know, though few outside of China understand it, that the ten most popular family names are *Li, Zhang* (with more than one hundred million in China), *Wang, Zhao, Chen, Yang, Wu, Liu, Huang,* and *Zhou.* These ten family names make up 40% of all family names in China and there are more than 250 million Chinese with the family name, *Li, Wang, Zhang,* or *Zhao*. Just as many Chinese believe that Western given names are actually their family names, as frequently occurs in Chinese bibliographies and reference lists, most westerners misunderstand that Chinese family names are typically one syllable and the given names are usually two syllables, and that in formal writing the surname is listed first. One reason that many young Chinese women who informally adopt a Western given name choose names of flowers, seasons, birds, composure, or jewelry is directly involved with their Chinese given names, such as *Ting* (graceful), *Mei* (enchanting), Hua (flower), *Feng* (phoenix), *Huan* (ring), *Yin* (silver), or *Yan* (beautiful). Chinese men's given names tend to honor ancestors, have a militaristic / revolutionary background, or have a name representing strength (Consulate General of the People's Republic of China in Houston, 2003). English given names are often chosen in Chinese middle school English classes by the teacher who often puts a list of English given names from an English dictionary on the chalk board and then students select their own names from the list. Other male or female English names are chosen by the general sound of one's Chinese name, for example, *Rui* becoming "Ray," *Zhou* or *Zou* becoming "Joe," *Zhang* becoming "John," *Mei* becoming "May" or "Mary," *Ting* becoming "Tina," or *Feng* becoming "Fiona."

1.2.4   Globalism, Globalization and Cultural Universals

We are well aware through the concept of globalism and the actual **process of globalization** that a new world order has begun to emerge in the recent past several decades, much different than international relations experts might have predicted even in the mid-1980s. *Encarta World English Dictionary* (1999) defines **globalism** as "the belief that political policies should take world-wide issues into account before focusing on national or state concerns, or the advocacy of this belief: and **globalization** as "the process by which social institutions become adopted on a global scale" or "the process by which a business or company becomes international or start operating at the international level." Evelin Lindner proposes: "A global culture and global institutions of social and societal cooperation can create meaningful life on planet Earth.... We need to seek optimization of balance within each individual's life, as one integrated life, embedded in one united global community.... Today, it takes a decent global society to give humankind a future" (2010: 141). As an optimist for a positively connected and interdependent global society, Lindner argues: "Global brotherhood and sisterhood, global connectedness, cohesion, mutuality, solidarity, and loving care for our human family and its habitat are desperately needed. In Europe, the term 'social cohesion' is preferred, while in Asia, the phrase 'the harmonious society' is more commonly used. Whatever the phrasing, the meaning behind the words is solidarity among all of humankind for the common good" (xvii).

William R. Slomanson, an international relations expert, says that none of the experts might have imagined in the mid 1980's that by the end of the decade the Soviet Union would begin to collapse, the wall separating East and West Germany would fall, that the two Germanies would be reunited, that Apartheid would begin to end in South Africa, or that China would begin to become a more and more important world power (2000). As Samuel P. Huntington wrote in his 1996 book, *The Clash of Civilizations: and The Remaking of World Order*, asks whether the Judao/Christian West and the Muslim Middle East and North African nations and cultures and the Asian Confucian/Buddhist/Hindu cultures are fundamentally different and at odds with each other. Can we engage in a "dialogue of civilizations" as suggested by Zhu Weilie instead (2007. September)? If China is a civilization state more than a nation state, it is an important intercultural issue for China and for other states to pursue, as well as for individuals interacting with Chinese citizens and the reverse.

Here is a question: does **globalization** bring us closer together as a "global village" as Marshall McLuhan, Canadian guru of communication, asked in the 1960s and early 1970s (1964 & 1970), or does it move us ever farther apart, as the newspaper and magazine entrepreneur Rupert Murdoch envisions with a "global city?" A village brings people together where all of the villagers know each other, often very well, and may collectively be opposed to **cultural change**, but it is often intrusive on one's privacy. A city allows for greater anonymity, where people don't know each other. In China, there are many streets that act as a type of close knit village, but when residents leave it to enter the city, their lives are constantly organized in the larger and broader society. Men and women wearing pajamas on the "village within the city" streets, as happens also in Japan and Korea, must give way to regular street clothing when they go even blocks away in the city. There are 200 cities in the world now with more than 5 million residents. The China International Urbanization Development Strategy Research Committee selected the following Chinese cities as China's top developing cities for 2009: Shanghai, Beijing, Tianjin, Guangzhou, Hangzhou, Chengdu, Nanjing, Fuzhou, Changsha, and Ji'nan, all which have more than 6 million inhabitants, except Fuzhou (*Global Times*, 2009: November 30). In contrast, the US with its 366 million residents has only four cities with more than 2 million residents: New York City, Los Angeles, Chicago, and Houston (US Census Bureau, 2000).Which society is more likely to fit the pattern of global cities, China or the United States?

The post WWII anthropologist George Murdoch stressed that certain **cultural traits** are common to all societies, such as the cycle of life: birth, adolescence, youth, courtship, mating, maturity, old age, and death are all **cultural universals**. He and other similarly oriented anthropologists also noted other universals, such as bodily care, bodily ornaments (especially for women), male and female bodily differences, cleanliness, hygiene, modesty, sexual customs and restrictions, relations with others in the community, including local governance, kinship, cooperative labor, community organization, education, law, status differentiation, and customs relating to a belief in the supernatural or a higher power and religious power (Murdoch, 1945: 123–145).

The **theory of cultural universals** offers important intercultural and cross-cultural insights. However, Geertz warns that having identified such concepts as **cultural universals**, we must test the most significant ones which are thoroughly grounded in particular biological, sociological, or psychological processes, empirically across cultures and cross-culturally. He believes that saying all people have a religious impulse, and we are aware that most Chinese do not recognize such an impulse, or have reasonably similar views on mating or marriage, or the concept that all people have a common interest in private property, for example, then "the question still remains whether such universals should be taken as the central elements in the definition of man [and woman], whether a lowest common denominator of humanity is what we want anyway ... In short, we need to look for systematic relationships among diverse phenomena, not for substantive identities among similar ones" (1973: 39–44). Geertz questions whether we can profitably consider such universals as the central elements in the definition of what it means to be human, "whether a lowest-common-denominator" view of humanity is what we want anyway (39–44).

1.2.5 Cultural Stability or Cultural Change

We can ask, "Which is more important, **cultural stability** or **cultural change**?" The **postfigurative culture** would totally resist change, unless forced by the onrush of modern culture intervening in their society. **Cofigurative** culture tends to appreciate old customs and traditions, while moving faster toward the perceived aspects of contemporary culture as its own civilization or culture advances technologically, often with the parent and child generations working together. Generally, such **cultural change** is evolutionary. On the other hand, the **prefigurative culture** members wish to rush toward a new Utopian society that has rid itself of old ways, ideas, traditions, and customs. The hippies in America, the student revolutionaries in Iran, the American push toward forced democratization in the Middle East, and the former student group of 800 who formed the Afghanistan Taliban, or even the early Al Quaida members, are also examples of utopian efforts to transform society. Nevertheless, B.F. Skinner (1971: 124) might have been correct when he challenged those who seek to create a totally **utopian society**, with the question: will it really work? Whenever new cultural patterns emerge, moving toward an ideal or utopian society, we have to recognize that we must start with what exists in the society which we wish to replace. Henry's argument in 1963 continues to be relevant in the second decade of the twenty-first century: "Today, when we think we wish to free the mind so that it will soar, we are still, nevertheless, bound by the ancient paradox, for we must hold our cultures together through clinging to old ideas lest, in adopting new ones, we literally cease to exist" (1963: 234). **Cultural creativity** often emerges in art, music, literature, drama, cinema, internet chat rooms, and even architecture but not so often in politics, religion, economics or nationalism.

1.2.6 Multiculturalism and Cultural Diversity

In John Walsh's early book, *Universal Education in the Community of Man*, when the study of **intercultural communication** was still relatively new, he stressed that "to be a universal man means not how much a man knows but what intellectual depth and breadth he has and how he relates to other central and universally important problems" (1973). It is a goal in the study and practice of intercultural communication to move from **monocultural individuals** towards becoming positive **multicultural individuals**, and in the process, **world citizens**. At about the same time, Peter Adler suggested that what is universal about **multicultural persons** is an ongoing commitment to the essential similarities between people in many different cultures, while at the same time recognizing that there are also significant differences among cultures and even between members of the same cultures. In a sense, as Adler indicates, **multicultural persons** are characterized by three major aspects: *being psychoculturally adaptive; always undergoing personal transitions*; and *maintaining indefinite cultural boundaries*. Adler believes that while there have often been **multicultural persons** in the past, for example with ancient Athens being a hub of multicultural activities and intellectual ferment, basically it is a contemporary phenomenon of internationally, transculturally, or dedicated interculturally oriented individuals who see the unity of all humans (Adler, 1974: 24). **Multicultural individuals** may be representative of what Mead has called **prefigurative culture**, in a state

of creative tension, dynamic, creative, critical, and passionate as they recreate themselves culturally, as well as seeking to recreate those around them to move from their old culture to an entirely new one. **Open-mindedness** is of course a major condition for an individual brought up in one, often isolated culture or society, to move toward multiculturalism or world citizenship. Additionally, we would argue that an intercultural sensibility is also important in this regard for being a multicultural person and intercultural tolerance as well.

Nonetheless, Condon and Yousef offer a warning for those who think that they can easily move from being monoculturally situated, or even reasonably able to be bilingual, bicultural or intercultural in their development, or seeing themselves through "the myth of the universal communicator." They argue that it is too much to believe that certain people will always be well liked, respected, understood, and effective in any cultural or societal culture that they visit. "The universal communicators" idealistically believe that their good will transcends other cultural problems or differences, but Condon and Yousef reject the idea that being an individual with **intercultural communication competence (icc)** in one culture means that he or she will automatically be as competent in an entirely different culture (1975: 252–253). When Prosser went to China in 2001, he was offered the following three recommendations: "1. Patience, 2. Patience, 3. Patience," because even those seeking to become multicultural individuals must recognize that entering a new society or culture can cause serious **culture shock** both for the hopefully multicultural individual entering the culture, and also for those within the culture itself confronting someone definitely not in the **in-group** but more clearly in an **out-group** status.

While many Westerners believe that communication has definite beginnings and endings and that time and space are entirely linear, Adler (1974) proposes that the effective multicultural individual is on the boundary of multiple cultures, crossing easily, but sensitively into other domains and values **the harmony of all cultures**. In a sense then, positive **multiculturalism** can be defined as valuing sharing of time, space, and power with other multiculturals. K.S. Sitaram writes that Asians believe there is no definite boundary, neither beginning nor ending but generally accepting the Chinese concept of *yin* **and** *yang*: light and darkness, male and female, dryness and moistness, good and evil, reality and illusion, endless blending of cultures, and a never ending harmony and stability (1995).

The social psychologist Edward C. Stewart held that the **principle of similarities and differences** is the central theme for the study of intercultural communication, and while the concept of similarities is such a strong assumption in American thought, society, and culture, the major reason for studying it in fact is because of sometimes very marked differences among cultures and societies (1984). Stewart's earlier *American Cultural Patterns: A Cross-cultural Perspective* (1971) illustrates these cultural differences in the assumptions and values of Americans and Filipinos in their perceptions on the self and the individual, the world, motivation, relations with others and forms of activity. Additionally, though many Filipinos do not speak very good English, it is a major part of the educational system there. Tapio Varis writes: "In the early days of

developing intercultural communication as a field of study, we focused on studies of cultural differences, stereotyping, ethnocentrism, and in general divergence. Now we are more likely to study cultural similarities, positive imaging, cultural relativism, and generally convergence" (1998: xiii). Ringo Ma proposes that what is actually happening in many cultures, including China, is that the **global society** is moving toward a situation with more "local diversity within international homogenization" (2002: 211).

At the same time, when Stewart compared Filipinos and North Americans across a value scale (1971), and Dean Barnlund argued that the Japanese and North Americans were at opposite ends of the cultural spectrum (1974), and Geert Hofstede initally created four societal dimensions out of his empirical work with IBM across many different cultures, the study of China from outside of China had also begun. It is obvious today however, that **multiculturalism** and **cultural diversity** might also be at different ends of a scale. Fourth century St. Augustine said that those who have not traveled have not yet opened the first book of life. But for those of us who have not done so previously, then we may also suffer severe **cultural shock** or **fatigue** when we find ourselves in a new cultural or multicultural environment and missing family and friends, having our own beliefs challenged, hearing our country criticized, or even by strange new customs. Many Chinese students keep connected by *Xiaonei*, which has been renamed Renren, QQ, Jhoos, email, messenger mail, Skype, or cell phone calls or text messaging. Additionally, in opening up to other cultures or travel, sometimes we find ourselves becoming critical of our own cultures, and perhaps even suffering severe **reverse cultural shock** when returning home. **Culture shock** or **cultural fatigue** often causes us as travelers in other cultures or countries to become excessively tired, weary, or even depressed, while when we are returning home we often find ourselves experiencing **reverse cultural shock**, seeing the new culture or country cross-culturally as better than our home country.

Lindner writes: "Unity in diversity is layered. The decision to treat everybody as equal in dignity defines unity at the core. While diversity can flourish at a more peripheral level as long as it does not destroy unity" (Lindner, 87), we must recognize, as Lindner postulates that "culture is not fixed but negotiable ... valid in the lifetime of a person, a community, a world, a region and humankind at large. We are free to create almost any culture we want within the limits of our biosystems" (28). In every society, she says we need: a culture of social connectivity.... We are also not slaves of history as it is mediated by genes or culture. Instead of enslaving ourselves we can create and advocate a wide range of new cultural scripts that are constructive for today's living conditions" (25–26).

1.2.7 Popular Culture

Culture can be described as **"high" or "low" culture**. **High culture** includes, for example: classical **art** such as the marble *Winged Victory*, *Venus*, *David*, *the Pieta*, or the Vatican Sistine Chapel by Michelangelo, Da Vinci's *Mona Lisa*, *The Last Supper*, or the *Vitruvian Man*; or Rembrandt's *The Night Watch*, or traditional Chinese art based on calligraphy and shadow; **music** by such composers as Beethoven, Wagner, Mozart, or Schuman, or the classical music of the Chinese erhu, Russian zither, or Spanish classical guitar or operas by Puccini or Mozart; **literature** such as Homer's *Iliad* and *Odyssey*, *The Canterbury Tales*, Jane Austen's *Pride and Prejudice*, Charles Dickens' novels, or the four Great Chinese classics, *The Dream of Red Mansions*, *Outlaws of the Marsh*, *The Romance of the Three Kingdoms* or *Journey to the West*, *War and Peace* by Tolstoy, or the prose and short stories of Lu Xun; **poetry**, such as Petrarch's or Shakespeare's sonnets, or Whitman's *Leaves of Grass*, or the Chinese poets Li Bai or Du Fu; **drama** such as that of the Greek playwrights, Sophocles, Euripides, and Aristophanes; Shakespeare's histories, tragedies, and comedies' or the plays of the Russian playwright Chekov. Religious **high culture** includes the Hindu *Bhagavad Gita*, the *Old Testament* and *New Testament* of the Bible, or the Qu'ran. We could even include classical architecture such as the Acropolis, Temple of Apollo, or the Parthenon, or, in the United States, Jefferson's University of Virginia Rotunda, Westminster in London, and in China the Forbidden City, the Temple of Heaven, or the Golden Buddha in Wuxi, in India, the Taj Mahal, or in Russia, St. Basil's Cathedral on Red Square. **High Culture** has permanence.

Low culture contains many of the same forms, but without necessarily having a timeless value. Many Chinese students list as their favorite Chinese TV programs MTV or Channel V for pop music and game or romance shows, Japanese cinema of anime, Korean soap operas, or American TV comedies and dramas such as *Friends*, *Desperate Housewives*, *Prison*

Break, Lost, or *American Idol*, animations such as *The Simpsons* or *South Park,* or American cinema such as *Forrest Gump, The Titanic, Star* *Wars, Saving Private Ryan, The Terminator, The Lord of the Rings, 2012, The Aliens,* or *Avatar.*

1.3 Case Studies

1.3.1 An Intercultural Chinese and British Marriage: Striking an Equilibrium, Lili Zhang, London

I had learned almost all the important aspects of communicating in an intercultural marriage from my grounded MA thesis study in Shanghai in 2006. But none prepared me thoroughly for my own intercultural marriage with James from London. We need patience, openness and determination to survive and thrive in the ups and downs of this closest form of relationship. James is from North England. I am from North China. We met on his business trip, visiting rather unglamorous paper mills in and around Shanghai back in 2005. I moved to London in April, 2007. We have been married since June of the same year.

Ups

I consider myself lucky to be able to assimilate into the English culture fairly naturally. James' existing friends circle keeps me occupied. I soon learned to utilize pub drinking as a social opportunity to network

with them and also my colleagues. The British love for antiques is also growing in me. And more importantly, I stopped thinking of him as a "foreigner" and rarely perceive myself as one either. This equilibrium eases the power struggle within the marriage. His attitude towards life to have fun regularly rather than waiting until he is rich fits very well with my own values. Sometimes to my slight disagreement, we spend much of our earnings on holidays, dining and other entertainment. This continuity of enjoyment is very uplifting, even after the wedding and possibly after the birth of our children. We attempt to have a balance of including each other's hobbies, with mine like movies and shopping and his like betting and football.

We have many examples of efficient communication. One case is that we keep each other informed of our own working time requirements, and manage each other's expectation on when any household administration will be done, such as calling a plumber. This minimum-noise communication has helped to build up our mutual trust and interdependence. Going further than that, we have been helping each other with analyzing our office politics and devising tactics to improve office relationships. Another example is our financial arrangement. My mother's ability to manage the family finances boosted my urge for control. James and I had a long discussion about whether or not to have a joint bank account back in 2007. Despite the psychological barrier, I realized the value of having separate accounts at that time due to credit record issues. Having a joint account would have brought down his hard-built credit score and would have meant less borrowing capacity for us. We made each other aware of our priorities and concerns. As a result, neither of us felt that we were being disadvantaged.

Downs

I used to find it a constant struggle between James' demand for privacy and my personal friends' time demand. Outside work, James usually likes us to spend time on our own. He enjoys privacy and freedom. And similar to many couples in the UK, he wants us to see our friends together as a couple. This was quite a shock for me, as England is a very individualized society. On the other hand, my Chinese friends and I enjoy going to Chinatown, and speaking Chinese without the need to speak a non-mother-tongue language. And what's more, it is just relaxing to have a girly gathering. We both have had to learn to compromise in this conflict of interests.

In terms of communication breakdown, it has to do with assumptions and not understanding different styles of communication. Once I was ill, and hence did not want to proceed with the tidying up of the flat (in order to be ready for the incoming tenants). I presumed that he would notice my illness himself and look after me. He didn't. The consequence was that he criticized my lack of determination to get things done. I became annoyed with his lack of care. After a three hour argument, I finally slipped to him that I was too ill to carry on. He apologized. Like many of my Chinese friends, I used to be keen to demonstrate my positive feelings, but reluctant to show any negative ones explicitly. Ever since then, if there is a problem, I would communicate it and its implications in a direct manner. On his part, he is becoming more competent in studying my subtle body language in discomfort and unwillingness.

1.3.2 Korean Taekwondo Master Lee Meets Ms. Ruth: Ruth Lee, Virginia, USA

I was taking Taekwondo, preparing to test for my 1st degree black belt. I entered the Dojang, noticing a young Korean, the new instructor Master Won Keun Lee. I was instantly attracted. He trained me to prepare for this test. I was so nervous I couldn't concentrate on Taekwondo. After a few weeks, I knew there was something more between us than just Taekwondo. Soon he left the school to teach elsewhere. I was heavily involved in martial arts through competitions, and teaching so I kept asking about him. After almost 5 years, one day at a party he came to me; we talked and he told me he was coming back. With his happy personality and always joking, I didn't believe him. But he told the truth. I thought "I am not going to let him go this time without at least being noticed." One day in Taekwondo he asked me for lunch. I knew his culture and coming from a traditional Korean family, I thought "why would this Korean man be interested in an American woman" as I believed that Koreans only dated Koreans. With his unclear English when he invited me I understood but didn't think he was serious. The next day at my mom's house she kept getting phone calls from "Lee". We didn't answer. I never thought it was "my" Lee trying to reach me. The next day at Taekwondo he asked me why I didn't respond. I explained that I didn't think he was serious. He was serious. His friends said "Before you decide to go out with him you should know he is a traditional Korean man." I didn't completely understand at the time but soon found out. We had lunch and spent hours just talking. I told him that I was looking for a husband so if he wasn't in that stage of life, I wasn't interested. He said "Ok, I understand." That's when it all began. He was very persistent as a traditional Korean with me and called so much that at one point I didn't answer the phone. One day I woke up and realized that this man really wanted to be with me for life. That was a big change that I realized between dating an American versus a Korean.

We married in September 2006 with a small wedding to get his green card process going and then celebrated with a big traditional American wedding in April 2007. While planning the wedding, we ran into some bumps. Normally, many American couples do everything together. Korean men don't want anything to do with the wedding plans. I tried to involve him in decisions but it frustrated him. He did not want to send out invitations as he explained that Koreans didn't do it that way. I told him why we needed to know how many people were coming for us to pay for the reception. Another thing worrying me was that Koreans do not RSVP; they just show up with all of their family. He invited so many people but promised that they would only come to the wedding ceremony. That started a big argument between us because Korean men appear not able to say no to their superiors or older people so I was concerned that he would just start telling them to show up. In the Korean wedding tradition, a box is placed in front of the wedding location for people to drop off money gifts. He didn't tell me about this tradition so I didn't include a box. Korean guests asked where to put the money. He was very upset with me, but didn't want to hear that he needed to communicate and explain to me what was needed. Because of the English barrier, such things were not communicated well between us.

In starting our normal daily lives, I noticed some cultural differences. Sometimes he would leave the house without telling me. When I would call to ask him about it he would be frustrated. If he got upset he would raise his voice and throw his hands in the air and then not speak to me. Most of the time he would swear in Korean and shut me out. I was so shocked that I would cry. Finally he explained that this is "just a Korean man." I said that I wouldn't be treated in that disrespectful way. We had arguments about getting the food on the table or making sure that everything was clean and organized for him. I was also working a full time job but I was very patient and loving with him.

We decided to have a baby soon after the wedding. He said that he would send the baby back to Korea to learn to be a Korean. I was so angered by that I insisted that we could visit Korea and his family could come to the US as much as possible but I would not allow the baby to go without me to Korea. In American culture we do not send our small children to other countries to live for a while and learn the native culture and I wouldn't do it. Now, our two year old daughter is learning both Korean and American culture. Perhaps soon she will teach Lee American English. Initially he was a very strong disciplinarian focusing on our daughter not being a boy as Korean culture favors boys. My husband kept saying he wanted a boy. I was very concerned that he wouldn't pay attention to her or love her the same way as a son. When she was born, however, I had no doubts that he was going to be the best possible dad.

I feel I have completely accepted his values and his way of meeting friends and family. Some differences are not surprising because the Koreans show respect for each other and my parents raised me the same way in our culture. I traveled to Korea with Lee to see his family. What an eye opener! I saw the way his father treated his mother, waiving his hand, yelling and walking away, just like my husband. Men in Korea make the women stand on the train if there are no seats. If the children are crying and screaming I've seen the fathers yelling at their wives to tell them to shut up. I couldn't believe it. But I realized that this was why my husband acted this way when he was angry. The saying "The apple doesn't fall far from the tree" is so true.

We were in Korea at the time of Chosun Korean "Thanksgiving." One big tradition is that the father lays out food on a table with incense for the deceased grandfathers, family members and ancestors. Only the men can ritually kneel, bow and pray, take the cup with wine and incense, and create circles. My father-in-law invited me to participate with them, a big honor because only men do this. My husband told me that his father asked deceased family members to accept me into this family and that I was loved. I bowed and participated, still feeling strange but happy to do that for them.

Korean women work all day and the wives are then at home cooking and cleaning. Lee wouldn't admit it but I think sometimes this has been hard for him. Currently, I work full time which pays a good salary and 100% of our health benefits. He recently opened a martial arts school and we are struggling. Part of his struggle as a Korean man is that he tries hard to be the main supporter in our family but it's not yet happening. I encourage him as much as possible. We have had differences with the way Korean families and American families handle discipline. In Korean families, everyone including grandparents, aunts, uncles, brothers and sisters take care of the child. Anyone can handle a problem as seems necessary including teachers. My American family does not handle things that way. The parents only handle the situation. When he first started visiting my family, he was shocked at how things were handled. It took him a very long time to learn not to say anything when nephews and nieces needed correcting. I had to make him understand that in America, at least among my family and friends, and when we were in Korea, I did not want his family disciplining our daughter if she needed it since only we as parents were responsible.

Lee and I are definitely still learning and are still very much in love. I wouldn't change my decision for anything. He makes me laugh, smile, sometimes become angry and sometimes cry but he is also very loving, dedicated, and very strong in his marriage beliefs. One big thing I feel being in love with and valued by a Korean man is that once he commits and marries, he likes to keep it that way. Even though Won Keun Lee and I have our intercultural differences and struggles, we are still together and pushing through it one day at a time.

1.4 Summary

In this chapter we have held our first interactive dialogue with an imaginary group of students in an intercultural communication class, an imaginary Professor Zhang, and Michael Prosser. You are a part of this dialogue too. Some might say that real Chinese students would not have made these statements so early in a class, but virtually everyone of the imaginary student statements have been made in one or another of Prosser's classes or talking informally to him outside of class. We have explored several definitions and the nature of culture, survival as a culture's chief goal, culture's spread both vertically downward and horizontally by spreading the culture outward geographically; cultural universals; objective and subjective culture; multiculturalism and cultural diversity and two intercultural marriages, as case studies, first a Chinese-British marriage, and second an American-Korean marriage.

1.5 Questions for Discussion

1.5.1 Perhaps you have read C.S. Lewis' *Tales of Narnia* or *Alice in Wonderland*. If so, you may have understood that they are fairy tales for adults. The dialogues in this and following chapters are similar. What is the advantage or disadvantage of such dialogues among an imaginary Chinese teacher, an imaginary group of Chinese students, and Michael as the actual American coauthor of this book as a teaching method in an intercultural communication class?

1.5.2 Are such imaginary dialogues realistic in terms of young adult Chinese learners' lived experiences, or are they simply fantasies without a realistic basis? Why? What is the value of an adult fairy tale in understanding culture?

1.5.3 Why is cultural survival a key element in studying culture itself? If you were to choose the second most important element for culture introduced in this chapter, what would it be and why?

1.5.4 Sometimes called the grandfather of intercultural communication, Edward T. Hall argued that "Culture is communication, and communication is culture." How can you compare this statement of another anthropologist, Clifford Geertz that "humans create culture, and culture creates humans?"

1.5.5 Margaret Mead speaks of three different cultural types: postfigurative, cofigurative and prefigurative. As young Chinese, which of these cultural types most clearly identifies you? Why do you think that this is true?

1.5.6 When we compare the terms globalism, globalization, cultural universals, multiculturalism, what are the most distinguishing characteristics that make them similar? And different? Why? How do multiculturalism and cultural diversity complement or challenge each other?

1.5.7 Which is more realistic for Chinese culture, the universalistic concept of multiculturalism or the particularistic concept of cultural diversity? Why? In Chinese culture, there is a feeling that China is civilizational rather than just as a nation state like other Asian cultures. What is the meaning of these two concepts for the Chinese?

1.5.8 Objective culture and subjective culture both are descriptions of culture. What are the major characteristics of each term? How are they similar and different? Why? What's in a name, objectively and subjectively?

1.5.9 Two case studies illustrate the positive and negative intercultural communication patterns of a Chinese-British marriage and of an American-Korean marriage. What do we learn cross-culturally about cultural similarities and differences in a Chinese writer's views, on one hand, and an American writer's views, on the other hand, towards their intercultural marriages? If we identified them as British-Chinese and Korean-American marriages, is there a subjective difference in the meanings?

1.6   Suggested Readings

Davis, L. (2001). Doing culture: Cross-cultural communication in action. Beijing, China: Foreign Language Teaching and Research Press.

Gao, G. & Ting-Toomey, S. (1998). Communicating effectively with the Chinese. Thousand Oaks, CA: Sage.

Geertz, C. (Ed.) (1971). Myth, symbol, and culture. New York, NY: Basic Books.

Geertz, C. (1973). The interpretation of cultures. New York, NY: W.W. Norton.

Inglehart, R. F. & Welzel, C. (2005). Modernization, cultural change, and democracy: The Human Development Sequence. Cambridge, England: Cambridge University Press.

Kuhn, R. L. (2010). How the Chinese leaders think: The inside story of China's reform and what this means for the future. New York, NY: Wiley.

Lustgarten, A. (2008). China's great train: Beijing's Drive west and the campaign to remake Tibet. New York: NY. Times Books, Henry Holt and Company.

Sitaram, K. S. & Prosser, M. H. (Eds.) (1998). Civic Discourse: Multiculturalism, cultural diversity, and Global communication. Stamford, CT: Ablex.

Zhou, M. (2009). Contemporary Chinese: Immigration, ethnicity and community transformation. Philadelphia, PA: Temple University Press.

Chapter Two

Communication and Intercultural Communication

2.1 Dialogue

Professor Zhang: Good morning, class. Now that we have discussed Edward T. Hall's notion of culture as communication and communication as culture, let's begin to discuss communication by itself, but of course connected back to culture, and begin to see how both ancient Greek and Chinese thought had an impact on communication, language and values. We will discuss language and nonverbal language a bit later, but this will just be an introduction. Also, Spring and Summer, as identical twins, you will be interested in the idea of identical twins having the most close communication patterns intraculturally.

Summer: Yes, Spring and I will be very glad in learning that. But what is the difference between intracultural and intercultural communication?

Professor Zhang: We will discuss it more fully in the class lesson, but briefly, intracultural communication happens within a culture, and intercultural communication happens between people in different cultures, often in an interpersonal setting. We will also discuss the correlation between cross-cultural, international and global communication, and some practical aspects of intercultural and multicultural communication.

Spring: Yes, we know about Confucius, but how do the ancient Greeks and Confucius have anything to do with each other?

Communication and Intercultural Communication

Professor Zhang: You have all heard of the great Greek philosophers, Socrates, Plato and Aristotle. Socrates was Plato's teacher; Plato was Aristotle's teacher. Socrates was offered the choice of exile or death as he was accused of corrupting the morals of the Athenian youth through his teaching. He chose death by drinking hemlock rather than going into exile, as he said that being a searcher for truth, wisdom, justice, and the good life was more important than living a life of dishonesty and deception in an unjust society. He said that he was like a gadfly on the back of a tired old horse, the state. Aristotle was not only an actual midwife, but also called himself the midwife of ideas. Do you know who was Aristotle's most famous student?

True Nation: I know—Alexander the Great. He conquered most of the world then. He was a true patriot and warrior for his country, Greece. I hear that a lot of college graduates in China are now joining the PLA, as it is modernizing and getting a more and more educated armed forces.

Tony: As a loyal CPC member, perhaps I will want to consider joining the PLA. As you and Michael have said, culture, technology, and modernization are all very important for China's development. A new more advanced military needs more people who are well educated to work with the advanced military technology.

Gloria: Personally, I want to take the Beijing and Shanghai civil service exams to work for China. What do you think, Michael, about that?

Michael: I have had several Chinese students who have successfully passed the civil service exams. As you know, Confucius was very involved in helping to create an educated set of citizens for the early Chinese civil service system. Earlier, we talked about Aristotle's book, *Nicomachian Ethics*, written to his son Nicomachias, about what makes a happy life. You remember that Aristotle considered the most important values: good family, good friends, good community, good education, good health, good patriotism, and a sufficient amount of wealth for one's station in life. He said that one does not know if he or she has had a happy life until it's nearly over. But he ended his list by saying that a final element of a happy life would be to die gloriously on the battlefield for one's country. So, he probably would have approved of his student Alexander's conquering most of the then known world for Greece.

Tony: China does not want to be a conqueror but to be an international leader in good ideas and technology for our less developed neighbors and international friends. So Aristotle would have approved of educated citizens joining the PLA?

Professor Zhang: Aristotle and Confucius both advocated a good education for a country's citizens and both wanted their citizens to serve their countries well. Let's consider Plato's Socratic Dialogues, where he had Socrates involved in dialogues with his well educated friends. Socrates' search was always for truth, justice, wisdom, courage and the good life. Aristotle agreed on these values, but added also happiness as the goal of any Athenian male oral communicator. Several of the ancient Greek teachers had the goal of making their young men students well rounded world citizens. Athens was the center of intellectual life in the Mediterranean world. The goddess Athena was both the patroness of wisdom and war. We all want to live happy lives, don't we?

Michael: Yes, Plato had several main virtues: ***truth, justice, wisdom, courage***, and ***moderation***, and later St. Paul added ***faith, hope***, and ***love*** to make the group eight. More recently, some writers consider the eight global core values: ***love, truthfulness, fairness, freedom, unity, tolerance, responsibility and respect for life***. We can recall Confucius' "Golden Rule": "Do not do unto others what you would not have them do unto you." The ancient Greeks and the New Testament say it slightly differently: "Do unto others as you would have them do unto you."

Catherine: What about the young women? Did Socrates and Plato leave them out? In China, we have the Women's Federation which promotes equality among men and women. It gives all Chinese women a voice and also helps us to know our rights and responsibilities. Chairman Mao said that men and women each hold up half the sky.

Professor Zhang: Even in Shakespeare's plays, women's roles were played by young men or boys. Do you remember the movie, *Shakespeare in Love*? Like in Shakespeare's plays, there is always a mix up between the men playing men's parts and those playing women's parts. In that movie, a woman was playing the role of a man playing a woman. Very confusing! Japanese Noh and Kabuki Theatre still uses men in woman's roles, and Peking Opera always has some men playing women's roles. Don't forget the Chinese movie, *Farewell, My Concubine* starring Leslie Cheung as the Concubine. It was awarded the Cannes Palme d'Or award, the first Chinese movie to win it. Perhaps you haven't seen it, except on your computers?

Ruby: I was little, but I thought that I was in love with Leslie Cheung. When he died in 2003, I wore a black armband the next day to school. My teacher thought someone in my family had died. When she heard it was for Leslie Cheung, I had to take it off. My mother scolded me.

Michael: Recently, when I was seeing a somewhat modernized version of Shakespeare's *Midsummer Night's Dream*, in the play inside the play, women played men's parts and men played women's parts, to make it a bit more interesting. In his comedies, *As You Like It, Love's Labors Lost*, and *Twelfth Night* men's and women's parts are mixed up too. Patrons at the Globe Theatre loved the intrigues.

Gloria: In the movie, *Shakespeare in Love*, I would have liked to play the part of the young woman. Oh! Glorious! Were women in the original Greek Olympics?

Michael: Women were not in the original Olympics, but some Greek art shows them participating in later Olympic games. You are right, Catherine. The Greeks considered the role of the women to be at home, bearing children, caring for the house and family, and teaching the girls to be good future wives. Later, the Romans had a very strong family structure, much like filial piety for Confucius with very strong bonding between fathers and their sons. It was the responsibility of the sons to make the death mask for their fathers when they died. Most of the more traditional societies give preference in education, prestige, and honor to the male children. However, the American anthropologist, Margaret Mead made an inclusive statement both for men and women: *"Never doubt that a small group of thoughtful, committed citizens can change the world. Indeed, it is the only thing that ever has."*

Jason: In Chinese society, we boys carry on the family name as the girls keep their family name after they get married.

Professor Zhang: Of course, also in Asia, including Korea, Japan, and Vietnam, the first born sons are usually assigned the ceremonial duties of honoring the ancestors. We Chinese, including whole families, celebrate the spring Tomb Sweeping holiday which we call "*qing ming jie*" or "Pure Brightness Festival." Many, especially in the rural areas, think that if the ancestors' spirits are not properly taken care of by sweeping the tombs and offering food and drink, they will become hungry ghosts who can create lots of trouble for the living.

Jade: I think that it is just a superstition but I return home each year and go with my parents to sweep the tombs of the ancestors because my grandma insists that we do it together as a family tradition. I like the autumn moon, lantern and dragon boat festivals better.

Spring: In our freshman year at the university, Summer and I stayed all night in Tiananmen Square with thousands of others for the early morning flag raising ceremony on National Day. How proud we were!

Gloria: Oh! It must have been glorious! I wish that I could have been a woman athlete in the later Greek Olympics! Or even in the Beijing Olympics!

Michael: Christian countries often have November 2 as "All Souls Day." In Mexico, families go to the cemeteries then have a big feast on the graves of those who have died, and provide lots of food for the dead. Many countries have a special memorial day for the dead, especially those who died in war defending their countries.

Iris: Do you celebrate a memorial day, Michael?

Michael: When I was a child, my parents and I always went on the US Memorial Day at the end of May down to the cemetery in southern Indiana where their families were buried. We brought many dozen peonies to put on the graves. Much of the Chinese art features peonies as you know. We had a picnic, and the high school marching band would play patriotic songs, like they do on our Independence Day, July 4 parades. All of the veterans buried in the cemetery would have an American flag placed at their gravesites and there would be patriotic speeches. Aren't peonies the national flower of China? Chinese traditional art has many examples of lovely peonies in their paintings.

Professor Zhang: In Luoyang, Henan Province, each spring there is a ten day peony festival and trade show. The tree peony is certainly one of our favorite flowers. So far, we do not have an official national flower.

Tulip: In Wuxi, we have many lovely flowers each spring, with many beautiful tulips. That's where I got my English name, Tulip. There are many tulips near the 80 meter tall golden statue of Buddha.

Jasmine: Hangzhou is so beautiful in the spring with all of its flowers. You know the Chinese proverb, Michael, "In heaven there is paradise; on earth there is Suzhou and Hangzhou."

Angel: Kunming is the spring capital of China, and we always have many beautiful flowers. My favorite flowers are the roses and tree peonies. My boyfriend who is at Yunnan Normal University always gives me a red rose when we go to a dance together. I like Gertrude Stein's poem, "A rose is a rose is a rose." My favorite western festival besides Christmas is Valentine's Day. Then he gives me six red roses. When we get married, I will wear the Western white wedding dress, and then I will change into the Chinese red dress for happiness.

Tony: Ha! I read a quote by the American writer, Toni Morrison: "Love is or it ain't. Thin love ain't love at all."

Jason: Angel, you should remember Qian Zhongshu's quote in *Fortress Besieged*, "Those who are out of marriage want to get in, and those in marriage want to get out!"

Class laughter

Angel: Then I want to get in!

Ben: Yes, Angel, you know the Chinese proverb, "If you want to be happy for one hour get drunk, if you want to be happy for three days get married, if you want to be happy for a week, slaughter a pig."

Angel: But Ben, the ending of that proverb is better: "If you want to be happy for a lifetime create a garden!" That's why Kunming is called the garden city or spring city! My boyfriend and I have thick love! I like better than your proverb the saying: "Love is the language of the Orient!"

Cherry: On Mother's Day in May I always call my mother in Hoh Hot. We don't do that much for Father's Day in June. They aren't so sentimental as our mothers and sometimes are more distant from us as our families' authority figures. We Chinese don't tell our parents that we love them and they don't tell us that they love us either, but our language is more subtle and indirect. Our mothers say that they are fixing our favorite foods for us and we tell them that we are glad to come home to taste their wonderful food. Michael, I think that you Westerners are much more direct than we Asians are about love.

Michael: My children and grandchildren and I always sign "Love" in our emails. Yes, we are very direct usually, but not always. Valentine's day gives romantic couples either a direct or indirect way to say "I love you." On Russian streets in several cities that I visited, romantic couples were often much more direct in their nonverbal aspects of love than either Americans or Chinese.

Lucky: I like Christmas as the main western festival. I hear Michael, you used to play Santa Claus or "old man Christmas" which we call in pinyin *"sheng dan lao ren"* every December when you have taught regularly in China. Do you think that I can grow a beard like you, Michael? Then I could be a fat Santa Claus too.

Laughter

Michael: People call me that on the Chinese streets in December because of my long white beard, "*Shengdan Laoren!*" One year, another American teacher and I both had our red Santa suits, made in China, and with our real beards, we led a Christmas celebration for our students, two Santas instead of one. Christmas is the most important Western celebration, both for those who are religious and those who just enjoy the secular celebrations.

Ali: Saalam! I really enjoy the feast of Ead, when our Muslim forty days of fasting for Ramadan ends. Then we eat lots of mutton. I hope to go to Mecca someday for the Hajj. It's one of the five pillars of our faith.

Michael: That reminds me to suggest to you class, that as some of you will want to travel or study outside of China, you should get yourselves your ten-year passports where your *hukou* is located. More and more young Chinese are traveling or studying outside of China. More than 100,000 are studying now in the US alone.

Eva: I have a passport and my parents took me to Thailand last year. It was great.

Professor Zhang: Some of the topics we have talked about today are very much related to our study of communication, both interculturally and globally and some very interesting cultural customs. As you know, we often celebrate our cultures by our behavior or our rituals. As humans, we cannot not help communicating symbolically and through our behaviors. Let's now begin to consider some of these subjects more fully. Shall we?

2.2 Communication

2.2.1 Definition and Nature of Communication

Communication is often called the process of interacting, and therefore is like culture, dynamic, interpersonally located, which in Chinese is called *jiaoji*, and constantly evolving, while **communications** are all of the **channels and often in a mass setting** which in Chinese is referred to as *chuanbo*, by which the communication takes place. The study of communication is by its nature interdisciplinary. Steve J. Kulich indicates that subjects of inquiry relating to the study of **intercultural communication** include as relative examples: anthropology; sociology; social, cultural, and cross-cultural psychology; speech and mass communication; rhetoric; discourse analysis; linguistics; semiotics; semantics; interpersonal and inter-group communication; comparative literature (primarily on China in contrast to its western placement in literature); legal and political studies; organizational communication; ethnic studies; international media and relations; and diplomacy (2007: 3–4). In Igor Klyukanov's 2010 book, *A Communication Universe: Manifestations of Meaning, Stagings of Significance*, he identities the study of communication theory more specifically, as coming from at least four sources for inquiry: "(a) the rhetorical tradition, (b) propaganda and media effects, (c) transmission and reception of information, as well as (d) group dynamics and interpersonal relational developments" all

of which are studied mostly in the context of the humanities and social sciences. At the same time, the natural sciences and other scientific studies also contribute, as Klyukanov claims (2010: 16).

No matter which major you are studying, both **communication** and **intercultural communication** are very important for your future as Chinese citizens. All human communication is based on the use of verbal or nonverbal symbols and signs (*semiotics*) and perceived meanings (*semantics*), incorporated into practical usage (*pragmatics*). Klyukanov, in his earlier book, *Principles of Intercultural Communication* (2005: 70–71) articulates three performance principles: (1) Intercultural communication is a process of playing out our identity by moving from rules to roles, (2) enactment of meanings constitutes cultural identity interactively, (3) interactive intercultural communication moves from activity through actions and then back to activity. Thus, he argues that "intercultural communication is a joint effort of creating and enacting meanings." Carolyn Calloway Thomas, Pamela J. Cooper, and Cecil Blake's 1999 book *Intercultural Communication: Roots and Routes* develops some of the same themes metaphorically and practically.

Kenneth Burke, who was actively engaged in studying communication and rhetoric until his death at 93 described humans, even earlier than Geertz, as symbol-making, symbol-using, symbol-misusing, inventors of the negative or moralized by the negative, and makers of tools that make tools. Burke contrasted the ancient Greek view of **persuasion** and the more contemporary view of **language** and **identification**, as those seeking to persuade others have to develop a mutual identity with them through the use of **symbolic language**. **Identity** with others compensates for their divisions, overcoming their separateness, and motivates others to cooperate (1962; See also Dai and Kulich, 2010). Burke's concepts about communication clearly fit well into the broader perspective of **intercultural communication**. The concept is refined further in Gudykunst and Kim's *Communicating with Strangers* (1984), which has been a very popular intercultural communication text in the US and which is now available in China. The internationally known author Evelyn Lindner (2010: xxi) reflects on her life: "I am an intercultural voyager ... a voyager uses the challenges of cultural diversity and intercultural conflicts as a stage for forging new relationships and new ideas. Consequently, I cherish meeting strangers and encountering strangeness with the entire range of my vulnerabilities."

Without the differences that come from interacting with those outside our "**in-group**," we would not need to consider intercultural communication as a subject for our study. Lindner remarks: "As long as neighbors are called neighbors, no matter how offensive their behavior may be, they are considered part of one's in-group. Even if we hate our neighbors, most of us will still treat them with a certain degree of care ... one will be aware that the children of neighbors have to live together." Continuing, she comments: "Before the world became interconnected, it was feasible to define an outside sphere [**out-group**] as a space

where enemies could be destroyed without consequences ... However, new technologies such as the Internet or multitasking mobile phones have changed everything ... Interconnectedness turns everybody into a vulnerable neighbor within a single inside sphere" (51). Lindner quotes a letter from the former President of the International Society for Intercultural Education, Training, and Research and expert on Native American (Indians), Jacqueline Wasilewski: "The ideal Native American love context is maternal ... inclusive as mother's arms, like mother earth, loving each of her children uniquely ... In the Comanche language, there is no direct translation for the English word 'love' but there are hundreds of words for 'respect' ... And in our work on Native American values, a Respectful society/world consists of the intersection between four other R's: Relationship, Responsibility, Reciprocity, and Redistribution. We are related to everyone and everything in some way. Out of that particular Relationship comes our Responsibility to one another, that is, all Relationships are Reciprocal [much like *guanxi* in Chinese society], and if the Relationships are in order, the system enables a Redistribution of all goods, physical, mental, emotional—in an equitable way throughout the entire society/world" (75). In the dialogue for this chapter, we have also seen that as Chinese students, you rarely tell your parents that you love them, or rarely that they tell you that they love you. In this way, the Chinese culture and Native American culture have some striking similarities, despite their overall differences.

All communication is **contextual**, that is "the set of circumstances or facts that surround a particular event, situation, etc" (*Random*

Communication and Intercultural Communication

House Webster's Dictionary, 1991). Lavandera (1988) summarizes **context** in sociolinguistics as either social and/or interpersonal (as we indicated in the dialogue, Chinese call interpersonal communication *jiaoji* versus mass communication *chuanbo*). The **social context** includes such factors as gender, age, race, and socioeconomic status, while **interpersonal context** may include intention, beliefs, or knowledge. In the same way, although **interpersonal oral communication** often disappears quickly "he said/she said," **media** and **mass communication** have a more lasting impact backwards and forwards, especially with such modern media as print, radio, television, and computer mediated communication. In American elections, statements made earlier by candidates in the mass media can be pulled up later to support or hinder their campaigns or their actions after the elections. Most **intercultural communication** is typically also highly **interpersonal** or **intergroup- oriented**. Edward T. Hall's description of the **high-context/low-context** range of communication explains that many societies communicate in a high-context format: "A **high-context** (HC) communication or message is one in which most of the information is either in the physical context or internalized in the person, while very little is in the explicit, transmitted part of the message. A **low-context** (LC) communication is just the opposite: i.e., the mass of the information is vested in the explicit code" (Hall, 1976: 91). Kulich discusses **the cultural influence of contexts** (2005): "The starting point for intercultural awareness is the identification of contexts and specific interactants (audiences). Then we can begin to more effectively psychologically process

the dynamic interaction that is taking place." Donahue and Prosser, (1997) discuss in detail **context** in both discourse analysis and rhetorical analysis in their application of contexts to the diplomatic setting at the United Nations.

In their book, *Business Communication* (1992) Michael Galvin, David Prescott and Richard Huseman note that the subject of communication has seven myths and realities:

(1) **Myth:** *We communicate only when we consciously and deliberately choose to communicate.*
Reality: *We communicate many times when we are not consciously aware that we are communicating.*

(2) **Myth:** *Words mean the same thing to our listeners as they do to us.*
Reality: *Words do not really have meanings; meanings are in large part determined by people's experiences and perceptions.*

(3) **Myth:** *We communicate primarily with words.*
Reality: *The majority of the messages we communicate are not based on words but rather on nonverbal codes and symbols.*

(4) **Myth:** *Nonverbal communication is the silent language.*
Reality: *Nonverbal communication is received through all the five senses.*

(5) **Myth:** *Communication is a one-way activity.*
Reality: *Communication is a two-way activity.*

(6) **Myth:** *The message we send is identical to the message received by the listener.*
Reality: *The message as it is finally received by the listener is never exactly the same as the message we originally thought we sent.*

(7) **Myth:** *You can never give someone too*

much information.
Reality: *There are times when people can be given too much information and thus suffer from an information overload (1992: 6–10).*

2.2.2   Chinese Communication and the Civil Society

Kluver writes that **civil society** allows citizens a voice in influencing social and political life outside the power of the state itself. He calls **civic discourse** the ability to define the nature of the society and its people, including economics, cultural and social issues, and popular culture, by which the national identity can be expressed. **Civic discourse** helps to create the society, and the **civil society** helps to promote **civic discourse**, much like Hall's claim that *culture is communication and communication is culture.* **Civic discourse** is seen not only in political matters in China, where those in power in the Party and government provide the substantial part of the discourse, but also in popular culture including the arts, music, books, TV, advertisements, the Internet both as a form of exercising communicative interactions and in a major way in China as entertainment. Given the ever increasing importance of education at all levels in China, not only do the political leaders exercise power in the **civic society**, but also intellectuals (*zhishifenzi*) from the major universities (1999: 12–13). In the tradition of the dynastic periods, the Confucian scholar-officials tended also to serve as "the conscience of the emperor." The cultural assumption that the scholars have a moral duty not only to innovate, but also to concern themselves about the progress of the society, remains true

today, Kluver believes "that intellectuals have been and will continue to be a vital element of Chinese civic discourse." Additionally, Kluver claims that the guiding principles of Marxism-Leninism/Mao Zedong Thought also contribute to the role that intellectual elites play in China's **civic discourse**, which Deng Xiaoping reinforced through the centrality of the Party to the development of social order, with a strong and well educated set of leaders leading and guiding the general population (1999: 12–20). Just as Martin Jacques (2009) has argued, Kluver also believes that the new Chinese society may develop some democratic tendencies quite unlike the Western model of democracy: "The future is likely to bring an even more diverse set of ideas into a culture and a society that is rapidly constructing a new identity, and a new Chinese world" (20–22).

2.2.3   The Spectrum or Continuum of Intracultural, Intercultural and Multicultural Communication

John Locke in his 1690 *An Essay on Human Understanding* proposed that at birth all humans are like a "tabula rasa" or "blank slate" to be written on. Over time in such fields as psychology and communication, many scholars have discussed whether **nature** or **nurture** is more important in a child's development. Was Locke right in his argument for **nurture** as opposed to what a child genetically is endowed with, such as intelligence? Additionally, Locke noted that the concept of moral values, passed down from generation to generation, as a key thrust of passing down one's culture in a vertical progression, was itself based on ***nurture*** rather than *nature*, but that these values were at best a trigger for human moral actions, as humans are more likely to need considerable persuasion to adapt to selecting these moral values and actions for themselves rather than their opposites. Also, in 1690, *Locke's Second Treatise on Government* argued that the goal of a **civil society** was to establish a **social contract** between those who govern and those who are governed. This **contract**, he would suggest, is based not on hereditary privilege and characteristics coming from his or her natural abilities derived from his or her parents, but from the nurturing that both his family and society have provided. Locke had a huge influence on Thomas Jefferson, the third president of the United States, the writer of the *Declaration of Independence*, and the founder of the University of Virginia. While the "Declaration" said that all men are equal, with God-given rights, "life, liberty, and the pursuit of happiness," unfortunately, Jefferson had 80+ slaves, many of whom came from different African tribes, and thus initially were unable to even understand each other interculturally, until they had acclimated to the American master/slave society in the southern parts of the country. What if natural slave brothers and sisters were reunited after a number of years, how would their lives have been similar or different?

In 1993, for the 250th birthday celebration of Thomas Jefferson, 80 African American students received permission from the University of Virginia president to walk through the outdoor ceremony on Jefferson's historic University of Virginia lawn, blind-folded, with their right hand on the shoulder of the one ahead of them, as a nonverbal symbolic protest that Jefferson, the writer of the *Declaration of Independence* and the University founder had enslaved 80 human beings. We remember from the earlier discussion that Kenneth Burke called humans "Symbol makers, symbol users, and symbol misusers." These students' nonverbal blind-folded procession provided a powerful nonverbal symbolism of the hypocrisy of Jefferson. Mikhail Gorbachev, the last president of the Soviet Union, was the convocation's principal speaker, and thus was a witness to this symbolic protest against Jefferson 250 years after his birth. Historical evidence demonstrates that Jefferson was far kinder to his slaves than many slave owners in the southern part of America. Nonetheless, although he promised to free all of his slaves at his death, he only freed half a dozen in his will, and his nearly destitute family members sold the rest, breaking up parents and children born on his plantation. Other early presidents, also born in Virginia, including George Washington, James Madison, and James Monroe, all nearby neighbors, additionally had large collections of slaves on their plantations. These early American presidents were "neighbors," but what about the slaves? Were they neighbors of their slave masters? Literally they were, but symbolically they were not in the same category as their masters since they were bought and sold as property. Theirs was the status of dependency on powerful slave masters. Even the sixteenth president of the US, Abraham Lincoln, and the Great Emancipator, did not initially believe that slavery was morally repugnant, but only that it should not be expanded out of the south because of its troublesome situation.

We can see intercultural communication on a spectrum or continuum of extremes. Perhaps identical twins have the most intracultural communication potential, followed next by fraternal twins, brothers and sisters and their parents. There is a story a number of years ago from Long Island in New York about three young men who each thought that they were single adopted children. Their friends started telling two of them that they had seen one of them in other locations but that there was no response to the greetings. They seemed to have very similar characteristics, like smoking the same type of cigarettes, laughing the same way, dating the same type of young women, and gesturing almost identically. After some investigation, the two young men met each other and saw a mirror image of himself. They learned that they were identical twins and became very close. Still later, they were being told by friends that they had been seen in another location where neither of them had been before. Amazingly, with more searching, the third identical triplet was found. Again, all three had very similar characteristics and each one was a mirror image of the others. It turned out that they were a rare case who had been separated after their births, and given to three different sets of adoptive parents living within several kilometers of each but without knowing that each triplet had two other identical brothers. After graduating from their separate colleges, they opened a restaurant called "The Triplets' Restaurant." Unfortunately, one of the three of them later committed suicide. Perhaps the pressure became too great for him, first believing that he was the only son of his adoptive parents and then later learning that he not only had one identical twin brother, but that he was one of three identical triplets. Despite their very similar characteristics, there were some very nurturing differences because they had grown up in different families and cities. **Here we can ask the question**, was John Locke correct that at birth each person is born with a "blank slate" which then must be filled in through **nurture** rather than **nature**? If you are critical thinkers, what does your analysis tell you, **nature** or **nurture** or a mix of both? We note that they had many similar characteristics. How did this happen, **nature** or because of culturally learned differences as well, **nurture**? It is a good example of **intracultural communication**.

If we think about practical examples of the opposing arguments about nature and nurture, let us consider a Russian girl, (Michael Prosser's granddaughter), adopted at eight months by an American couple, but who has living Russian parents and four natural Russian brothers and sisters, or the many Chinese girls who have been adopted into American families (Evans, 2000). The Russian girl, Dasha, has no memory of her natural parents or brothers and sisters, and has become a thoroughly Americanized teenager, blond and blue-eyed, speaking no Russian, and growing up with an American single mother and the mother's natural son and daughter as her younger brother and sister. One or both of her adoptive parents, now divorced, have been told, without people knowing her background that she looks just like the [adoptive] parent. She is smart and intelligent. She knows that she was born in Russia and her adoptive mother has said that when she is eighteen, she can make a trip to Russia to meet her natural family, if possible. Where does this intelligence come from, the birthright from her natural parents, or from her nurturing American family, location, and educational opportunities? Or, again, is it

Communication and Intercultural Communication

a combination of both **nature** and **nurture**? If she were to go back to her natural family in Russia, would she and her natural family members, parents, and siblings, be so different from her as to be unrecognizable as a family, or would there be certain characteristics that would be as similar as those discovered by the three originally separated identical triplets on Long Island? Is she more American by **nurture** than Russian by **nature**? Or, down deep, is she potentially more Russian than American, despite never having lived in Russia since she was 8 months old? In contrast, two Chinese girls being adopted at different times into a white American family, and possibly not being blood sisters, certainly do not look like their adoptive American family and possibly not even like each other. When they grow up and perhaps marry young Caucasian or African American men, what characteristics will emerge for them and their mixed race children? What part will be **nature** and what part will be **nurture**? Like Dasha, they might never speak their native language, nor even visit their home country. Are they inherently more American than Chinese, despite their Chinese looks, or still more Chinese despite their adoptive American heritage? Intercultural marriages are increasingly occurring in China, and many foreigners coming to China to study, work or teach have taken native Chinese spouses, usually foreign men and Chinese women. In China, there are more than 50,000 such marriages annually. The basketball superstar, Yao Ming and his wife returned to the US while she was pregnant with their first child, and as the baby was born in the US, the child automatically became an American citizen as well as a Chinese citizen. In this case, the parents are Chinese, speak fluent Mandarin, and would provide considerable Chinese cultural heritage characteristics to the child. At the same time, if the family lives a long time in the US, then the child would adapt many American cultural characteristics. Would the child remain more Chinese, but living in the US, or more American than Chinese because of also adapting to American cultural patterns? In the chapters' dialogues, we have two identical twins, Spring and Summer. What would happen if they had been adopted by two different sets of parents in another country at an early age? Coming to visit China as young adults, how would they feel, perhaps not speaking Mandarin, being raised in another cultural environment, and being different? Many Chinese American or Chinese Canadian young adults come to China to study, travel, and perhaps meet relatives who stayed in China. Some of these young people cannot speak Chinese. Can they inculturate easily into Chinese society?

As we progress on the spectrum between the extremes of **intraculturalism**, **interculturalism**, and **multiculturalism**, except for those growing up in Quebec Province where there is great pride in their French culture and speaking French rather than English, many native-born and native-speaking English Canadian citizens or residents really seem very much like their American neighbors to the south, especially the closer that they live near the 4,500 kilometer Canadian-US borders. Sometimes Americans from the region of New England and Canadians from Eastern Canada do have both very similar accents and spoken patterns, which might be different from the midwestern Canadian provinces' or midwestern

American states' accents or cultural patterns. Americans, Australians, British, and New Zealanders who are native English speakers may have some difficulty in understanding the spoken English of the others, but all of them generally can easily understand the written English of the other native speakers. It is sometimes more difficult to understand the spoken English of those countries or cultures where "new Englishes" have been adopted as a standard "lingua franca," such as India, Pakistan, or former British African or West Indian colonies, though with some minor differences, their written English can generally be understood by other English speakers. Many Europeans speak and write fluently in English, especially the farther north one goes in Western Europe, causing little or no problems in understanding, plus often having at least one more European language. However, Dean Barnlund argued that on the cultural spectrum, Japanese and English- speaking cultures are at the opposite extremes of the **cultural spectrum** (1974), and if he had also made cross-cultural comparisons of English language speakers and cultures with those of the Chinese, with Mandarin as the major dialect, or Koreans, he probably would have seen the differences between the groups also to be at the far left and far right end of the **entire spectrum of cultural differences**. How might he have felt about Chinese and American young people? Would it be the same as the opposition on the **cultural spectrum** for Chinese or Koreans and Americans or different? How would he place Chinese and Japanese on the spectrum? After all Chinese and Japanese share many cultural aspects such as their roots in Confucianism and the similarities of their ideographic

characters in language. Still, perhaps the cultural differences might also be very large. What do you think as **critical thinkers**? After all, we can expect all of you to graduate from college or university, and thus be identified as educated citizens. Educated citizens should also be **critical thinkers**. The more intercultural or international that you become, the greater your world expands.

American, Canadian, Malaysian, and Singaporean cultures are more or less multicultural or heterogeneous in nature, while China, Japan, and Korea are basically monocultural or homogeneous, despite having a number of ethnic identities in their broader cultures. We have already identified several characteristics of the **multicultural individual** in Chapter One. The dialogue in Chapter Seven provides a brief multicultural look at the guests who have come to talk to the intercultural communication class, and the content includes several cultural views of contemporary youth by which we could explore some cross-cultural comparisons and contrasts.

Let us ask the question: Are there any significant differences between **intercultural** and **multicultural communication**? Often **intercultural communication** occurs just between two or three individuals from different cultures interacting, while **multicultural communication** typically involves an assortment of individuals from several cultures in interaction. A key concept, both in effective and genuine effective intention-oriented **intercultural** and **multicultural communication** is using **power** in a positive manner with a sense of equality among those in dialogue. Although differences might bring the individuals together, similarities on shared topics offer a fruitful exchange between them. It is not a utopian goal to have **multicultural dialogues** in the context of shared topics, but of the utmost practical nature. Generally speaking, it would be a positive enhancement of Chinese higher education to make at least some classes **multicultural**, especially if there are foreign students on campus.

Michael Prosser and young people in Kuala Lumpur

Stereotyping, prejudice, ethnocentrism, and **power** combined also undermine the positive relationship in both **intercultural** and **multicultural encounters**. Kenneth D. Day (1998: 133–144) recommends for fostering respect for other cultures, both in **intercultural** and **multicultural** settings: "Consideration for other cultures involves perceptions of worth and the belief that accommodations should be made for cultural differences ... Learning the expected expressions of respect in another culture is, of course, a particularly relevant aspect of cultural knowledge ... Ethical intercultural communication [should] be based on the principle of dialogue in which

participants understand their own beliefs to be merely beliefs rather than the truth ... to understand what a member of another culture is communicating." He argues that both **low ethnocentrism** and **low prejudice** are essential for positive **intercultural** and **multicultural** effectiveness and that direct and regular contact with those from other cultures may be the most effective ways of developing respect for the other cultures.

2.2.4 Cross-Cultural Communication

Later, we will see an example of **international** and **global media** as well as "media diplomacy" in Chapter Eight as an example of **international** and **global communication**, and a fuller example of **cross-cultural communication** study and research in Chapter Ten. At the moment, we can understand **cross-cultural communication** to mean considering comparative or contrastive linguistic or non verbal codes, behavior, attitudes, beliefs, or values between two or among several cultures. This can take place within a culture, for example, in comparing two or more of the 56 "nationalities" in China, or in Singapore and Malaysia with three distinct cultural groups, Chinese, Indians, and Malay, or in North American society among Arabic, African American, African Canadian, Asian, Caucasian, French Canadians, Asian Americans and Asian Canadians, and Hispanic cultural groups in the two societies. Additionally, as both Canada and the US are heavily multicultural, they can include many citizens or resident aliens living there from other countries and cultures. Unlike the US, for example, which seeks more and more to restrict immigration, Canada, as well as Australia and New Zealand specifically seek to recruit new immigrants because of their relatively small population bases. Or, it can occur in comparing cultures from an international viewpoint between countries. In China, Beijing Language and Culture University is often called "The little UN" as among the more than 1,500 international students studying there annually, more than 142 countries are represented. Your campus may also have many international students, just as in the US, there are currently more than 100,000 Chinese students. At the same time, it is estimated that in the not too distant future, 40% of those living in the US will be of Hispanic (Latin American) and Spanish-speaking background, making cross-cultural comparisons with other Americans, whether African American, Asian, or English speaking Caucasians, a major national issue.

Robert L. Stevenson, in his book, *Global Communication in the Twenty-first Century* (1994: 59–80) explains that among the problems in **cross-cultural communication or cross-cultural miscommunication** (which could even exist for example between native English, French, or Spanish countries), words often have double or multiple meanings, with **denotative** meanings (literal dictionary meanings) and much more complex **connotative** or **cultural** meanings (developed both collectively within cultures and individually and based on personal perceptions and experiences). He suggests that when we consider abstract words such as justice, peace, freedom, or love, cross-culturally it might be very difficult to agree to a precise and common understanding: "Cultural meanings overlap but are never exactly the

same for any two people even in the same culture. Between two cultures, the differences are larger, sometimes to the point that common understanding is extremely difficult." Stevenson notes the differences in **psycholinguistics** (the effect of a specific language influencing how we think and perceive the social environment), **cultural linguistics** (differences in connotative or cultural meanings), and **sociolinguistics** (the social factors related to the use of language such as accents, dialects, pronunciation, and vocabulary), and **nonverbal** aspects (which often transmit more information in culturally specific, unwritten, and not subject to easy control or repetition). All of these aspects, several which we will discuss later in Chapters Four, Five, and Six, can cause serious **cross-cultural conflict**.

As we will discuss more fully later, Geert Hofstede's **cross-cultural national cultural dimensions**, we can briefly note them here. Initially, he had four **cross-cultural national dimensions**: **individualism** versus **collectivism**; **low** versus **high power differences**; **low** versus **high uncertainty avoidance**; and **masculinity** versus **femininity**. Then he and Michael Harris Bond added **Confucian dynamism** in 1984 which they later called **short term** versus long term **orientations**. More recently, he has explored two new dimensions: **monumentalism** versus **flex-humility** or **self effacement**, and **self restraint** versus **self indulgence**.

Sometimes, **cross-cultural comparisons** infer superiority of one culture versus inferiority of the compared culture. Considering **international and global communication cross-culturally** at the level of individuals, Evelin Linder (2010: xvii) insists

Communication and Intercultural Communication

Sheldonian Theatre in Oxford University, England

that "global brotherhood and sisterhood, global connectedness, global cooperation, cohesion, mutuality, solidarity and loving care for our human family and its habitat are desperately needed. In Europe, the term 'social cohesion' is preferred, while in Asia, the phrase 'the harmonious society' is more commonly used. Whatever the phrasing, the meaning behind the words is solidarity among all of humankind for the common good." You are probably already competent individuals, and are in the process of becoming competent interculturalists and multiculturalists. Thus, as some of you will be **future Chinese leaders** and potentially **multiculturalists**, you personally are called upon to foster respect for other cultures in solidarity with other humans of good will from various cultures and societies, in support of the common good and

an all-round harmonious society for China and more broadly. **Are you ready to assume your role in making the world a better place through your own actions and interactions**? Early starting points include making friends with people from other cultures.

In Andrew Kelly's article on Ben Wildacky's 2010 book, *The Great Brain Race: How Global Universities Are Reshaping the World*, he writes that Wildacky "argues that nations should embrace the emergence of a global higher education market, not fear it … The existence of an academic 'free market' promises to pay dividends that are not nation-specific. World leaders should therefore endeavor to remove barriers to the free movement of people and ideas to and from the world's colleges and universities." Concluding his article, Kelly says: "In the end, The Great Brain Race is very convincing: the world is a far better place when we embrace the transnational flow of people and ideas, limit the urge to engage in academic protectionism, and to expand the reach of the global meritocracy" (2010).

2.2.5 Intercultural Communication Competence (ICC)

Guo-Ming Chen (2009: 529–532) has long been a leading scholar on many aspects of intercultural communication, and especially on **intercultural communication competence (ICC)** which he calls an extension of communication competence, but with the addition of the critically important cultural aspects of communication in "promoting productive and successful communication among people from different cultural, racial, and religious backgrounds." He notes that his original work on ICC began in 1987, with his own doctoral study at Kent State University in the United States, and incorporated four elements: (1) **personal attributes**, which include self-disclosure, self-awareness, self-concept, and social relaxation; (2) **communication skills**, including message skills, social skills, flexibility, and interaction management; (3) **psychological adaptation**, including frustration, stress, alienation, and ambiguity; and (4) **cultural awareness**, including social values, social customs, social norms, and social systems. In 1996, William J. Starosta reconsidered the four dimensions and recommended the study of **ICC** from the three aspects of **human ability**: **cognitive** (intercultural awareness), **affective** (intercultural sensitivity) and **behavioral** (intercultural effectiveness).

Still later in 2005, Chen began to relate ICC to **global perspectives**, arguing that "successful global citizens must foster the ability to negotiate their status in and among local, national and global communities." In other words, Chen claims, "on the global level, communicating competence requires people to cultivate the ability to acknowledge, respect, tolerate, and integrate cultural differences in order to become enlightened global citizens." He proposes that the four dimensions of **global communication competence** include: (1) **having a global mindset** (sensitive toward cultural diversity, open minded, locally and globally knowledgeable, critical and holistic thinkers, and conceptually and behaviorally flexible; (2) **unfolding the self** (the ability to expand one's personal identity attributes and also consider the broader world around

them; (3) **mapping the culture** (acquiring the cognitive ability to acquire as much cultural knowledge as possible or to "map the culture," and (4) **aligning the interaction** (with behavioral skills suitable to adjust to the new patterns of global interaction).

Former UN Secretary General Kofi Annan stressed that two of the greatest global problems in the world are both civil and interstate war, which brutally discriminate especially against the elderly, women, and children, including the widespread use of child soldiers, and abject poverty, which again affects the most vulnerable in society, the elderly, women, and children, who are often sold into slavery or for the women and girls who are sold into prostitution in the traffic of human beings. The current UN Secretary General Ban Ki-Moon, reflecting in a similar vein, laments that the biggest global crisis "is a lack of global leadership" and "there are too few citizens with an entirely new vision for the world, a vision that is informed by a sense of global responsibility" (Lindner, xviii). Lindner promotes the individual as "the most influential of the new forces in the global village. The voice of every person has more potential impact today than ever before" (xxxiii).

2.2.6 Intercultural and International Ethical Communication

Confucius, in *The Analects*, stipulated a Chinese "Golden Rule" which is "Do not do unto others as you would not have them do unto you." The Graeco-Roman-Christian ethical code is "Do unto others as you would have them do unto you." Later, the first century Roman poet, Horace, cautioned that the pilot of a ship should not steer it too far out into the ocean, lest it be overcome by the huge waves, nor too close into the shore, or it might be capsized on the rocks. By this he meant that we should always find a middle way, avoiding extremes, and pursuing a moderate set of principles and life. **Do you live an ethical life filled with integrity and moderation?** The Russian author Igor Klyukanov's book, *Principles of Intercultural Communication*, argues that among many approaches to **intercultural communication ethics**, there are two main broad approaches: the **universalist approach**, on one hand, in which people's actions should be similar for people in all cultures and societies, for example, the Jewish *Ten Commandments* which have been adopted world-wide by Christians as part of their ideal ethical code, or in Kale's essay, "Peace as an Ethic for Intercultural Communication" (1994) and on the other hand, the **relativist approach** which proposes that people's actions, and thus also their sense of ethics, are a part of their **cultural diversity** and can only be judged according to the ethics of a particular culture. Klyukanov finds both positive and negative aspects in each approach: "Universalist ethics is proposed as a desirable moral option for today's multicultural world because it provides a set of moral standards for all cultures to follow.... A relativist ethics is also proposed as a desirable moral option for today's multicultural world because it allows different culturally diverse moral standards, which preclude various cultures from judging one another (242–243). Klyukanov indicates then that both approaches are ethnocentric, as the universalist approach reduces all cultures to one specific standard, while relativist standards

negate all other moral standards except its own. Klyukanov cites B. Hall's 2002 (343) statement: "Ethics may be viewed as a compound of universalism and relativism. All ethical systems involve a tension between what is universal and what is relative.... The challenge, then, is to understand the nature of this compound and its implications in intercultural settings."

John C. Merrill, a famous theorist in international mass media and communication, argues that **international communicators** should pursue "overriding ethical commonalities" such as "empathy, open-mindedness, sincerity, and mutual respect." He offers two major guidelines for ethical behavior in practicing ethical journalism and international communication: (1) "Communicate only to willing others those things and employing only those techniques which you would be willing for others to use in communicating with you. (2) When in Rome use Roman ethics if such ethics do not do mischief to you own ethical standards" (1989: 286, 287, 288). In his essay, *Ethics in Intercultural Communication* (1991), he recommends four principles as a universal basis for ethical intercultural communication: (1) "Ethical communicators address people of other cultures with the same respect that they would like to receive themselves." (2) Ethical communicators seek to describe the world as they see it as accurately as possible. (3) Ethical communicators encourage people of other cultures to express themselves in their uniqueness. (4) Ethical communicators strive for identification with people from other cultures (Kale, 1991; 424 quoted by Day, 1998: 22).

2.2.7 Intercultural Conflict Resolution

As early as the 1970's, communication scholars began to consider **communication conflict theories**, and Anne Maydan Nocotera (2009: 164–170) recommends that it be called **communication management** rather than **conflict resolution** because the earlier theories suggested "an ongoing communication process focusing on interaction, whereas the latter suggests episodes that must be dealt with as they occur, focusing attention on the discrete content of each episode." She identifies several theories and concepts: **uniting conflict and communication** as interdependent, simultaneously defining each other; **conceptualizing conflict and communication**, defining conflict that allows for a constructive and continuous view of conflict; **early conflict models**, including game theory and social exchange which analyzes rationally conducted conflict between players, each of whom pursues well-defined interests and chooses from among alternative actions; **integrative negotiation models**, developing theories of collective bargaining, mediation and interpersonal conflict; **dual concerns**, which focuses on conflict management styles, predispositions, and behavioral tendencies; an **mediation competency**, where a third person intervenes to manage the conflict. Among continuing traditions, Nicotera indicates that the **interpersonal context theory** includes personal relationships, among which are the **social-ecological model**, which focuses on environmental and interpersonal relationships, the **relational order theory**, which deals with mediating in marital conflicts, the **family conflict socialization process**; the **cascade model** which predicts the likelihood of divorce from a cascade of interrelated processes; **social knowledge/cognition** which includes various beliefs, rules, and problem appraisals; and **strategic conflict**, in which it is seen that competent conflict behavior is mindful, mediated by individual differences, interpretations of the conflict, and goal assessments. Nicotera also discusses **organizational conflicts**, which occur in an institutional setting, often such as a workplace; **the community context**, which is conflict in the public arena; and in the **intercultural/international context**, which occur between two or more different cultural or identity groups, which is of interest to us and you in a course on intercultural communication. She concludes her essay by saying that the study of communication and conflict is broad and diverse, but it also emerges from such presumptions as the **inevitability** and constructive **nature of conflict**; the **dynamic nature of goals**; and the **mutual relationship** between **communication** and **conflict**. If you find yourselves becoming involved with conflict in your communication with others, remember that **all problems also have potential solutions**. Guo-Ming Chen and Ringo Ma have written an excellent book entitled *Chinese Conflict Management and Resolutions* (2002). In Chapter Ten, Zhang Rui provides us a short essay and the abstract from his MA thesis about his study on intercultural communication conflict in a university setting.

2.2.8 "Personal Motivational Persuasion" by the President of the United States to Michael Prosser

Michael —

It has now been well over a year since the near collapse of our entire financial system that cost the nation more than 8 million jobs. To this day, hard-working families struggle to make ends meet.

We've made strides—businesses are starting to hire, Americans are finding jobs, and neighbors who had given up looking are returning to the job market with new hope. But the flaws in our financial system that led to this crisis remain unresolved.

Wall Street titans still recklessly speculate with borrowed money. Big banks and credit card companies stack the deck to earn millions while far too many middle-class families, who have done everything right, can barely pay their bills or save for a better future.

We cannot delay action any longer. *It is time to hold the big banks accountable to the people they serve, establish the strongest consumer protections in our nation's history—and ensure that taxpayers will never again be forced to bail out big banks because they are "too big to fail."*

That is what Wall Street reform will achieve, why I am so committed to making it happen, and why I'm asking for your help today.

Please stand with me to show your support for Wall Street reform.

We know that without enforceable, commonsense rules to check abuse and protect families, markets are not truly free. Wall Street reform will foster a strong and vibrant financial sector so that businesses can get loans; families can afford mortgages; entrepreneurs can find the capital to start a new company, sell a new product, or offer a new service.

Consumer financial protections are currently spread across seven different government agencies. Wall Street reform will create one single Consumer Financial Protection Agency—tasked with preventing predatory practices and making sure you get the clear information, not fine print, needed to avoid ballooning mortgage payments or credit card rate hikes.

Reform will provide crucial new oversight, give shareholders a say on salaries and bonuses, and create new tools to break up failing financial firms so that taxpayers aren't forced into another unfair bailout. And reform will keep our economy secure by ensuring that no single firm can bring down the whole financial system.

With so much at stake, it is not surprising that allies of the big banks and Wall Street lenders have already launched a multi-million-dollar ad campaign to fight these changes. Arm-twisting lobbyists are already storming Capitol Hill, seeking to undermine the strong bipartisan foundation of reform with loopholes and exemptions for the most egregious abusers of consumers.

I won't accept anything short of the full protection that our citizens deserve and our economy needs. It's a fight worth having, and it is a fight we can win—if we stand up and speak out together.

So I'm asking you to join me, starting today, by adding your name as a strong supporter of Wall Street reform:
http://my.barackobama.com/ StandForWallStreetReform

Thank you,
President Barack Obama

2.2.9   Analysis of President Obama's "Personal Motivational Persuasion"

Aristotle wrote one of the early treatises on persuasion, Rhetoric, in which he proposed that rhetoric is finding all of the available means of persuasion, through **logic (logos), credibility of the speaker (ethos)**, and **emotional appeals** received by the audience through the emotional identification of the communicator to the audience **(pathos)**. **Persuasion** is used to convince others on issues that relate to deliberation of policies, actions, and motivation, attitude, beliefs and values, that illustrate the **author's credibility**, and the **audience's willingness** to hear or read the author's message through various channels. The **source's credibility**, according to Galvin, Prescott, and Huseman (1992: 70), includes his or her expertise, trustworthiness, dynamism, objectivity, and good will toward the audience. They identify the following characteristics for getting the audience's attention and motivating it, based on Abraham Maslow's categories of **human needs: physiological, safety** and **security, belonging; esteem, status**; and **self-actualization needs**, plus direct and indirect rewards that might be achieved by following the **motivational appeals** of the speaker or writer. **Persuasion** is often framed in terms of problems that need to be solved with reasonable or emotional solutions being offered to the audience.

In the example above, we have a "personal message" from the President of the United States to Michael Prosser about the **problem** of excessive profits by Wall Street financial institutions and the struggles that ordinary American families have faced because of the 2008–2010 recession, and the proposed **solution**: reform of the Wall Street financial system. The message offers **refutation** for counter arguments that others might make against his proposal. Obama seeks to identify in general with Americans who have suffered through the most serious 2008–2010 recession. However, **we can also ask**: why has the President of the United States written personally by email to Michael? President Obama makes the following "urgent" appeals: "**We cannot delay action any longer**" and "**Please stand with me to show your support for Wall Street reform.**", and thus "**So I'm asking you to join me, starting today, by adding your name as a strong supporter of Wall Street reform**" and he even provides a very specific website: **http://my.barackobama. com/StandForWallStreetReform** by which Michael can express his support. Before finishing his message, President Obama makes the situation very personal in terms of his own commitment to Wall Street reform: "I won't accept anything short of the full protection that our citizens deserve and our economy needs.

Communication and Intercultural Communication

It's a fight worth having, and it is a fight we can win—if we stand up and speak out together." Then when Michael goes to the website, first, there is the statement: "Stand with the President on Wall Street Reform," with an attractive photo of President Obama, and we find these hoped for commitments by Michael and those others who open their personal message:

> *"I stand with President Obama to:*
> *Create the strongest consumer pro-tections in history so that Americans always get the information they need to make smart financial decisions; and rein in Wall Street abuses, hold the big banks accountable, and ensure that taxpayers never again have to bail them out; and prevent lobbyist loopholes or exemptions from weakening reform."*
>
> *An invitation is provided to join the group with first and last name, email address and zip code, and a final request: "Add Your Name."*

In doing so, another linked message appears and requests: "**Please Donate to Support Wall Street Reform**" and at the bottom of the page, the request is repeated: "**Please donate today.**" Then, on the right side of the page, there is information for contributors, including Michael Prosser's name already filled in, with requests for his email address, mail address, and phone number, and suggested donation amounts:

$10	50	250	1000
$25	100	500	Other
Credit card:	Visa		
	Mastercard		
	American Express		
	expiration date		

Finally, six legal compliance regulations are provided, including the statement: "I am a United States citizen or a permanent resident alien." At the bottom of this form is a provision for sending a check offline to "Organizing for America," and then "**Submit.**" At the very end of the third page, we are told that Organizing for America has paid for this message, and that it is a project of the Democratic National Committee, with its address listed.

Should Michael be flattered to have received this personal message from the President of the United States? To be honest, Michael receives a couple of personal messages like this one from President Obama or his staff weekly related to different issues of national importance. Why does Michael receive such messages? Perhaps, Michael signed up for such messages during the 2008 presidential campaign, when Barack Obama received more than one billion dollars for his campaign through the Internet alone for "Organizing for America." Michael signed on the second page of the current message in supporting the initiative, but did not proceed to support the third page request for a donation. Did the President's three-step motivational approach then not succeed with Michael? Or did Michael's curiosity or interest motivate him to agree generally in principle to support the President on this issue, and thus at least indicating his attention to the message and partial support? How many people actually received this personalized message? Out of the millions in the total number of personal emails sent out, what percentage would be likely to move to the third step and donate to Organizing for America? Statistics for such messages often demonstrate that the number is as low sometimes as 10%.

Was Obama's expertise considered credible or noncredible? He has some very strong emotional language in the message. Is it effective? Are there other national issues which might successfully motivate Michael or like-minded individuals to fully support the President's requests? If Michael did not donate for this issue, is it possible or likely that he has done so in the past or will he do so later because of the President's personalized appeals? Did Obama meet the needs of Michael and others in his persuasive and recipient identification efforts? Since the email request is a project of the Democratic National Committee, how would Republicans in general opposition to the President's policies and initiatives react if they received such a message? Is financial reform on Wall Street a topic of interest to both major American political parties and to ordinary Americans and permanent resident aliens? Would those who identify themselves as independents be more or less likely to be motivated to respond positively to such requests than Republicans? After all, Obama won office not only by the votes of many Democrats, but also of enough independent voters and Republicans who may have been disenchanted with the campaign of John McCain/Sarah Palin to become elected by a 53% to 46% popular vote in 2008.

However, although Obama had a very high poll approval rate in his presidential election, his polled approval ratings have dropped considerably. Is it likely to go up or down in later polls? In fact, the legislation was passed with only Democratic legislators voting for it, and it became a major political and divisive issue in the 2010 US midterm elections, which was a serious loss for many Democratic candidates. And its divisiveness is likely also in the 2012 elections, when President Obama and other Democratic candidates for state governorships, state legislators, US senators and congressmen will face challengers from the Republican Party (The GOP or Grand Old Party) and other minority parties such as the rather unfocused "Tea Party."

Janet A. Bridges (2009: 2004–2008) identifies **corporate campaign theories** as the study of corporations when they develop **campaign communication** because either existing or new legislation is being advocated or challenged. She points out that such corporate campaigns can be seen from either of two perspectives (1) **promotional or service advertising campaigns** and (2) **corporate issues campaigns**: "In the corporate environment, issues campaigns focus on either opportunities or threats." She argues that "the issues both attract and compete for attention in the public arena, including media coverage. An issue may also attract activist interest groups. Management of these corporate issues campaigns therefore involves negotiations with activist groups included in the theoretical framework of powerful stakeholders."

Thus, **we can ask in this context**, how many groups of powerful stakeholders were signficantly included in the campaign? In a sense, Obama's appeals involved as stakeholders on the opposition side, Wall Street bankers and Republican members of Congress, and on his other side Democratic members of Congress, and in this particular case, American citizens and resident aliens who could contact the legislators to pass the regulations that he sought to limit the influence of the Wall Street bankers. In fact, among the legislative victories of the

Obama White House in 2010 was the passing of the regulatory legislation which he requested.

Now, **we can also ask**, why is Obama's **three-step motivational message** of interest to Chinese students who live in China and who could not vote for President Obama or his intiatives in any case? In fact, we have learned that in order to donate to "Organizing for America," one must be an American citizen or a permanent resident alien in the United States. Thus, if Michael was a Chinese citizen living in the United States as a temporary resident, such as a student, he could support step two by endorsing President Obama's position, but he could not donate to this cause. Why should reform of excessive Wall Street financial practices be of concern to Chinese in China? Generally speaking, Obama has been very popular among many Chinese young people, but that alone is not a good reason for you to be interested in this campaign.

As President of the United States, and in the context of the recent nearly world-wide financial crisis, there are multiple intercultural, cross-cultural, and global implications for policies which he proposes or signs into law, and which are also significant for China's fairly rapid financial recovery from the recent recession. Thus, solutions to financial emergencies in the United States are also very important far more broadly than just in America.

While President Obama's arguments were validated in the passage by Congress and the Senate of strict laws regulating Wall Street, the Democratic Party had huge losses in the 2010 US election, with more than 60 seats in the House of Representatives moving into Republican hands, the election of enough Republican senators to change the Democratic senate seats down to 53 versus 47 for the Republicans, and the loss of several governorships of individual states and major Republian gains in state legislatures. The conservative, mostly independent voters, swung broadly against the Obama policies as going too far, while the very liberal Democratic voters and liberal independents felt that he was too timid in his measures to make a historic change in health care for the Americans and in terms of stabilizing the American economy. President Obama admitted in a press conference the day after the November 2, 2010 election that he and his party had received a major "shellacking" (a decisive defeat). Many media pundits argued that he must make significant changes in his administrative goals and policies if he would have any chance to win the 2010 presidential election. Towards the end of December 2010's "lame duck" Congressional season after the election, President Obama did win several important legislative compromises, again resulting in Republicans saying that he won too much and Democrats and disinfected independents who helped him win the presidential election in 2008 who said that he was being too weak to win more concessions. It is in the nature of electoral politics in the US.

2.2.10 Becoming Critical Thinkers

Francis Bacon's statement "**Knowledge is power!**" is still true today. Rene Descartes' famous words "**Dubito, ergo cogito! Cogito, ergo Sum!**" ("**I doubt, therefore I think! I think, therefore I am!**") called us all to be **skeptics**, and then **thinkers**, and then **independent thinkers**. During the Enlightenment, Immanuel Kant exclaimed: "**Dare to know! Dare to think independently!**" To be really effective in understanding persuasive, intracultural, intercultural, international, cross-cultural or global communication and media, we need to become, as the American educator John Dewey suggested, *critical thinkers*, or as the Brazilian educator for the oppressed, Paulo Freire, called it, holding a **critical consciousness**, as the communication is often of a critical nature, especially in the direct editorials in major newspapers for or against a specific candidate or policy, or widespread on the Internet, blogs, or social networks.

Lindner proposes that developing a policy or vision comes first, followed by creating strategies to implement the policy, ideally through a process of dialogue. Then she suggests that the ideas need to be promoted as widely as possible through network building. After this the strategies can be formulated and logistically put in place (Lindner, xxvii). Even if Obama and his team had done all of these things, if Michael were a Republican,

for example, he would probably be very likely not to accept President Obama's expertise on this issue, however, and possibly would even consider that Obama was being untrustworthy or untruthful, unless with a very open mind the President would convince him of the merits of his persuasion. The Republican Senate Minority Leader, Mitch McConnel of Kentucky, following the 2010 election, claimed that the major Republican goal for the second two years of Obama's first four year in office should be to prevent him from winning a second four-year term.

This is a topic worth discussing as an aspect of **motivational persuasion** on one hand, and as Chinese students in studying **intercultural** and **cross-cultural communication** and becoming both **critical thinkers**, positive **multicultural** and **global citizens** on the other hand. It also represents the President of the United States in what can be considered a "**corporate campaign communication**" by his administration in this case, since such **campaign communication** often occurs when legislation is occurring or anticipated.

2.3 Case Study: The United Nations as an International Communication Forum

Following the unsuccessful League of Nations founded after World War I, which the US as an emerging major power did not join, and failing to prevent World War II, British Prime Minister Winston Churchill, Soviet Chairman Josef Stalin, and US President Franklyn D. Roosevelt in the Atlantic Charter conference of 1942

agreed to establish the United Nations. After World War II and the San Francisco Charter preparation conference in 1945 with 50 nations present and signing the Charter, the first session of the General Assembly was held in 1946 in war torn London. The UN Charter reads:

Communication and Intercultural Communication

We the peoples of the United Nations, Determined to save succeeding generations from the scourge of war, which twice in our life time has brought untold sorrow to mankind, and to reaffirm faith in fundamental human rights, in the dignity and worth of the human person, in the equal rights of men and women, and of nations large and small, and to establish conditions under which justice and respect for the obligations arising from treaties and other sources of international law can be maintained, and to promote social progress and better standards of life in larger freedom, and, for these ends, to practice tolerance and live together in peace with one another as good neighbors, and to unite our strength to maintain international peace and security, and to insure by the acceptance of principles and the institutions of methods, that armed force shall not be used, save in the common interest, and to employ international machinery for the promotion of the economic and social advancement of all peoples, have resolved to combine our efforts to accomplish these aims (UN Charter, 1945).

Five organs were established: the Security Council, as the major binding decision-maker on issues relating to international security and peace, including the People's Republic of China since 1971 (initially the Republic of China), France, the Soviet Union (becoming Russia in 1991), the United Kingdom, and the United States plus 4 two-year terms for national delegations and rising to 10 nations with two-year terms in 1955; the General Assembly including all 192 nations belonging to the United Nations; the Trusteeship Council (no longer functioning since there are no longer any trust territories); the UN Educational, Scientific and Cultural Organ (UNESCO); the International Court of Justice (World Court); and the Secretariat, headed by the Secretary General, presently Ban Ki Moon of Korea, beginning a second five-year term in 2012.

UNESCO Ethical Issues of the Information Society

The commitment of UNESCO to the crucial issue of the free flow of information and access to knowledge sources is very much inspired by its Constitution which states: "the wide diffusion of culture and the education of humanity for justice and liberty and peace are indispensable to the dignity of man and constitute a sacred duty which all the nations must fulfill in a spirit of mutual assistance and concern." Acceptance of these principles while developing creative multilingual content and universal access to information and communication means is central for achieving an equitable presence in, and access to, cyberspace. Embracing coherent ethical guidelines is essential in face of increasing globalization.

Thus, the definition and adoption of best practices and voluntary, self-regulatory, professional and ethical guidelines should be encouraged among media professionals, information producers, users and service providers with due respect to freedom of expression.

Access to information for all remains a fundamental right which should be upheld with greater efficiency and imagination in a spirit of equity, justice and mutual respect. (UNESCO)

As an aspect of international and global communication, UNESCO has established 936 World Heritage Sites throughout the world.

Until July, 2011, China ranks third in such sites since1985, with 41 world heritage sites. Each of these sites are protected as a part of the world (and cross-cultural) heritage. Besides honoring these sights as world treasures, each one assists the indigenous populations to earn livings by protecting and demonstrating them through tourism.

2.4 Summary

In Chapter Two, our initial dialogue has started to become richer with more and more students entering into the conversation and on various topics which do in fact relate closely to the study of intercultural and cross-cultural communication, despite what some might consider as irrelevant interventions. We have investigated the **nature** and **definitions** of **communication**, especially as socially interactive behavior. We have noted more than once so far in the text that humans are uniquely **symbol-makers**, **symbol-users**, and **symbol-misusers**. We have seen that there is a **spectrum** or **continuum** of levels of **cultural communication**, **intraculturally** between twins or family members, **interculturally** between members of two different cultures, and in a **multicultural setting** with participants interacting from several different cultures. We have seen that **cross-cultural communication** is typically comparative or contrastive, but that the goal for all levels of **cultural communication** is to respect other humans and to unite in solidarity for the common good. We will return to the subjects of **international** and **global media** in Chapter Eight and **cross-cultural research** in Chapter Ten. Guo-Ming Chen has offered us the dimensions that make **intercultural communication competence (ICC)** possible and productive. Both in the chapter's text and in the case study discussing UNESCO, we have seen that ethical communication is an important ingredient. Later, in Chapter Ten, we will return to the concept of **ethical student behavior**. We have noted that a barrier to intercultural and international communication lies in **intercultural communication conflict**. A substantial case study within the text itself has been the presentation and analysis of a personal persuasive message to Michael Prosser (and others) by the President of the United States, Barack Obama. This analysis, as well as the dialogues, and the chapter questions have led you to move toward becoming **critical thinkers** by exploring different viewpoints and making a serious analysis of the topics under consideration. Finally, the case study discusses the role of the United Nations as a **universal communication forum**.

2.5 Questions for Discussion

2.5.1 In the imaginary dialogues, we can see that both the imaginary Chinese teacher, Professor Zhang, and the real American teacher, Michael, have different styles of teaching the class. Considering the cross-cultural similarities and differences between the two teachers, how would you describe each of their teaching styles? Do they represent your typical views of a Chinese and an American teacher? Why or Why not?

2.5.2 In this chapter's dialogue, we find considerable discussion of Chinese and Western significant days and holidays. What are the differences between the Western Christmas and the Chinese Lunar New Year celebrations? How do the two broad cultures remember those who have died? Why is Mother's Day, an important Western event, influential in China, but not Father's Day, also a Western special day? Though not discussed in the dialogue, Labor Day in China and the US fall on different days and periods of the year: the Chinese Labor Day on May 1, and the American Labor on the first Monday of September. How do you account for the differences?

2.5.3 The early anthropologist practitioner of intercultural communication, Edward T. Hall, often called the grandfather of intercultural communication, says that "communication is culture" and "culture is communication." Compare Chapter One: Culture and Chapter Two: Communication. What are the overlaps between the two chapters? What is the meaning of such an apparently repetitious explanation of culture and communication? Do you agree? Why or why not?

2.5.4 We have suggested that there is a spectrum or continuum of intracultural, intercultural, and multicultural communication. There appears to be substantial overlap between the three terms. What are the similarities and differences that exist in the three different levels of the spectrum? How are homogeneous versus heterogeneous cultures similar and different at the same time?

2.5.5 Guo-Ming Chen provides us with four dimensions which help individuals become interculturally competent in their communication: **personal attributes, communication skills, psychological adaptation**, and **cultural awareness**. How are these attributes linked? Which is the most important among them? Why?

2.5.6 In our discussion about interculturally and internationally ethical individuals, Kenneth D. Day provides several steps for leading a life filled with integrity and living in moderation. Why is self-respect and respect for others in solidarity with other humans so important in learning and practicing effective intercultural communication?

2.5.7 Assuming that you and your dorm mates may come from different parts of China, and that your intracultural differences might lead you to interpersonal conflicts, what are the ways that you can find solutions to overcome these communication management problems and conflicts? If your dorm mates instead were multicultural in nature, perhaps the communication conflicts might become even more severe. How can you achieve a harmonious situation in this case? If you needed mediation in either case, where the dorm mates are from a different part of China, or if they come from perhaps two or three different countries or cultures, what steps would you take to seek solutions to potential communication conflicts?

2.5.8 In President Obama's "personal" motivational persuasive message to "Michael" (and many others with personalized greetings), why is Michael, also a Democrat, rather than his youngest son, Louis, who is a conservative Republican and financial analyst, more likely to click the place where he can agree with Obama's message? Why would Louis who accepts very few of Obama's monetary persuasive arguments or policies be unlikely to submit a response that says that he agrees with Obama's attacks on the financiers on Wall Street?

2.5.9 Why should you, as Chinese students, be interested in President Obama's financial persuasion or policies? What are the financial implications of Obama's policies on the international financial markets? What are they for the Chinese economy? What are the impacts of Chinese fiscal policy on other international financial markets, or those of the United States?

2.5.10 *Encarta World English Dictionary* (1999) describes **critical thinking** as "giving comments or judgments, containing or involving comments and opinions that analyze or judge something in an analytical way," such as "a critical analysis of modern economic theory." What are the ways that you as Chinese students can become effective **critical thinkers** on topics which are important to you as Chinese citizens, and potentially as "world citizens?" You have long been taught to memorize information that has been presented, but as you get older, your critical thinking and analysis seeing topics from more than one side have increased more and more. How do you sharpen these skills progressively as you become more and more mature?

2.6   Suggested Readings

Casmir, F. (1998). *Ethics in intercultural and international communication.* Mahwah, NJ: Earlbaum.

Chen, G. M. & Ma, R. (Eds.) (2002). *Chinese conflict management and resolution.* Westport, CT: Ablex.

Chen, G. M. & Starosta, W. J. (2007). *Foundations of intercultural communication.* Shanghai, China: Shanghai Foreign Language Education Press.

Dodd, C. H. (2007). *Dynamics of intercultural communication.* Shanghai, China: Shanghai Foreign Language Education Press.

Gao, G. & Ting-Toomey, S. (1998). *Communicating effectively with the Chinese.* Thousand Oaks, CA: Sage.

Gudykunst, W. B. & Kim, Y. Y. (2007). *Communicating with strangers: An approach to intercultural communication.* Shanghai, China: Shanghai Foreign Language Education Press.

Gudykunst, W. B. (2007). *Cross-cultural and interpersonal communication.* Shanghai, China: Shanghai Foreign Language Education Press.

Heisey, D. R. (Ed.) (2000). *Chinese perspectives in rhetoric and communication.* Stamford, CT: Ablex.

Hofstede, G. (2008). *Culture's consequences: Comparing values, behaviors, institutions and organizations.* (2nd edition). Shanghai, China: Shanghai Foreign Language Education Press.

Jia, W., Lu, X., & Heisey, D. R. (2002). *Chinese communication and research.* Westport, CT: Ablex.

Kulich, S. J. & Prosser, M. H. (Eds.) (2007). *Intercultural perspectives on Chinese communication.* Shanghai, China: Shanghai Foreign Language Education Press.

Lu X., Jia, W., & Heisey, D. R. (Eds.) (2002). *Chinese communication studies: Contexts and comparisons.* Stamford, CT: Ablex.

Lustig, M. W. & Koester, J. K. (2007). *Intercultural competence: Interpersonal communication across cultures.* (5th edition). Shanghai, China: Shanghai Foreign Language Education Press.

Prosser, M. H. (1970). *Sow the wind, reap the whirlwind: Heads of state address the United Nations* (two volumes). New York, NY: William Morrow.

Prosser, M. H. (1978, 1985, 1989). *The cultural dialogue: An introduction to intercultural communication.* Boston, MA: Houghton Mifflin; Washington, D.C.: SIETAR International. Trans. into Japanese by R. Okabe. Tokyo, Japan: Tokai University Press.

Samovar, L. A. & Porter, R. E. (2007). *Intercultural communication: A reader.* (10th edition). Shanghai, China: Shanghai Foreign Language Education Press.

Samovar, L. A.,Porter, R. E., & McDaniel, E. R. (2009) *Communication between cultures* (6th edition). Beijing, China: Peking University Press.

Ting-Toomey, S. & Oetzel, J. (2001). *Managing intercultural conflict effectively.* Thousand Oaks, CA: Sage.

United Nations Charter (1945). New York, NY: United Nations.

Universal Declaration of Human Rights. 1948. New York, NY: United Nations.

Chapter THREE

Creating Our Own Cultural Stories

3.1 Dialogue

Professor Zhang: Good morning, boys and girls. I hope that you are now ready to consider "Creating Our Own Cultural Stories." Before we can clearly understand the nature of intercultural communication as it applies to ourselves, we need to have a sense of our own special cultural stories. We need to know who we are as Chinese, in our own families, communities and society. You have your own cultural stories which will be different from others as you come from different parts of China, with 56 different nationalities, the largest of which is Han. Call your grandparents and your parents and learn more about their cultural stories. Their stories are a part of your own cultural stories. Are you one of China's minorities? You come from different cities and towns. Is your culture different from that of your grandparents or parents, or cousins growing up in different Chinese locations? Or even from that of your classmates in this intercultural communication class? Even the twins, Spring and Summer, have similar but still also unique cultural stories.

Michael: I am an only child, chosen by my adoptive parents when I was two. Occasionally I have wondered if my natural parents each separately had more children, and if I would then have half-brothers and half-sisters both by my natural mother and by my natural father whom I never knowingly met.

Creating Our Own Cultural Stories

Ivy:	Michael, what's a half-brother and a half-sister? It doesn't make sense.
Michael:	We would each share only one natural parent. Stepsisters and stepbrothers occur in a second marriage where the spouse is not related to the other spouse's family. Recently, on a cruise around southern Latin America, an old man poked me with his cane and said, "Hi, Larry." Then he realized that I was not his own son Larry, but when I met Larry later on board, there certainly was a considerable resemblance, both of us are bearded and heavy. Now, I have a Russian-born granddaughter. My daughter, Michelle and her former husband were encouraged by my cultural history of being adopted, to seek a Russian child, who might more or less resemble them.
Tulip:	How does it feel to be adopted, Michael? Did you ever try to find out who your natural parents were?
Maria:	How does your granddaughter feel about being adopted, Michael? Would she rather grow up in Russia or in America?
Michael:	There are lots of very good comments and questions here. What about you, ladies and gentlemen, what do you think about children being adopted by parents overseas?
Tony:	It shouldn't happen. Children should grow up in their own country.
Fiona:	But if they are orphans, and a couple from overseas wants to love them as their own daughter or son, that's good.
Joy:	Actually, I am an orphan from Fujian. My real parents died in a flood when I was a small child, but my adoptive parents love me very much. That's why I took the English name Joy.
Michael:	No doubt you know Beethoven's *Ode to Joy*. It's your song.
Tulip:	As I said before, I am just an ordinary Chinese girl. I don't have any cultural stories that are very interesting. I am twenty, but nothing interesting has ever happened in my life or that of my family.
Professor Zhang:	The Chinese culture is very rich and vibrant. There are very few cultures and societies in the world that can match or surpass our history. Tulip, you are too modest.
Michael:	Yes, when I said that I only know English and very little Mandarin, at the same time, I have worked hard to learn as much about the Chinese culture as I can. We can consider aspects of Asian culture, and then of Chinese culture, and then our own individual cultures. Though I am not Chinese, and never can be, some of my

Chinese student friends have called me a "Chiamerican" since I have blended my life-long American and more recently Chinese cultures.

Laughter

Mike: That's funny. Yes, I think you probably are a Chiamerican, Michael.

Cherry: Let's test you on some of the top proverbs or sayings in Chinese culture. In a study for a Master's thesis by a friend, Weng Liping, he found out that the Chinese women students preferred the three top proverbs or sayings: "Follow your own course; let others do the talking." "Impossible is nothing," and "Just do it." Where do you think that these sayings come from, Michael?

Michael: Well, that's amazing, don't you think, Cherry? The first one I think is from Dante, so it is a western saying. The other two are easy. One is the advertising slogan for Adidas and the other is the advertising slogan for Nike. We can see that these women students are fairly westernized.

Iris: Here are two more Chinese proverbs, Michael. "Honoring contentment brings enduring happiness," and "Where there's a will, there's a way."

Michael: Yes, the first one certainly sounds like a Chinese proverb, but we Americans use the second one all the time. I do think though that the saying "A journey of 1,000 miles begins with the first step." definitely is a Chinese saying.

Laughter

True Nation: We Chinese university students place a lot of value on our own independence, which we didn't do so much in middle school. We are more self-confident, and ambitious. I am proud to be a highly nationalistic Chinese. If I start a tee shirt company, I could call it the True Nation Ping and Pong, Ltd. with little sayings by both of them on each tee shirt.

Laughter

Angel: A lot of our Chinese pop songs say that "tomorrow is another day" but we know that "the past is prologue." Are those Chinese or Western proverbs? I am not sure, but we certainly know that the saying "the kindness of a drop of water will be repaid by a flowing spring" is Chinese.

Professor Zhang: This is an interesting discussion, class. Maybe these sayings or proverbs are cross-cultural in nature. It's like the short story: "The Lady or the Tiger" which many of you know. I always believed that it was a Chinese story, but I learned that an American, Frank Stockton, had written it in the late 1800s. So, we see that

Creating Our Own Cultural Stories

proverbs and stories cross back and forth between and among cultures. When faculty members, students, or business persons, and their accompanying families, live in a new society for a long period, we can consider them "third culture persons" since they incorporate both aspects of their own culture and also that of their new culture. We also have the concept of "third culture kids" for a young person who has lived a long time in a new culture, or perhaps even more than one new culture, for example, in the case of diplomatic, military, or business families living and working or studying in new cultures, such things often happen when families move from culture to culture.

Michael: As humans, we are story-tellers by nature. We all have stories to tell, some more than others. In digging more deeply into your family and community backgrounds, it becomes clearer that your cultural stories are important to your own lives. We all need to "map" our cultures before we start to understand other cultures. Many members of non technological cultures believe that the very stones tell stories. If stones have important messages, then so do our families, our communities, and ourselves.

Professor Zhang: As you know, there are many foreigners living in China, some with the expectation of spending much of their lives here, often in intercultural marriages, that we can call "settlers," and others who are here for a shorter time and who then may shift to another society or culture, and we can call them "sojourners." Your goal is to acknowledge that each of you really do have a rich individual culture through your communities and families. Some of you have family names that are a part of the old one hundred names in Chinese culture, such as mine. This is a simple form of qualitative intercultural research.

Jason: Yes, I have the same family name as yours, Professor Zhang. Perhaps we are related?

Laughter

Michael: Since I have lived longer than all of you and Professor Zhang, and have traveled widely, I have many interesting cultural stories to tell. In fact, since I came to China several years ago, I have kept a journal as often as it is convenient, and I have now filled more than 36 notebooks, which expand on my cultural experiences, allowing me to retrieve my memories, and to provide them for my sons and daughter and my grandchildren if they should choose to read them later. It would be wise for all of you to keep a regular journal in English, and by doing so you can have a record of your own cultural story and can look back at how much more your current cultural experiences are meaningful now and later in your life. If culture is a memory chain from the past to the present to the future, then your present cultural life is important too. Just think, what if the centenarians in Ru Gao had kept journals for half of their lives or much longer since they were young. What a rich historical and cultural legacy they would leave!

Professor Zhang: Now, Professor Li Mengyu of Ocean University, the first author of this book, has kindly agreed to give you some of her own cultural story, and Professor Michael will give you some of his own cultural story. Then we will share a few cultural stories of other young people in and out of China and an interesting case study about three generations of Chinese women: grandmothers, mothers, and daughters. You should each write your own cultural stories.

The Typical Japanese Bar

Creating Our Own Cultural Stories

3.2   Li Mengyu's Cultural Story

I was born in the late 1960s, I grew up when education was gradually becoming important. My mother was a middle school teacher, and my home was in the school. I was a good student in the teachers' eyes and studied very hard. I passed the college entrance examination smoothly, an important step in my life. Higher education changed my life direction. I continued pursuing my graduate and doctoral study and I now teach in the Ocean University of China. Another important issue in my life is English which I studied as an English major. English has given me a keen interest in Western literature such as Shakespeare's sonnets and Wordsworth's poems. My graduate paper focused on Steinbeck's *Long Valley* and my doctoral dissertation compared Shen Congwen and William Faulkner's novels. I have participated in many international conferences on intercultural communication in the USA, Japan, and Singapore. My horizon has been broadened by meeting scholars from different parts of the world and getting to know different cultures and people.

When I first attended a 2007 intercultural communication conference in Harbin, I met American Professor Michael Prosser, a distinguished expert in intercultural communication as well as one of the founders in the field. I greeted him by saying "Hello, Professor Prosser", he smiled and said, "Everyone calls me Michael." I was shocked, since in China, I addressed respectable professors by their titles and surnames. However, several years later, when we met

again in Kumamoto, Japan, I greeted him by saying "Hello, Michael," and he responded with "Hello, Professor li." Each of us had learned well the greeting differences in Chinese and American cultures. At the Harbin conference, I met another American Professor Tom Bruneau whose research includes brain communication, nonverbal communication in time and silence. Inspired by his research, I also research these topics, particularly focusing on the Chinese perspective. I also met scholars from Europe, Russia, Japan, Iran, South Africa, and Mexico, experiencing real and unique intercultural communication with people from very different cultural backgrounds. Once I met an Iranian professor who carried a camcorder with him and asked me to say something to his students. I had a friendly chat with a South African professor. When talking about nonverbal communication issues, he said in his culture his children could not gaze at him when he spoke and women whose positions in families and society were quite low were not even allowed to wear trousers as many women do in China. Two Norwegian female scholars remarked that they found it quite interesting when I told them what I and other Chinese women have for breakfast.

In September 2008, I was a visiting scholar at the University of Louisville. I felt very excited to visit the US for the first time. Generally speaking, my life there was thrilling and pleasant. I learned more about American people and culture, making many nice friends there and visiting many wonderful places. I also experienced several culture shocks. When I first arrived at the Louisville airport, I felt upset that my small suitcase was missing. Searching for it for a long time, I was the last one entering the luggage claim area. Two American service women were surprised to see me turning up late and they discussed it secretly and suspiciously. I sensed their unfriendliness and mistrust.

Another culture shock in Louisville was the safety issue. I was surprised to hear that one should not go out alone after sunset. "If you go outside alone you surely take the risk of losing your life," one of the Chinese students said. I could not believe it, since in China, I often shop and walk in the evening as other Chinese do, and I had never thought of safety problems. However what happened on one night really terrified me. Suddenly someone knocked heavily at my door a for long time. I phoned my landlord, who eventually took me to a safer apartment. What's more, he told me not to speak to strangers after that, "since there are some bad guys who would stop you and even knock you down by taking your purse away. How can you figure out who is good or bad from their appearances? So never speak to any strangers for the sake of your safety." Perhaps he exaggerated the issue, but safety was a serious problem in that city. It raised a question in my mind: "I have thought of the United States as a free country, why is there no freedom of taking a walk as one likes in the evening in Louisville?" Maybe the allowance of buying guns freely causes part of the problem. The United States is such a free country that it allows its citizen to buy guns freely. But those who have no guns may become victims. Still, I longed for the freedom of walking in the morning and at night as I had enjoyed in China.

Michael Prosser Is Demonstrating the Importance of Opening Up One's Horizon

However, I appreciate the kindness, politeness and earnest attitude of American people and their sweet smiles. When I asked Americans the way or something else, they were always very friendly and talked to me patiently and politely. Another good American quality is their earnest attitude towards work. Once a secretary in the University's International Center said that she loved her work and regarded it as exciting and creative. In short, I think Americans' sincere and earnest attitudes towards work and people are worth learning.

In the US, I saw many wonderful things and different people. Particularly, I cherish my visit to Washington D.C. The short experience and trip organized by the International Center of the University of Louisville were marvelous. In Washington, scholars and students from different parts of the world had friendly chats and a good time together on the bus. Seeing American girls laughing loudly and sometimes walking on the bus with bare feet surprised me. In China, girls seldom behave like that. I also found that the Brazilian students liked to gather as a group. We visited some famous free

Creating Our Own Cultural Stories

Smithsonian museums, such as Natural Science, National Gallery of Art, and the National Air and Space Museum. When I walked around the Washington and Lincoln Memorials, I had great respect for the outstanding American presidents, and I was particularly inspired by Lincoln's famous Gettysburg address sculptured on the wall: "and that government of the people, by the people, for the people, shall not perish from the earth."

In 2009, I attended a conference held in the Kumamoto Gakuen University. In southern Japan, it is not easy to ask the way in English if we get lost, since many people there cannot understand or speak English well. However, in Tokyo, it is totally different. Once I lost my way at midnight in Tokyo, but I found my way easily as many people in Tokyo can speak very good English. Japanese culture has been greatly influenced by Chinese culture, while keeping the tradition quite well. There are many Japanese lanes with the Chinese Tang Dynasty architectural style with a calm and silent atmosphere. As we know, Japanese tea originated from China during the Tang and Song Dynasties by monks who studied in China. However, the Japanese tea ceremony has developed into a unique style by combining daily activity with a profound philosophical and aesthetic pursuit. The inside of the tea room at Kumamoto Gakuen University was very simple but quite nice. On a wall there was a calligraphy with the four characters "harmony, respect, silence and solitude." It showed that the tea philosophy was greatly influenced by the Chinese Taoism and Buddhism cultures. Some young women in kimonos warmly welcomed us. When we finally left the tea room, we felt happy and peaceful.

In the University, we also appreciated another performance of Bushido. As it is known in China, there are seven virtues of Bushido: *Gi* (doing the right thing), *Yuuki* (bravery and courageous energy), *Jin* (benevolence). *Rei* (politeness and respect shown in social behavior), *Makoto* (truth in word and action), *Meiyo* (a good reputation and honor), and *Chuugi* (loyalty). Here we see again the impact of Confucianism culture as these virtues are all fundamental virtues of Confucianism. However, in Japanese Bushido culture, the virtues have been greatly stressed. Ruth Benedict in her book *The Chrysanthemum and the Sword* was puzzled about the paradoxes she observed in Japanese culture, by a people so ready to die by the sword and yet so concerned with the beauty of the chrysanthemum. I think the two symbols of the Chrysanthemum and the Sword illustrate perfectly the Japanese people's innate sense of love for beauty and deep obsession with the virtues of Bushido. On June, 2010, I was also invited to attend the 60th Annual International Communication Conference and experienced the wonderful cultural diversity in Singapore.

Ever since 1980s, Chinese scholars have become more and more active in the field of intercultural communication, and the voices of Chinese scholars have been uttered more and more. Nevertheless, we still have a long way to go. Therefore, in writing my professional intercultural communication papers, I have a strong sense of speaking out the Chinese voice. I have written on the topic of the unique values of Chinese traditional cultural time orientation in comparison with the Western cultural time orientation, underscoring my view that the subjective, flexible and relative approaches of the traditional Chinese culture time orientation can provide meaningful revelations to the western world. I have also discussed the Chinese viewpoint of harmony which advances the view that creating a harmonious communication relationship among people from diverse cultures is of vital importance to our successful intercultural communication, while the traditional Chinese notion of "harmony" underscoring the value of difference, reconciliation and creation can provide the field with the new and illuminating resources I have also discussed in my papers on cultural time, space and values between Chinese and American novels. Recently I have finished another paper reexamining perceptions of silence in Chinese culture. In short, I hope through my teaching and professional writing efforts, I can make a little contribution to the field of intercultural communication by expressing a distinct Chinese voice. My husband, Professor Wen Fenqiao, and I hope that our own cultural and professional background will encourage our son Wen Haiqi, who has adapted the English name, Kevin, to undertake postgraduate studies in the US after he graduates from a Chinese university.

3.3 Michael Prosser's Cultural Story

Monocultural to Multicultural

My adoptive mother and father grew up in a small town in southern Indiana, and lived across the street from each other. My grandfather Fred Prosser had several brothers and sisters. My grandmother Kate Prosser had two brothers and one of them was a manager at the cement factory there. When my father, Marshall, an only child, was in the seventh grade, he jumped out of the classroom window and never went back to school. When he was grown, he first sold new cars from Detroit, Michigan one at a time; then just before the Great Depression, my adoptive parents moved north to a city where he worked in the auto parts factory for General Motors for the rest of his working life. I don't ever remember him reading a book. My mother had two years of college and wanted to teach primary school, except that the Ku Klux Klan in the small town area where she and my father grew up wouldn't allow her to teach because she was a Catholic. The KKK hated Catholics, Jews, Negroes, as black people were then called, and all foreigners. The xenophobic KKK members often wore white robes and hoods to intimidate those whom they hated. The small town had a handmade and very offensive sign on the roads going into the town saying: "Nigger, don't let the sun set on you." The KKK (Ku Klux Klan) when my parents were young often hanged black men who paid too much attention to young white women.

I grew up *monoculturally* in a small city, Muncie, Indiana, where there was a teacher's

Creating Our Own Cultural Stories

college, Ball State University, in which I later received both my BA and MA degrees. In high school, I studied away from home in boarding schools, planning to become a priest. Some much older students were being sent to Rome or Austria to continue their studies, and my parents took me for a three week trip to Canada after my high school graduation.

Somewhere here was perhaps a spark that ignited a fire within me to become more intercultural and international and to see more of the world. As a college student, I worked in a hospital and doctors' office as a cleaner, and in two of my summers for a public utility company, I earned enough money to take an independent two month trip to Europe at twenty-two, traveling there by a student ship crossing the Atlantic Ocean with 1,000 students on board, visiting about a dozen countries in Western Europe, hitchhiking auto rides and staying in international youth hostels, returning to the US by plane, and entering the MA program. In this event, later travels with my own family to Europe, then more trips there, and even traveling into Eastern Europe, I began to become *Eurocentrically* oriented as much of my education had also promoted.

In 1962, my daughter Michelle was born; in 1964, my son Leo was born; and in 1965, my son Louis was born. Now, each of them have three children: thus I have nine grandchildren: Christine Ann, Elizabeth Marie, and Mary Catherine Rose, daughters of my son Louis and his wife, Bernadette; Darya Serenity Michelle, Sanders Stephan Gabriel, and Sophia Lily Grace, children of my daughter Michelle; and Conner Michael, Jordan Faith, and Luke Patrick, children of my son Leo and his wife Hope. **My family is my greatest cultural legacy**. If each

grandchild has three children, then there would be twenty-seven great grandchildren; if each of them has three children, there would be 81 great great grandchildren. (Michael's dynasty!)

During the 1980's, I was host father for international high school students from Sweden, Belgium, France, and Spain, a year at a time, a Brazilian exchange student for a half year, I had a sixteen-year old El Salvadorian refugee boy living with us for nearly a year, and I was the local leader of an international youth exchange program, hosting an Indian South African student. The boys from Brazil, El Salvador and South Africa encouraged me to develop more interest in developing countries and thus expanding my global enthusiasm still more and traveling on a faculty study tour to Lebanon, Jordan, and Israel. I taught a year in Swaziland in South-east Africa, bringing two high school students back to the US for additional high school education, and still later, I had several young adults from Sudan living in my home, thus making me more *Afrocentrically* inclined. In my teaching at the University of Virginia, increasingly about one third of my undergraduate students were African Americans, and about 10% were either Asian American, or international students.

I led several conferences to help create the field of intercultural communication during the early to mid 1970's. In 1974, I participated in a Japanese-American bicultural research conference in Nihonmatsu, Japan; in 1980, returning to Japan, and giving lectures in South Korea and Singapore, I began to focus my attention on becoming *Asiacentrically* oriented. With an already developing enthusiasm for China, in 2000 at a conference in Seattle, Washington, knowing that I was retiring in

2001 from two American universities, some of my Chinese colleagues suggested that I should teach in China. My response was, "Why not?" In the first decade of the twenty-first century then, I expanded this interest exponentially, by teaching 2200 Chinese students in three Chinese universities in eight years. I visited Cambodia and India twice, plus Vietnam, Japan, and Thailand, the Philippines, Australia, and New Zealand. Coincidentally, my first visit to Russia was when I was twenty-three as a rather rare American tourist, with my second visit thirty years later for a satellite and computer communication conference. However, while I was teaching in China and more recently, I have returned to Russia three more times, twice taking two young Chinese friends along, attending Russian communication conferences and giving lecture series in two Russian universities.

My daughter, Michelle, visited me in Beijing and traveled with me and two Chinese students in 2005 to Xi'an, and in 2008, she and her three children, Darya, Sanders, and Sophia came to visit me in Shanghai, traveling with us to Suzhou, Changzhou, Yangzhou, Yellow Mountain, and Maanshan, Anhui Province. Most recently, I have begun to explore South America more than I had done in the past, with Michelle and I going to El Salvador and Peru in 2007, and more recently going by myself to Argentina and Chile. I have traveled with Chinese student friends to many places in China and young Chinese have traveled with me to Vietnam, Cambodia, the Republic of Korea, India, Europe, the Philippines, Russia, Australia, New Zealand, Thailand, Japan, Singapore, Malaysia, and Indonesia.

My research has centered on rhetoric and public discourse, intercultural and international communication and media, and the United Nations. At this moment in my life, I have become a much more *multicultural* individual, and the goal of Socrates, whose famous quote: "I am neither a citizen of Athens, nor of Greece, but of the world," leads me so that I can also become a world citizen, having begun with a *monocultural* orientation, developing in an *Eurocentric* orientation; becoming *Asiacentric* and *Afrocentric*, and emerging with a *multicultural* world view. I have now been to sixty-two countries and look forward to visiting several more. I have spent nearly nine years in China and have returned three times after retiring.

My cultural story goes forward with my three children, and each family's three children. As Bertrand Russell espoused: "**Culture is a memory chain linking the past, present, and future.**"

Creating Our Own Cultural Stories

3.4 Cultural Stories of Several Young People

Throughout the dialogues we are learning snippets of both the cultural stories of Professor Zhang and Michael and their imaginary students. Professor Steve Kulich at Shanghai International Studies University has for a number of years made the first assignment in his intercultural communication classes the student writing of their own cultural stories. His view and that of many others in the study of intercultural communication contend that we must first acknowledge our own cultural stories before we understand others. Humans by nature are narrators of their own and other stories, symbol makers, users, and abusers, capable of truth-telling and falsification, often depending on our perceptions through our own lived experiences and others of what is an illusion and what is reality in our or their stories.

We are devoting an entire chapter to this topic of *Creating Our Own Cultural Stories*, including the cultural stories of the two co-authors of the book, and also a number of different Chinese young people. All of the young writers of cultural stories, or various other narratives in this book, are mostly written by young people, who like yourselves are after all members of the **post-80s generation** or even now the **post-90s generation**. Your own stories are also cultural, and whether grand or small are important contributions to your understanding of intercultural communication. Consider the post-90s generation as the "weathercock of a society in transition."

3.4.1 My Cultural Background (William Zhu, Shanghai International Studies University)

Believe it or not, I have never seriously as well as thoroughly considered who I am and what constitutes my cultural background for the past twenty two years. Admittedly, every human being in this unprecedented changing era might be caught in the confusion as I am when I take painstaking efforts to draw my cultural context and materialize it in words. No single element could epitome my culture for it is influenced by multiple aspects interacting with each other. Some dominant influences I deem important are Confucian thought, religious beliefs, the reform and opening up policy, and the information age and globalization.

To begin with, Confucian thought carves a deep notch in the cultural heritage of all Chinese people. Its profound impact is

The Assembly Hall in the United Nations, Geneva, Switzerland

witnessed in every aspect of our life: humanity, benevolence, courtesy, respect for the old and love for the young, family hierarchy, filial piety, diligence, harmony, thrift, and obedience, to name a few. Though those attributes were proposed by Confucius thousands of years ago, they stand the test of time and are passed down from generation to generation with alterations. When I was a small kid, I was taught by my parents and teachers to respect the old and pay due deference to people senior of my age. I should not call my parents, elder brothers and sisters, uncles and aunts their names; instead, I should greet them by their appellations respectively. However, when addressing my younger brothers and sisters, I enjoyed the privilege to call their names directly. In terms of respecting the old, particularly my grandparents, I have to carefully observe many rules. For instance, when eating together at the same table, the arrangement of seats is fixed and I should sit accordingly. Usually, my grandpa or grandma's seats are considered the dominant ones and signify authority. If they happen not to be present, their seats are taken by my uncles or senior male family members. It seems to me that the rules at the table are observed not only at home but also in society. When having dinner with friends, colleagues or people who are not our relatives, the senior, powerful one always sits above the salt. The same seating arrangement pattern is also demonstrated in meetings. I remembered that whenever our family had something to discuss or decide, we would customarily have an informal meeting with my grandparents sitting in the middle of the crowd and supervising the process. Small kids like me did not have a say as all we had to do was to listen attentively and carry out the

The Moscow University

decisions to the letter. We were not supposed to raise any doubts or challenge the decision; if we did, we would end up receiving either verbal or physical punishment. Besides, to sustain a harmonious state is of vital importance as I learned from my own experience. It is common that some discord or friction exists among family members. Despite dislikes or even resentment, we try to achieve, at least, a superficial harmony by avoiding obvious conflict. By doing so, we are giving each other face and being gentle. Also, I grew up in an environment of diligence and thrift which also typifies the characteristics of the majority of the Chinese. Being a spendthrift, waste, laziness and idleness are considered evils and people who are extravagant or slothful are labeled with derogatory epithets, condemned and even chastised. I once received a good beating because I bought something from a neighborhood grocery on credit. My mother considered the incident to be extremely serious and thought I might end up as a spendthrift idler if no intervention was carried out. Another example is that as a kid, I had to eat all the food in my bowl and if there were any leftovers, my

Creating Our Own Cultural Stories

parents or relatives would repeat the invariable story how precious rice is and how hard farmers work to harvest it under the scorching sun. One salient traditional breakfast in south China is "*paofan*," rice soaked with water. Actually, they are the leftovers of the previous night's supper. In addition, diligence is a great virtue that my parents tried their best to cultivate in me. With the proveb that the early bird gets the treasure, diligence is the means by which one makes up for one's dullness.

Those adages are carved into my head as a stimulus to urge me to get up early and study with might and main. My parents were excessively proud of me as I was a top student through primary school to university. They often tell me that as my genetic makeup might not be very favorable because neither of them has obtained a bachelor's degree, I have to be much more industrious than others and spend ten times as many efforts on study than my smart peers.

As Confucian thought may exert a positive influence on my cultural context, the Cultural Revolution, a devastating political as well as social catastrophe, has taken its tolls. Both my grandfathers on my mother's and father's side were put into prisons and forced to reform through labor, and were displaced and tortured. My mother's father at that time was a graduate from one of the leading universities working in a bank; he was persecuted because as a liberal and young person with high aspirations, he voiced many discontentments and disagreements with the authorities. As a consequence, he was sent to a remote backwoods province laboring in the field, enduring unspeakable ordeals which affected him physically and psychologically all through

his life. It is by no means exaggerated to say that his life had been totally transformed. My father's father, who at that time worked as a cadre in the local government, had a very promising future for he was eloquent, charismatic and knowledgeable. Unfortunately, due to his dishonorable family background, he was dismissed, jailed and forced to cut his connections with all the family members. The tragedy did not end up here as my mother and father, and their brothers and sisters, as the offspring of the rightist, underwent tremendous humiliation, unfair treatment and hardships. They were deprived of the right to receive a higher education; they were also forced to labor after school to be educated. All these experiences left a great impact on their life. They are apolitical, distrustful of the government and place enormous expectation on us. My parents, since I could remember things, instructed me not to be too aggressive, not to voice discontent in public, not to offend others, not to get involved in politics, to study hard and be in a low key. Actually, the golden rule seems to be "reticence is better than eloquence" and "a ready tongue is an evil." Evidently, they drew the lesson from their parents. They did all they could to ensure that I get the best education which they were deprived of. They know how horrible and painful a political upheaval could be and their last wish was that I should not repeat what they went through during those turbulent years when nobody trusted each other and human evil was revealed to the most as even spouses set up against each other. There is no doubt that the psychological aftershock of the Cultural Revolution will exert its power not only in my generation but also my offspring.

Another point that I want to elaborate on is religious belief as it is very closely connected with culture and it has a powerful impact on my cultural background. My mother is a Buddhist, so is my mother's mother. The first thing my mother and grandmother do after they get up every morning is to offer incense to Buddha. And each first as well as fifteenth day in the lunar calendar, they will put some fruits, pastry, and a bowl of rice in front of the Buddha statue, which is placed in the living room to serve as a tribute. Whenever a family member has to travel to a far away place, or I have to sit in for an exam, or some family member has some trouble, be it illness, misfortune or whatever, my mother or my grandmother will pray before the statue, kneeing and kowtowing. Bad times are interpreted as a test that Buddha has for us and achievement or luck is interpreted as a blessing of Buddha by my mother and grandmother. Our lives are considered to be predestined and all we have to do is to accept our destiny and act accordingly (this perspective is quite paradoxical in Buddhism for we both accept our destiny and pray for good things to happen). As Buddhists, we have a pre-life and after-life, we have to engage ourselves in philanthropic undertakings and good deeds; those are the tenets of Buddhism that my mother and grandmother hold. Though I am, at least at the present time, an atheist, I have undergone constant struggle as I have tried to strike a balance between its influence on my life and the impact of science. I am totally aware that being over-obsessed with the potency of some imaginative figure or resigning ourselves to our destiny mapped out by a fortune teller is absurd and highly detrimental as that might result in a pessimistic worldview. Nevertheless, strangely

enough, each time I have achieved something or whenever I have had some very hard time, I would spontaneously make some connotation as some unseen power might manipulate all the things that happen to me. I would under some circumstance, when I am extremely unhopeful, lost or depressed, resort to Buddha and pray though I know exactly it is of little avail. Thus, I think I am very much affected by my mother and my grandmother and some Buddhist tenets and thoughts have already become one part of my cultural background.

Three watersheds that divide my generation and my parent's or grandparent's generation are the reform and opening up policy and the information age and globalization. The former one, which unleashes productivity and brings about unprecedented economic benefits is by no means parsimonious in its impact on my cultural context. Compared to my parents who are more traditional and a bit invulnerable to change and adaptation due to the immense influence of Confucian thought, I, like my peers, tend to be more flexible and receptive to fresh things or phenomenona. Improvement of

The Sydney Opera House in Australia

life, diversity of goods, consumption economy, swollen pockets: all these factors strongly transform our lifestyles, outlook of the world, and they corrode some traditional virtues such as thrift and integrity. Unlike my parents who still prefer a relatively self-restrained lifestyle which features "saving for a rainy day" and not wasting money on luxurious goods, I am more willing to purchase brand names. In addition we have different views on eating and spending money. For instance, if I really loath the food or the food goes bad, I will refuse to eat it and I make great efforts to urge my parents to give up some unhealthy lifestyle such as eating the leftovers, buying cheap, poor quality products or using expired daily necessities. Another case in point is that I always have a heated argument or debate with my parents whenever we go shopping as I like to buy the brand names such as Nike or Adidas but they are very reluctant to spend money on those expensive clothes for they think cheaper ones will also do. When my friends and I hang out, we like to go to Starbucks, KFC or some upscale restaurants to dine, and we prefer TV or some other entertainments to have fun and to socialize.

The second and third factors that divide my generation and my parents and grandparents' generations culturally are the information age. A large number of novel words, phrases, epithets and things pop up. QQ, iPod, 3-G, netizen, on-line shopping, and so on. All these fresh novelties profoundly affect our socializing forms, behavior, linguistic competence, viewpoints, way of thinking, relationships and communication patterns. decency, social responsibility and individuality make my generation more vocal and voluble to express ourselves, to show great concern on

the inequality or dark side of the society and to gather momentum for change. Unlike my parents who pay undue importance to family members, I consider friendship more important and I want that more attention should be directed to me. I correspond with my friends with emails, short messages or on socializing web networks, while my parents still prefer to make phone calls. In terms of my future career, my parents want me to take a stable job in the government or some public institution, but I want to do some really creative and rewarding tasks.

In a word, it is really difficult to fully summarize my cultural background in this increasing diversified world in which numerous factors interact with each other in constituting my specific cultural context. Nevertheless, the above mentioned characters, Confucian thought, the Cultural Revolution, Buddhism, the reform and opening up policy, the information age do approximately generalize my cultural background by offering a panorama view of who I am.

3.4.2 From the Mini UN to the Real UN (Zhang Jing, the United Nations, New York City)

Before I came to the US, I studied at the Beijing Language and Culture University (BLCU), whose nick name is "the mini United Nations" as it has international students from more than 170 countries. I enjoyed studying and living in this pretty campus for three years. This was the place where I made many international friends and experienced cross-cultural communications by exchanging languages and going out together. This was also the place where I heard about a small European country called Moldova for the first time.

Now I am a Public Information Assistant at the Department of Public Information at the United Nations (UN) headquarters in New York City. UN is such a multicultural organization. Take my office for example, my colleagues are from 5 continents. One Italian lady had studied Mandarin at BLCU before! What a small world! One day I even came across my high school math teacher from Shenzhen. You never know whom you will meet next! At the UN not only do I have opportunities to work with people from different cultures, but I also have opportunities to meet visitors from around the world. I have noticed that Asian people like to take photos a lot, while Europeans tend to want to know more about the organization. French and German people are critical and always have questions. I have met people from places such as Kosovo, Palestine, and the Democratic Republic of the Congo, where the Security Council has deployed the peacekeeping operations.

My most unforgettable experience at the UN was to work for the 64th General Assembly (GA) in September, 2009. This is the time once a year that the New York Police Department blocks the road up to the Second Avenue as heads of state and heads of government attend the General Debate. I was lucky to work for three different departments during the week of the General Debate. Working for the Meeting Service Department enabled me to hear speeches from many big-wigs such as President Hu Jingtao, Barack Obama, and Nicolas Sarkozy. I came across famous ladies like Hilary Clinton and Carla Bruni just by randomly walking inside the building. Of course I should say the security was very tight; not every staff member could enter the General Assembly building and you need a special pass besides the work ID. I also experienced some unique moments such as seeing Muammar Gaddafi make the second longest speech in the UN history (the longest speech was made by Fidel Castro for more than 4 hours); witnessing the voting whether to let the so-called president of Madagascar to speak in the GA or not as they had a coup and apparently the voting result didn't recognize the current government.

Working for the Media Relations Department made it possible for me to attend press conferences and meetings hosted by Tony Blair, Al Gore, and Hugo Chaves. Moreover, I once escorted a FOX news reporter to interview Iranian president Mahmoud Ahmadinejad. We had argued where to wait for him: the reporter thought we should wait at the elevator as Ahmadinejad was going to the 38th floor to meet with the Secretary General. I didn't agree with him as no one else was waiting there and suggested that we should wait at the Delegates' Entrance. I was right. He showed up on his way to meet the SG. We had been waiting for him for more than 2 hours, but in the end he only talked to an Iranian reporter in Persian when he left. My third duty was to work at the Bilateral Meetings. During my tenure, I witnessed many agreements that were reached as a result of the meetings or negotiations.

As I am new and still learning the ropes, I feel proud to work for such a great organization which has gone so far since its creation in 1945. At the same time, I feel that I have responsibility to let more people know about the work of the UN, because it's our world.

3.4.3 The Value of Family, Education, and a Girl with a Russian Passport (Anya Klyukanova, University of Oregon)

My name is Anya Klyukanova and I am a sophomore at the University of Oregon in the midst of obtaining a degree in political science and journalism. I was born in Tver, Russia and I moved to the United States when I was just a toddler. However, I started returning to Russia every summer since I was about four. Because of the careful upbringing of my parents and my repeated returns to the motherland, I proudly consider myself to be Russian and I have many traits that are characteristic of Russians. Many of these traits are not prevalent in the American culture but they are still a major part of my life.

A big difference I've noticed between the Russian culture and the American culture is the value placed on family. I consider my parents to be the two most important people in my life and I interact with them a few times a day, whether by phone, e-mail or Skype. However, none of my American friends seem to place such high importance on family values; most talk to their parents once a week for five minutes and do so begrudgingly. Although I never resent talking to my parents, I argue with them often. This is another difference I have noticed between the two cultures. In America, it seems to be considered almost a taboo to argue with anyone but in Russia, arguing is simply a part of life. A quiet discussion can turn into a loud argument and back to a peaceful discussion within a matter of minutes and no one will think twice about it.

Next to my parents, I value my education as a critical part of my life. I take school very seriously and try very hard to excel in my studies. However, many of my American peers seem to view college as a place to party and socialize. Their lack of concern for their grades has always appalled me but if they put in half the amount of effort they put into beer ping pong and sports, they would have straight A's. Unfortunately, this lack of concern for grades is also shown through their lack of respect for authority. In Russia, students must stand up when a teacher enters the room and are only allowed to sit back down when told to do so. In America, students are playing games on their computer and texting on their cell phone with their feet on top of their desk when a teacher enters the room. In a Russian institution, this sort of behavior would cause a student to be expelled.

Although these are just a few of the cultural differences which I have encountered in America, I also have many traits which I share with my American friends. I have become accustomed to living with constant hot water, a full refrigerator, a laptop, a car as a mode of transportation, etc. Ultimately, I have a higher standard of living than many people in Russia. Also, I keep up with both Western fashion and media much more than I do with Russian fashion and media; I shop at American stores and my favorite source of information is *The New York Times*. But even though I've become more accustomed to the American way of life, I will never forget my roots and I will continue to live as a girl with a Russian passport.

3.4.4 Open Heart and Immense Patience (Michelle Cui, Trading Manager, Omicom Group, Chicago, Illinois)

When my dear friend Professor Prosser first asked me to write a piece on intercultural communication to be included in Professor Li's and his book, I did not know where to start. However, I was well aware of the reason why he asked for my insight for this essay. Having spent my teenage years in Seattle, Washington, I went back to China to continue my studies in senior middle school, majored in English Literature at Beijing Language and Culture University, worked as a spokesperson for a multinational corporation for a year before I left China again for two master's programs in the United States. And here I am, sitting in my apartment on the north side of Chicago, IL, writing something that seems to be my everyday life.

Sometimes I believe with increasing information shared on the Internet, intercultural communication has become easier than ever before. It is common to witness a conversation between a Chinese and an Indian student about the latest US TV show. It is never too hard to gather hundreds of blog entries on a single event such as an American global company, Google, pulling out of Chinese market and moving its search engine to Hong Kong. It is no surprise that on the same day, thousands of reviews are available online from all corners of the world on one product. Yes, advanced technologies and new communication tools provided many more topics and materials to talk about among people with different cultural backgrounds.

However, I still find it difficult to understand American's enthusiasm toward sports: Why do they celebrate the night of the American football Super Bowl as a major national festival, and why do they look forward to the night with such exuberant passion regardless of their race and religion? No machine today can help us to comprehend social phenomena like those mentioned above. Simple answers such as a nation's nature, or a country's political structure cannot be the solutions to every question arising from intercultural communication. I wish my friends could live part of my life to understand my country and my people, and vice versa, so that I could truly share their joys, cheering for the sporting event considered to be the most watched TV show in the US and widely throughout many parts of the world.

Before that life-exchanging machine is built, the mission of producing effective intercultural communications falls onto the shoulders of people like you and me: People who are attracted to foreign cultures because they are so different from our own, breaking out of our comfort zone, walking the extra mile to learn and understand, and hope to bring understandings between countries and nations to avoid unnecessary conflicts. New technologies are the tools that we use to reach out and learn, but the essence of communication still lies within us. The key, as my dear friend Professor Prosser told me, is an open heart and immense patience.

Creating Our Own Cultural Stories

3.4.5 From an Ordinary Family (David Xu, Tongji University)

I am David Xu, from an ordinary family in a small county, Hubei Province, central China. In my early age of the late 1970s, China was very poor, and even though my parents were working for the government we could only have a dish with a little meat or egg every one or two weeks. The early experiences made me decide to work first to release the burden of my parents and then to look for opportunities to upgrade myself. After finishing the study of pipe fitting in a petrochemical technical school affiliated to Sinopec, I was assigned to a petrochemical engineering and construction company. The first four years were tough, day or night with labor intensive and overtime work, mostly outdoors, so I did jobs in the rain or snow, a hot and stuffy environment, and in dangerous situations like poison gas leaks, reparations after explosions, up on a 40 meter high tower, walking on thick pipes without a protective fence. But my pay was alright then, around 200 USD a month in the later 1990s, even higher than my mother whose ranking was the same as a 15-year town leader. The job did not make me stop my study, and I studied part time to finish my associate degree in accounting in three years. I had another three years in the company as an X-ray QC inspector, and comparatively it was a good job for me then. A large scale State Owned Enterprise (SOE) reform started in 2001 where over 3,000 workers were laid off with 3–4 years of salary as compensation.

I started to think again about my future and an English class for adults gave me a chance to learn English. In 2003 I left the company with two years' salary paid in advance as a laid-off worker. I went to Beijing's New Oriental School for learning English full time. There, my eyes were opened for the new world since a lot of students there were planning to go abroad. The Internet also was an access to get in touch with the world-wide information. In 2005, I came to Shanghai alone. I tried to get trained in English at the Shanghai International Studies University and found a new job in such a metropolis. Michael was my teacher in SISU, and I traveled over one month with him in Europe from St. Petersburg, Russia to Rome, Italy, which let me first walk out of China to get a direct touch with Western cultures.

English learning and the trip changed my life. In SISU in a model UN Security Council course, I declined to speak for Syria about the nuclear issue. An unexpected thing happened that I was assigned to be a manager in the Syrian oil fields by the new company in Shanghai after our European trip. It was my first time working abroad and in the Gobi desert, I got live intercultural experiences with Arabic, Kurdish, Canadian, Hungarian. I got more confident and brave after the experiences abroad, and landed jobs mostly in foreign companies, which allowed me to practice my language ability as well as having a higher salary. My tough technical experience also let me have a deep understanding of engineering practices.

In Shanghai we may learn all kinds of things, and I dare not let the chance go. I am close to finishing both English literature and purchasing and supply management Bachelor degrees. I took the national test applying for the MBA program of Tongji University. I hope I can make it, although I am not so young any more.

3.4.6 The Story of My Nearly 30 Years (Jacky Zhang, Dezhou University)

Complicated feelings filled my mind for I had to look back at my life carefully and seriously. I was born in the 1980s, the period for China to start the "One Family One Child" policy. In China, we young people born in the 1980s are called the "Post-80s Generation." Most are only children who usually stress self-value, pursue their own personality and enjoy love from their family members, but lack the ability for self-care and a sense of social responsibility. In many people's eyes, we are the "spoiled" generation. Unfortunately, I am one of the "spoiled" group. Fortunately, I have a younger sister, and many cousins, so my childhood was not so lonely as the only child of most families. Actually, I don't think I was spoiled. My grandparents were not rich when I was born, living in a rural area in Shandong Province. My father told me that life at that time was poor. My grandparents had three sons and two daughters, and five grandchildren already before me. As a result, I haven't ever received any gifts or red envelopes from my grandparents. But I haven't complained because they still loved me very much, especially my grandmother who died in my junior middle school period. I want to show my great appreciation to my parents because they made a great decision as soon as I came into this beautiful world that changed my life to do whatever they could to support my education. My mother told me her greatest wish when I was an infant was that I could enter the best university one day. I didn't let my parents become disappointed. I entered a good university, although not the best one in China. Later,. I entered Shanghai International Studies University (SISU) to pursue the master's degree in international relations from 2006 to 2009 and completed my thesis, entitled *USCC's Cognition on China and Its Influence on Sino-US Relations.* My experience in SISU changed my life again because I met my lasting teacher and friend Michael H. Prosser who brought me abroad to experience the colorful world and culture.

A wonderful cruise trip opened the curtain for me to experience various cultures. Michael and I went to Australia and New Zealand, visiting ten different cities. I am still excited when I think of the trip. All the things in the cruise are as clear as if I am still enjoying it. After arriving at our Sydney hotel, we visited the Sidney Museum and the world-famous Opera House. At the Bondi Beach I swam while Michael talked to two beautiful young Indian women. I wanted to get stuffed kangaroos, koala bears, and Tasmanian devils for my roommates and nephew, but we soon realized that all of them were made in China as were most souvenirs or clothing. This really makes me happy for China and being a Chinese. We watched the biggest Chinese Lunar New Year parade outside of the Asian continent, with many schools and other groups participating.

We boarded the Holland America Line ship MS Volendam for the 14 day cruise where many guests appeared to be in their sixties, seventies or older, and from several different countries including Australia, Canada, China, Japan, and the United States. So I felt so honored to have Michael as my best friend helping me to have an international view and think broadly. We travelled to Melbourne and Tasmania and through the Tasmanian Sea, the roughest sea in the world, to New Zealand, another fantastic experience. Both New Zealand and

Creating Our Own Cultural Stories

Australia left deep impressions on my mind. What I thought most about is when China could have as clear a sky as those two countries. Particularly, China still has a long way to go in environmental protection.

Back in Shanghai, we planned to go to Japan in September 2009 to attend the 15th International Association for Intercultural Communication Studies conference. We met in the Fukuoka, Japan airport, and surely another cultural experience awaited me. I did better than in my first trip outside of China because I had become more mature in international travel. Different from the first one, the Japan trip meant more to me. Since this was my first time to attend a formal international academic conference, I learned a lot in doing my power point presentation for the conference. I made a cultural mistake about cross-cultural communication as I wore a black tie the last day of the conference. But when I walked into the auditorium, some Japanese stared at me surprised, confusing me by the looks on their faces. At that moment, the conference leader kindly told me that a black tie in Japan is only for funerals. Realizing my mistake, I apologized and I didn't wear the tie in the closing ceremony. Then we traveled to several places in southern Japan where the clean environment impressed me greatly. I noticed Japanese children are very shy when they say hello to western people. A lot of Japanese we met couldn't speak very fluent English which surprised me.

After the Japan trip, Michael and I developed another trip to Thailand in November 2009. So the unique and traditional Thailand culture filled my mind closely. On our 7th day in Thailand, we went to Cambodia, staying there for three days and two nights. The strong contrast between Thailand and Cambodia touched me greatly. Cambodia is such a poor country and the basic construction is underdeveloped. But the poverty couldn't stop people to pursue a better life. Our young Cambodian guide at Angkor Wat, a UNESCO World Heritage spot, told us that most Cambodians live a satisfactory life. I didn't know how to describe my feelings when I wandered in the ancient castle and Hindu temples. This wonderful place caused a very strong sense of history.

I know the world is full of variety and mystery. But my cultural experience outside of China strengthens it. All my international travels make me think more globally. I love the world and I love more the people who made everything become interculturally real for me.

3.4.7 Seattle and Christchurch: Twin Cities (Zizi Zhao Zhao, Christchurch, New Zealand)

I was born in 1983 at Shenyang, China. Shenyang is a typical industrial city in the north, once the focus of the nation in the 1980s. Due to the growing role of light industry in China, the influence of my hometown has faded, but it is still playing an important role. I had an impeccable childhood, which I became conscious of years later. I have had a complete family to depend on, little homework to do and plenty of time playing in the yard. I never escaped classes and listened to my mom for extra English lessons after school every day. I was still not a good student, never among the top students, and had been at the bottom for two years. I'm terrible at exams all the time.

I got accepted by Jilin University and started my college life in 2001 in Changchun, which is far more north and shares the same culture with where I'm from. I had my happiest, most productive and glorious four years of life in my university. At that time almost everyone in my school knew my name as an outstanding student, a successful society leader, a popular hostess, a flashy singer and a skillful ping pong player, not to mention the ideal ending that I was guaranteed to further my education in the Shanghai International Studies University without taking the national examination.

That is where everything began to change unfavorably. I began to realize that northern Chinese culture contradicts with Shanghai's local culture in many aspects. Most of the time I had to discard old beliefs and welcome a new set of living philosophy to fit in, which I did not totally agree with. I felt increasingly lonely, depressed and tired of life. The only thing that made me feel I was still blessed is that I got involved in the MA intercultural communication program and met Michael, with whom I made some choices that did change my life forever. Through his eyes, I got the whole picture of the world and he also showed me the most beautiful human virtues. I made my first overseas tour to the United States in 2007 for intercultural communication training because Michael insisted that I should not miss this chance.

My intercultural adventure in the US lasted only for one month. I was eating western food, speaking the English language, behaving the way they'd like to accept and dealing with intercultural misunderstandings everyday. This intense experience paid me back in many ways later academically and practically.

As a turning point, I lived a more solitary life thereafter, according to my friends, but I enjoyed my company. I didn't plan my future as anything to do with my university (SISU) and I kept searching to join a company where I could do the same training as the one I had experienced in the US, until I received a call from my supervisor who offered me a position in her SISU college.

Now I worked in SISU for almost two years. But I fell in love with teaching and being with my students. Currently I'm very keen on being a good teacher and it is a treat to me if I can advise my students on life at times.

At the beginning of 2010, I embarked on a new journey of adventure to Christchurch, NZ. I will have the longest overseas experience ever in my life for over a year. Michael thinks I'm lucky enough to have another overseas trip soon after the first one. Christchurch is best-known for its natural beauty, which did not leave me such a brilliant impression as Seattle first did. As the sister city of Seattle, Christchurch reasonably has the most friendly and helpful citizens. I think I'm lucky enough to live for a while in both cities and at peace with the world.

3.4.8 A Third Culture Child? (Nick Deng, Yunnan Normal University)

I often feel like that I am a "third culture" child in many ways, even if my overseas life experience is relatively limited (a year or so in Thailand, less than half a year in the USA) and my family background is nowhere near an

Creating Our Own Cultural Stories

intercultural one. I grew up in a small town, a few hours drive away from Chongqing. Even today, after decades of fast growth, it is still counted as a rather backward place. I never knew I was going to study English and had the slightest idea of how it would change my life altogether. I made up my mind to learn English intensively back in high school when I sensed that I might want to live and work abroad. This seemed to be a rather odd idea to many around me at that time when nobody even knew what was TOEFL or IELTS. But somehow, to me, it was a brave and exciting decision. This preceded a really important stage in my life, my time at BLCU, where I met some of my lifetime friends and of course, Michael. I experienced many shocks as I started to learn English from a whole different approach. It was just about grammar, vocabulary and countless English tests. I was totally immersed in a whole new culture. I can still remember some of the chapters vividly: arriving at my first British friend's party at six to help her out when the party started at seven; calling foreign friends at eight in the morning on a Sunday; waiting for my buddies outside of a tea house when they thought I meant inside, etc. There were many times when I thought about withdrawing from all this because it was getting emotionally hard for me to take all of this in while my Chinese fellows started to call me a "fake foreigner." Not to my regret, I soldiered on. Before I knew it, at a party during my senior year, for the very first time, an Australian asked me which state I came from. It was surreal! I knew that he took it that I was an American because of not only my Spoken English but also the way I presented myself. But that was hardly the only occasion. When I was traveling with Michael to Vietnam,

it took me literally five minutes to convince a German lady that I WAS a Chinese. My American roommate asked me last year: "Are you sure you are a Chinese? You are not shy and don't camp in the library." What happened? I don't know. Some wild guesses are: hours after hours of American TV shows, talking with friends like Michael, and probably most importantly an open mind to the outside world without much resistance.

In 2009 after completing my MA degree in Thailand, when I was sitting in my dorm at Georgetown University in Washington, D.C., skyping with one of my American friends and talking about my real American experience, he suddenly asked me what was the biggest shock I had by that time culturally. Ironically, my answer was "You know what? I don't think Americans and Chinese are THAT different." It was not until then I realized that deep down inside the two nations probably share more similarities than I previously thought: the drive to succeed, the appreciation of diligence and intelligence. However, after that summer, when I came back to China for my teaching job, I experienced culture shocks again, reversed ones: I sound incredibly and painfully blunt to some of my colleagues and many times I have to figure out the real messages that people are trying to deliver with their words.

So, here I am, 27, at a cultural crossroad.

3.4.9 Lotus Seeds (Cindy Zhao, Shanghai)

I was born in a Chinese family, I mean, both my parents majored in Chinese literature in college. My close relationship with classic Chinese culture can be proven by a tape produced on the first anniversary of my birthday. It recorded my lisping recitation of some ancient poems. My grandpa, the eldest son of an old time wealthy family and a journalist after the foundation of the PRC, used a scarcely seen Chinese character as my name, which literally means "lotus seeds." In traditional Chinese culture, lotus is a symbol of nobleness, integrity, and purity. It is adored by many men of letters. My father was one of those typical young men who left their home villages and found a new life in the city with their ambition and capability. His good temper, diligence and moral character set up my standard for a good man.

It is lucky for me to have grown up in a family with a tradition of open-mindedness. I can make my own decision in most cases. Yet there seems to be an inherent sentimentality in me, and my high school years were spent in great depression with my loathing toward the usual Chinese exam-oriented education. Then I went to Yunnan, a southwestern province far away from my hometown, to start college study. Yunnan is famous for its natural beauty and diversity in population. Fifty-two ethnic groups live in this land of 390 thousand square kilometers, each with their own culture and values. Their passion, friendliness and art talent were quite admirable. They seemed to have a closer relationship with nature, and their lives were simple and happy. Although I can't be one of them, I can learn to be more cheerful and optimistic toward life.

In the summer vacation of 2003, I traveled to Emei Mountain, a famous Buddhist mountain in Sichuan Province. It was my second time there. Just outside the door of a temple, I casually picked up a small book

about Buddhism, and it became a starting point of my contact with the religion. From then on I read lots of related books and tried to find possible answers for some unresolved questions in my mind. I cannot say that I'm a believer of Buddhism, but it surely offered me another point of view, helping me to calm down and find what I really want in my life. I also found much mental nutrition in ancient Chinese wisdom such as Lao-tzu and *Cai Gen Tan*. At the same time, since my major has been English, I have read lots of English books which opened another door for my world.

In 2009 I graduated from Shanghai International Studies University with a master's degree in intercultural communication. Until now, I've worked in both multinational companies and local ones, feeling the subtle differences between those places. The more people I meet, the stronger my feeling is that no matter wherever you come from or whoever you are, people are essentially similar.

Creating Our Own Cultural Stories

3.5 Case Study: Contemporary Chinese Women

A Glimpse of the Life of Contemporary Chinese Women—by Studying a Certain Group of Them (Joanna, Beijing)

Chinese women are quite unique in the world. On one hand, they are much more free in some aspects than their sisters in other ancient developing countries. Sometimes even some developed countries. On the other hand, they are facing a lot of pressures. Pressures come from both the ancient Chinese tradition and the rapid changing of modern Chinese society. To give a general description and analysis of Chinese women's lives is too big a subject to me and to this report. Because just like a lot of other things in China, women's rights and pressures are extremely unbalanced. They differ from area to area, generation to generation, and are influenced by financial conditions, education, tradition, etc. So I'll have to limit my topic to the life of women living in the suburban district of southeast China, which is quite familiar to me and which to my opinion, is quite representative. I'll divide women and their lives into three general groups, the grandmothers, the mothers and the daughters. Then I'll focus on two things which have played and are playing important roles in their lives, Family Planning and the Women's Federation.

The Grandmothers

They are generally housewives more than 55 years old, with more than three children and are now living with one of their children. Having never taken up any formal jobs all of their lives, they are now mostly financially depending on their children, especially sons. So if their children treat them badly, their lives are sure to be miserable. Most of the time, the money they get from their children is quite limited. Because of this and their habits formed in the hard old days, they now live a quite thrifty life and are strongly against any form of so called wastefulness and extravagance.

If they are healthy enough, they take as much of the housework as possible and take care of their grandchildren and even great grandchildren. Sometimes, it is quite heavy work for an elderly woman. But both they and their children take it for granted. Once they are not able to help their children anymore, they tend to consider themselves as useless and a burden on their children. With little education, they have no interest in books, radios, newspapers and TVs. They travel little and know few people except for family members. The only way they get and exchange information is the gossip among themselves. Therefore, their minds are quite narrow and out of date. They are the most faithful guards of the old tradition from which they have suffered the most.

The Mothers

They are women aged from 35 to 55, with less than three children and are mostly the women of families now. Very few of them are full time housewives. They work with their husbands in the local family business. Their salary is not very high but it is an important part of the family income. This earns them a comparatively important position in the family. These days, the town and township enterprises are not as prosperous as before, and the older and poorer educated of them are facing the danger of losing their jobs. Those who really lose their jobs are forced to take up temporary jobs with lower salaries or become housewives.

Though they work, they have to do much more housework than their husbands. Things are not so bad for those who have their mothers or mothers-in-law to help them. Quite a lot of them have to work, to take care of the whole household and take care of their grandchildren and the old people of the family at the same time. So they are usually quite busy and tired.

Most of the mothers have finished their primary school but went no further. Because they work and take care of the education of the children and deal with all kinds of social affairs of the family, they have the basic knowledge of the society, but have no interest for more things. They spend their leisure time playing mah-jong, watching TV series, swearing and gossiping. But you cannot say that they are intellectually inferior to their husbands. At least, they have equal common sense with them. I know a lot of mothers who are the mainstays of the family. They make almost all the important decisions. They are energetic, hardworking and smart, and some of them in my opinion, are the most respectable women I've ever seen.

The Daughters

They are the daughters and young mothers, living with or near their parents' family. Usually, they don't care much about money; they have their parents and husbands to support them. They take up easy jobs and, as it is more and more difficult to find a proper job, they feel quite happy to stay at home and enjoy themselves, if possible.

Most of them have finished their middle schools. Those who haven't gotten the opportunity to go on studying will take up a life more or less similar to their mothers, but with few burdens. Some of them are required to work hard on their books since they were little girls. They pass their examinations and get the opportunity to receive further education in technical schools or colleges. After graduation, they'll choose to stay in cities and start their own lives. They will live independently and become new women who are completely different from their grandmothers, mothers, and sisters.

Now, we can see some of the basic features of contemporary Chinese women. Compared to their husbands, they are more bound to the family. The young generation women have gotten the opportunity to work and are able to support themselves, but when jobs are in a shortage, they are the first to lose them and the most difficult to get them. They have basic education, but many of them have little interest in developing themselves because they think it's unnecessary, or they themselves are too old, too busy, too stupid or something else. Most of the daughters, as the only child of the family, are supported as well as the boys. They are more well-educated, more independent, and believe themselves not to be inferior to boys. They are the new women of this country. The mothers and the daughters benefit a lot from the policy of the new China, especially in family planning and the Women's Federation, which enable them to live more freely and to get more opportunities than their mothers and grandmothers.

Family Planning

Many Westerners criticize the family planning in China for depriving women of their rights of giving birth to more children. They have their reasons. But it's beyond all doubt that the family planning policy greatly frees women, at least in two ways.

First, it frees the mother. Giving birth to a child is quite a time-consuming and energy-taking work. If a woman gives birth to seven to eight children, which was quite common in old China, and takes care of them until they can take care of themselves, it will cost her the best 20 years of her life, from 20 to 40. Now, because of the family planning policy, she is allowed to have one child, and with the help of her mother and mother-in-law and kindergartens set up by the government, she can bring up her child and as well as keep her job. If she wishes, she can also develop herself by further study.

Second, it frees the daughters in a family with sons and daughters, if the money and energy are limited, parents will do their best to support the boys, and sacrifice the rights of the daughters, because they are considered to be sure to leave the family one day. And the girls are the most likely to stay at home to look after their younger sisters and brothers and help their mothers with housework, when they ought to be in school. But if a family has an only daughter, the parents will concentrate their strength on her. These girls are not only

provided with equal opportunities, but also have a sense of equality to anybody.

The Women's Federation

Another thing which is quite unique and important in Chinese women's lives is the Women's Federation. Any woman, no matter where she lives and where she works is taken care of by a certain Women's Federation. The Women's Federation enjoys vast rights from the carrying out of the family planning, issuing marriage licenses, to judging the complaints of a mother-in-law to her daughter-in-law. The Women's Federation is an important part of the local government and has its own voice, usually the voice of women, in all of the local affairs. Many able women start their careers as government officials with positions in the Women's Federation. The most important function of the Women's Federation is to provide women with a place to go when they are treated badly by their families or colleagues.

Conclusion

Most of the material of this report is from my own experience and from my aunt, who has worked for our local Women's Federation for 15 years. It is too weak and too limited to be a scientific report of the contemporary Chinese women, but I've done my best to convey the lives of the women whom I am most familiar with and whom I love the most, hoping to provide a way to understand their lives and understand our own lives as young women.

3.6   Summary

To be sure, we all are part of several cultures: global society, our national society, our own specific culture, and our own individual culture. All cultures constantly change just as we do ourselves, and our interpersonal communication is usually spontaneous, unless it is frozen in time by being recorded, videotaped, or printed on a page. Heracletus, the ancient Greek, made the enduring statement: "You can't step in the same river twice." In the same way, our culture when we, or our parents, or our grandparents, were young is no longer the same, and in fact, might itself be cross-cultural. Our cultural changes happen all the time, but we don't easily notice those developing changes on a daily basis. If we have a birthday, we don't really feel a year older, but if we compare this birthday with the last year's birthday, the change noted is considerable. However, in the south part of China, when the child is born, she or he is already one, and depending on when the Lunar New Year falls, he or she might already be considered to be two. Being one at birth does make sense, since the child has been inside his or her mother for nine months. Nonetheless, in Western societies, the child is not considered to be one until a full year has passed after birth. Internationally, the China principle is often culturally confusing.

Before we can easily understand other cultures, we need to have a clear sense of our own culture, who are our parents and grandparents, or have been. What was our youth like, and that of our parents, and that of our grandparents, our cousins, and if we have a brother or sister, aunts and uncles, great aunts and uncles? Then we need to expand our notion to our neighborhood, to our friends at different stages of our lives, then to the village, town, or city where we live and the schools where we study. What about the society in which we grow up? Parents, relatives, neighbors, teachers all teach us early how to live in our own society.

Additionally the cultural characteristics of your society, for example "with Chinese characteristics" becomes a part of your own memory chain backward and forward. In the traditional society, people may never move willingly out of their own small area, perhaps never more than 150 kilometers in diameter, whereas in a modernizing society such as China, your eyes keep seeing broader visions. In the 2010 World Expo in Shanghai, the Chinese media said that more than 73 million visitors descended on the Expo site. The vastly largest proportion of these visitors were naturally Chinese, curious to get a small glimpse of the world beyond Chinese borders without leaving China. In a symbolic sense, each Chinese visitor to the Expo had his or her own passport to travel freely among the national pavilions, hindered only by the excessively long lines at many of them. We can assume that all of these visiting Chinese obtained a broader intercultural, international, and global view of the world, just as did those Chinese attending the Beijing Olympics or The Sixteenth Asian Games in Guangzhou.

In this chapter, we have seen a variety of cultural stories by young Chinese and the young Russian woman student in America, ranging in age from 20 to about 31. Among the young authors in this chapter, William begins philosophically by identifying Chinese societal cultural influences in his life, and on the lives of other young Chinese. Zhang Jing studied both in China and in the United States, plus a semester in France, and now works for the United Nations in New York, while Michelle Cui was a middle school student in Seattle, writing a popular book in Chinese after she returned. When she graduated from the university, she was the spokeswoman for a major Chinese company in Beijing, and then pursued two different masters' degrees in the United States. Anya Kyuklanov was born in Russia, but went to the United States as a toddler. She returns to Russia each summer to maintain a balance between both her Russian and American cultures. Zizi Zhao Zhao had the opportunity to undertake a brief intercultural training in the United States and more recently has studied in New Zealand. Cindy Zhao and William have not yet gone out of China, still looking forward to such a chance. David Xu, Jacky Zhang and Nick Deng all have traveled outside of China with Michael Prosser. Writing the case study of the chapter on the role of women, grandmothers, mothers, and daughters in southeast China, Joanna's case study considers three different generations of women in southeast China. Each individual included here and elsewhere in this book has his or her own unique cultural story. **So do you. Why not write your own cultural story?**

3.7 Questions for Discussion

3.7.1 In this chapter's dialogue, there is a discussion about adoption, both within China and the United States, as well as from one country to another. Would you agree or disagree with the student statement that orphans should stay in their own culture? Why? Why not?

3.7.2 Michael has provided considerable self-disclosure in discussing his own adoption. Until he was in his thirties, he never spontaneously acknowledged that he was adopted. What are some possibilities for why he was reluctant to do so earlier? Why might he have become willing in his thirties to use self disclosure in acknowledging that he was adopted?

3.7.3 Professor Li Mengyu, in her cultural story relates her academic development, visiting the US and Japan, and the thrust of her professional intercultural writing. Are there clear signs of her future developing as an expert on intercultural communication from the cultural story of her earlier life? Which event in her adult professional life appears to be the most significant? Why?

3.7.4 In his cultural story, Michael identifies himself as a monocultural individual, then as a Eurocentric individual, then as an Afrocentric and Asiacentric individual, and finally as a multicultural individual. What does this progression culturally mean? If it is his goal and that of students in the imaginary class in the dialogues is to become world citizens, what steps must be taken to achieve that status?

3.7.5 Zhang Jing used her English name, Sherry, as an undergraduate student at Beijing Language and Culture University, and then her Chinese name, Jing Zhang, at her American college and at the United Nations. Now, for her essay in this book, she has asked that she be listed as Zhang Jing. How can we explain this progression with her name changing from Chinese to American to Jing Zhang, and now to Zhang Jing?

3.7.6 Which is more powerful in the cultural essays by the young Chinese in this chapter, the early influences in their lives or the more recent experiences that they have had as more mature young adults? Why?

3.7.7 Almost all of the cultural stories in this chapter by the young Chinese writers were written by former students of Michael. What characteristics tend to be similar in all of these essays? What characterisitics are dissimilar?

3.7.8 If your cultural story were included in this chapter, how would it be similar to the other young Chinese writers? How would it be different?

3.7.9 What cross-cultural comparisons and contrasts can be made between the young Chinese writers and Anya, a Russian brought up in the US?

3.7.10 Three of the young men writers in this chapter have traveled outside of China with Michael. Are there special insights that they have identified by their indication of having traveled with Michael in contrast to the writers William and Cindy who have not yet traveled outside of China?

3.7.11 Which of the cultural stories by the young writers in this chapter have most inspired you if you were to write your own cultural story in about 500 words? Why? Which one comes closest to your own cultural story? Why?

3.7.12 Joanna, in her case study about grandmothers, mothers, and daughters in Southeast China makes very strong contrasts among the different age groups. How are the three groups similar? Despite being potentially members of the same three generation families, why are the contrasts so strong between the grandmothers and the granddaughters? Would the same conditions exist among the generations in different parts of China? Why?

Creating Our Own Cultural Stories

3.8 Suggested Readings

Dixon, D. (1993). *Writing your heritage: A sequence of thinking, reading and writing assignments*. Foreword, S. Blau. New York, NY: National Writing Project.

Levett, M. (2010: March 20). www.thirdculturestories.com

Pollock, D. C. & Van Reken, R. E. (2001). *Third culture kids: growing up among worlds*. New York, NY: Nicholas Brealey.

Useem, R. (1993: January). *Third culture kids: Focus of major study—TCK "mother" pens history of field. Newslinks—the Newspaper of International Schools Services*. Vol. xii. No. 3. Princeton, N.J.

Useem, R. (1999). *Third culture kids biography: Studies in third cultures*. London, England: Academic Press.

Zhang, Y. & Goza, F. W. (2006). *Who will care for the elderly in China? A review of problems caused by China's one-child policy and their potential solutions*. Journal of Aging Studies: 20(2), 151–164.

Chapter FOUR

Perceptions, Beliefs, Worldviews and Values

4.1 Dialogue

Professor Zhang: Class, what do you think about Descartes' quote, "I doubt, therefore I think; I think, therefore I am"?

Catherine: What does it mean? Why does he say that you have to doubt before you can think? I don't doubt something every time that I am thinking.

Echo: Yes, and what does it mean that because I think, therefore I am? Is this related to the ancient Greeks and Confucius and Mencius' ideas? You talked about Plato's, where he discussed illusion versus reality and the different ideas of the cave that different men might see if they only saw one shadow in the cave. Didn't Socrates and he argue against illusion?

Professor Zhang: We discussed in the text the idea that one of your goals is to become critical thinkers. Remember that being or becoming critical thinkers requires us all to try to see more than one side to an argument or proposition. When Michael received the online message from President Obama about his efforts to curb the Wall Street excesses and lack of regulation, Michael asked how it might be different if he were a Republican rather than a Democrat.

Perceptions, Beliefs, Worldviews and Values

Michael: One of my sons whose career is linked to financial planning and insurance is a Republican. He believes that almost everything that President Obama promotes is wrong. During the 2010 US midterm elections the Democrats lost badly with the Republicans gaining more than 60 seats in the House of Representatives, several seats in the Senate, several state governorships, and a lot of state legislatures. So, my son Louis's perceptions about Obama and the Democrats are a lot different than mine. What do you think it means to have different perceptions about an event or issue?

Jason: Perhaps, Michael, you and your son have had different experiences and therefore even though you are his father, you and he see things differently. Maybe you are both right with your own perceptions, but from your different experiences. After all, you must be a lot older than your son.

Laughter

Michael: Well it is true. I was born at a very early age.

Laughter

Michael: Good! You are beginning to catch the puns well. We agree completely on some things, for example about a very good education for his three daughters, and we completely disagree on other things, such as politics. In my family, my daughter and other son tend to vote Democratic, but Louis and his wife vote Republican, and their three daughters, when they reach 18 will probably vote the same way that their parents do. The three teenage girls' perceptions are shaped by their parents. So we see that perceptions are selective. Louis' three daughters have been shaped by their nurturing about religion, education, and politics by their parents. The two brothers, Leo and Louis, had similar experiences when they were children and teenagers, but now they are each fathers of three children. Now their later experiences have been different and so they have different selective perceptions.

Professor Zhang: This is a good discussion, class. So if our perceptions are shaped by our experiences, can we relate to the Sapir-Whorf hypothesis about language which says that "Language shapes perception and perception shapes culture which shapes language?"

Echo: That sounds like Gertrude Stein's "A rose is a rose is a rose is a rose." It seems like a very circular argument, doesn't it? I know that we Chinese and other East Asians have the ability to do more circular reasoning than many Westerners, and that as we become more Western, we move toward the logic of Socrates. I remember that he talked about a major premise, then a minor premise, then a conclusion.

Professor Zhang: Indeed, we Chinese are also familiar with Aristotle's famous statement: "Socrates is a man, all men are mortal, therefore Socrates is mortal."

Tulip: That sounds all right, but what if we use the statement: "Elsie is a cow, all cows are green, therefore Elsie is green."

Laughter

Tulip: Maybe that makes sense for Westerners, but perhaps our way of seeing things or our perceptions about events should be seen through Chinese eyes and logic rather than the Western ideas. What do you think, Professor Zhang?

Professor Zhang: You are right, Tulip. This is one of the reasons that we believe a lot of the ideas of Confucius still today, here in China, in Japan, Korea, Vietnam and other Asian countries. For example, we have such terms as harmony, face, and filial piety. This shows us that both our perceptions and our beliefs may sometimes be similar to those of the Westerners, but at other times may be more exclusive in our own Asian societies. You know, perhaps, that China has developed more than 150 Confucius Institutes overseas to teach Confucius' ideas, Chinese culture and language. As we discussed Descartes' skepticism, Confucius was also a skeptic.

Gloria: What you have told us makes a lot of sense to me.

Professor Zhang: When we deal with perceptions, we come from our own experiences, and those of others whom we trust. At the same time, when we talk about critical thinking again, it means that we have to have an open mind and see the idea from different angles. Perhaps each side has some good points that we can perceive the same, and then that we can believe in, too.

Michael: Now we are back to the different perceptions that my son and I and the Republicans and Democrats have about politics and some social issues. My son and I disagree with each other on many political issues and policies, but we can then continue to be loving and friendly toward each other, and there are many things that we hold in common. We also share many of the same religious beliefs. The UN Charter, you know, talks about having tolerance for different views. In fact, while coming from different cultures we may have some different values and world views between the East and the West, still we can not only have tolerance for different political, educational, cultural or religious world views, but we can also have empathy for the other person's views. You have heard the saying, "You have to walk in another person's shoes or sandals to truly understand his or her values." We call that empathy.

Perceptions, Beliefs, Worldviews and Values

Bernard: You would have a hard time walking in my sandals, Michael. Your feet are far too big!

Laughter

Michael: Actually, Bernard, we have to see that as a metaphor and not literally in my case. Kenneth Burke calls language the soul of culture, and metaphors the soul of language. Most Chinese feet are in fact much smaller than those of many Americans.

Professor Zhang: What are some of the things that Chinese or other Asians and Americans or Europeans would seem to both value? For example, do we believe that both Western and Eastern parents have as a high value their family relationships? Or that the parents from these countries believe in encouraging their children to respect their parents and elders, and have filial piety toward their parents and grandparents?

Cherry: We have talked about values that the Greeks had, such as justice, wisdom and the courage such as Socrates had when he had to decide whether to go into exile or die. The Greeks also believed in moderation, truth, and certainly the good life. Don't you think that Confucius also had many of the same values?

Michelle: Then Aristotle had as a major value also happiness. He listed several causes of becoming happy, and for me friendship is one of my major reasons that I am happy. I am a Christian and so I would add perhaps faith, hope, and love.

Professor Zhang: In her book, Evelin Lindner talks also about eight core universal values: love, truthfulness, fairness, freedom, unity, tolerance, responsibility and respect for life.

Joanna: I really liked the case study that the other Joanna gave us about the women in southeast China—the grandmothers, the mothers, and the daughters. Her story is very much like mine with the three generations, even though I come from Inner Mongolia. I value my parents and my grandparents. So that might be a value that we hold in common in China, and I think that is probably true in the West as well. What about you, Michael? You said that you have three children and nine grandchildren. Do they all respect you and value their time with you?

Jason: That's sure a lot of grandchildren! Do you all live together or at least in the same city?

Michael: No, my three children each have three children and I live with my daughter and her three children, but my two sons live several hours by car from us and from each other. Still, I have strong positive feelings for my three children and their children, and I think that they all have the same for me. In the US of course, we are a multicultural country, just as Canada is and Singapore and Malaysia are here in Asia. So different families might have different family structures and relationships, depending on their original cultures and as their cultures become a part of what we call "the salad bowl" or the Canadians call their "mosaic." That is, we retain our distinct characteristics within the broader and shared national cultures values. In Canada and the US, many single mothers raise their children. Sometimes two people of the same sex live together and raise the children.

Catherine: If I were to express my stereotypes about young Americans, I would say that they lead a much easier life in their education than we Chinese do and that they are more likely than we are to think for themselves. We do a lot of memorization in school. But I also think that in subjects like math we may be ahead of the American students. Is that prejudice?

Michael: We make stereotypes based usually on not enough evidence, perhaps just a small sample. For example, many Americans believe as you do that Chinese students are very good in math and science, and much better than they are. But, because the US and Canada are fairly isolated by two oceans, young Americans often have lots of misperceptions about other cultures. Factually, there was a recent reliable report that fifteen-year olds from Shanghai had the best math and science scores of more than forty groups of fifteen-year olds in different countries. Unfortunately, the fifteen-year olds in the US who were sampled came in at number 22 or 23. So in this case, it appears that the Shanghai educators and students value math and science very highly. Such information then creates the perception of Chinese being so strong in math and science. At the same time, then there is both a perception and stereotype that American students are rather weak in math and science. This is a cross-cultural comparison.

Ben: Sometimes I think that we Chinese know more about the US, for example, its geography, the American presidents, American history, and American literature than many of the young Americans do. We learned about all of the American presidents, where the Rocky Mountains were, where the Great Lakes are, and the size and shape of America.

Michael: You are quite right, Ben. Unfortunately, many young Americans don't have much sense of the rest of the world or sometimes even our own geography. It is a pity.

Tony: However, some common values that we Americans all tend to share are what Thomas Jefferson said in *The Declaration of Independence*: that all men (and

Perceptions, Beliefs, Worldviews and Values

women) are created equal and endowed with certain inalienable rights—life, liberty and the pursuit of happiness. These are common values on which the American society is founded. But when the founders of America were promoting these values, there were still stereotypes, which can be good or bad, and prejudice which almost always is bad because it involves power and looking down on others whom we consider inferior to us.

Ben: But you Americans had slaves until Lincoln's *Emancipation Proclamation* in 1863. How could Jefferson's *Declaration of Independence* saying that all men were created equally support slavery?

Michael: Yes, as we have already mentioned, early US Presidents from Virginia, George Washington, Thomas Jefferson, James Madison, and James Monroe all made great strides to create a country based on these beliefs of equality and freedom, but all of them owned a large number of slaves. There was a lot of hypocrisy. American women at the Seneca Falls Convention of 1848 called for the right of women to vote, but it took until 1920 before that happened. So, while values are always something desirable, we don't always match the values with reality. Brazil had the largest number of African slaves in the western hemisphere, and did not abolish slavery until in the 1880s. Now, it has reasonably good interracial relations.

Jade: In China, we have equality of men and women. As Chairman Mao said, "Women hold up half the sky." We saw in the case study by Joanna about the importance of the Women's Federation in protecting women's rights in China.

Professor Zhang: What are some other common values that we Chinese all seem to have in common?

Catherine: Well, we have already mentioned that we consider a lot of Confucius's ideas from the *Analects* important like filial piety, benevolence, kindness, proper conduct, correct rituals, face, and harmony. Since we are part of the post-80's generation, we may have more modern ideas than our parents, and surely more modern ideas and beliefs than our grandparents, just as Joanna said in the case study.

Professor Zhang: Those are good values for each culture. We may not agree on all of them as our cultures are quite different, but we all certainly want to be happy and to have many of these very desirable values. So, let's stop and continue our lesson for the day about perceptions, beliefs, attitudes, values, and world views, shall we?

Tony: Ok! Let's do it, Professor Zhang and Michael!

4.2   Perceptions

4.2.1 Defining Perception

Samovar, Porter and McDaniel (2009: 129) define perception as the means by which we make sense of our physical and social world as well as the process whereby we convert the physical energy of the world outside of us into meaningful internal experiences. Teri Gamble and Michael Gamble (1999) further state, "Perception is the process of selecting, organizing, and interpreting sensory data in a way that enables us to make sense of our world." Here we can see perception involving a three-step process: **selection, organization** and **interpretation**.

First, **perception is selective**. Since we are exposed to too many stimuli every day, we "allow only selected information through our perceptual screen to our conscious mind" (Adler, 1997). For instance, when picking up a newspaper, the politicians or those interested in politics might pay great attention to political news, and young people will focus more on the entertainment, sports and movie issues, while some of the housewives may show great interest in items for daily use.

The second step in **the perception process is organization**. Organization is a process of categorization. Taking number categorization as an example, in China, people do not like the number four since its pronunciation is similar to that of death, while the numbers six and eight are preferred since they are categorized as lucky numbers which can bring people good fortune and wealth. In some western countries, the number 13 is perceived as unlucky. In the US, some hotels have no thirteenth floor. But many Americans perceive the numbers 7 and 11 as lucky numbers and the convenience food chain store 7/11 has that partial implication. Therefore, we unconsciously put things and people in categories in our cultures.

The third step is **interpretation**. **Interpretation is a process of organizing the selected information in some meaningful ways**. As Jandt points out, "This refers to attaching meaning to sense data and is synonymous with decoding" (2004: 57). For instance, when we encounter a stranger, we often make judgments and interpretations by his or her age, appearance, personality, social status, and the like.

4.2.2 Culture and Perceptions

When talking about the different **perceptions of reality** in different cultures, Samovar, Porter and McDaniel (2009: 128) offer us a very vivid illustration:

Some people in Korea and China put dogs in their ovens, but people in the United States put them on their couches and beds. Why? People in Tabris or Tehran sit on the floor and pray five times each day, but people in Las Vegas

Perceptions, Beliefs, Worldviews and Values

sit up all night in front of video poker machines.

Why? Some people speak Tagalog; others speak English. Why? Some people paint and decorate their entire bodies, but others spend millions of dollars painting and decorating only their faces. Why?

Some people talk to God, but others have God talk to them. And still others say there is no God. Why?

The answer lies in the fact that **culture strongly influences the way we perceive our reality and the world**, and there are direct links between culture and perception. As Adler (1997) points out: "perception is culturally determined. We learn to see the world in a certain way based on our cultural background." Thus, due to our different cultural backgrounds, people perceive the world in different perspectives, Sitaram and Cogdell (1976) offer a similar view of point when they write: "Members of different cultures look differently at the world around them. Some believe that physical world is real. Others believe that it is just an illusion. Some believe everything around them is permanent while others say it is transient. Reality is not the same for all people."

We can make a further illustration of the different **perceptions of reality** in philosophical and religious spheres. Plato's views of "**Logos**" or "**Ideas**" have exerted far-reaching influence in the western culture. Plato did not regard the physical world as real, but he thought it was just an illusion, and he believed the realm of **Ideas** (or **Logos**) to be real and permanent by stating "The beauty of Logos is eternal, it operates without beginning or ending,

without victory or defeat, without increase or decrease." Hinduism also holds the same belief of reality, and believes that "What we say as reality is the merest illusion, a game, a dream, or a dance" (Kolanad,1994: 56). However, it regards Nirvana as the real reality which denotes a "state of spiritual enlightenment." As for Hindus, they hold the belief that "Nirvana releases man from the cycle of birth, suffering, death and all other forms of worldly bondages" (Usha, 1971: 52). While in Chinese Taoism (Daoism), the reality is viewed from another quite different concept "Tao" or "Dao", and "Tao" is believed to be the origin of the world. In Lao Tzu's interpretation of the beginning of the universe, "There was something formed from Chaos, before the creation of heaven and earth. It is silent and formless. It stands alone always and never ceases coursing. You could consider it as the source of all things. I don't know what it is called, but if forced to name it, I would say "Dao." Therefore, "Dao" is a crucial concept in Chinese culture which is interpreted as the operating force in the universe. From Dao, we also get the figure of **Yin** and **Yang**: opposites, such as male/female, light/darkness, moist/dry, and black/white.

Not only do people in different cultures perceive reality in different ways, but also we interpret many other issues in different perspectives. Taking the perceptions of "**dragon**" as an example, we can see they differ quite strikingly in the Chinese and Western cultures. ***Dragon*** in the Chinese culture is viewed as a positive creature which symbolizes magic, power and prosperity. **First**, dragon (*long*) in Chinese culture is perceived as a mysterious creature, which is the combination of different parts of animals, such as snakes, beasts and fish, and in the Chinese legend, **dragon** is believed to be a magic creature which can bring rain and clouds and get rid of drought. **Second, dragon** was once considered as a symbol of power. Particularly in the feudal society in China, emperors were often addressed as dragons. **Third**, the Chinese **dragon** is still highly valued in China and even today the Chinese people call themselves the "the descendants of Long," since they think it denotes prosperity and good luck. Thus the Chinese **dragon** has become the cultural and spiritual symbols of magic, power, harmony, prosperity and good luck. For this reason, the Chinese scholar Guan Shijie suggests using "**Lung**" as the right term for the western word "**Dragon**" in order to avoid misunderstanding. It is also interesting that the wife of the Dragon is the Phoenix bird, who destroyed her nest by fire, and then rebuilt it. Michael's first Chinese purchase in Hong Kong before he had come to the mainland was an embroidered Phoenix bird being visited by 100 other birds (for example as an analogy to the old 100 Chinese names). At that time, he did not perceive the power of either the Dragon or his wife, the Phoenix bird.

However, **dragon** in the western culture is often perceived as a negative symbol of evilness, at least in the past, and **dragons** from the west are said to be wicked and dangerous monsters who breathe fire. In the famous British national epic *Beowulf*, the hero Beowulf was eventually killed by a fire dragon. There are also images of St. George killing the dragon with his sword. Furthermore, in the west, there is also a story of punishment related to the **dragon**. According to the story, a prince killed his father for the purpose of gaining kingship, and the dying king put a curse on his son that turned him into a dragon; later the dragon was killed by his greedy brother, who also became a dragon by receiving the same curse. Therefore, in the historical western culture, **dragon** has, mostly in former times, often been perceived as a kind of fierce and threatening monster that will bring misfortunes to people. Probably very few westerners today are concerned much about this image. In contrast, unicorns are seen to be a very favorable image, and appear on many children's bedding items in the US.

4.2.3 Perceptions and Media

Marshall McLuhan (1967) believed that **media** can change the way people think and he regarded the **mass media** as the important shaper of culture by asserting the famous saying "The Medium is the Message." Carley H. Dodd (2006: 240) further interpreted the phrase by pointing out, "The clear implication is that a medium dominates our perceptions of an event, since it is precisely through some medium that we become aware of many events in our world." The interpretation illustrates the influential role that the **media** play in determining people's perceptions of the reality of events as well as the outside world.

Particularly, mass media have exerted great influences on peoples' perceptions of both illusion and reality today. Many communication books focus on the **effects of mass media**, for instance, starting from the 1930s and 1940s American scholars argued the **all-powerful mass media theory** by comparing mass media as a hypodermic needle which has a tremendous force in affecting people's attitudes and behaviors. Later, **the limited effects of** media theory as well as the mediating effects theories developed, since some scholars regard media effects only as one dependent variable among a complex set of variables. However, although many scholars argue that the effects of mass media are not as enormous as the early researchers have assumed, there is no doubt that the mass media play a tremendous role in determining people's experiential perceptions of the reality they live in as well as the outside world. Many young people see their own reality through the most contemporary media such as the Internet, social networks, blogs, chat rooms and mobile phone texting. We will discuss several of these and other media theories more fully in Chapter Eight.

Media have exerted an enormous influence on cultural awareness as well as on cultural perceptions. It is well known that mass media can set agendas for the intended information that they want to focus on, and this is so called "agenda-setting" theory in the communication field. For instance, during the Beijing Olympic period in 2008 and even before that, Chinese media broadcast a vast amount of news and information related to the topic, concentrating on the enhancement of China's national pride, Chinese prosperity and economic power. As a result, the Chinese people were very proud of the Olympic Games as well as being Chinese people. It has been the same case with the Shanghai World Expo, because of the extensive broadcastings of the Chinese media, millions of Chinese people paid visits to the Shanghai Expo. Before the Expo closed on October 31, 2010, according to the Chinese media 73 million people, mostly Chinese, had visited the Expo. Additionally, the 2010 Asian Games in Guangzhou brought great pride to many Chinese throughout China and overseas, enhanced by the media.

Some researchers maintain that media could provide the audience with consumption satisfaction, and this leads to the famous "uses and gratification" theory, which holds the view that mass media could create the entertainment needs of the audiences and then satisfy their needs. Nowadays in Chinese media, there appear various entertainment programs, which serve to meet and cater for the needs of the Chinese audiences, especially the urban and youth audiences in China. Thus as Dodd (2006: 243) analyzes, "Some evidence suggests that media satisfaction may be connected to a culture's overall satisfaction with its vital information. Ultimately, we may discover that media consumption and satisfaction link with a culture's stress among its members."

Do the media exert positive or negative influences on our perceiving of the cultural reality? It depends. Obviously, the media could provide us with useful and instructive information and knowledge as well as insightful outlooks. Moreover, Eliot Aronson (1980) believed that the influences of mass media were sometimes subtle and unintended, but they really worked. The following were cited by Dodd (2006: 239):

Historical evidence is compelling. The 1977 showing of Alex Haley's Roots on ABC television to over 130 million viewers, the largest television audience at that time to watch any one program in the United States, captured attention and inspired African Americans to increased pride in their heritage. The number of people in the United States to trace their genealogy increased, indicated by the genealogical inquiries after that showing. In 1978, NBC showed Holocaust, a dramatization documenting the Nazis' execution of millions of Jews.

When the same program was telecast in West Germany, it was credited with providing the motivation for the passage of a law stiffening Nazi prosecution. The 1974 showing of the NBC television movie Cry Rape, in which a rape victim went through more trouble in trying to press charges than the horror of the rape itself, may account for the decreased number of rapes reported to the police in the weeks that followed.

As the above examples indicate, **media** can wake up and reinforce one's ethnic identification in many positive ways; however, **media** can also affect the audience in negative ways. One serious issue about the **media** lies in its stereotyping towards certain groups of people, such as the minority groups. For instance, in the United States, the images of African Americans, Hispanics and Asians on television have been sometimes twisted. As Dodd states (2006: 239), "According to a news story released in June of 1993 by George Gerbner and associates at the Annenberg School of Communication, after a ten-year study, these minority stereotypes and media usage of minorities have changed little." We can speculate that more than fifteen years later, the same situation is prevalent. Many Chinese protested at the CNN coverage of the attacks in several countries on the Olympic torch relays, saying that CNN "had hurt the feelings of the Chinese people."

Furthermore, a large number of people, particularly teenagers have become obsessive to various forms of **media**, such as Western, Korean and Chinese TV series, movies and music videos or MTV as well as computer games. As for the adolescents, their addiction to computer games and Wii has become a serious problem even in China today. Critics and educators warn that the **media** have exposed some adults and a large number of teenagers and children to the highly imaged violent world; as a result, they have made the violent imaged-world stronger than a more positive harmonious and peaceful reality and this leads to the continuing increases in adolescent crimes. We will discuss this concept more in Chapter Eight.

4.2.4   Defining Belief

From the Hindu *Bhagavad Gita*, we read that "Man is made by his belief. As he believes, so he is." The British writer Thomas Henry Huxley argued: "It is not what we believe, but why we believe it. Moral responsibility lies in diligently weighing the evidence. **We must actively doubt; we have to scrutinize our views, not to take them on trust.** No virtue is attached to blindly accepting orthodoxy, however 'venerable.'" The great French essayist Michel de Montaigne, expressed the nature of belief this way: "Traveling through the world produces a marvelous clarity in the judgment of men. We are all of us confined and enclosed within ourselves, and we see no farther than the end of our nose. This great world is a mirror where we must see ourselves in order to know ourselves. There are so many different tempers, so many different points of view, judgments, opinions, laws and customs to teach us to judge wisely on our own, and to teach our judgment to recognize its imperfection and natural weakness." Albert Einstein's view was that "During the last century, and part of the one before, it was widely held that there was an unreconcilable conflict between knowledge and belief" (from *The Value of Perspective*, 2010).

Cultural beliefs are closely related to **cultural perceptions**, and in a sense, **beliefs** are the assumed **perceptions** by which people view the world. To be more exact, **beliefs** are the commonly held norms and moral standards of right and wrong doings, as Rogers and Steinfatt (1999: 81) point out, "Beliefs, therefore, are a set of learned interpretations that form the cultural members to decide what is and what is not logical and correct." **Beliefs are deeply rooted in the core of a culture**, as they further illustrate, "Beliefs serve as the storage system for the content of our past experience, including thoughts, memories and interpretations of events. Beliefs are shaped by the individual's culture." Therefore, **beliefs** derive from a culture's inheritance. For instance, people who grow up in a Chinese culture background who have been greatly influenced by Confucianism find it quite difficult to believe in the western Christian culture's concept of original sin, salvation and heaven. On the other hand, some Western people who hold a firm belief towards Christianity might also find it hard to understand some doctrines of Confucianism in Chinese culture.

4.2.5 Stereotypes and Prejudices

In 1922, journalist Walter Lippman (1957: 79–103) first used the term **stereotyping** to refer to a means of organizing our **perceptions** of other people into fixed and simple categories which we use to stand for an entire collection of people. He illustrated the feature of **stereotype** by saying "It is the projection upon the world of our own sense of value, our own position and our own rights. The stereotypes are therefore, highly charged with feeling that are attached to them." His statement reveals that **stereotypes** involve not only cognitive and selective perceptions, but that they also have something clearly to do with our **value assessments** as well as our **emotional attachments**. Hewstone and Brown (1986) think that **stereotypes** are often built on the basis of easily definable characteristics such as sex or ethnicity. They analyze the three characteristics of stereotypes in more detail:

(1) A set of attributes is ascribed to all (or most) members of that category.

(2) Individuals belonging to the stereotyped group are assumed to be similar to each other, and different from other groups, or this set of attributes.

(3) The set of attributes is ascribed to any individual member of that category (1986: 29).

Lustig and Koester (2007: 148) share a similar view by stating the basic feature of **stereotypes** in the following analysis, "When people stereotype others, they take a category of people and make assertions about the characteristics of all people who belong to that category. The consequence of stereotyping is that the vast degree of differences that exist among the members of any one group may not be taken into account in the interpretation of messages." In some sense, **prejudices** are closely related to **stereotypes**, and they turn out to be deeply held negative feelings towards a particular group. Macionis (1998: 217) provides us with a detailed definition: "Prejudice amounts to a rigid and irrational generalization about a category of people. Prejudice is irrational to the extent that people hold inflexible attitudes supported by little or no direct evidence. Prejudice may target people of a particular social class, sex, sexual orientation, age, political affiliation, race or ethnicity." Stereotyping and prejudiced assumptions toward a certain group of people often occur in our daily lives. For instance, when talking about the American people, British people, French people as well as the Japanese people, many Chinese would hold some stereotyping views. American people are supposed to be open-minded, liberal, energetic and cordial, British people are thought of as conservative, formal and polite, French people are perceived as romantics as well as artistic.

It is the same case that people from other cultures would often also hold **prejudiced and even stereotyped perceptions** about people of other nationalities. Axtell (1991: 83–84) made a particular study on American businessmen's impressions of the English, French, Italians, Latin Americans and Asians and the results showed as follows: English people are supposed to be "conservative, reserved, polite, proper, formal," being quite similar to the Chinese people's assumption of the British people. French are portrayed as being "arrogant, rude, chauvinistic, romantic, gourmets, cultural,

artistic." Here "arrogant and rude" descriptions towards the French people are negative comments, being different from what has been assumed positively above in many Chinese people's minds about French people. In regards to the impressions of Asians in many American businessmen's minds, they are "inscrutable, intelligent, xenophobic (fear/hatred of strangers/foreigners), golfers, group oriented, polite, soft-spoken." Hence, these impressions are both positive and negative portrayals and stereotypes of the Asians. As to the negative ones, such as the descriptions of "inscrutable, xenophobic (fear/hatred of strangers/ foreigners) these **perceptions** are endowed with a sharply **prejudiced connotation**. In fact, from the perspective of many Asians, the Asian people are not so difficult to understand and get along with. Besides, most Asian people do not see themselves as xenophobic; instead, Chinese believe that they are kind, warm-hearted and willing to help and make friends with strangers as well as foreigners.

Bryan Hall and W. Pitt Derryberry in their study's abstract (2010) discuss the differences of **aversive racists** versus those with **high explicit racial prejudice**:

> *Aversive racists are those low in outward expressions of racism that nonetheless possess negative feelings (i.e. implicit prejudicial attitudes) toward out-groups such as African or Asian Americans.*
>
> *This study examined whether those meeting the criteria of aversive racism were more advanced from those who are high in attitudes favoring explicit racial prejudice in moral judgment*

development, moral identity, universal orientation, empathy, and social desirability. Conversely, this study examined whether those meeting the criteria for aversive racism were statistically less advanced from those who are high in attitudes favoring explicit racial prejudice in authenticity, nonprejudice, authoritarianism, social dominance, and authoritarianism. Significant differences were observed in authenticity, nonprejudice, authoritarianism, social dominance, and postconventional reasoning. The findings support that aversive racism appears to be a phenomenon distinct from high explicit racial prejudice. However, findings also suggest that though aversive racism may impact day-to-day decisions, it does not appear to be as detrimental to the self and social functioning overall as is high explicit racial prejudice.

4.2.6 Attitudes and Values

Milton Rokeach argues that **attitudes** long held the central position in the scholarship of social psychology and sociology, but that the **value concept** should move ahead of **attitudes** as social psychology's and sociology's central focus: "First, value seems to be a more dynamic concept since it has a strong motivational component as well as cognitive, affective, and behavioral components. Second, while attitude and value are both widely assumed to be determinants of social behavior, value is a determinant of attitude as well as behavior. Third, if we further assume that a person possesses considerably fewer values than

attitudes, then the value concept provides us with a more economical analytical tool for describing and explaining similarities and differences between persons, groups, nations, and cultures" (1972: 157–158). He notes that while **attitudes** seem to focus in the study of social psychology and sociology, the study of **values** crosses many more disciplines, thereby creating the possibility for interdisciplinary scholarly collaboration. Rokeach defines **attitudes**, which are **an organization of several beliefs focused on a specific object or situation as predisposing one to respond in some preferential manner**. However, he postulates that: "Values, on the other hand, have to do with modes of conduct and end-states of existence ... Once a value is internalized it becomes consciously or unconsciously, a standard or criterion for guiding action, for developing and maintaining attitudes toward relevant objects and situations, for justifying one's own and others' actions and attitudes, for morally judging self and others, and for comparing self with others. Finally, a value is a standard employed to influence the values, attitudes, and actions of at least some others ..." (159–160). He sees **two types of values**, *instrumental*—which may be centered around one or a small group of beliefs, and *terminal* values—which suggests: "I believe that such-and-such an end-state of existence (for example, salvation, a world at peace) is personally worth striving for" (160).

Rokeach later suggests that in the **polarity of values** in terms of social relations as they relate to the *criteria of desirability*, different dimensions or modes of valuing may emphasize: "*equality or inequality; collectivity or individual interest; acceptance or rejection or authority; individual* *autonomy* or *interdependence*; *expressiveness* or *restraint* (affectivity/neutrality); *diffuseness* or *specificity*; *ascribed qualities* or *excellence of performance* (ascription/achievement); *particularistic relationship relationships* or *categorical memberships*; *personalized* or *universalistic standards*; *hostility* or *affection* or *indifference*; *dominance* or *submission.*" [italics added] Because **values** are learned culturally, a densely filled "value space" can be represented reasonably well by four factors: "(1) the extent of acceptance of authority, (2) need-determined expression or value-determined expression or value-determined restraint (3) acceptance or rejection of egalitarianism, and (4) extent of acceptance of individualism ... The communication of common appraisals eventually builds value standards, which often become widely accepted across many social and cultural boundaries ... "(1979: 22). Arguing that in any **ideal value system**, Rokeach says that if pressed to extreme limits, unexpected and undesired implications and consequences may result: "Example 1: Who does not want freedom? Who does not believe in some aspects of equality of human right? But what happens if we demand instant and total freedom, or instant and total equality? Total freedom is chaos, and the end result always is a dictatorial order. Total substantive equality requires a tight system of social control" (1979: 43). In this **context**, we must note that the universalism of human rights may in certain circumstances conflict with other views in the specific cultural or particularism context, basically a contrast between Western and Eastern/Middle Eastern/African perspectives.

4.2.7   World Views

Rapport and Overing note that **world view** "is the common English translation of the German word *Weltanschauung*, meaning overarching philosophy or outlook, or conception of the world." (2000: 394) Samovar and Porter (2004) explain the term by saying "World view, therefore, is a culture's orientation towards such things as God, humanity, nature, human existence, the universe, death, life, suffering, sickness, and other philosophical issues that penetrate all phases of human existence." That is to say, **world views are life philosophies** that deal with all phases of the world and human existence.

The Virgin and Child

Religion is the predominant element found in almost every culture and has given their people a **worldview**. For instance, Christianity, Judaism, and Islam are all monotheistic religions which believe in one God. However, the interpretations of God and the relationship between God and human beings in the three religions are different. In Christianity, as Hale illustrates, "God is the eternal creator who can transcend creation and yet is active in the world and God became incarnate—fully human—as Jesus of Nazareth, who is believed to be the as the savior and redeemer of human kind." (1998: 54) While Judaism, as Ehrlich summarizes, "believes in one universal and eternal God, the creator and the sovereign of all that exists. God has entered into a special relationship or covenant with one people, the Jews, or Israel, and given them the task of being a nation" (1998: 16); last, Islam holds the beliefs that "There is no God but Allah, and Muhammad is the prophet of Allah." We can figure out the commitment to God from two Arabic words *Islam* and *Muslim, Islam* means "to submit", *Muslim* refers to the person who submits to the will of Allah. Besides, Muhammad is regarded as God's messenger who delivers the final religious message and establishes a social order, both spiritually and politically.

In contrast, Hindu philosophy, with many gods and goddesses, puts more emphasis on the discovery of oneself instead of relying on an outside force of God. According to Hammer, Hinduism believes that "The ultimate cause of suffering is people's ignorance of their true nature, the self, which is omniscient, omnipotent, perfect and eternal" (1971: 170). Here the omniscient, omnipotent, perfect and eternal self instead of God is perceived as the true nature of life. Furthermore, in Hinduism, there is the very important term "Nirvana," which means "a state of spiritual enlightenment." (1971: 79–80) and the spiritual enlightenment is a process of the exploration of the true nature of self.

However, in Taoism and Confucianism, Chuangtse and Mencius underscore the importance of finding oneself. Lin Yutang once wrote: "Who are we? That is the first question. It is a question almost impossible to answer. But we all agree that the busy self occupied in our daily activities is not the quite real self. We are quite sure we have lost something in the mere pursuit of living" (2008: 151). In Chuangtse's view, what we have lost is a state of Naiveté with the burden of civilization. Mencius, the follower of Confucius says "A great man is he who has not lost the heart of a child." As Lin Yutang further states, "Mencius agreed with Chuangtse that we have lost something and the business of philosophy is to discover and rediscover that which is lost-in this case, a "child's heart" (2008: 152). Hence, according to the traditional Chinese culture's view, the true self is a state of naiveté and innocence.

4.2.8 Defining Values More Fully

Geert Hofstede regards **values** as a key mental software and states that "a value is a broad tendency to prefer a certain state of affairs over others" (2008: 5). Kluckhohn gave a more detailed illustration of the term, "A value is a conception, explicit or implicit, distinctive of an individual or characteristic of a group, of the desirable which influences the selection from available modes, means and ends of actions" (1967: 395). This definition underscores the fact that **value is kind of abstract conception** which can be held by individuals and groups. *Explicit or implicit* indicates that **values** can be either clearly perceived or remain unnoticed. *Desirable, selection* and *available* denotes what conceptions and behaviors are more preferred, desired, appreciated and hoped for by individuals or groups. Albert highlights the point when she proposes "a value system represents what is expected or hoped for, required or forbidden. It is not a report of actual conduct but is the system of criteria by which conduct is judged and sanction applied" (1968: 32). At last, Nanda and Warms summarize the **concept of value** in a more concise way, "Values are shared ideas about what is true, right, and beautiful that underlie cultural patterns and guide society in response to the physical and social environment" (1998: 49). Hofstede states that **values** deal with such things as the following (some of which are analogous to the **Yin and the Yang** in a binary sense):

> *Evil versus good*
> *Dirty versus clean*
> *Dangerous versus safe*
> *Decent versus indecent*
> *Ugly versus beautiful*
> *Unnatural versus natural*
> *Abnormal versus normal*
> *Paradoxical versus logical*
> *Irrational versus rational*
> *Moral versus immoral (2008: 6)*

Hofstede further illustrates the **unique role of values** in the structures of culture by drawing an "onion diagram." In the diagram, according to Hofstede, symbols such as words, gestures, objects, and pictures are put in the outside layer of the onion; Heroes such as persons, real or imaginary, who are highly prized in a culture are placed in the second layer of the onion. Rituals which are supposed to be socially essential and collective activities are placed

in the third layer and values are placed in the innermost layer of the onion, **since values are considered as the core of a culture**. Among the four layers of culture, symbols, heroes, rituals are visible to an outside observer, while **values are invisible**, nevertheless, their cultural meanings can be interpreted by insiders through the channel of practices. As to the outsiders, the most difficult issues are the invisible concepts or ideas hidden behind the veils of values (2008: 10). **Ritual** often is the explicit conduct of shared values, as well as our daily behaviors. Most cultural ceremonies are ritualistic in nature. For example, the opening of the Beijing Olympics Games occurred on August 8, 2008 at 8 pm, which is a highly auspicious numbering for the Chinese people, and 2008 Chinese drummers helped to open the ceremony.

4.2.9   The Significance of Values to Intercultural Communication

Values serve as the core of culture and play a significant role in **intercultural communication. Culture** is often compared to an iceberg, in which only a small part above the iceberg is visible and perceivable, such as landscape, dress, clothes, architecture, painting, and customs (**as aspects of objective culture**); however; the larger part hidden under the iceberg of culture is invisible and unperceivable; among them are ideas, beliefs, attitudes, stereotypes, and prejudice as well as values and cultural thought patterns (**all aspects of subjective culture**).

As we have mentioned above, **values** are also addressed by Hofstede as "the software of the mind." We are all familiar with the software of computers, which serve as the operating programs of computers. McLuhan early saw the software of computers as analogous to a human nervous system. Hofstede proposes "Nearly all our other mental programs (such as attitudes and beliefs) carry value components. **Man is an evaluating animal** (Kluckhohn, 1951/1967: 403). Judaic, Christian, and Muslim biblical legends, mythology, assumptions, and prescriptions put the choice between good and evil right at the beginning of humankind's history (with Adam and Eve), thus indicating the fundamental impossibility of humans' escape from choices based on value judgments" (Hofstede, 2008: 6).

Prosser puts **values** in a still broader cultural context by illustrating that: "Values are the patterns in individuals and groups which are structured primarily through cultural communication. They are the most deep-seated aspects of culture, and we assume that all humans have values." (1989: 174) Munro S. Edmonson embraces the view of **Cultural Functionalism** which underscores the most important result of culture is the creation of structure, and proposes that among the many kinds of cultural structures, values are "the most cultural of cultural structures" (1989: 174).

4.2.10 Comparing Eastern and Western Values

In terms of the comparison of Eastern and Western values, K.S. Sitaram (1995) identifies two primary values and value orientations: **Eastern responsibility vs. Western individuality**. He regards that many Easterners see themselves collectively, with modest respect for responsibility, authority, benevolence, and propriety for their groups and others as well as loving care for family members, while Westerners see themselves first as individuals which leads to the importance of values such as competitiveness, aggressiveness, challenges to authority, public opinion polls, political differences, court-protected individual rights, success, high personal earnings, private property, personal identity, self-centeredness, and ethnocentrism. Prosser would challenge that those which are negative aspects should be called **values**; instead he calls them **drives**.

To be more specific, Sitaram lists the following **contrasting values and goals** in Asian and western cultures. In Asian culture, the **key values** are authoritarianism, brotherhood, collective responsibilities, education, gratefulness, loyalty, respect for elders, and hospitality. While in Western culture, the **primary values** are human dignity, individuality, firstness, frankness, directness, punctuality as well as respect for youth. According to his illustration, the following are several **key values** stressed in the Eastern cultures.

Authoritarianism:	It is a primary value in Asian, African, and Middle Eastern cultures. Eastern societies with respect for authority have established a set of hierarchical systems. For instance, birth may predict status in Hindu caste system; and Confucianism underscores hierarchical order as well.
Brotherhood:	It is a value cherished by Confucianism as well as Islam. Chinese culture speaks highly of brotherhood, and it is the same case in Islam. According to Qu'ran in Islam, all Muslims are brothers.
Collective responsibility:	It is the Hindus and Buddhists' highest value, which is also cherished in Chinese culture.
Cooperation:	Qu'ran-value of brotherhood results in cooperation (and sometimes Jihad) among all Muslims. It is also a primary value in Chinese culture.
Education:	Eastern cultures place high priority on education and shows great respect for teachers. According to Sanskrit saying: "The teacher is god." Chinese and Japanese culture value education as well.
Gratefulness and loyalty:	It is an Eastern and long-lasting value.
Hospitality:	To some extent, the guest is god in Eastern sacred books. For instance, in Hindu weddings; the hosts serve the best food to guests.
Respect for elders:	Both African and Asian cultures hold the values of ancestor worship; showing respect and caring for the elderly.
Sacredness of the land:	In the Hindus' eyes, "Sacred cow like mother who nurses her children." Taoists also hold the view of earth as mother.

Sitaram contrasts the key values underscored in the western culture as human dignity, individuality, firstness, directness and respect for youth:

Human dignity:	It is a basic concept in the UN Charter, and equality among persons is highly valued in western culture.

Perceptions, Beliefs, Worldviews and Values

Individuality:	It is a clear western value which stresses achievement, success, winning, and competition.
Firstness:	Westerners want to be first. For instance, the Soviet Sputnik was a great shock to US in 1957. (First to land on the moon, to make an auto, to fly a plane.) (Guinness Book of World Records.)
Frankness and directness:	Most Western people prefer the direct way of speech. Particularly, Americans like frank and direct expressions instead of vagueness or ambiguity in communication. Many Western leaders announce: "I mean what I say, and I say what I mean."
Respect for youth:	Western cultures are youth-oriented. The value of youth is highly appreciated.

4.3 Case Study: On the Traditional Chinese Value of "Harmony"

Resources for the Study of Intercultural Communication, Li Mengyu

Intercultural communication is a field which focuses on the exploration of the relationship between communication and culture, as we have noted earlier. The ultimate aim of the discipline is to help people from diverse cultural backgrounds communicate more effectively with one another and to establish a harmonious relationship. To some extent, to create a **harmonious communicative relationship among people from different cultures is of vital importance to the successful intercultural communication**. The traditional Chinese value of "**harmony**" can provide the field with new and illuminating resources either on a theoretical basis and/or practical usage.

In the traditional Chinese culture, the notion of "harmony" is often interpreted as a dialectical and dynamic term. The conception of "Supreme Harmony" or "Great Harmony" (*tai he*) was first mentioned in *The Book of Changes* (*Zhou yi*). Fung Yu-Lan in his book, *A Short History of Chinese Philosophy*, stated: "Harmony of this sort, which includes not only human society, but permeates the entire universe, is called the Supreme Harmony. In Appendix I of the *Yi*, it is said: "How vast is the originating power of [the hexagram], Ch'ien ... Unitedly to protect the Supreme Harmony: this is indeed profitable and auspicious" (2007: 286). The term "*Ch'ien*" (also translated as "*Qian*") denoting the ultimate way the universe operates, is regarded as the perfect reconciliation of opposing forces of nature. As Yu Dunkang illustrated: "It explains that all beings find the ultimate and proper purpose of their existence by transformations of the *qian* path: hard and soft are reconciled and united, producing the perfect harmony by which all beings are created and on which they thrive, and bringing a state of ultimate peace to the world" (1991: 53). The notion of **harmony** is also elucidated in *Tao Te Ching*: "Tao gave birth the One: The One gave birth successively to two things, three things, up to ten thousand. These ten thousand creatures cannot turn their backs to the shade without having the sun on their bellies and it is on this blending of the breaths that their harmony depends" (90). Hence, the conceptions of "*Ch'ien*" in *The Book of Changes* (*Zhou Yi*) and "*Tao*" in *Tao Te Ching* can be respectively interpreted as the originating power or intrinsic principle of the universe which involve the **harmonious interaction** of opposing forces such as *yin* and *yang*, light and dark, hard and soft, water and fire. "The Supreme Harmony" is thus regarded as the dynamic balance of the forces. The notion of **harmony** is also illustrated in *Chung Yung*, (or *the doctrine of the Mean*), within which *Chung* and *Ho* serve as the two crucial terms. It explains: "To have no emotions of pleasure or anger, sorrow or joy, welling up: this is to be described as the state of *Chung*. To have these emotions welling up but in due proportion: this is to be described as the state of *ho* [harmony]. *Chung* is the chief foundation of the world. *Ho* is the great highway for the world. Once *chung* and *ho* are established, Heaven and Earth maintain their proper

position, and all creatures are nourished" (284). Therefore, **harmony** (or *ho*) in *Chung Yung*, can be perceived as the perfect state of appropriateness, which lays great emphasis on the proper position and due proportion of the various elements being involved.

In another famous Chinese ancient book called *Tso Chuan*, Yen Tzu further expounded the **notion of harmony** by employing the famous analogy "Seeking harmony is like making a soup. One uses water, fire, vinegar, soy source and prunes all together to stew with fish and meat. The chef mélanges harmoniously all the ingredients for a tasteful soup" (47). **Harmony is also a key word of understanding Confucius's thought**, the term has appeared in *The Analects* eight times. Confucius's entire life was engaged in the perfection of one's virtue and personality as a gentleman (or a perfect person). "*Ren*" (humanism) and "*li*" (ritual) were two main concepts in *The Analects*. Confucius particularly interpreted the two concepts in terms of harmony. *Ren*, according to Confucius, is "the ideal relationship which should pertain between individuals" (Smith, 1994: 110). And he stressed "In practicing the rules of propriety, it is harmony that is prized" (Pan, et al. 2004: 6). Confucius had further broadened the thought of **harmony** by stating "The gentleman harmonizes his relationship with others but never follows them blindly (*he er bu tong*). The petty man just follows others blindly disregarding any principle (*tong er bu he*)" (45). Thus, in Confucius's eyes, a gentleman (or a perfect person) is a person who has accomplished the maximum development of one's virtue and personality by being kind and considerate to others on the one hand and maintaining his or her independent mind on the other hand, and this reflects Confucius's unique interpretation of the **harmonious relationship among individuals**. Above all, **harmony is a very important conception in traditional Chinese culture**, and it embodies the supreme ideal of Chinese culture that regards "All things are nurtured together without injuring one another; All courses are pursued together without collision" (Fung, 2007: 286).

Although the above typical views of **harmony** quoted are illustrated in different ways, they express the common dialectical and **dynamic interpretation of harmony**, which underscores the value of difference, reconciliation and creation. First, they do not regard **harmony** as a category denoting sameness, uniformity and conformity; instead they underscore in particular the value of difference, diversity, multiplicity and plurality within the concept. Next, they lay great emphasis on the reconciliation of the heterogeneous things rather than contestation, conflict and strive among them. Finally, they conceive **harmony** as a source of constructive creativity which can bring mutual benefit for all in the process of transformational synthesis of various components. The interpretations of **harmony** in traditional culture mentioned above have offered rich revelations to the intercultural communication study.

4.4 Summary

In this chapter, we have held a dialogue on perceptions, beliefs, attitudes, stereotypes and prejudice, world views and values between our imaginary intercultural communication class, the imaginary Professor Zhang, and Michael. We have further explored the definitions of **perceptions, beliefs, attitudes, stereotypes, prejudice, world views and values**. On this basis, we have also discussed topics such as **culture and perceptions; media and perceptions**, the **significance of values to intercultural communication** as an ongoing theme of *Communicating Interculturally*. We have seen comparisons and contrasts of Asian and Western values. At the end of the chapter, in Li Mengyu's case study, the illustration of the traditional Chinese value of "**harmony**" as well as its resources for intercultural communication are provided. **Now, we can ask**, as emerging **critical thinkers, interculturalists, multiculturalists, and world citizens**, how should you perceive your own culture and society, your role in **international** and **global** affairs, and the role of China as an **international stakeholder** and as an increasingly important power?

4.5 Questions for Discussion

4.5.1 In our opening dialogue for this chapter, we can see that the students are becoming more and more capable as **critical thinkers**. Several of them speak with confidence and authoritatively. Can you provide several examples of the development of their **critical thinking** through their comments and questions?

4.5.2 In the dialogue, we have seen the expression of the circular Sapir-Whorf hypothesis: "Perception shapes language; language shapes culture; culture shapes perception." Would you agree with this hypothesis or not? How can you defend your agreement or disagreement as a **critical thinker** yourself?

4.5.3 Since **perception** is closely related to **experience**, why is it that the experiences of some cultures in terms of the same events or opinions leads one cultural group in an opposite direction than that of a different cultural group?

4.5.4 A famous early intercultural communication scholar, Edward C. Stewart, describes his own "selective perception." As a little child in a small Brazilian town with a university, he went with his mother to the "red brick" gymnasium to care for individuals wounded in a civil uprising. Later in his fifties, he returned to the town and looked for the "red brick" gymnasium, but couldn't find it. A very old worker told him that there never had been a red brick gymnasium. Why do you think that this scholar always thought that the university had had a red brick gymnasium when he was a little boy, when in fact there never had been such a red brick gymnasium at that university?

4.5.5 Edward T. Hall, often called the grandfather of intercultural communication, says that he was lodging as he often did at the same small hotel on a back street in Tokyo, and one day he returned to his room only to find that someone else's belongings were there. When he asked the clerk what happened, he was taken to another room where his items were laid out exactly as in his first room. "This is your new room, sir," he was told without further explanation. Considering the role of Western and Eastern cultural **perceptions** and **attitudes** in this situation, why do you think that this happened?

4.5.6 **Beliefs** are clusters of assumptions, usually based on reasonable evidence, or sometimes simply faith. Most westerners and easterners believe that the sun will rise in the east and set in the west. However, our Muslim student, Ali, in the dialogue, believes that Allah could easily decide to have the sun rise in the west and set in the east. What sort of **perception** and **belief** has led him to express this assumption?

4.5.7 If **beliefs** are generally based on some sort of faith, how can we see that three major religions, Judaism, Christianity, and Islam accept the concept of a monotheistic God, while Hindus have, and even the ancient Greeks had, a belief in many gods and goddesses. Why is it that one group of religions believes in only one God and another group believes in many gods and goddesses? Why do most Chinese athiests believe in no God?

Perceptions, Beliefs, Worldviews and Values

4.5.8 In the discussion on **attitudes** and **beliefs**, we see that Rokeach describes them quite differently what are these distinctions and how do they relate to this particular chapter as we develop our understanding of **intercultural communication**?

4.5.9 How are **world views** similar or different to **values**? Do people in a culture first have **values** or **world views**? What is the importance of **world views** and **values** to the understanding of **intercultural communication**? Do you have any general or specific **world views**? Are they different from those of your parents and grandparents? If so, what are they and how do you think they have been formed?

4.5.10 If **values** relate to what is desirable or good or to be appreciated in a culture, how can we distinguish cultural patterns on such topics as love, respect, justice and kindness, versus competition, aggressiveness, freedom, and debate, as either Eastern or Western? Do both cultures support all of these norms in some way? If so how can they be reconciled? If not, why not?

4.6   Suggested Readings

Dai, X. D. & Kulich, S. J. (Eds.) (2010). *Identity and intercultural communication: Theoretical and contextual constructions: Intercultural research. Vol. 2.* Shanghai, China: Shanghai Foreign Language Education Press.

Dai, X. D. & Kulich, S. J. (Eds.) (2011). *Identity and intercultural communication: Contextual applications: Intercultural research, Vol. 3.* Shanghai, China: Shanghai Foreign Language Education Press.

Kulich, S. J., Prosser, M. H., & Weng, L. P. (Eds.) (2011). *Value frameworks at the theoretical crossroads of culture. Intercultural research. Vol. 4.* Shanghai, China: Shanghai Foreign Language Education Press.

Kulich, S. J., Weng, L. P., & Prosser, M. H. (Eds.) (2011). *Value dimensions and their contextual dynamics across cultures. Intercultural research, Vol. 5.* Shanghai, China: Shanghai Foreign Language Education Press.

Chapter FIVE

Cultural Patterns and Cross-Cultural Value Orientations

5.1 Dialogue

Professor Zhang: In our last set of questions, we noted that a famous scholar in intercultural communication had been as a little boy with his mother at a university in a small Brazilian town who was caring for wounded fighters in a civil uprising in what he remembered as a red brick gymnasium. However, when he returned many years later, he could not find the red brick gymnasium, and an old guard said that there never had been a red brick gymnasium. We called it "selective perception." What is the reason that he had a misperception about the red brick gymnasium?

Vivian: I think that he was too little to remember exactly where the wounded men were being cared for. Perhaps they were not being cared for in a gym at all.

Professor Zhang: That's good, but keep thinking.

Fiona: Maybe he just remembered the story because his mother mentioned it a lot after she and he were there?

True Nation: You said that he was an American scholar, right? Well, then perhaps he was at a lot of American universities as an adult, and most of them had red brick gymnasiums? Perhaps the military aspects also were a part of his memory as the men were wounded soldiers in a civil uprising. I have seen photos of an American university with a red brick gym.

Professor Zhang: Good for you True Nation! So over his life he had been to a lot of American universities and having regularly seen red brick gymnasiums, his misperception tricked him to believe that when he was a small boy at the Brazilian university the gymnasium there was indeed also a red brick gymnasium. Perhaps the military situation also clouded his memory.

Sara: That brings up another question. You talked about Edward Hall having all of his things moved in a small Japanese hotel to another room, and even Hall couldn't figure out why that happened to him. Did they dislike him as a guest at the hotel?

Maria: I have an idea, but I am not sure that it is correct. Perhaps someone else had booked the room and so it wasn't available later after he had moved in.

Professor Zhang: Very good thinking, Maria. That is part of the answer, but there is still more to this story.

Jason: You said it was a small hotel on a side street. Then, maybe the hotel manager felt that since Hall had come to that hotel several times he wouldn't mind being moved with all of his things to another room.

Professor Zhang: You are right, Jason. In fact, he had stayed there enough that the hotel manager thought he was like family, and wouldn't mind the change. However, the manager didn't tell him because family members would not mind the change, and there would be no real reason to explain it to him. This is high-context communication. Hall's mini-cultural story got more complicated, as at a later time, his things were moved to still another small hotel nearby, without explaining it to Hall, as he should know that he was actually being given special treatment as a family member.

Michelle: So, Hall is showing how the Japanese had intuitive logic, but Hall was working with a Western style of logic or what Hall calls low-context commuication? The Japanese logic would be Chinese logic too, right?

Professor Zhang: Good thinking, Michelle. Hall calls this very high context behavior—indirect and with the meaning found more in the manager's pleasant but vague treatment of Hall, where Hall, as an American professor, expected more direct and explicit information about his situation or low-context communication. Still, he found the other hotel to be even a better experience, with no other foreigners present, than the first hotel and when he came back to Tokyo again, he always went to the second hotel which was owned by the same people.

Michael: I had an interesting experience in Beirut, Lebanon in 1981. While the PLO controlled a large part of the city, there was a New Year's parade, and I saw what seemed like the same red haired boy pass by three or four times. In this case, the parade circled around several times or it would have been much smaller. But, a young soldier accidentally brushed the bayonet on his rifle against me and pulled my shirt open. Later in the week, I foolishly went by myself to the bombed out Christian area. A uniformed soldier stopped me and spoke to me in French, so our conversation was very vague, as he had very little English and I had very little French. I was a bit nervous both because of the language barrier, but also because of the rifle with the bayonet that I thought he was carrying. Fortunately, I was writing a daily journal, and perhaps a year later, I was rereading my writing about the incident with the French-speaking soldier. To my surprise, I had not written about him having a rifle with a bayonet. Again, because of the earlier experience, I had had my own selective perception since the young soldier at the parade did indeed have a rifle with a bayonet, but while the soldier in the bombed out area may have had a gun, if so, it was a pistol instead of a rifle with a bayonet.

Amelia: That was scary! Why were you walking anyway by yourself in that bombed out area, Michael?

Michael: Hall writes that it is good to get lost in another culture, unless it is dangerous, as it gives us unexpected insights into the culture more informally. I was being foolish, as I said, and perhaps feeling too individualistic rather than collectivistic as I should have stayed with other members of our group. In the years later in Lebanon, Americans and British were taken hostage and held for more than a year, Teffy Anderson, a British hostage negotiator, was held for nearly seven years. He wrote a very popular cultural story of his experience, *The Den of Lions*.

Professor Zhang: That's a very interesting and sobering cultural story, Michael.

Tony: It's lucky for you that you were always safe while you were living in China.

Sophia: I have been reading about cultural and value orientations, but I am not quite sure what the term means. Can you explain it for me?

Michael: Basically, Sophia, it means that there is what we call a cluster of values, or a more generalized way of looking at a collection of values, or what some of the writers, like the Dutch management researcher Geert Hofstede called national

Cultural Patterns and Cross-Cultural Value Orientations

dimensions. Hofstede developed a whole set of these clusters. For example, one of his dimensions was called high and low power distance, and he speculated that in a collective and more traditional society, power is hierarchical, while in more individualistic societies, power is more egalitarian and vertical.

Sophia: So, he might think that China has a larger power distance, for example, between teachers and students than America might have?

Michael: Yes you are thinking well about this concept. However, curiously in my case, I always was called by my last name when I taught in the US, which would suggest that I was then more high power distance. But in China I am always called Michael, which gives the impression that I am more collectivistic. Have I become more Chinese and less American? There is a saying, however, "You can take Michael out of America, but you can't take America out of Michael." Perhaps this would be true too, Sophia, if you were studying in the US, where it would still be hard to take China and your Chinese culture out of you.

Echo: But you are still our teachers. Perhaps this is why we call Professor Zhang by the family name here in our collective society, but because you are a foreigner, you can change the rules for yourself here to be more egalitarian while you are more high power distance when you teach in the US. And we respect both of you as our teachers because of our Chinese and Confucian background.

Mike: Michael, as I have said before, maybe you are a "Chiamerican!"

Laughter

Michael: Yes, it's a good idea. Thanks, Mike. You might be right. Perhaps I am a "Chiamerican."

Professor Zhang: We see from the comments of our students and you, Michael, that as humans we are all storytellers, who develop our own cultural stories, as we saw in Chapter Three. We are also seeing a lot of humor in this class which is a part of good story-telling and interactive communication. Today, however, we want to explore culture patterns, values, and value orientations more fully. Shall we move on to our key topics for today?

Tony: Professor Zhang and Michael, let's do it!

5.2 Understanding Cultural Patterns and Value Orientations

According to Samovar, Porter and McDaniel, **a cultural pattern** is "a system of beliefs and values that work in combination to coherent, if not always consistent, model for perceiving the world" (2009: 132). So the main elements in **cultural patterns** are **beliefs** and **values**; they are **the cores of each culture** which reflect and determine different cultures' perceptions of the world. For instance, in regard to the value of credibility, Chinese think in American culture most people consider that a person should be direct, rational, decisive, unyielding and confident, while Japanese have often conceived a creditable man to be indirect, sympathetic, prudent, flexible, and humble. (2009: 129) Therefore different cultures have different belief and value systems, and in a word they have different **cultural patterns**. However, we acknowledge that in every society there are many variations to the usual cultural patterns or perceived patterns. We also acknowledge that times are changing quickly, so that some of these assumptions have been supplanted by newer trends more similar to western cultures.

Ruth Benedict made a particular study on Japanese cultural patterns (without visiting Japan) in her 1934 book *The Chrysanthemum and the Sword*, and she found that Japanese culture is a typical **shame culture** in comparison with European and North American cultures which tend to be **sin cultures**. That is, in Japan, China, Korea, and other East Asian, or Confucian-oriented **cultures**, our failings, weaknesses, and misdeeds are seen as bringing shame to our family, neighbors, ancestors, and our motherland. In Asian cultures, such as the Chinese, Japanese, Korean, Vietnamese and Thai cultures, **shame** is often perceived as a negative situation, since **shame** is often associated with disgrace, loss of face and personal dignity. This **shame culture** can be traced back to Confucianism which stresses the **values** of loyalty, filial piety, benevolence, courtesy, righteousness, face, and harmony. In contrast, the European and North American cultures are often regarded as typical types of **guilt culture** which are under the great traditional influence of Christianity's view of original sin and redemption. The *Old Testament* of the *Bible* relates that in the fall and expulsion of Adam and Eve from the Garden, it placed an original sin on all humankind at birth, and The *New Testament* identifies that the freely chosen death of Jesus Christ as both divine and human provided humans with redemption and salvation. Dodd further summarizes the **guilt** and **shame** cultures as "characterized by their perceived sense of personal **guilt** (usually found in individualistic cultures) and **shame** usually found in collective cultures" (2006: 96).

People and cultures are naturally rather complex. As Evelin Lindner says, "humans are naturally cultural" (25), therefore, **cultural pattern research** offers us insights into the diversified cultures and different people. Many scholars who are interested in culture study endeavor to explore different **culture patterns** underlying the surface of reality. We should review the extensive **cultural pattern research** by the Chinese scholars as well as the western scholars.

5.3 Chinese Scholars' Emphasis on Cultural Traits and Cultural Orientations

The Chinese scholars' ways of thinking and research perspectives are intuitive and unsystematic, their studies mainly concentrate on cultural traits, yet their analyses are instructive and illuminating.

5.3.1 Gu Hongming's Study on Cutural Traits

Gu Hongming, in his study of **cultural traits**, speaks highly of Chinese civilization and people, describing the unique personalities of the Chinese people as having depth, broadness, simplicity and delicacy. He highlights that "In fact, in order to understand the real Chinaman, and the Chinese civilization, a man must be deep, broad and simple, for the three characteristics of the Chinese character and the Chinese civilization are: depth, broadness and simplicity." Gu thinks it is hard for people from other cultures and countries to fully understand the real Chinese people. He has made such a statement:

The American people, I may be permitted to say here, find it difficult to understand the real Chinaman and the Chinese civilization, because the American people, as a rule, are broad, simple, but not deep. The English cannot understand the real Chinaman and Chinese civilization, because the English, as a rule, are deep, simple, but not broad. The Germans again cannot understand the real Chinaman and the Chinese civilization because the Germans, especially the educated Germans, as a rule, are deep, broad, but not simple. The French,—well the French are the people, it seems to me, who can understand and have understood the real Chinaman and the Chinese civilization best.

In Gu's mind, the French do not have the depth of nature of the Germans, the broadness of mind of the Americans as well as the simplicity of mind of the English, but the French people have a quality of mind which is necessary to understand the real Chinese people and Chinese civilization; it is the quality of delicacy. Obviously, Gu puts delicacy as the most important quality of the Chinese character, and he speaks highly of the Chinese by calling for other nations to learn from the Chinese people and Chinese civilization:

It will be seen from what I have said above that the American people if they will study the Chinese civilization, will get depth; the English, broadness; and the Germans, simplicity; and all of them, Americans, English and Germans by the study of Chinese civilization, of Chinese books and literature, will get a quality of mind which, I take the liberty of saying here that it seems to me, they all of them, as a rule, have not to a preeminent degree, namely, delicacy. The French people finally, by the study of the Chinese civilization, will get all,—

depth, broadness, simplicity and a still finer delicacy than the delicacy which they now have. Thus the study of the Chinese civilization, of Chinese books and literature will, I believe, be of benefit to all the people of Europe and America. I have therefore added to this volume an essay on Chinese scholarship,—the Sketch of a program how to study Chinese, which I made for myself when I made up my mind and began, after my sketch of a program on how to study Chinese which I hope will be of help to those who want to study Chinese and the Chinese civilization.

We understand that his statement is culturally different and far more intuitive than might be likely by a North American or European scholar whose comment might be more direct and less intuitive. **We can ask**, which is better, the intuitive Asian approach or the Western logical approach? Probably the answer is that it depends upon which cultural background you come from.

5.3.2 Lin Yutang's Study on Cultural Characteristics

Lin Yutang in his book, The Importance of Living (2005), highlights four key words "Realism, Dreams, Humor and Sensitivity" to measure the different characteristics of different nations. His formulas are:

R3D2H2S1 = The English
R2D3H3S3 = The French
R3D3H2S2 = The Americans
R3D4H1S2 = The Germans

R2D4H1S1 = The Russians
R2D3H1S1 = The Japanese
R4D1H3S3 = The Chinese

As he explains in the book, "R" stand for a sense of reality (or realism), "D" for dreams (or idealism), "H" for a sense of humor, and "S" for sensitivity. While "4" stands for "abnormally high, " "3" stand for "high, " "2" for "fair," and "1" for "low." He spoke frankly that his ways of observing and analyzing the different nations' characters are "pseudoscientific:"

We have the following pseudo-chemical formulas for the following national characters. Human beings and communities behave then differently according to their different compositions, as sulphates and sulphides or carbon monoxide and carbon dioxide behave differently from one another. For me, the interesting thing always is to watch how human communities or nations behave differently under identical conditions. As we cannot invent words like "humoride" and "humerate" after the fashion of chemistry, we may put it thus: "3 grains of Realism, 2 grains of Dreams, 2 grains of Humor and 1 grain of Sensitivity make an Englishman."

Lin Yutang's "findings" are interesting and enlightening, as here he proposes that his Chinese character formula is "R4D1H3S3"; that is to say, the Chinese people score high in reality, humor and sensitivity approaches, but have low scores in the "dream" approach. It is quite true that the Chinese people are very realistic in national character on the one hand, but quite humorous and sensitive on the other hand. From the Chinese scholars' research approaches we see that these two Chinese scholars prefer to adopt a qualitative

Cultural Patterns and Cross-Cultural Value Orientations

A Deer Is Crossing the Road

and observational method of analyzing cultural patterns; this shows their unique ways of thinking.

5.3.3 Hui-ching Chang's Study on Interpersonal Communication

Hui-ching Chang (2007), noting that while relationships are central to the concept of **interpersonal communication (*jiaoji*)** study, especially in the US, "due to the Confucian emphasis on five ethics, Chinese relational systems are more hierarchically differentiated, extending from kin to non-kin relationships, as compared to Americans' more equal and less tangled relational positioning.... The Chinese perspective on 'communication' is more connected to their views about the universe.... Fundamentally, the existing-along American 'self' must be revealed through communication, whereas the Chinese 'self' lies in a network of inter-connectedness in which communication is primarily a lubricant" (2007: 104–105). Further, she asks: "Do we know enough about

Chinese culture to give in-depth analyses?.... To use 'harmony' as an example, it is less important to decide if 'harmony' is indeed a core cultural value and central organizing concept that helps define and interpret Chinese communication, but more central to address how it is played out in actual interactional encounters and in mediating Chinese relationships" (121–123).

5.3.4 Kwang-kuo Hwang's Study on Interpersonal Relationships

Kwang-Kuo Hwang (2007), an indigenous Taiwanese psychologist, refers also to Confucius in his statement of the Golden Mean to establish guiding cultural traits for the Chinese, and subdivides ethical arrangements for **interpersonal relationships** as **ethics for ordinary people** and for scholars. Using Confucius' and Mencius' views about benevolence (*ren*), propriety (*li*), and righteousness (*yi*): "It is righteous to decide who has the power of decision-making by the principle of respecting the superior; it is also righteous for the resource allocator to distribute resources by the principle of favoring the intimate.... *Yi* is generally used in connection with other Chinese characters like *ren-yi* (benevolent righteousness or benevolent justice) or *qing-yi* (affective righteousness or affective justice, (2007: 266–267). Hwang proposes that the five cardinal rules in Mencius' thinking must be followed to define standard **cultural traits** for the Chinese: "Between father and son, there should be affection; between sovereign and subordinate, righteousness; between husband and wife, attention to their separate functions; between elder brother and younger, a proper order; and between friends, friendship." Hwang interprets these cardinal rules of "face" and "favor" that those who are superior (emperor, father, elder brother, or husband) should deal with the principles of kindness, gentleness, righteousness, and benevolence. Those having the subsidiary role should follow the principles of filial duty and piety, obedience, submission, deference, loyalty and obedience (266–269). It is important to note, however, that while many of these principles remain valid in contemporary **Chinese collectivistic society**, still, as young Chinese become more and more westernized (partly through languages such as English), they are more and more likely to become increasingly **individualistic** and **independent** of these noble principles.

5.4 Western Contributions

In the Western academic circles, especially in the fields of anthropology, sociology, intercultural communication, and cultural psychology, Western scholars have made long-term studies of **cultural patterns**. Their studies are based on quantitative analysis, in combination with qualitative research. In general, the main and representative early findings were Milton Rokeach's study of beliefs and values (discussed in Chapter Four). Kluckhohn and Strodtbeck's value orientations, Hall's high and **low context communication modes**, Hofstede's **national value dimensions**, Trompenaars' **value dimensions** oriented toward business and international trade, and more recently Schwarts' **universal value orientations**.

5.4.1   Clyde Kluckhohn's and Fred Strodtbeck's Value Orientations

Clyde Kluckhohn and Fred Strodtbeck in their book, *Variations of Value Orientations* (1961) defined cultural value orientations as "complex but definitely patterned principles … which give order and direction to the ever-flowing stream of human acts and thoughts." They thought that different cultures had different patterns of thought and behavior when facing some fundamental issues. Based on their study on Latinos, Navajo Indians, and European Americans in the southwest, they put forth five orientations, respectively: **people nature orientation, human nature orientation, time orientation, activity orientation** and **relational orientation**. We have also included the **space orientation** which Kluckhohn and Strodbeck considered but did not study.

5.4.1.1 People Nature Orientation

The **people-nature orientation concentrates on the study of human beings' relationship to nature**. Kluckhohn and Strodtbeck classified the **human beings' relationship to nature** into three categories: **the human beings subject to nature, cooperation with nature** and **controlling nature**. In regard to the human beings' subordination to nature relationship, this orientation's first classification believes that nature is a kind of mysterious and awe-inspiring force, human beings are under the control of various powerful forces; they must obey or accept the force. This approach can be observed in ancient Chinese culture and even still today among many traditional Chinese. When faced with a harsh environment, people at that time felt that nature was a kind of force outside their control, particularly when they met with droughts, floods, starvation and illness, they were left so helpless that they often resorted to some mysterious forces in nature, whether the forces were a god, fate, or magic.

In terms of human beings' cooperation with nature, the value orientation regards that nature instead of being a hostile force, is a part of a person's life and people should live in cooperation and harmony with nature. Again this value orientation can be observed in Chinese traditional culture. As we have discussed in the first and this chapter, **harmony** is a very important conception in traditional Chinese culture, and its appeal is that "All things are nurtured together without injuring one another; All courses are pursued together without collision." (Fung, 2007: 286). Eventually, both in Taoism and Confucianism, the **harmony with nature philosophy** is

considered as one of the highest goals of Chinese culture.

The Chinese traditional culture has a cult of loving nature. The ancient Chinese culture was proud of its richness in poetry. And poetry has become a unique way of expressing the poets' feelings of oneness with nature. For instance, in his famous poem *Drinking Alone Under the Moon*, the famous poet Li Bai once wrote:

Amid the flowers, from a pot of wine
I drink alone beneath the bright moonshine,
I raise my cup to invite the moon who blends,
her light with my shadow and we're
  three friends.

Li Bai was once called "the poet of moon." Li Bai was a poet with great talent; however, he had no chance to carry out his ideals, so his life was not a satisfactory one. He felt so lonely and resorted to the moon for consolation. To him, the moon was his only friend that accompanied him. It was said that Li Bai eventually fell into a river when he attempted to seek a shadow of the moon in the river when he got drunk. Li Bai's fate is actually the fate of the ancient poets, who had talents but no opportunities to use them. Therefore, they chose to retire from the reality and dwell in deep seclusion in nature.

Jacqueline Wasilewsky, in writing to Evelin Lindner, explained the role of nature in the native American Comanche culture as "maternal ... inclusive like a mother's arms, like mother earth, loving each of her children uniquely ... there are hundreds of words for respect ... and a respectful society/world consists of the intersection between four other R's: relationship, responsibility, reciprocity, and redistribution." She notes that from relationship "comes our responsibilities to one another, that is, all relationships are reciprocal, and if the relationships are in order, the system enables a redistribution of all goods—physical, mental, emotional in an equitable way throughout the entire society/world. (Quoted in Lindner, 2010: 75)

The third approach is the controlling nature orientation, which stresses the conquering and directing the forces of nature to human beings' advantage. This value orientation is typically reflected in the Western culture, which has a long tradition of valuing human beings' power, technology, and science. The Western culture has also been greatly influenced by the Hebrew civilization as well as Christianity. In the Bible, God had arranged an authoritative and controlling role of human beings over other creatures in the world: According to God, "Let us make man in our image, after our likeness: and let them have domain over the fish of the sea, and over the fowl of the air and over the cattle, and over all the every creeping thing that creepeth upon the earth (Genesis, *Bible*)." Obviously, Judaism and Christianity have provided a major approach of human beings' control of nature with philosophical and theoretical bases.

The different religious approaches have exerted a far-reaching influence on the people's views and behaviors in different cultures. For instance, Ting-Toomey (1999: 61) in *Communication across Cultures* has cited a good example of Trompenaars's survey on the relationship between people and force in nature. Trompenaars (1993) asked managers in 38 countries to make a choice between the following two statements. One is "What happens to me is my wrong doing", another one

is "sometimes I feel that I do not have enough control over the directions my life is taking." The finding was that 89% of the surveyed US managers and of the 82 % of surveyed German mangers and only 56% of the Japanese mangers in the survey as well as 35% of the Chinese managers chose the first one. Obviously, we see that most European countries in Western culture appear to have a high score in the first choice while Chinese managers have a low score in that option. This suggests that the people in the Western world tend to believe they can control their own fate while the Chinese managers in the survey do not have enough confidence in controlling their life direction.

To sum up, in terms of the people and nature orientation, **Chinese traditional culture lays more emphasis on the first and second approaches, which accept that nature has either mysterious or charming power, or that peoples' attitudes towards nature are to respect and become one part of it. However, in the Western culture, many people tend to think that there is a clear separation between human beings and nature and that people have domination over nature.**

Jandt remarks on the American way of dealing with the relationship between man and nature by pointing out "American people typically make a clear and separate distinction between human life and nature, valuing nature but clearly placing a higher value on human life." (2004: 213) and he makes a further sarcastic analysis: "This belief that humans have 'dominion over nature' has made it possible for the United States to change the course of rivers, harvest forests for wood and paper, breed cattle for increased meat production, and destroy disease-causing bacteria. There can be little doubt that this belief has contributed to the material wealth of the United States" (2004: 213).

Maybe the traditional Chinese Daoist attitude ("For Daoists, the power of water is predominant against the hard and the strong/ nothing excels it") towards nature should be adopted. As long as we hold a respect and loving attitude toward nature, we can live more peacefully with nature; or either wise nature might take a revenge on our careless and hostile attitude towards it.

5.4.1.2 Human Nature Orientation

This orientation focuses on the different cultures' **perceptions of human nature**, and it generally classifies **human nature** into three types: **a basically evil approach**, **duality (good/evil) approach** and **intrinsically good approach**. Judaism, Christianity, and Islam share a common belief in the first approach, which regards people as basically evil, but redeemable. In the Arabian world, where Islam is strong, it believes that people have a tendency for evil if they disobey the laws of Allah. This dimension clearly relates to a belief in some supreme power or god.

To an extent, Judaism, and Christianity cannot be entirely separated. Christianity particularly adopted the teaching of the *Old Testament* in Judaism, and they both hold a firm belief in the concept of original sin of human beings. The beginning of the *Bible* tells us a famous story of Garden of Eden, when Eve and Adam, the legendary Jewish and Christian ancestors of human beings, ate the fruit of the tree of knowledge of good and evil that God

had forbidden; they committed a grave sin, which symbolized the original sin of the whole human beings. Since Christianity has had a great influence in the western world with more than 1.2 billion adherents, a large number of Christians in the western countries hold strong beliefs that people are born evil , despite the fact that Matthew Fox's book, *Original Blessing* (1996) disputes this "fall/redemption" concept with its reference to creation spirituality. In England and the United States, this orientation had once developed into a unique Calvinism/ Puritanism, which accentuated the people's initial sin to a larger extent. However, it also believed that self-discipline, hard work and education could help people achieve goodness.

Some cultures take a duality (good/evil) approach to **human nature**. For instance, many Christian European cultures think that people are born with a tendency for evil, but it is through learning and education that people gradually become "good." It should be noted, however, that Western European churches are emptying in alarming rates, and so young Europeans may also be discarding this value orientation. In traditional Chinese culture, Daoism regards that there are two forces of good and evil in this universe, which are in a constant process of struggling with each other, and the operation of the universe is a balanced and dynamic interaction between the two forces. In Chinese and other eastern Asian societies, and demonstrated in the national flag of Republic of Korea with the *taijitu* symbol, we can see the ***yin and yang,*** as we have mentioned before, as complementary opposites such as emptiness/fullness, dark/light, cold/hot, moist/ dry, man/woman, all transforming each other like an undertow in the ocean where every advancement is marked by a retreat and every rise transforms into a fall.

The approach of innate goodness of human nature can be found in the philosophies of Confucianism and Buddhism. Confucius was very optimistic about human nature. Buddhism also maintains that "you are born pure and are closest to what is called 'loving kindness' when you enter this world." From the analysis above, we can see that the Chinese and East Asian cultures again differ greatly from western cultures in terms of the **human nature value orientation**. Both Confucianism and Buddhism hold a quite positive attitude towards human nature, whereas, the Western cultures, under the influence of Christianity have taken a more negative attitude towards human nature, with many Christians accepting the concept of "orginal sin" which Jesus came to cleanse.

5.4.1.3 Time Orientation

The time orientation classifies different cultural focuses into past, present and future. Cultures differ widely in their temporal orientation of the past, present and future. The past orientation holds a firm belief in the significance of history, prior events, tradition, ancestors, and established norms and religions, and it regards that the past serves as a valuable guide for the present and future. Indigenous people in much of tribal Africa, China, Japan, Korea, Great Britain, France and native America have a strong sense of valuing the past. Present orientation cultures believe that the present moment has the most significant value as is exemplified in the Mexican saying: "Eat, drink and be merry for tomorrow you

Laughing Buddha

may die." This orientation can be observed in people from Mexican, the Philippine and Latin American cultures. However, African Americans tend to value both the past and the present. Future-oriented cultures such as those of many English—speaking Canadians, from the US and some other western countries underscore the importance of the future and lay greater emphasis on youth and devalue aging. Nevertheless, even in the western world, as Ting-Toomey has observed, sometimes the **time focus differs greatly**. She (2006: 63) analyzes that "the larger French culture has been classified as past–present oriented," while "in the larger US culture, its view of the future is that the individual can control it by personal achievement and inner-directed accountability." Many American politicians like to espouse their humble roots but take pride in their ability to solve problems.

As to the **time focus** of Chinese culture, the situation is more complex. **In terms of the traditional Chinese cultural time orientation, it is a mixture of past and present orientations,** and the focus can still be observed in the vast areas of rural places where more than 50% of the Chinese population still lives and in some developing or transplanted cities in China. However, with the quickening pace of Chinese modernization, in the big cities such as Beijing, Shanghai, Guangzhou, and Shenzhen, people have become more and more future-oriented as seen in the rapid rise of entrepreneurial enterprises. As Jandt has described (2004: 219) in the lifestyle of many Americans, "Most will admit to being motivated by the future in how to act in the present: going to school to get a degree and a satisfying job, working to be able to provide for oneself and one's family in the future, dieting so as to have a better figure and more friends in the future, training so as to be better at sports in the future, and living the future in the present." He thinks that the expense of living for the future in the present leads people to have "less time and appreciation for what is happening at the moment." This future-oriented focus has brought modern people more substantial satisfactions, but more spiritual pressures and sufferings. This fate is what the modern Chinese and Westerners both have to face. Hofstede and Bond developed a time orientation concept related to "Confucian dynamism," later distinguishing between long and short time orientations.

5.4.1.3.1 Cultural Time

The cultural setting is a key element in intercultural communication, as Wood (1994) notes: "The largest system affecting communication is your culture, which is the context within which all your interactions take place" (Wood, 1994: 29). There are numerous cultural variables worth studying in intercultural communication, and the time dimension as an example of nonverbal communication most broadly is one of the most important ones. For this reason, the American "time" research scholar Bruneau (1990) uses the concept of cultural time to describe the cultural differences in time orientation (1990: 309). The cultural time and space orientations in the context of intercultural communication are of vital importance to intercultural communication research since they act as mirrors of reflecting a culture's deep value structure, life philosophy as well as lifestyle. Particularly, **the traditional Chinese cultural time orientation has its unique values**, which has a striking feature contrast with the popular western cultural time orientation.

5.4.1.3.2 The Time Orientation in Chinese Culture

Confucianism played a major role in shaping the Chinese culture for thousands of years. As Chen and Watson noted (1960), "If we were to describe in one word the Chinese way of life for the last two thousands years, the word would be 'Confucian'" (Barry et al., 1960: 17). Confucius advocated good virtues and manners in which ren (humanity) and Li (ritual) were two main concepts; his entire life was engaged in the perfection of one's virtue as well as the prosperity of his state. Thus, he maintained a very positive attitude towards life, and considered time to be valuable and to be put to good use. According to the Confucius Speaks (Tsai: 2005), once Confucius stood by a river and made a deep sigh in front of the passing water: "All things that pass are just like this!

Night and day it never stops" (Tsai, 2005: 79). However, he kept a very calm mind before the endless flow of time and thought he had done quite well by making positive remarks towards the life he had spent: "At fifteen I set my heart on learning. At thirty, I could stand firm. At forty I had no doubts. At fifty I knew the Decree of Heaven. At sixty, I was already obedient (to this decree). At seventy I could follow the desires of my mind without overstepping the boundaries (of what is right)" (Pan et al, 2004: 11).

Another aspect of the time orientation in Confucianism is the past-time focus, which should not be simply understood as conservativeness. Confucius lived in the spring and autumn period, a time when wars broke out frequently and there was a decline in social morality. Hence, he was very dissatisfied with the situation and intended to reform society by looking back to the past for a good model. Although Confucius seemingly pointed out some shortcomings of the ancient men in the following statements, what his real intention was that he wanted to express his appreciation of the ancient men and pass criticisms upon the moral degeneration of the men in his time: "In old days, men had three failings, which have perhaps, died out today. The impetuous of old days were impatient of small restraints; the impetuous today are utterly insubordinate. The stern dignity of old days were stiff and gravely reserved" (Pan et al, 2004: 215).

Confucius and other philosophers of his days had different approaches to the solutions of problems. The dominant view of that time espoused by legalists was for strict law and severe punishment, while Confucius resorted to Zhou rituals by delivering the following famous saying: "The rituals of the Zhou dynasty are inherited and developed from the two preceding dynasties Xia and Shang. How complete and elegant its rituals are! I follow upon Zhou" (Pan, et al, 2004: 215). Confucius interpreted the rituals of the Zhou dynasty as a cultural legacy inherited from the former dynasties Xia and Shang, which developed through generations of human wisdom; thus he addressed himself as a "transmitter" but not "an originator" because of his "believing in and loving in the ancients" (Pan, et al, 2004: 65). Although Confucius had established a unique system of social and ethical philosophy whose thoughts have exerted a profound influence on the Chinese culture for thousands of years, nevertheless, he frankly attributed his thoughts to the Zhou rituals. Therefore we see that the past-time orientation in Confucianism contains many more positive connotations than negative ones. It is due to Confucius' preference to the "Zhou rituals" that he developed his own concept of Li, a term not only referring to outside rites and ceremonies but also denoting graceful and civilized manners in one's personality. Now Li has remained one of the main Confucius' important teachings.

Confucianism holds a flexible attitude towards time. It accentuates "the right occasion" and "the right opportunity" in dealing with affairs. Whatever things they might be, whether they are issues concerning big events of the state or trivial household matters, they should all be performed on the right occasion. Confucius' follower Mencius further promoted Confucian thoughts. The text, *Mencius Speaks*, relates the fable, "Helping rice grow," which is a good example; it illustrates the importance of handling affairs on the right occasion: "There was once a man in Song Kingdom who was terribly worried that his rice had grown slowly; he was so impatient that he went to the field to help his rice out by pulling them up a bit; the result was conceivable when all the rice died." The flexible handling of time in Confucianism has exerted a profound influence on the Chinese culture; even at the present time the Chinese people seek the right occasion for dealing with affairs in business, politics and daily life. In short, the time orientation in Confucianism is multidimensional, its past-time focus enables its ethical core to be established upon the rich legacy passed down from the former dynasties, and its positive and agile attitude towards time is also enlightened.

Lin Yutang (2004) thought that Confucianism was not "sufficient for the Chinese people" since it was "too decorous, too reasonable, too correct" (113); hence Taoism arose in Chinese culture. Lin also made a comparison between Confucianism and Taoism: "Confucianism, through its doctrine of propriety and social status, stands for human culture and restraint, while Taoism, with its emphasis on going back to nature, disbelieves in human restraints and culture" (Lin, 2004: 114). Taoism in essence is a philosophy of perusing the limitless freedom by breaking through various boundaries and restrictions. Being one of the most famous sages of Taoism, Zhuang Zi, (Tsai, 2005) pursued freedom his entire life and resented worldly fame. Because of his great talent, he was once asked whether he was willing to be the prime minister of the Chu Kingdom, and he did not reply directly; instead he told the two messengers sent by the king of Chu Kingdom a story. It was said that there was kept in Chu Kingdom's temple

the bone of a wonder tortoise which had been dead for three thousand years, and then Zhuang Zi asked them a question: "If they were the tortoises, would they be willing to be killed and have their bones kept in the temple, showing off their nobility or to swim freely in the mud with their wobbling tails?" The messengers' reply was the latter. Zhuang Zi said he would also prefer swimming freely in the mud with his tail wobbling like the tortoise to enjoy a happy life without restriction. He further wrote another famous prose, *The Dream of the Butterfly*, imagining that he had turned into a carefree butterfly and wondering "Maybe Zhuang Zi was the butterfly, and maybe the butterfly was Zhuangzi" (Tsai, 2005: 27). In fact, the butterfly had become Zhuang Zi's unique perception of freedom.

In Taoism, the Tao is one of the most important concepts reconstructed by Zhuang Zi after he adopted the main idea put forth by Lao Zi, who was actually the founder of Taoism. Lao Zi regarded Tao as the origin of the universe while Zhuang Zi treated Tao as the highest principle of the world, in which there was no clear division between life and death, beauty and ugliness, and past and present. Thus, based upon the concept of Tao, Zhuang Zi had established his unique philosophy of relativity towards life. As far as the time dimension is concerned, because of Zhang Zi's pursuit of freedom and his unique philosophy of relativity towards life, Taoism advocates the relativity and limitlessness of time. Tsai Chih Chung (2005) wisely interpreted: "It is a philosophy which takes life and hurls it into the limitless time and space in order to be experienced to the fullest" (Tsai, 2005: 5). In his famous prose *Carefree Travel of Zhuang Zi*, Zhuang Zi tried to illustrate his relative view concerning time by citing a series of metaphors. Here is one excellent example of his prose:

People say that once there was a man named Peng Zu, who at 800 years old had lived the longest life ever. In contrast, there is a small bug called Zhaojun that was born in the morning and dead by nightfall. There is also an insect called the winter cicada, which is born in the spring and dies in the summer. However, in the southern part of Chu, there lived the giant wonder tortoise, to whom five hundred years was a mere Spring. And a long, long time ago, there lived the Geri-tree, to which eight thousand years was a mere Autumn. The Zhaojun and the winter cicada are called 'short lives', while the wonder tortoise and the Geri-tree are called 'long lives'. To the wonder tortoise and the Geri-tree, wasn't Peng Zu just another 'short life'? People see Peng Zu as having lived a long life, but wasn't he really just another tragic 'short life'"? (Tsai, 2005: 6–7).

Considering our comments below, **according to Aristotle and Isaac Newton's view, time was an absolute physical concept**; eight thousand years and five hundred years were real physical time; and their lengths were definitely longer than one spring, autumn or a day. Nevertheless, in Zhuang Zi's eye, there was no clear division among them when compared with the endlessness of time and space. Hence, what Zhuang Zi pursued in his entire life was the limitless freedom beyond various restraints; either they are the limitations of the definite time and space, or the bondages of a mundane world. Time to Zhuang Zi was no longer the dominant force in the control of human beings' lives, but rather the issue being freely handled at the hands of human beings, which could enable human beings to enjoy more freedom of an easy-going time.

Furthermore, **the time orientation in Taoism which places more emphasis on the subjectivity and relativity of time has helped cultivate the unique Chinese temperament as well as the carefree life style of the traditional Chinese culture**. In his book *The Importance of Living*, Lin Yu Tang (2005: 145) spoke highly of "this divine desire for loafing in China" and he praised "that carefree, idle, happy-go-lucky—and often poetic—temperament" (2005: 149) in the Chinese scholars as well as the Chinese ordinary people. He thought that the temperament could be traced back to "the Taoistic Blood" (Lin, 2005: 150). Indeed, Taoism's carefree philosophy towards life has made a great impact on the Chinese carefree manner of spending time, which has been well reflected in a large number of the Chinese ancient poems.

In the famous, *An Anthology of Popular Ancient Chinese Poems*, (Guo, 2004) there are poems here and there depicting pictures of an easy-going and idyllic life of the Chinese scholars and ordinary people. For instance, the first poem entitled, "An Impromptu Poem Composed in Spring", is one good example:

Pale clouds and gentle breeze near midday,
I pass the stream by the willows and flowers.
You folks don't know my heart young and gay,
And say I follow a lad to enjoy his free hours. (Guo, 2004: 2)

When the poet/philosopher Cheng Hao wrote his poem, he was no longer young; however, a spring outing had made the poet forget his real physical age and his heart became "young and gay."Another famous Chinese poet Su Shi in his poem, "Spring Night" even expressed the feeling that "A moment of joy on a spring night is better than gold." (7). Thus, Lin Yutang (2005: 148) showed his great appreciation of the Chinese scholars and poets' easy-going manner of spending time and stated that "The wisest man is therefore he who loafs most gracefully." The cult of idle life can also be observed in the ordinary Chinese people's lives at the present time although more and more Chinese people, especially people in the big cities, are beginning to have a quicker life pace. Nevertheless, many ordinary Chinese people of an older age still prefer to spend some time in chatting with their friends, relatives or neighbors to enjoy the carefree life, perhaps as a later reflection of Taoism.

5.4.1.3.3 The Time Perception in the Western Culture

In a sense, time is a kind of philosophical issue, which has something to do with the essence of human beings' existence. The famous Greek philosopher Heraclitus once compared time to a boy who was playing games. However, he regarded the boy not as an ordinary boy, but the authoritative king in the game. Thus, according to Heraclitus' interpretation, human beings were subordinated to time and time was the real king of the world that had a dominant role in controlling human beings' lives. The concept of the overwhelming power of time is pervasive in the Western culture, which has deep roots in Western civilization. Ever since the ancient Greek time, time had often been perceived from the physical aspect. **Plato classified the world into two categories: the phenomenon and noumenon**, and he perceived the phenomenal world to be unreal, which was only the shadow of the absolute logos world, since it symbolized the mutable realm of reality, while he believed the noumenal world to be real, since it stood for the immutable realm of eternal form (in Greek, "idea"). Although Plato debased the value of the phenomenal world, yet he considered the phenomenal world to be controlled by the mutable movement of time. Aristotle in his famous book *Physics* further defined time as a measurable object in motion, but unlike Plato, he began to accept the authenticity of the phenomenal world and further probed into the physical, objective features of time.

The scientists and philosophers after the Renaissance followed Aristotle's suit, and they thought of time as a kind of object in linear motion as well. The famous scientists such as Galileo and Newton regarded time as a certain quantity, which was used to calculate the speed of the object in motion, and most philosophers at that period such as René Descartes and John Locke also interpreted time from the physical aspect. Among them, Newton's perception of time is the most influential and far-reaching. In his famous book *Natural Science*, he emphasized the concept of absolute time. As a result, the physical interpretation of absolute time as the object in motion had been the main time orientation in the Western civilization.

The physical interpretation of time established by Aristotle and Newton underscored regularity, absoluteness, and progress of time, and these features of time were reinforced in the process of western industrialization. As Mumford (1962) stated: "The first characteristic of modern machine civilization is its temporal regularity ... From the moment of waking, the rhythm of day is punctuated by the clock. With regard to time, he claimed that Irrespective of strain or fatigue, despite reluctance or apathy, the household rises close to its set hour" (Mumford, 1962: 269). What's more, we see in the Western culture that time is often believed to be something definite, absolute and valuable, which is even used to measure profit and achievement, and there are many famous sayings which express the importance of time: "The early bird catches the worm (the United States), "Never put off to tomorrow what you can do today" (England), "lose an hour in the morning, chasing it all day long" (Jewish culture). Time has become an absolute, determinant force in the Western culture. As Edward T. Hall (1959) noted: "People of the Western world, particularly Americans, tend to think of time as something fixed in nature, something around us and from which we cannot escape; an ever-present part of the environment, just like the air we breathe" (Hall, 1959: 19).

The physical interpretation of absolute time in linear motion, together with industrialization and civilizational progress helps cultivate the future-time orientation in most countries of the Western world. Taking the American people as an example, who particularly value the future and believe they can control the future, Hall used "M-time" (monochromic time) to describe the characteristics of Western cultural time orientations mentioned above. Of course, the

M-time orientation has its own advantages, and according to Hall (1990), M-time people concentrate on the job, take time commitment (deadline, schedules) seriously, adhere to plans, are concerned about not disturbing others, and follow rules of privacy (1990: 15). In general, M-time culture places more emphasis on efficiency and promptness.

However, it has its disadvantages and limitations, and is even sharply criticized by some scholars. As Kim has observed (2001): "Life is in constant motion, people consider time to be wasted or lost unless they are doing something" (115). M-time people under the great pressure of time are often controlled by the "invisible hand of time" and their individuality and freedom have been severely damaged. As Wright had pointed out (1968): "This is the history of increasing, unchecked, and now intolerable chronarchy. That word is not to be found in The *Oxford English Dictionary*. Its coiner should be entitled to define it. Let chronarchy, then, be not merely 'rule by time', but 'regimentation of man by timekeeping" (1968: 7). Lin Yu Tang (2005) used another term "working animal" to describe the wretched situation in which people in a more civilized world have been confronted. He thought of civilization as a matter of seeking food: "But the essential fact remains that human life has got too complicated and the matter of merely feeding ourselves, directly or indirectly, is occupying well over ninety percent of our human activities" (2005: 144). In contrast, the Chinese traditional cultural time orientation reflects quite a different attitude towards life and it can help resolve some problems which the Western culture is confronted with. Unlike the Western time orientation that accentuates

Cultural Patterns and Cross-Cultural Value Orientations

An American Rural House

the objectiveness, absoluteness and fixation of time, the Chinese traditional cultural time orientation conceives time to be subjective, relative and flexible.

In contrast, the Chinese traditional cultural time orientation reflects quite a different attitude towards life and it can help resolve some problems the Western culture is confronted with.

5.4.1.4 Space Orientation

Clyde Kluckhohn and Fred Strodbeck, in their study of five southwestern US communities on which they did their research in the 1950s, noted but did not precisely consider the **space orientation**. Condon and Yousef in their 1975 book, *An Introduction to Intercultural Communication*, gave consideration to this dimension, as Hall had earlier, explored, for example, the nature of space in housing in several different cultures. Globally, as we have suggested earlier, goods, people, currency and ideas, particularly those factors representing "pop culture" move rapidly in space across cultural boundaries. American suburban homes are very spacious, and are set

on areas that have much more land surrounding them than even many European homes. Cities typically have to move upward spacially, as is seen in major world cities and many Chinese megacities and smaller cities, which in fact are quite large by the sizes of most American cities. The early term "skyscraper" suggested initially buildings of fifty stories or more. In contrast, in many countries, several families may be forced to live together, or with a very limited amount of space. Earthquakes, floods, hurricanes, tsunamis and conflict situations often force many local people to find shelter in small tents, as occurred in Sichuan earthquake of 2009 and the Haiti earthquake of 2010. A great danger in very tall buildings, of course, can be seen in the inability to save many stranded people on higher floors in the 2001 September 11 destruction of the World Trade Center Towers leading to the loss of life of more than 3,000 persons. Hall considers proxemics or space to be an important aspect of hidden culture, and very important in the study of nonverbal and cultural communication. How we consider the aspect of space, both as a cultural orientation, and as a nonverbal factor determines the sort of lives that we live. While Chinese students generally expect to live often for four years with the same three or four roommates in a relatively small space, the American expansiveness of time tends to lead toward many university students having only one roommate, or none.

5.4.1.5 Activity Orientation

An **activity orientation** involves the approaches by which different cultures view **activity**. Generally speaking, they can be divided into three views: *Doing orientation*, *Being orientation*, and *Being-in-Becoming orientation*.

5.4.1.5.1 Doing Orientation

This orientation is a kind of achievement-oriented approach which lays great emphasis on activity and action. It can be found in the dominant American culture, middle-class African Americans, Asian Americans and the European Americans. Much of the western "doing" orientation can be traced back to early Christianity. In the *New Testament*, Jesus was a doing person, who traveled from different places helping the poor and sick and whose authority was established in his action. Peter, one of Jesus' disciples, once remarked on Jesus by saying, "He went about doing good." In short, the doing activity is closely related to Christianity, but even before it was based on Greek and Roman characteristics. However, the doing-activity cultures mentioned above may vary in different directions. For example, according to Ting-Toomey's observation, European Americans, the African Americans and Asian Americans have different focuses: "For European Americans, a 'doing' mode means focusing on tangible accomplishments for personal gains such as a converted job promotion or a bigger salary to take care of self and immediate family" (Ting-Toomey: 65), but "For the African American groups, a 'doing' mode means to fight against adversity and to combat racism through social achievements and activism for the good of the community," (64) while "For Asian immigrants in the United States, the 'doing' model is typically associated

with working hard and making money in order to fulfill basic obligations toward family and extended family networks" (Ting-Toomey: 65). In fact, it is well known that many Asian immigrants have their whole families working with discipline to help some members of the family move ahead in good jobs or education, especially in North America.

5.4.1.5.2 Being Orientation

The Being orientation holds the view that the current activity is the most important. Many cultures such as the African and Latin American cultures share this view. African Americans enjoy "having a sense of aliveness, emotional vitality and openness of feelings ... African American culture is infused with a spirit (a knowledge that there is more to life than sorrow, which passes) and a renewal in sensuousness, joy and laughter. This symbol has its roots in African culture and expresses the soul and rhythm of that culture in America" (Collier & Ribeau: 1993, 102–103). In the Latin American/Hispanic culture including the Mexican culture, people enjoy the happy moment spending with their family members and friends, and Mexican people would spend several hours chatting with their friends to enjoy the moment to the fullest.

Michelle Epiphany Prosser, in her book *Excuse Me, Your God Is Waiting* (2008) writes that **being is from the soul and its very essence which "celebrates connection."** When we are "being," we understand on the soul level, *that everything is connected. The Taoist book of wisdom, the Tao Te Ching, praises this quality and compares it to the fluidness of water. It* *urges us to "do" without "doing." "Taoists believe the path of action through inaction, wu-wei, is superior."*

She also stresses that: "The Asian notion of *wu-wei* has been greatly misunderstood because of translation and Western resistance to the word 'inaction.' Instead of being passive, *wu-wei* means intuitive cooperation with the natural order and the belief that everything is perfect and harmonious. When we can come from the perspective that everything is perfect and harmonious, our suffering over how we think people and things 'should' be ends. We stop wading upstream in our river. Instead, we turn and go with the flow. We do not consume our energy with trying to figure out why something happened. Instead, when we regard everything as perfect, our question becomes 'What do I need to learn from this?'" (Prosser, M.E., 2008: 176).

5.4.1.5.3 Being-in-Becoming Orientation

The Being-in-Becoming orientation underscores spiritual development and growth, stressing spiritual introspection and renewal. In a word, it values spiritual life more than material achievements. Some religions such as Hinduism, Buddhism, and Islam, as well as some in Christianity are involved in spiritual meditation, growth and renewal. Among them, Hinduism is a typical example. Hinduism believes "What we see as reality is the merest illusion, a game, a dream or a dance." Therefore it advocates that one should seek the spiritual existence beyond reality by the means of Nirvana, which is a state of spiritual enlightenment and happiness. There are also some other cultures holding **the Being-**

in-Becoming orientation. For instance, both the Latino and Native American people also devote themselves to religious and spiritual pursuits.

As far as Chinese culture is concerned, the **three activity orientations** can all be observed. In traditional Chinese culture, such as Confucianism, it tends to be **Being-in-Becoming orientation**, which stresses the importance "ocontemplatio" (I contemplate or meditate) and self-cultivation in spirit. While ordinary Chinese people concentrate more on the *"Being" approach*, they would enjoy their moments of spending time with their families, neighbors and friends. Since the retirement age is early by Western standards, this may be quite true. In the case study in Chapter Three, we see elements of the mothers and grandmothers following such a path, as the daughters are more likely to be active and "doing." However, as time is passing on, Chinese culture in the present era has turned into more and more of a kind of **doing activity orientation**, and the mainstream of the Chinese culture focuses more on material pursuits and personal achievement than in the past.

5.4.1.6 Relational Orientation

The fifth orientation developed by Kluckhohn and Strodtbeck is the relational one. This orientation describes the human's relation to other persons. It has three subdivisions: the individualistic, the collateral, and the linear orientation. When individualistic principles are dominant, each individual's responsibility and place in the total society are defined in terms of goals and roles which are structured as autonomous. A dominant collateral orientation calls for a primacy of the goals and welfare of the laterally extended group. Finally, since all societies and cultures are related culturally and biologically through time, there is always a linear relation according to Kluckhohn and Strodtbeck.

5.4.2 Geert Hofstede's National Value Dimensions

Geert Hofstede, a Dutch management researcher, social psychologist and well-known scholar of communication study, researched IBM (identified initially in his study as Hermes) business employees' work-related values in 72 countries. In 1980, he first published his research results based on his study of 116, 000 employees in IBM from 70 countries, but eventually centering on 40 countries. He argued in, *Culture's Consequences*, and more broadly in his 2001 version that in national cultures or societies, people develop certain mental dispositions which are learned and shared among the group, and thus they share a specific **national character orientation**. He has earlier identified five **value dimensions** across all multinational cultures, and his dimensions have exerted a far-reaching influence in the field of **western cultural** pattern study. These dimensions are identified as **individualism versus collectivism**, **high** versus **low power distance**, **high** versus **low uncertainty avoidance**, **masculinity** versus **femininity and Confucian dynamism** or **long term orientation** versus **short term orientation** which he and Michael Harris Bond jointly later developed in 1984. Very recently in 2008, Hofstede has added two new dimensions for studying national culture

values: **monumentalism** versus **flexhumility or self-effacement** and **indulgence** versus **self-restraint**. Steve J. Kulich (2009: 989–994) gives a brief summary of the first four empirically tested dimensions:

(1) **Power distance** *(the extent to which less powerful members expect and accept that power is distributed unequally)*,
(2) **individualism-collectivism** *(from loose self directed ties to integrated, cohesive loyal in-group ties)*.
(3) **Uncertainty avoidance** *(the extent to which members feel threatened by ambiguous or unknown situations)*, and
(4) **masculinity-femininity** *(from distinct gender roles, assertive-tough-successful men and modest-tender-caring women to the overlap of emotional gender roles and both genders are more concerned with the quality of life)*.

Later, Kulich notes that Hofstede's cooperation with Bond studied values of students in 23 countries, with a **Chinese Values Survey**. This led to a new dimension first called the **Confucian dynamism** and later renamed:

(5) **Long-term/short-term orientation** *(from societies in which members primarily seek future rewards through adaptation-thrift-perseverance to those who focus on the present by maintaining face-fulfilling social obligations and the traditions of the past.*

Kulich indicates that Michael Minkov produced three dimensions: "**exclusionism** versus **universalism**," which closely corresponds to **individualism** versus **collectivism**, and that Minkov then identified two more dimensions, which Hofstede has subsequently explored for his list of dimensions.

(6) **indulgence** *versus* **restraint** *(for the first time confirming what [Talcott] Parsons foresaw as a range in affectivity and discipline) and*

(7) **monumentalism** *versus* **self-effacement** *(Minkov called it flexhumility, a combination of self-flexibility and humility).*

However, Geert Hofstede has finally decided not to follow the dimension related to monumentalism and flexhumility. He now has only six cultural dimensions.

5.4.2.1 Individualism and Collectivism

This dimension attempts to describe how people in each culture identify themselves and others. **Individualism** places the greater emphasis on the individual, and "I" consciousness prevails in that culture. Competition rather than cooperation is encouraged, personal goals and interests take precedence over group goals and interests. Hofstede (1991) defined **individualism** as "societies in which ties between individuals are loose; everyone is expected to look after himself or herself and his or her immediate family." Therefore, in an **individualistic culture**, an individual or "I" identity is regarded as the most important unit in society, and the value of each individual is placed in the first position, often in a very egalitarian manner. While in a **collectivistic** or **communitarian culture**, "we" consciousness prevails over individuals, group goals and interests take precedence over personal goals and interests. Consequently,

Hofstede (1991) explained **collectivism** as "societies in which people from birth onwards are integrated into strong, cohesive in-groups, which throughout people's lifetimes continue to protect them in exchange for unquestioning loyalty." Samovar and Porter (2004) analyzed the feature of **collectivism** in a similar view, "Collectivism is characterized by a rigid social framework that distinguishes between in-group (relatives, clans, organizations) to look after them, and in exchange for that they believe they owe absolute loyalty to the group." Thus, in **collective cultures**, the concept of "group" and "we" is of great importance; each person's identity is established on the social system; and the individual has a close tie with the organizations and institutions in which he or she belongs.

According to Hofstede, **individualism** and **collectivism** are central to all the cultural values. According to his research, the United States, Australia, Great Britain, Canada, the Netherlands and New Zealand are among those most **individualism-oriented** countries, while Pakistan, Indonesia, Colombia, Venezuela, Panama, Ecuador, and Guatemala are highly **collectivistically-oriented**. That is to say, **individualism** can be found in most northern and western areas of Europe and North America, while **collectivism** can be observed in Central and South America, the Middle East, Asia, Africa and the Pacific islands. However, even in the same **individualism** or **collectivism** categories, there are some differences. Listed below are the scores of nine countries/areas' samples for **individualism** and **collectivism**.

In the table, among the **individualism** category, the US has a very strong individualism tendency among all countries examined.

Nevertheless, in the European region, England occupies the position of a country which has a very strong individualism tendency, the other two countries such as France and Germany have less strong individualism tendencies. We are aware, however, that English belongs to the Germanic language families, and there may be a correlation linguistically, and that France has a romance language family basis which may suggest that such countries might have a lower relationship than those in the Germanic language family. In the **collectivism** category, Guatemala in Central America has a very strong collectivism tendency, and Asian areas such as Japan, Hong Kong (China) and Korea have less strong collectivism tendencies.

It seems that western cultures and eastern cultures have gone to the opposing directions of **individualism** and **collectivism**. The two different approaches can be traced back to their different civilizational origins. As is well known, the Western cultures hae been greatly influenced by the Graeco-Roman/Judao-Christian civilizations' roots. The sometimes harsh geographical and mountainous environment in Greece has helped its inhabitants to develop a value based on individualism, stressing the individual's great capacity in fighting with the harshness of the surroundings, and paying little attention to authority and formality. The value of the individual in the early Greek culture was rediscovered in the Renaissance period after

Nation / Area	Value	Range	Conclusion
United States	91	1	Very strong individualism tendency
England	89	3	Very strong individualism tendency
France	71	10 / 11	Less strong individualism tendency
German	67	15	Less strong individualism tendency
Japan	46	22 / 23	Less strong collectivism tendency
Hong Kong (China)	25	37	Less strong collectivism tendency
Repubic of Korea	18	43	Less strong collectivism tendency
Taiwan (China)	17	44	Less strong collectivism tendency
Guatemala	6	53	Very strong collectivism tendency

it had moved through the Middle Ages. In the Enlightenment period, the notion of personal freedom and independence was underlined; in short, the **individualism** which stresses independence, freedom and equality had its rich resources in western culture.

On the other hand, the **collectivism dimension** of the Eastern cultures owes its origin to the traditional Chinese culture and Confucianism. Confucianism, for thousands of years, has had a major role in shaping the culture and history of the people in East Asia, such as Korea, Vietnam, Japan, and especially China. As Meyer remarks, "With individual rights severely subordinated, group action has been a distinctive characteristic of Chinese society." Confucius, as the founder of Confucianism once stated: "If one wants to establish himself, he should help others to establish themselves." With the passage of time, Chinese culture has been moving toward modernization, especially since the opening up in 1978 and following, and some of the old teachings of Confucianism have been considered less important. However, a strong sense of **collectivism** still prevails in today's Chinese culture. Most Chinese people believe that they should make contributions to their families, their groups they belong to (in-groups), as well as the whole nation.

This **collectivism orientation** is reflected in various aspects of Chinese culture. Chinese proverbs serve as a good example, which lay great emphasis on the cooperation and unity among persons. Here are some typical ones: "A fence has three pile, a real man has three gang.", "Unity is strength.", "A single flower does not make a spring)." If we compare them with the western proverbs such as "God helps those who

help themselves", "You made your bed, now lie in it", "You'd better look out for yourself; no one else will," or "the squeaky wheel gets the grease," we can figure out metaphorically a striking distinction of the opposite **collectivism** and **individualism dimensions**.

The opposing **collectivism** and **individualism** approaches can also be reflected in family education of the Chinese culture and Western culture. Family education plays a very important role in shaping a person's values and behaviors. As Bridenthal, Kelly, and Vine (1989) stated: "Here is where one has the first experience of love, and of hate, of giving, and of denying, and of deep sadness ... Here the first hopes are raised and met—or disappointed. Here is where one learns whom to trust and whom to fear. Above all, family is where people get their start in life."

Children in the western cultures are taught and encouraged to "decide for themselves," "do their own things," "develop their own opinion," and "solve their own problems." The **value of individualism** can be traced back to the structure of nuclear family made up of parents and children, and the nuclear family tends to emphasize independence and individual autonomy. Therefore, in individualistic cultures in the west, children are taught at early ages to do things by themselves, act independently and be responsible for their actions as well as make their own decisions. While in Chinese culture that has traditionally stressed the collective view, the value of responsibility, loyalty to the family and group are considered important as we discussed in the last chapter. Samovar and Porter (2004) point out, "The value is learned from an extended family in these cultures. (big family, among its members are parents, children, grandparent, uncles, and aunts in laws, cousins of varying degrees, a large network of family), in such a family, the children and parents have strong ties and obligations to relatives." In a collective culture like China, the parents are more likely to make the decisions for the child, and the children are not supposed to make their own decisions when they are young. We are aware of the concept of the "little emperor" or "little empress" in many one-child families where parents and grandparents go to great lengths to cater to the needs of the child so that he or she can devote more time to study, without being responsible for activities for which children in the west would be responsible. For some Chinese university students, before they enter university, they have no idea about what majors they should choose and they have to follow the advice of either their parents, caring little about their own interests.

However, the situation has changed gradually, especially in the urban cities, young people now are given more and more freedoms to make their own choices and decisions. Certainly, as we have mentioned earlier, more and more young Chinese are increasingly independent and individualistic especially in their university study. **We can ask**: as Chinese university students which approach best describes you—**being indivualistic and independent** or **collectivistic and dependent**? **We also can ask**: which approach do you prefer in your own mature development? If you have chosen the first approach, we need to remember, however, that there are good points in a **collective culture**. It can reinforce a nation's coherence and strengthen the power of unity and emphasize the mutual love and caring among people, particularly when faced with a great disaster, the collective power is enormous. For instance, on May 12, 2008, when the severe earthquake in Wen Chuan, Sichuan Province, took place, in order to rescue more victims, the Chinese government made good use of the whole nation's resources; a large number of army helicopters, soldiers, and excavation machines were sent to the Wen Chuan and related areas. Thousands of volunteers, medical staffs from every province and cities of China were dispatched there. In addition, tent mills from different parts of China worked day and night to produce sufficient tents for the people in the earthquake area. As a result, an overwhelming rescue and relief work swept the whole of China. People from all over China, as well as other governments and nationals, offered their selfless help in various ways. Not only did different organizations and companies, but also the ordinary people, including school children, donated their money, clothes and quilts, books, and toys to the victims of the earthquake. Many Chinese people were involved in the earthquake event in their own ways. The collective power helped China undergo a great disaster. People felt that they were the family members in a huge family of the Chinese civilization and nation.

5.4.2.2 High Versus Low Power Distance

For Hofstede and Bond (1984), **power distance** is "The extent to which the less powerful members of institutions ... accept that power is distributed unequally." There are two types of **power distance, high power distance, low power distance**. Samovar and Porter (2004) defined **high power distance** as "Both

Cultural Patterns and Cross-Cultural Value Orientations

consciously and unconsciously, these cultures teach their members that people are not equal in this world and everybody has a rightful place, which is clearly marked by countless vertical arrangement. Social hierarchy is prevalent and institutionalizes inequality. "While a **low power distance** culture holds "that inequality in society should be minimized. Subordinates consider superiors to be the same kind of people as they are, and superiors think in the same way." **High power distance** cultures can be observed in Malaysia, Guatemala, Panama, the Philippines, Mexico, Venezuela, Arabian countries, Ecuador, Africa, Singapore, and Brazil whereas low power distance cultures can be found in the United States, Great Britain, Switzerland, Finland, Norway, Sweden, Ireland, New Zealand, Denmark, Israel and Austria. Hofstede has further analyzed the following factors that have exerted influences in **power distance**: geographic latitude, population and wealth. Higher latitudes are associated with **low power distance**, countries with a large population are associated with **higher power distance**, while national wealth is associated with **lower power distance**. We note of course, that since Hofstede conducted his studies, many changes may have occurred in these and other countries which he describes as having **high** or **low power distance**.

Confucian cultural inheritance countries score high, countries with a Romance language (Spanish, Portuguese, Italian, and French) score medium and Germanic language countries (English, German, Dutch, Flemish, Afrakaans) score low on Hofstede's **power distance index (PDI)**. The former two groups of cultures were ruled in ancient times from a **single power distance**, whereas the Germanic language countries now (German, English, Dutch, Danish, Norwegian, and Swedish) remained "barbaric" during the Roman days (Jandt: 1997). As far as the historical factor is concerned, Confucianism has exerted a profound influence on the East and South East Asian cultures, particularly on the Chinese culture and civilization in terms of high power distance and **hierarchy**. As Samovar and Porter stated (2004), "Since ancient times, Chinese philosophies have respected an ethical hierarchy in human relationship, and we must not forget that a salient characteristic of China thought is its ethical nature." Confucianism puts forth "an ethical hierarchy in human relationship" known as *wu lun*, they are respectively as follows:

(jun Chen): the emperor over the subject
(fu zi): the father over the son
(fu fu): the husband over the wife
(xiong di): the elder brother over the younger one
(peng you): friend and friend

In Confucianism, **the family relation** is the basis and model for other social orders, which is a typical mode of **hierarchy relation** and as a result, it has produced a **high power distance culture**. As to the relationship of father and son, the son has to obey the father; with regards to the relationship of husband and wife, the wife should obey her husband. In terms of the relationship of *Xiong di* (brothers), the younger brother should obey the elder bother. The whole ancient Chinese nation is an extended, larger family, with the emperor acting in the role of a father, and all his subjects acting as sons who should obey him. Among the "*Wu lun*", only the relationship of *pengyou* (friends) is equal.

This kind of **hierarchical relationship** can be traced back to "*Li*", as Feng Youlan) remarked: "The most important thought of ancient China is the idea of *Li* (rules governing the way of life) which Confucius gave to the whole system of political and social customs handed down from an early age." And he further explained: "The ethics of *Li* gave a high value to the order of social position. The **ethics of Confucianism** was one for the governing class, namely, for people who were ranked in high positions in society. These people were the governing class politically and intelligentsia culturally. Superiority in society and states in the governing class was the important thing. A one-sided obedience of the lower class to members of the upper class was emphasized" (265).

However, the **power distance** in China has turned out to become smaller at the present time. A relatively open and free atmosphere is more pervasive in most of Chinese people's relations. In family relations, particularly in cities, children are more and more considered as equal individuals to their parents, and greater considerations have been paid more attention to their views and feelings, smiling coyly and saying "Isn't he a naughty boy?" Americans have the saying "Boys will be boys."

The United States is supposed to be a country where people can enjoy the benefit **of low power distance**. Communication between American people tends to flow both upward and downward and horizontally regardless of rank and class. In many corporations, each person has the freedom of sharing his or her views, suggestion and feeling with others and there are suggestion boxes for the employees to place their ideas. In schools, the students feel fairly free to interrupt the teacher's lecture by

Occupy Wall Street Demonstration in the USA

asking questions and stating their own views. Nevertheless, some people regard the United States as becoming **higher in power distance**. There is a big gap between the rich and ordinary people, let alone the poor with the top 5% having more wealth than most of the rest of the 95% of the population. The social wealth has been under the control of the wealthy people. According to Jandt (2004), "In the United States in 1980, the average CEO salary was 42 times as much as the average worker. In 1990, it was 85 times as much. In 2000, it was 531 times as much…. In 1977, the top 1% in the United States had an after-tax income equal to the bottom 100 million." This remains true today, despite the 2008–2010 severe depression. The December 2010 Obama-Republican senators' agreement to continue to give the richest Americans another two-year tax break, along with the middle class tax-break extension, is expected to cost more than $70 billion.

Cultural Patterns and Cross-Cultural Value Orientations

5.4.2.3 High Versus Low Uncertainty Avoidance

The **uncertainty reduction theory** (Knobloch, 2009: 976–978) defines **uncertainty** as the inability to predict personal behavior or that of others: "Cognitive uncertainty arises when individuals are unsure about their own beliefs or the beliefs of others. Behavioral uncertainty occurs when people are unsure about their own actions or the actions of others. In sum, uncertainty exists when individuals lack information about their surroundings." The **theory of managing uncertainty** (Afifi, 2009: 975) proposes that those seeking to overcome uncertainty go through six stages: first, experiencing uncertainty triggered by some event; second, making cognitive or logical efforts to reduce the uncertainty; third, making motivational attempts to reduce the uncertainty by seeking new information; fourth, being stopped by competing motives; fifth, selecting from a range of communicative behaviors; and sixth, recognizing that this process typically has a dramatic effect on reducing the uncertainty.

According to Vijai N. Giri (2009: 532–537), "Members of high uncertainty-avoidance-cultures resist change more, have higher levels of anxiety, have higher levels of intolerance for ambiguity, worry about the future more, see loyalty to their employer as more of a virtue, have a lower motivation for achievement, and take fewer risks." On the other hand, Giri notes that "Members of low uncertainty avoidance cultures appear to engage in more vocalization of anger toward out-group members and to control their anger toward out-group members less than do members of high uncertainty avoidance cultures."

Roberta Bell Ross and Sandra L. Faulkner (1998: 33–34) identify Hofstede's **Uncertainty Avoidance Index (UAI)** which demonstrates that **uncertainty avoidance** moves on a continuum from a low to high structure, suggesting that "cultures registering high on the continuum have a tendency to rely on structure and rules to cope with uncertainty…. Employees in the study tended to worry more, have higher job stress, mistrust foreign managers, be less ready to compromise with opponents, view conflicts in organizations as undesirable, and be less emotionally resistant to change." In contrast, Ross and Faulkner identify **low-uncertainty avoidance participants** in Hofstede's study as being "more willing to take each day as it comes, feel less stress, show less aggression and emotions, and face difference with curiosity. Students are comfortable with open-ended learning situations, time constitutes a framework for orientation. People in low UAI cultures generally are more tolerant of deviant and innovative ideas and behavior. "They note that among countries identified on the UAI, Greece had the highest ranking at 112 and Singapore with the lowest at 8, while the US was at 31.

Igor Klyukanov (2005: 43–44) defines the **Uncertainty Principle** as follows:

"First, we cannot be absolutely confident that our understanding of intercultural interactions is certain and complete. Intercultural com-munication is inherently variable and subject to reinterpretation…. Second, intercultural communication can be presented as a process of disclosure, or simultaneous opening up and closing down of the

windows of awareness.... Third, different experiences form the basis of intercultural communication, as shared order is created out of uncertainty."

Klyukanov formulates the Uncertainty Principle as "Intercultural communication is a process whereby people from different cultures constantly search for knowledge of how to interact with one another against the background of uncertainty."

5.4.2.4 Masculinity and Femininity Dimensions

Hofstede uses the terms **masculinity** and **femininity** to distinguish the differences in **gender values, behaviors and modes of communication**. He defines **masculinity culture** as "societies in which social gender roles are clearly distinctive (namely, men are supposed to be assertive, tough, and focused on material success whereas women are supposed to be more modest, tender and concerned with the quality of life)." While **femininity** culture pertains to "societies in which social gender overlap (both men and women are supposed to be modest, tender, and concerned with the quality of life)." (Hofstede, 1991: 82–83) Samovar and Porter (2004) further explain the **masculinity** and **femininity dimensions** by interpreting "masculinity is the extent to which the dominant values in a society are male oriented, which defines very different social roles for men and women, and expect men to be assertive, ambitious and competitive and to strive for the material success. Cultures that value femininity as a trait stress nurturing behaviors, maintains that

men need not be assertive and that they can also assume nurturing roles; it also promotes sexual equality and holds that people and environment are important." Countries such as Japan, Austria, Venezuela, Italy, Switzerland, Mexico and Ireland are masculinity-oriented, while countries like Denmark, Netherlands, Norway, and Sweden are **femininity-oriented**. Both mothers and fathers can often take off long periods from their work to care for their children.

In the **masculinity culture**, the **masculine personality** such as assertiveness, toughness and ambition are highly valued, and economic growth, business performance and achievement are placed in a primary position, while females are regarded as the second priority, the **female personality** such as tenderness, caring and nurturing are devalued. Furthermore, a **masculine culture** places great emphasis on the value of work and regards the life goal when a person comes to the world is to work, and it also differentiates the roles of male and female distinctively in performing work. Males are supposed to undertake some important jobs in political, scientific, and economic areas, while females are supposed to be service persons or housewives who are at home taking care of children and doing housework.

But in the **feminine culture**, people attach much importance to the quality of life, nurturance and environmental issues. People think that the most important thing in life are not material issues, but the mutual caring relationship and that people should enjoy life and value the quality of life. As far as the work attitude is concerned, its principle is to "work in order to live" rather that to "live in order to work." A **feminine culture** holds an equal and flexible view towards gender, and regards that not only females but also males could perform the role of nurturing. Owing to its stressing the value of nurturance and caring, it also lays great emphasis on environmental issues.

5.4.3 Edward T. Hall's Value Orientations

Hall provides us with **high-context** and **low-context orientations** in examining different cultural patterns. He distinguishes among cultures on the basis of the role of **context in communication** by categorizing cultures as being **high-** or **low-context**. He defines **high-context** and **low-context communication** in the following manner: "A high context (HC) communication or message is one in which most of the information is already in the person, while very little is in the coded, explicitly transmitted part of the message. A low context (LC) communication is just the opposite i.e., the mass of the information is vested in the explicit code (1976: 91)."

Thus we see in **high-context cultures**, many of the meanings being exchanged do not have to be communicated through words. People in **high-context cultures** such as those of Japan, Korea, China, Vietnam, and among the Chinese diaspora tend to make inferences from their surroundings and their environment and do not rely too much on verbal communication as their main information source, but often more on facial or other gestures. The context of the message is well understood by both sender and receiver. While in low context cultures, people rely more on the spoken and specifically direct words to communicate with one another. For instance, Germans and Americans often speak up directly; most of the information is contained in their verbal message; and very little is embedded in the context or within the participants.

Ling Chen (2007) proposes that in studying Hall's quote "culture is communication and communication is culture," and **high-** and **low-context orientations**, we can identify some goals of Chinese communication studies. She isolates four major perspectives: the traditional **humanistic, interpretative, critical-cultural** and **neo-positivist perspectives**. The first scholars approach the topic by "examining the texts produced in scholarly writings, historical documents, literature, or other mediated messages as rhetoric." The second set of scholars study "social interactions in interpersonally or organizational contexts as verbal communication." The third group examines "public communication in different forms as the social structure and social process for power and control." The last group measures "internal states or external factors in relation to human communicative behavior and activity" (338–341). She remarks that: "Chinese communicating studies contribute most to a clearer understanding of Chinese, the Chinese and Chinese societies in the first two aspects, presenting reflection of culture in mediated and non-mediated communication as well as the extent to which communication is part of the Chinese culture ... Much less attention has been on communication processes that help form, constitute the Chinese culture and change the culture.... Once again, there are currently talks in the mainland society ... on the state of Chinese consciousness in this respect compared to Western societies in an increasingly globalized world" (345–346). As we note her point which she makes specifically in reference to Hall's quote "culture is communication and communication is culture," then of course Hall's ideas of **high** and **low context**, and **polychromic time management** (multitasking at the same time) and **monochromic time management** (managing one task in a linear time pattern) processes in Chinese communication makes sense as the Chinese (and other East Asians, Middle Easterners, and Africans) are quite often involved in indirect and inferential communication while the Westerners are frequently used to direct and confrontational communication, both verbally and nonverbally.

5.4.4 Fons Trompenaars's Value Dimensions

Another recent research for the understanding of culture patterns was raised by the Dutch researcher Fons Trompenaars and the British scholar Charles Hampden-Turner, whose books focus more on **intercultural business management**. Based on research questionnaires to over 150,000 managers from 28 countries which cover 47 national cultures, they find that cultures differ in the specific solutions they choose to problems. They then identify seven fundamental dimensions of culture. There are five orientations covering the ways in which human beings deal with each other.

5.4.4.1 Universalism Versus Particularism (What is more important, rules or relationships?)

Universalism consists of the general ideas, rules, and practices shared by people universally (*etic*), while **particularism** (*emic*) is the specific circumstances that govern ideas, rules and practices. In cultures with **high universalism**, formal rules, legal systems, contracts rather than relationships are underscored, whereas in culture with **high particularism**, the focus is more on personal systems, interpersonal trust, as well as duty to friends and families. According to Trompenaars' research, countries such as the United States, Australia, Germany, Sweden and the United Kingdom are **universalism-oriented**, while countries such as Venezuela, Nepal, Republic of Korea, the former Soviet Union, China, and Indonesia are **particularism-oriented**.

5.4.4.2 Individualism Versus Communitarianism (Do we function in a group or as individuals?)

This approach is quite similar to the **"individualism and collectivism" value dimension** raised by Hofstede and discussed above. However, their findings differ slightly in terms of some countries' value dimensions tendency. For instance, Mexico and Argentina are focused on collectivism in Hofstede's findings but in the individualism focus in Trompenaars' research.

5.4.4.3 Neutral Versus Emotional (Do we display our emotions openly?)

The approach concentrates on to what extent emotions or feelings are displayed. A neutral culture focuses on "subtle communication" in which "physical contact [is] reserved for close friends and family." The emotion in the neutral culture is often hidden and "hard to 'read.'" An affective culture is the one in which people tend to be more "expressive" and "vocal," and the physical contact is more "open and free." According to Trompenaars' **relationship orientations** on **value dimensions research**, Japan, the United Kingdom, Germany and Sweden are **neutral-oriented**, while the United States, France, Spain, and China are **affective-oriented**.

5.4.4.4 Specific Versus Diffuse (Is responsibility specifically assigned or diffusely accepted?)

The **specific** versus **diffuse orientation** is related to the involvement in relationships among people. In specific cultures; individuals' personalities are more open and extroverted; people deal with issues in direct and confrontational ways. While in diffuse cultures, individuals' personalities are more closed and introverted, people try to avoid direct confrontation and like to separate their work and private lives. The United Kingdom, the United States, France, Germany, and Italy are **specific cultures**, while Japan, Sweden, Spain and China are **diffuse cultures**.

5.4.4.5 Achievement Versus Ascription (Do we have to prove ourselves to receive status or is it given to us?)

This approach discusses the criterion on whether individuals are judged by their **personal achievement or social ascription**. According to Trompenaar, in terms of **achievement cultures**, status is based on competency and achievements, whereas in **ascription cultures**, status is based on position, ages, schooling, or other criteria. As far as the female and male position in the work force is concerned, in an **achievement culture**, women and minorities are visible in workplaces, while in **ascription cultures**, there appears to be a more homogenous workforce, mainly occupied by the males. Besides, we see in an **achievement culture**, since the personal achievement is highly valued, newcomers, young people and outsiders gaining due respect if they prove themselves to be talented and capable. While in **ascription cultures**, deference is based on specific criteria. Moreover, there is a different way in which societies look at time. The United States, the United Kingdom, Sweden, Germany and France belong to achievement cultures, while Italy, Spain, Japan and China belong to **ascription cultures**.

5.4.4.6 Sequential Versus Syncretic (Do we do things one at a time or several things at once?)

In addition to the five relationship orientations on value dimensions, Trompenaars also found out the two types of different perceptions and ways that people deal with time: **sequential** and **synchronic approaches**. The **sequential** and **synchronic approaches** are quite similar to the **monochromic (M-time)** and **polychromic (P-time)** classifications raised by Hall (1990); M-time people prefer to do one thing at a time, concentrate on the job, and take time commitment such as deadlines, schedules and plans seriously. (1990: 15) In general, the sequential approach has the similar characteristics with that of the **M-time**. While **P-time** people like to do many things at once and change plans often and easily. It is the same case with synchronic people, who tend to do more than one thing at a time, and people and relationships appear to be more important than schedules and plans.

5.4.4.7 Internal Versus External Control (Do we control our environment or are we controlled by it?)

The last important difference is the attitude of the culture to the environment. This approach is quite similar to the **person-nature orientation** by Kluckhohn and Strodtbeck, discussed above. Particularly it matches the two "**human being subject to nature**" and "**controlling nature**" approaches in Kluckhohn and Strodtbeck's **value orientations**.

In summary, we see that Trompenaars's **Value Dimensions**, also based on studies related to the workplace as were those of Hofstede, are generally identified in three different categories: namely **the relationships with people**, attitudes to time and attitudes to the environment. **Relationships with people** have been further differentiated into five dimensions: As has been discussed above,

some of Trompenaars's findings are very closely related to the ones put forth by Hofstede, Hall, and Kluckhohn and Strodtbeck.

5.4.5 Shalom Schwartz's Societal Orientations

Based on extensive research in sixty three countries, with more than 60,000 individuals taking part, the Israeli values scholar Shalom Schwartz studied a range of values. He identifies ten universal value types which could act as the central beliefs within a culture. They are power, achievement, hedonism, stimulation, self-direction, universalism, security, benevolence, tradition, and conformity. In his study, similar value types are located next to one another, whereas opposing value types are placed across from one another. For instance, in traditional Chinese culture, conformity as well as tradition are the core values, correspondingly, benevolence and security are also highly valued, while stimulation and self-direction are not underscored.

Above all, Schwartz' **societal orientations research** provides another good resource in **value orientation study** and serves as an instructive approach in evaluating values across cultures. Kulich (2009: 984–989) reminds us that following Hofstede, Schwartz "is often credited with developing the most carefully constructed a priori study of values. Since putting his integrated theory of values forward in 1992, he and his associates have collected extensive and carefully controlled data sets primarily from teachers, high school students, and workers in over 77 national cultures and regions (using both his more conceptual **Schwartz Values Questionnaire (SVQ)** as well as a simplified **Portrait Values Questionnaire (PVQ)** for less educated or more implicit societies) to analyze values both on individual and cultural levels." Kulich notes that Schwartz's potential 45 value items out

of the 57 tested appear to have some level of meaning interculturally: "They meet the basic requirements of human existence: (a) individual needs as biological organisms, (b) requisites of coordinated social interaction, and (c) survival and welfare needs of groups." (See also this Chapter's Case Study.)

5.5 Chinese Value Orientations

5.5.1 The Influence of the Traditional Chinese Value Orientations

China is a country with an approximately five-thousand-year history, in which Confucianism has exerted a major influence in shaping its unique culture and values. Confucius (550 BC–478 BC) and all his followers throughout the centuries have been very much concerned with the secular life of the real world or what Kwang calls the "life world," and the Chinese people as a whole have been practically-minded, exhibiting an unquenchable interest in **pragmatism** and **rationalism**.

Confucianism basically holds the beliefs of "Five Constant Virtues" (*wu chang*), as we have discussed before, known as "benevolence" (*Ren*), "personal loyalty" (*Yi*), "courtesy or politeness or propriety" (*Li*), "wisdom" (*Zhi*) and "faith" (*Xin*). As a result, the **beliefs and doctrines of Confucianism** have served as the cores of Chinese values. As has been discussed above, generally speaking, Chinese culture is **collectivism-oriented**, which pays

more attention to group identities, emphasizes **interpersonal** and **mutually dependent relationships** within the group, shows great concerns for **mutual faces, stresses consensus, cooperation** and **harmony**. These value orientations have provided a rich cultural legacy to Chinese, other East Asians, and Southeast Asians. June Yum (1988) has identified five influences that Confucianism has had on **interpersonal communication** (*jiaoji*) both in China and elsewhere: **particularism** (opposite universal patterns); **role of intermediaries** (heavy influence of ritual); **reciprocity** (*huhui*); **in-group/out-group distinctions** (freer and deeper talk for the in-group versus more superficial talk for the out-group); and **an overlap of personal and public relationships** (with business and social life intermixed).

However, Confucianism also has its negative influences, even among some that Yum mentions. The traditional Chinese culture is a typical **patriarchal ruling model**, in which "Gang Chang" ethics acts as the basic value principle. Confucianism lays great emphasis on the family, and regards it as the basic unit of the society. The clan system constitutes the basic structure of the country, in which the nation is regarded as the extension of the family. In terms of relationships among the family members and society members, it belongs to a kind of **patriarchal type**, in which the emperors, rulers, fathers, and elder brothers are endowed with controlling powers, while female members, such as wives and daughters are placed in low positions. These have led to the tragic fates of the womens' lives in the old China. The most famous contemporary Chinese writer Lu Xun once criticized the negative feature of Chinese in his masterpiece *The Wildman's Diary*.

5.5.2 The Contemporary Chinese Value Orientations

5.5.2.1 Pursuit of Life

With the rapid contemporary development of the Chinese economy and the process of **modernization** and **urbanization**, now the Chinese people pay great attention to their **material life**. In most of the Chinese people's minds, houses, cars, money and related material things are their major concerns for themselves and their family. Owing to the influences of the traditional Chinese value of owning personal houses, most Chinese people own their own houses or apartments; hence, there has been a thirst for buying houses or apartments. From big cities like Beijing, Shanghai, and Guangzhou to medium cities like Qingdao, Hangzhou, Chengdu, to the small cities and towns, there have been new apartments and new buildings

being rapidly built, leading to a housing glut in the 2007–2009 international recession. This is one factor that leads to the rapid increase of the house prices in China at the present time. Besides, now it is a fashion for Chinese people, particularly urban people to buy cars, world famous brand clothes, cosmetics, and other luxurious items. Today's Chinese people, in particular the youth, attempt to seek a life of material satisfaction and quality. They desire success, and spend more time in traveling, entertainment and group gatherings. They prefer personalizing things and an enriched life; they love music and sports, and long for more personal freedom and happiness.

5.5.2.2 The Family

Contemporary Chinese people still cherish their **family** and there is a caring, loving relationship among family members in most Chinese families. Unlike traditional extended family patterns, now most Chinese families tend to be nuclear families with parents and one child in each family due to the Chinese government's one child policy, perhaps with grandparents included. In most families, especially in cities, children are often spoiled, ("The Little Emperor" or "Little Empress") since much attention is paid to them. In most cases, children are not trained to be independent from their families; instead, parents and grandparents try their best to take care of their children, almost doing everything for them. An emerging problem in Chinese families is that often when young people marry, they become responsible over time not only for their child, but also for their parents and one or two grandparents.

5.5.2.3 Education

There has never been such a time that the Chinese people have attached so great an importance to **education**, with the most students in any country in the world. Since the 1978 opening up to the outside world, Chinese people have held the firm belief that **knowledge can change people's fate**, "**knowledge is power**" as Francis Bacon said. Both in the city citizens' and rural peasants' minds, education is the first important thing. However, their understandings of education are sometimes quite narrow-minded, as to most of them, they hope that their children can be accepted by good or even prestigious universities and colleges, especially the famous ones, since they believe these are the right ways in which their children could have the opportunities of finding good jobs. In cities, in addition to the regular school learning, most parents send their children to attend various classes, such as piano, drawing, singing, dancing, ping pong, and English classes to help them gain more competitive skills. While at school, the middle school students have a large burden of learning, memorizing knowledge and taking exams. At colleges and in universities, some students are also very practical in learning as their quests for learning have some personal purposes of finding satisfactory jobs with high salary and a stable life. In China, there is a saying: "The hardest working people are the students." Unfortunately, due to various reasons including the greater and greater number of university and college students and graduates, the students are under great pressure to find suitable and well-paying work.

5.6 Case Study: Universal Human Rights as Universal Values

By Michael H. Prosser*

When we review the many values which may have been or were considered universal at different times and in different traditions, we can see that among these major values found in the Old Testament as a pseudo history, chronicles, and poetry for the Israelites were the sacredness of life, the covenant with God, forgiveness by God to humans and forgiveness-seeking from humans by God, as in the Psalms of David, the brotherhood of man (but often in a particularistic dimension exclusively for them

---

* Michael H. Prosser (constituting the Summary of the essay, *Universal Human Rights as Universal Values*, in S. J. Kulich, M. H. Prosser, and L. P. Weng (Eds.) (2011), Value Frameworks at the Theoretical Crossroads of Culture. Intercultural Research Series, Vol. 3 Shanghai, China: Shanghai Foreign Language Education Press.)

as God's chosen people), dependence upon God, and a guide for righteous living among others. Basically the Old Testament was written over 1,500 years, and represented for early and modern Jews as the Torah or Law and the first of the world's major religions of a monotheistic God. *The Ten Commandments* given by God to Moses have become a near universal standard of conduct, at least in the Western world. It was accepted by the Christians as a part of their sacred texts along with the New Testament and later was modified somewhat as a part of the historical development of Islam as the final revelation from God through the Qu'ran. The Christians saw and still see the Israelites or Jews as their fore fathers in faith, and the Muslims saw and partially see the Jews and Christians as their predecessors in faith, but with the conviction that the Islamic Qu'ran is the final prophetic realization given to Mohammad in the sixth century.

The early Christian texts in the New Testament were identified as the new covenant between God and his people, but with the universalistic command "to go and teach all people." Jesus Christ claimed that he was in himself, (sui generis) "the way, the truth and the life." While accepting the Old Testament as the Law or Torah, he offered a new and more inclusive covenant and gave a new universal value to love God with one's full heart, mind, and soul, and also to love his neighbor as himself. Both Jesus and St. Paul placed major attention on the three chief virtues, faith, hope, and love. Jesus and St. Paul identified love as the most important and enduring of all virtues, and thus clearly universal in nature. Forgiveness of others' wrong doing and mercy were central themes in his teaching. In his

"Sermon on the Mount," Jesus annunciated a series of positive values and negative contrasts to these values. The Old Testament, the New Testament, the Qu'ran, and the sacred writings of the polytheistic religions and philosophies, all consider prayer, fasting, and alms giving to the poor as central to the development of a good life for all.

Hinduism, and later Buddhism, accepted the concept of a divine supernatural being, just as the Jews, Christians, and Muslims did, but added other divinities as also the Greeks and Romans accepted. The Hindus, without a definite founder or time for its initiation, accepted as universal principles four broad categories based on moksha—the search for liberation from unhappiness and a past chain of lives, and samsura—one's involvement in the universe. These four broad categories included kharma—the central role in life of having a sense of doing right, but which had both positive and negative aspects, artha—the pursuit of material well being, kama—the pleasure of the senses, and dharma—leading a right and virtuous life. These combinations, accepted at least as near universals, all have the power in Hinduism and Buddhism to lead one ultimately to happiness or linkage with Brahman or unity with the divine spirit.

Buddhism, enriched first by Sidhartha, and later living Buddhas, articulates for "all humans" "Four Noble Truths: "Life is suffering; all suffering is caused by ignorance of the nature of reality and craving for material well being and attachment; suffering can be overcome by overcoming ignorance and attachment (which Schwartz might call hedonism). Buddhism adopted the Hindu notion of life as cyclical. The "Four Noble Truths" can lead to the

Cultural Patterns and Cross-Cultural Value Orientations

"Eightfold Way": which consists of right views, right intention, right speech, right action, right livelihood, right effort, right-mindedness, and right contemplation. These eight are usually divided into three categories that form the cornerstone of Buddhist faith: morality, wisdom, and samadhi, or concentration.

Confucianism, based in *The Analects*, provides a hierarchical system of five universal values: and proposes such concepts as *ren*—benevolence, kindness, filial piety, love of kind (a particularistic value), respect for authority and elders, social stability and harmony, goodness in life, courteousness in public life, diligence in relationships, and loyalty to family or superiors; jen or humaneness, *li*—moral propriety through established rituals which include several of the characteristics of *ren*; *di*—moral righteousness or moral power; *lian*—one's internalized dimension including face practices; and *mianzi*—one's externalized images, including also face practices, or more broadly harmony or creating a harmonious society. While we do not necessarily see happiness as a central factor such as Hinduism, Buddhism, and the Greeks provide in their belief systems, it certainly must be a result in Confucianism in the process of being benevolent or kind, in having moral righteousness or power, and in both the internalized and externalized images which the Confucian lifeworld illustrates. Despite setbacks, the Confucian world view remains a dominant philosophy in societies such as China, Japan, Korea, and others. Justice (and social justice) is certainly a major value in Hinduism, Buddhism, and Confucianism and may indeed be a universal value.

For the ancient Greeks, and to an extent the ancient Romans who followed them, their perception of universal values were truth including the ultimate truth, truth-telling, wisdom, the overcoming of ignorance, goodness, justice, idealism, reality, happiness, forgiveness and reconciliation and the initiation of scientific rationalism. The goddess Athena represented both wisdom and physical power, strength, and war—as contrasting drives. Early developments of individualism were encouraged by the Greeks whose young male citizens were taught and encouraged to be direct, to argue for their own rights and positions, to debate forcefully, as well as to be fully involved in civic life through the courts, the theatre, the arts, poetics, and sports, in contrast to young ancient Asians who were taught to respect authority and only to speak when they had obtained wisdom and their own respected position in society. The Greeks saw themselves as like the gods and goddesses whom they had created anthropromorphically to have all of their own human attributes and failures.

Noting that what is called the high medieval period in the West continued to place God at the center of their universe, at the same time, it led to the creation of great European universities as early as the thirteenth century, extraordinary art and architecture, an evolving middle class, an enriched literature, dissident thought in the development of the Protestant Revolution, and global exploration. Often considered the greatest Westerner of the second millennium, Johannes Gutenberg, with his printing press, had a great opportunity to promote values not just as cultural, but as truly universal. As the Renaissance, or rebirth of classical knowledge, art, literature, and architecture, began in the West, and spreading widely, it led to the eighteenth century as the Age of Reason. In John Locke who pondered the concept of the social contract and civil society and later Thomas Jefferson, Benjamin Franklin, John Adams, and James Madison, we see life, liberty and the pursuit of happiness emerging as universal rights and values in the United States Constitution and the Bill of Rights. The 1789 French Rights of Man and of the Citizen declaration based on these ideas and certainly those of Jean Jacques Rousseau in the French Revolution in 1789: freedom, equality, and fraternity (or later called the brotherhood of man), included also universal notions of popular national sovereignty, religious tolerance, and the separation of powers as universal values and rights other values perceived as universal in the French document included equality of all persons before the law; equitable taxation; protection against loss of property through arbitrary action by the state; freedom of religion, speech, and the press; and protection against arbitrary arrest and punishment all which found their way into the *Universal Declaration of Human Rights* and the *International Bill of Human Rights* established by the two binding treaties in 1966 [civil rights and political rights].

Most likely, the term human rights was first fully developed in the 1815 *Treaty of Vienna*, when the international slave trade was abolished as a fundamental violation of the rights of those who were enslaved. However, the actual abolishment of slavery in the West did not occur until President Abraham Lincoln's Emancipation Proclamation in 1863. Unfortunately, although slavery has been identified more recently in United Nations treaties, documents, and declarations as a "crime against humanity," it still exists in many societies in the world. Universal values such as peace, national sovereignty, social justice, dignity, tolerance, and equality all have been stressed more and more in modern times and as central to the *Universal Declaration of Human Rights*, and subsequent United Nations treaties, covenants, documents, and declarations..

The Hague Conventions, the League of Nations, and the United Nations all set the stage for the *Universal Declaration of Human Rights*, and subsequent treaties, conventions, and declarations for a broad set of universalistic principles, norms, values, and ideals to be accepted, at least theoretically, on a world-wide basis. The universal search for international peace and security, as well as the rights and values noted above, in contrast to particularistic and culturally selective values and rights have been at odds in modern societies, especially in Eastern, Middle Eastern, and African contexts. Universal values are clearly linked to universal human rights in the principles of the United Nations, although often not in the practice in individual societies.

While Clyde Kluckhohn, Frances Kluckhohn, and Fred Strodtbeck were not explicitly concerned in their formulation and study of universal human values and value orientations specifically with universal human rights, the connections above linking universal values and value orientations and universal human rights are at least implicit. The values and value orientations that they have accepted and studied, and those added by Condon and Yousef and others such as Geert Hofstede, Michael Harris Bond, and Shalom

Schwartz later have at least implicitly offered the foundation for merging the tenets of the *Universal Declaration of Human Rights* and the later human rights treaties, covenants, and conventions with universal values. Rokeach clearly identifies the dimensions between universalistic and particularistic dimensions of universal values and universalistic versus particularistic or culturally diverse views of human rights.

Henk Vinken's discussion (2011) about human rights coming from two different camps, universalism and particularism is very appropriate and in terms of human values, his view is supported by Shalom Schwartz' studies of universal, regional, and culturally specific values. We note that in principle the *Universal Declaration of Human Rights* is an ideal standard for all of humanity, at every time, and in every place, and for every individual in society. The subsequent UN treaties, covenants, and conventions remain in contrast to the view by Asian, Middle Eastern, and African countries that certain human rights are not universal but can only be seen through the perspective of particularism or cultural diversity. A number of authors have considered the relationship between multiculturalism, cultural diversity, (leaning toward particularism), and global communication (leaning toward universalism). Shalom H. Schwartz's theory of the basic values that people in all cultures recognize, identifies ten motivationally distinct value orientations and specifies the dynamics of conflict and congruence among these values which were measured by his SVS test: benevolence (clearly identified in Confucianism), universalism (established in the *Universal Declaration of Human Rights*, and its subsequent treaties,

covenants, and conventions) , self-direction (also proposed by the Kluckhohns and Strodtbeck considerations of values and value orientations and identifying all persons as independent individuals worthy of dignity and respect in the UN Charter and Universal Declaration of Human Rights), stimulation, and hedonism (seen in Greek, Hindu, and Buddhism as potential contrasts to higher ideals), achievement and power (relating to physical versus moral power as found among the Confucianists, Greeks, and early Christians, and recognizing social esteem and dignity for all individuals), security (seen in developing the social contract, popular sovereignty, and national sovereignty), conformity (seen in the Universal Declaration of Human Rights in its call for all states and individuals to adhere to its principles), and tradition (the development over time of perceived universal values, rights, and later human rights versus culturally, philosophically, or religiously different traditions).

Schwartz notes that: "The values theory describes aspects of the human psychological structure that are fundamental, aspects presumably common to all humankind. Consequently, its propositions should apply across cultures." This statement certainly relates to the Universal Declaration of Human Rights and other universal values as perceived historically. There are four issues for consideration proposed by Schwartz: "(1) Is there a near universal set of values differentiated by motivational content? (2) Is the set of values identified by the theory comprehensive, leaving out none of the broad values to which individuals attribute at least moderate importance? (3) Do the values have similar meanings in different groups (e.g. ethnic, national, gender, etc.) thereby justifying comparison of value priorities across groups? (4) Is there a near universal structure of dynamic relations among values? Though it is obvious that the governments from an Eastern, Middle Eastern, and African context might disagree sharply with me as they come from a

particularistic and culturally diverse framework for human rights and human values, the UN Charter, the *Universal Declaration of Human Rights*, and the subsequent treaties, covenants, and conventions demand a universalistic approach to human rights, and thus in my perception also to the even broader framework of universalistic human values.

5.7   Summary

In this chapter, we have explored the definition of cultural patterns and discussed the values, and value orientation research done by Chinese scholars such as Liang Shuming's and Lin Yutang's cultural traits concepts, Hui-ching Chang's questions about Chinese values, Ling Chen's contribution to understanding Edward T. Hall's high and low context, Kwang-Kuo Hwang's development of psychology from a Confucian perspectives, as well as Western scholars such as Kluckhohn and Strodbeck's

value orientations, Geert Hofstede's national value orientations, Edward T. Hall's concepts of high- and low-context cultures, Fons Trompenaar's value orientations, and Shalom Schwartz's societal and universal orientations. At last, the traditional and contemporary Chinese value orientations are illustrated in particular. The case study is an excerpt from Prosser's essay, *"Universal Human Rights as Universal Values."*

5.8 Questions for Discussion

8.1 This chapter's dialogue begins with a discussion about Descartes' "I doubt, therefore I think; I think, therefore I am." What is the importance of this quote to the concept of critical thinking? Did the students handle this and other topics that were introduced in the dialogue well or not? Why or why not?

8.2 In this chapter's dialogue, we have a continuing but curious situation. Professor Zhang appears to be strongly focused on a firm organizational pattern in a Western logical pattern, which some would think is an American characteristic, while Michael seems to allow the conversation to go in an almost circular fashion, which we would think would be more intuitively Chinese or Asian. In fact, some of his students have called him a "Chiamerican." How can we understand this apparent reversal of roles between Professor Zhang and Michael? What does it mean when he is called a "Chiamerican?"

8.3 The dialogue includes considerable discussion about selective perceptions, going back to the questions in the preceding chapter and developing the concept more fully. What is the difference between perceptions, attitudes and beliefs? How can we see the concept of selective perceptions as an important aspect of the study of intercultural communication?

8.4 In discussing the Chinese scholars' ideas about cultural patterns and dimensions, which one seems to be most useful in studying intercultural communication? Why? How are these Chinese scholars' ideas different from those of western scholars whom we have been discussing in this and earlier chapters?

8.5 When we discuss scholarly intercultural theories and concepts, how do you see the discussion about Hall's notion of high and low context? Is he developing theory or offering a concept? If it is the former, how can it be tested in a research study? If it is the latter, what needs to be done to move a concept to a theory?

8.6 A critique of the development of the national value dimensions by Geert Hofstede argues that we cannot validly and reliably ascribe certain values to entire nations, especially in multicultural nations like Canada, much of Europe, Singapore, Malaysia and the US. Also, since he was conducting surveys in countries initially which had IBM branches, his early study was unable to gather any information about the mainland Chinese. How would you support or reject this critique for his very large study of more than 100,000 IBM employees?

8.7 If you were interested in conducting a study of cultural patterns, values, and value orientations in your own university locality, what research questions would you want to begin with? What hypotheses might you develop? What predictions might you want to make if you studied employees in a large business or industry as you consider any of such dimensions as individualism versus collectivism, high and low power distance, high and low uncertainty avoidance, or masculinity versus femininity?

8.8 Both Hofstede and Trompenaars's national value studies are organized around workers in individual nations while Schwartz's societal or universal values are directed toward a much broader conceptualization of cultural traits and value orientations. How can we compare the potential results which these studies might find since they are based on different premises?

8.9 We have made various comparisons and contrasts between Chinese or East and South East Asians and Westerners such as in the US or Europe. What are these major comparisons and contrasts in terms of values, cultural patterns and value orientations? Why?

8.10 In the case study for Chapter 4, Professor Li Mengyu offers a discussion about the Chinese concept of harmony and in this chapter, Prosser provides a case study about universal human rights as universal values. Compare the main ideas of these two case studies. Are they complementary in their focus or are there disimilarities which can be considered culturally different, based on Li being a Chinese scholar and Prosser being an American scholar?

5.9 Suggested Readings

Hofstede, G. (2008). *Culture's consequences : Comparing values, behaviors, institutions and organizations.* Shanghai, China: Foreign Education Press.

Kluckhohn, C. (1967). *Values and value orientations in the theory of action: An explanation in definition and classification.* In Parson, T. & Shils, E.A. (Eds.) *Toward a general theory of action.* Cambridge, MA: Harvard University Press. (Original work published in 1951).

Lin, Y. T. (2004). *My country and my people.* Beijing, China: Foreign Language Teaching and Research Press.

Lin, Y. T. (2005). *The importance of living.* Beijing, China: Foreign Language Teaching and Research Press.

Pan, F. E. & Wen, W .S. X (2004). *The Analects of Confucius.* Jinan, China: Qilu Press.

Prosser, M. H. (2011). *Universal human rights as universal values.* In S. J. Kulich.M. H. Prosser, & L. P. Weng (Eds.). *Value frameworks at the theoretical crossroads of Culture, Intercultural Research, Volume 4.* Shanghai, China: Shanghai Foreign Language Education Press.

Rapport, N. & Overing, J. (2000). *Social and cultural anthropology: The key concepts.* New York, NY: Routledge.

Rogers, E. M. & Steinfatt T. M. (1999). *Intercultural communication.* Prospect Heights, IL: Waveland Press.

Chapter
Six

Verbal and Nonverbal Communication

6.1 Dialogue

Professor Zhang: Class, today we want to talk about cultural verbal and nonverbal communication with an emphasis on language. Many of you have studied English since you were quite young and may have an understanding of various forms of linguistics, such as sociolinguistics and psycholinguistics. The Ministry of Education has made it essential that the Chinese educational system has the communicative learning of English as a major goal for all of our students. All of you are fluent in Chinese, mostly Mandarin and some regional dialects, and English. Many of you have also taken a second foreign language such as French, German, Japanese, Russian or Spanish. Ali, perhaps you have learned some classical Arabic to be able to read the *Qu'ran*?

Ali: The classical Arabic that the holy *Qu'ran* was written in, as passed down by the followers of the Prophet Mohammed, Peace and blessings be upon him, is very hard for us Chinese Muslims to understand. I need a holy *Qu'ran* in Chinese or English. My third language that I am learning now is Arabic, but it is hard and it is not the same as classical Arabic. Have you read the holy *Qu'ran* in English, Michael? Do you have one in English?

Michael: Yes, Ali, I usually bring two or three copies of the *Qu'ran* in English when I come to China after my US holiday. I have read it once in English. I can give you a copy.

Verbal and Nonverbal Communication

Yolanda:	I need a holy *Qu'ran* too Michael, if you please in English. Remember, I am a Uighor and Muslim too.
Professor Zhang:	Some scholars stress that even with the importance of learning our own native language, and the second language such as English or the third language that Chinese students majoring in English must learn, about 30% of our communication is based on verbal language, but 70% comes from our nonverbal communication, facial expressions, and gestures.We even have paralanguage which is a mix between real language and nonverbal communication, like "umm," "ah," "eh," "uh," or "uh huh."
Cherry:	Do you speak Chinese, Michael?
Michael:	I speak English very well.
Robin:	Since you teach intercultural communication, how many languages do you speak?
Michael:	I speak English very well. I have studied and taught Latin, which was abandoned in China after 1949 as a non practical language. I have also learned some French and German, but not enough to speak, read or write it. I can read a very little French, but I have no vocabulary any more except words that are rather common to English.
Ava:	I started learning English when I was nine. My mother was an English teacher too.
Michael:	As you know, when you were in first grade, you could all perfectly form 750 Chinese characters, and by the time you ended the second grade, you could all perfectly form 1,500 Chinese characters. Now, you can perfectly form more than 6,000 Chinese characters. For an adult foreigner, and even some Chinese born abroad, coming to China to learn Chinese, we would need to take classes 15 hours a week for a year, plus extensive homework, to be able to form 3,000 characters, and to be able to speak Chinese at a most basic level. It's a cultural difference. I can only form the characters for my first name "Mikai." My Chinese written characters for my first name are rather primitive. Let me write it on the chalk board, or is it a black board, or really a green board?

Laughter

Peter:	We know that English is supposed to be important for us, but it is not always easy to learn as there is so much vocabulary. Anyway, when we talk among ourselves we always talk in Chinese, or if Professor Zhang was just teaching us alone, we would speak in Chinese a lot. It takes an extra effort when you are talking with

us Michael, as you speak fast and have a much bigger English vocabulary than we have. Can you slow down and use simpler vocabulary?

Ava: When I was younger, I liked Li Yang's *Crazy English*. He has everyone always shouting the English expressions in English: "HELLO, ARE YOU FROM BRITAIN? MY NAME IS AVA AND I AM FROM CHINA!" Now, I realize that I don't have to shout when I speak English.

Laughter

Michael: It seems that every child and teenager in China, and also in Japan, answers the question: "Hello, how are you?" with "I am fine, thank you, and you?" No doubt, this expression comes from the Oxford English texts for children to learn English, an important medium for learning English. I have found that when I ask the same question of American children and teenagers, they respond "Good!" or "Great!" "How about you?"

Jason: That's probably because they have learned American English instead of British English.

Michael: One time when I was having an interview with Yang Rui on CCTV International's *Dialogue*, I told him that some of my students asked if we could speak more simply and slowly on the program. Yang Rui responded, "Tell your students that it is their responsibility to gain more English vocabulary and to learn to keep with the speed of educated English speakers. This program is designed for intelligent conversations on important topics between a Chinese interviewer with a broad international background and either Chinese experts with excellent English or foreigners fluent in English.

Vivian: I heard you once on China Radio International's *People in the Know* but I didn't know who you were then.

Professor Zhang: In October, 2010, the one millionth English dictionary word was developed. *The Oxford Dictionary of the English Language* now has 600,000 words. As a well educated and older American, language scholars speculate that you may have used 150,000 different words in your lifetime at least once, Michael. In your case, though class, if you have learned 10,000 words for IELTS or TOEFL, you have an extraordinarily rich vocabulary. There is what we call Basic English with about 600–800 words, but it isn't very rich or varied as a vocabulary. Esperanto was hailed at one time as the universal language, but very few people in the world can speak it. While Chinese is the most spoken language in the world, English is the most written language.

Jade: I am very proud to be Chinese and to speak Chinese, but I like to learn English too. Lots of people in Nanjing speak good English. I hope that I can study overseas in an English speaking country later. I have taken IELTS and TOEFL, and have gotten good scores. I also practice my English by watching *Friends* with my dormitory roommates, and then, we watch it again and practice the English of the women characters like Monica, Rachel, and Phoebe. But often some of the jokes are hard to understand.

Michael: It's true. Jokes are not easy to transfer from one culture to another, and even between different generations in the same culture. Puns are sometimes easier. Not long ago, I was driving past a cemetery with two of my grandchildren, Darya and Sanders, and I said, "You know, people are just dying to get in here." They were silent for a few seconds, and then one of them said, "Now, I get your pun, but it is pretty lame." Do you understand that pun, Jade?

Jade: Yes, but it is rather silly. Excuse me for being so frank.

Michael: Puns are often silly, like a play on words. You all laughed earlier when I said that my Spanish speaking friends sometimes call me Migueleito—little Michael, since I am about 1.95 meters tall. Recently, I received a box of chocolates, and I had eaten most of them. I told my youngest granddaughter, Sophia, that a tall man with a beard had gone into my refrigerator and had eaten most of the chocolates. After thinking a moment, Sophia said, "Oh! You are the tall man with the beard who ate the chocolates?" She caught my pun. Our case study today has a whole series of puns and curious English idioms contributed by Richard Lederer, a famous writer about these strange English expressions.

Forest: As Forrest Gump's mother said, "Life is like a box of chocolates. You never know what you are going to get!" I should have been there to eat chocolates with you.

Laughter

Professor Zhang: Class, you know that many scholars say that language is the soul of culture and the metaphor is the soul of language. Professor Michael, which do you think is more important in learning English, to be able to use sophisticated, elegant, and clever language or simple language in our writing and speaking? I try to have my students write their bachelors' theses in elegant and sophisticated language.

Michael: I think that as the Roman Cicero said, sometimes it is appropriate to speak or write in a grand manner, for example in very important occasions, as he did in his orations in the Roman Senate against the Roman conspirator Catiline. Often we speak or write in a more moderate tone, and sometimes for example in letters, email, or text messages, we write in a much more simple tone. However, many Chinese students try to affect a clever and overly complementary tone when they are applying for admission to American universities. Did you know that Cicero was the first Western writer to speak seriously about humor?

Eva: You are teasing us?

Michael: No, Cicero was very serious about humor.

Laughter

Michael: American admissions officers like more direct language. In his essay, "Politics and the English Language" George Orwell, author of *Animal Farm* and *1984*, said: "(1) Never use a metaphor, simile or other figure of speech which you are used to seeing in print. (2) Never use a long word when a short one will do. (3) If it is possible to cut a word out, always cut it out. (4) Never use the passive when you can use the active. (5) Never use a foreign phrase, a scientific word or a jargon word if you can think of an everyday English equivalent. (6) Break any of these rules sooner than say anything outright barbarous.

Professor Zhang: Well, Orwell makes some good points, but the best rule, as Aristotle and Cicero said is probably moderation. When we consider Orwell, his 1984 is itself a pun as it is the reversal of 1948 when he was writing his book.

Michael: Yes, I agree. I wonder, ladies and gentlemen, if any of you ever write poetry in English?

Sunny: No, as a preschool and primary school pupil, we all memorized a lot of ancient Chinese poetry and other material.

Michael: Some of the poetry of Lu Xun is very powerful and creative in English. This is one of the reasons also that I like Walt Whitman's *Leaves of Grass*. Both poets have a lot of spontaneous creativity when talking about fields of grass. In this sense, they are both called pastoral poets, just as William Wordsworth was, though his poetry was very structured. Perhaps two of the most significant words in the English language are also the simplest ones For example, "I do" or "I will" are both very simple, but in American weddings, the couple is asked if they will take each other as husband and wife, and each one agrees, "I do" or "I will." A binding commitment!

Angel: I'll remember that when my boyfriend asks me to marry him! "I will!" "I do!"

Laughter

Michael: We have read some poems by Chinese poets. Let's try a very simple poem style, the Japanese 17 syllable haiku. It usually is about nature, has 5 syllables in the first line, 7 syllables in the second line, and 5 syllables in the third line. Of course syllables in ideographic Japanese, Chinese, or Korean characters are very different than in English or the romance languages such as French, Spanish, Italian, or Portuguese.

Cherry: Can you give us some examples of haikus? It seems strange as Chinese students that we should learn Japanese haikus in English. It sounds very cross-cultural.

Michael: Yes, it is. Here are several examples first from ancient haiku masters, *Haiku for People*, but not in the 17 syllable pattern:

"Harvest moon / around the pond I wander / and the night is gone."

"A whale! / Down it goes, and more and more / up goes its tail!"

"A sudden shower falls / and naked I am riding / on a naked horse."

"First autumn morning / the mirror I stare into / shows my father's face."

"Green frog / Is your body also / freshly painted?"

"Without flowing wine / How to enjoy lovely / cherry blossoms?"

Jasmine: Oh, how nice! Michael, have you written any haikus yourself?

Michael: Yes, here are some of my own simple 17 syllable haikus.

"Tadpoles in the pool / swim most lazily about / will they become frogs?"

"The running tiger / catches the helpless rabbit / and enjoys dinner."

"In the autumn chill / I hurry quickly along / shivering slightly."

"Moon cakes in autumn / our own harvest moon glowing / warming all our hearts."

"Deep winter in Harbin / ice sculptures being created / snow falling lightly."

"Spring brings new flowers / the very beautiful world / shimmers and glistens."

"A summer evening / brings us happiness again / walking together."

"Kittens and puppies / play happily in the grass / the wind is stirring."

"Sea gulls are flying / above the Qingdao beach / Spring winds are blowing."

"At the yellow sea / in Qingdao I relax / enjoying sea air."

Gloria: Those haikus are lovely. How about this one?

"Beijing Olympics / a new green environment / glorious China!"

Tiger: Ok. Let me try one.

"Hong Kong is my home / China welcomes World Expo / our own happy land."

Mike: "Spring breeze kisses trees / slumbering land wakes from dreams / my old friend is back."

"The eagle traveling / spreads knowledge from north to south / a world professor."

Michael: Very good, Gloria, Tiger and Mike! As you see, the haiku, being such short poetry, has to keep it simple. As Professor Zhang has said, language is the soul of culture, and Aristotle also said that the metaphor is the soul of language (but only if it is used well). This is what George Orwell meant too. He wasn't against metaphors, but only the ones that are worn out or overused. In American English we have many sports metaphors that get overused a lot:

"Get on the ball!"

"He didn't get to first base with his girl."

"Keep your eye on the basket."

"Shoot straight with me."

"You are fishing for a compliment."

"Strike three and you are out!"

"Go for the gold, not the bronze!"

Professor Zhang: In Hall's early books, his 1959 *The Silent Language*, 1966 *The Hidden Dimension*, and *Beyond Culture* in 1976 which those of us teaching intercultural communication often consider the early Bible of the field, and this is a metaphor too, he spent a lot of time on nonverbal communication, gestures, facial and eye movements, touch, time and space. They are all so important in intercultural communication. Often people are saying one thing with their language meaning yes, but their eyes, facial expressions, or gestures are saying no. Or, what is acceptable nonverbal behavior in one culture is taboo in another culture. Japanese have a very hard time saying

Verbal and Nonverbal Communication

"no" in their language, but in English debating clubs, then it is easy to represent the negative point of view to win against the affirmative side.

Michael: When we raise our eyebrows at something said by another person in our own culture, or in a different culture, perhaps it can be very insulting. A slap in the face tends to be very insulting across cultures. Desmond Morris conducted a field study in Europe about how middle-aged men in different cultures had very different weak or strong gestures. For example, the farther south in Europe, especially near the Mediterranean, the gestures were more powerful and obscene and in Northern Europe, they were more placid, less powerful, and more polite.

Professor Zhang: The early values investigators like Clyde and Florence Kluckhohn and Fred Strodtbeck, just as Hall's books do, discuss time and space as important nonverbal factors between cultural groups, and the Sapir-Whorf hypothesis is about perception leading to culture, culture leading to language, and then all over in a circular fashion. Perceptions about time and space are very different in opposite cultures. Hall says that once he was in a small African village, with only one little and rather shabby hotel. As he was considering whether to stay or not, the lone hotel clerk blurted out: "Hurry up! Time is money!"

Michael: Yes, think about space in your own lives, for example in your 4 or 6 person dormitory rooms. American dormitory rooms at colleges and universities usually have only two people living together, and often only one living alone. There is an interesting book called *Bowling Alone*. Condon and Yousef's book, *An Introduction to Intercultural Communication*, illustrates the different dimensions of homes in different cultures such as in collectivisic and individualistic societies. For example, when I lived in Rochester, New York in 1994–2001, we lived in a one hundred-year old eleven room house, plus 3 $\frac{1}{2}$ bathrooms, halls, and a full basement. Early in its history, the third floor was the living quarters for a maid and butler couple, and the basement even had a wine cellar. There was a large front corner yard, and a 90-year old sycamore tree, plus bushes and flowers that were planted so as to bloom over several different weeks. Interestingly enough, the house was less expensive to buy than a much smaller new house or an apartment in Shanghai.

Jason: What is a $\frac{1}{2}$ bath room? Is half of it missing?

Laughter

Michael: It's an interesting metaphor, isn't it? If there are 3 major features that a home bathroom has to have in America, you would need a sink and toilet and a shower or tub. But a $\frac{1}{2}$ bath doesn't have a shower or tub, since it is primarily a guest bathroom. Culturally, bathrooms are very interesting. The Japanese TOTO brand of bathrooms is very elegant. Many Japanese homes or apartments often have an area for bathing quite separate from the toilet room. Have you seen the Chinese movie, *Shower*, about the professional young Chinese returning home where his father was managing a traditional bathhouse? It pits traditional and modernizing culture against each other.

Fiona: I saw it. At first the older brother returning home was arrogant about the bath house. The younger retarded brother sent him a postcard with a picture of him standing over their father, as though dead, to get the older brother to come home. Eventually, the older brother, who was used to taking showers, warmed up to their father and the traditional bath house, which eventually was sold as there weren't enough customers any longer.

Professor Zhang: Many European homes and hotels also have a bidet in the bathroom, designed long before the modern shower was developed, and still present in many modern European homes or hotel rooms, and sometimes also in South American homes or toilets with a European flare.

Maria: I've read that there are a lot of interesting names for toilets, depending on the culture: bathroom, restroom, the powder room, the John, toilet, the WC, and the Loo to name a few. The Belgians like to say that they are going to sit on the throne where the king sits alone. It's a pun.

Michael: Now after he has been out of office since January, 2009, Bush's new memoir, *Decision Points*, has been published. Perhaps it is available in China? Personally, I prefer Obama's *Audacity of Hope*, but then after all I voted for Obama in 2008 while teaching in China and two of my young friends named Zhang certified that I had voted and a third young Zhang took it to the post office.

Professor Zhang: They were probably some of my many nieces or nephews?

Laughter

Tiger: Maybe it was another pun.

Laughter

Professor Zhang: Don't forget though, Lucky and Tiger, Confucius' saying that sometimes silence is better than speech.

Michael: These are good puns. Some American puns are really old one in the US like those in the 1920s from the stand-up comedian Groucho Marx. By the way, what is a

Verbal and Nonverbal Communication

"stand-up comedian?" Does he or she not sit down? Richard Lederer asks this in his "English is a crazy language" in our case study. Here are some more of Groucho Marx' funny sayings: "Behind every successful man is a woman, behind her is his wife." "Marry me and I'll never look at another horse;" "Outside of a dog, a book is man's best friend. Inside a dog, it's too dark to read." "Why was I with her? She reminds me of you. In fact, she reminds me more of you than you do." "Either he's dead or my watch has stopped." "I don't care to belong to a club that accepts people like me as members." "I must confess that I was born at a very early age."

Lucky: So was I, born at a very early age? How about you Michael?

Laughter

Professor Zhang: Michael and the class are certainly clever today. Later, we have Richard Lederer's case study about "English Is a Crazy Language" which you will enjoy. Some of the crazy English that he looks at may be hard to understand culturally, but you should find it challenging. But now shall we move forward to our main discussion for this class, verbal and nonverbal communication, with ancient and modern versions, and the role of English now in China?

Tony: Let's do it. Shall we? Why not!

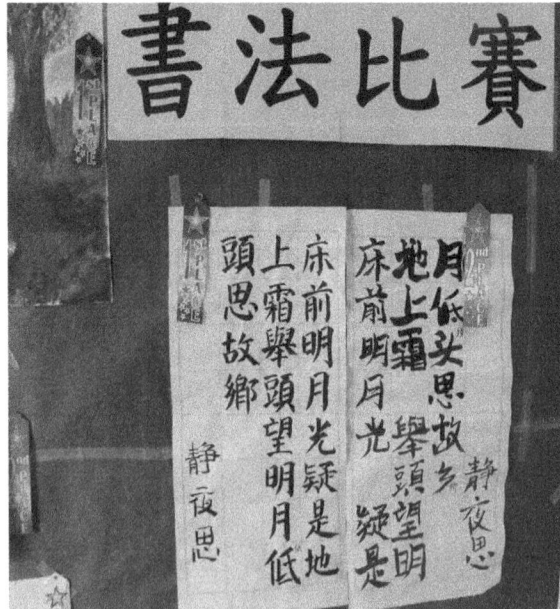

Chinese Calligraphy

6.2 The Nature of Language: Linguistic Aspects in Intercultural Communication

6.2.1 Defining Language

The Athenian poet and dramatist Aristophanes once said, "By words the mind winged." Henry Beecher believed that: "Thought is the blossom; language is the opening bud; action is the fruit behind." Language plays a very important role in our daily communication as well as in our intercultural communication. **In fact, language is the soul of culture. Language is a set of symbols shared by a community to communicate meaning and experience**. As Rubin earlier stated, "language is a set of characters or elements and rules for their use in relation to one another" (1922: 92). Samovar and Porter added that "these characters or elements are symbols that are culturally diverse." By stressing this point, they underscore the fact that language differs from culture to culture. DeVito defines language as "a potentially self-reflective, structural system of symbols which catalog the objects, events, and relations in the world" (1970: 7–9). Here he illustrates two basic features of language as sets of symbols. On the one hand, language being "potentially self-reflective" indicates that it is discretionary. For instance, the referent "chair" in English is named "椅子"in Chinese ,"silla" in Spanish, and "isu" in Japanese. On the other hand, DeVito says that the term "structural system of symbols" denotes that language is established by usage. As Kluckhohn points out, **a symbol is anything that carries a particular meaning** recognized by people who share culture. For example, "purple" is often linked with royalty in African culture, but in Roman Catholicism and other liturgical churches which follow a specific ritual annually, it is used during the penitential period of Lent, while it is the color of death in many Latin American countries.

The famous sociolinguist Joseph Greenberg offers his view of language in a more vivid description:

Language is unique to man, No other species possess a truly symbolic means of communication and no human society, however simple its material culture, lacks the basic human heritage of a well developed language. Language is the prerequisite for the accumulation and transmission of other cultural traits.

Such fundamental aspects of human society as organized political life, legal systems, religion and science are inconceivable without that most basic and human of tools, a linguistic system of communication. Language is not only a necessary condition for culture; it is itself a part of culture. It, like other shared behavioral norms, is acquired by the individual as a member of a particular social group through a complex process of learning. Like other aspects of human culture, it characteristically varied from group to group and undergoes significant modification in the course of its transmission through time within the same society (1971: 156).

Verbal and Nonverbal Communication

Greenberg not only illustrates the significant role of language in human beings' lives, but he underscores the fact that language is subject to our cultural background and differs from group to group. Thus, our language behaviors are also culturally diverse.

6.2.2 The Importance of Language to Intercultural Communication

Kenneth Burke calls **humans symbol-makers, symbol-users, and symbol-misusers** and **creators of the negative** as a unique human characteristic. Intercultural communication is a kind of interpersonal interaction between groups of people from different cultural backgrounds. During the process, language has played a highly significant role and frequently causes the breakdown of many intercultural encounters. Language includes the linguistics and nonverbal codes built upon the diverse cultural settings and systems, and it is of vital importance to successful intercultural interaction. As Prosser says: "Both the verbal linguistics and the nonverbal codes which we use in human communication are of considerable interest to the intercultural communicator and cross-cultural researcher" (1985: 89). In this chapter, we will discuss linguistics and nonverbal aspects in intercultural communication, both in ancient and modern views, and the role of English in China.

Just as culture and communication are complementary, **so too are language and culture inseparable**. It is hard to understand a language outside of its cultural context and it is equally hard to understand a culture without taking into account its language. Language is not only a set of neutral codes and symbols, but is also very connotative, and is regulated by different cultural settings, behaviors, and rituals. As Colin Cherry points out, "Man has endless uses of language, signs and ritual, significant of the fact that he is a member of a nation, or a class, or a tribe, or a race, of this or that group; but he has no common language, few signs, and virtually no universal ritual significant of the fact that he is a member of the human race" (1971: 3–7). Therefore, as many scholars have agreed, **language forms the basic identity of a people**. Ting-Toomey proposes that cultural orientations drive language usage in daily lives; she illustrates this with the following example: people in Germany and the United States, who have high individualism value orientations would more likely to use words and phrases such as "I," "me," "my goal," "I believe," "my opinion," "self-help," and "self-service" in their daily conversations, while people from China, Japan, and Korea who have a high collectivism orientation prefer to use the phrases such as "we," "our work team," "our goal," "our unit," "our future together," and "we as a group" (2007: 85). In fact, Confucius' *Analects* expressly identifies "love of one's kind" as a key aspect of culture, with special attention to "in-groups" versus "out-groups."

Since the world's more than 4,000 different languages have widely systems of the linguistic and nonverbal codes, even within the context of language systems such as the Indo-European language family, or the Chinese, Korean, and Japanese ideographic character system of language, **it often makes it rather difficult and complex for people from different cultures to understand one another and it even**

may cause serious misunderstanding and communication breakdowns in intercultural communication. In Genesis 11: 6–7 in the Biblical Old Testament, the unknown author had God claiming: "If as one people speaking the same language they have begun to do this, then nothing they plan to do will be impossible for them. Come, let us go down and confuse their language so they will not understand each other." It was known as "the tower of Babel" and we have the modern saying "a babel of languages."

Ting-Toomey further states that intercultural friction can easily occur when people catalog the different groups by using "outsiders" and "insiders," "strangers," "foreigners," and "hosts" classifications (2007: 85). She points out that "our primary identities such as cultural and ethnic identities are often expressed through the symbols and styles we use in our interactions with others" (2007: 84). Nevertheless, she also believes that it is possible for people to overcome the language barriers through mindful language usages, "While language and verbal communication can easily create misunderstandings, it also fortunately can clarify misunderstandings. Sensitive language usage is a pivotal vehicle in reflecting our mindful attitudes in communicating with dissimilar others" (2007: 85). Kenneth Burke argues that "communication is compensatory to division, and language becomes the essence of communication to induce humans toward cooperation … a new view of rhetoric is identification…. His concepts of symbolic linguistic and nonverbal communicative methods are important in the founding and maturation process of intercultural communication as a field of study or discipline." (Prosser, 2007: 48)

6.2.3 The Functions of Language and Transmitting Culture

Samovar and Porter believe that "language is significant because it is capable of performing labeling, interaction, and transmission functions" (2004: 139). They argue that the labeling function serves to identify or name a person, an object, or an act. The interaction function is concerned with the sharing and communication of ideas and emotions. The transmission function is the process by which we pass information to others (Samovar and Porter, 2004: 139). To be more specific, we say that language serves as the following main function: **language is a very significant element within the cultural system.** As we have discussed in Chapter One, an important characteristic of culture is that it can be passed down vertically from generation to generation and horizontally from one area to another area. During the process, **language acts as the main means of preserving history and transmitting culture vertically and horizontally.** Crystal underscores the function: "is an essential domain of language because the material guarantees the knowledge-base of subsequent generations, which is a prerequisite of social development of culture" (1997: 10).

6.2.4 Communicative Interaction

Language serves one of the fundamental forms of communicative interaction. As Drew indicates: "It is largely through conversation that we are socialized, through which institutional organizations such as the economy and the polity are managed, and through which we manage our ordinary social lives" (2005: 74). Bonvillain further emphasizes language's communal function by pointing out that **language is the primary means of interactions between people.** Speakers use language to convey their thoughts, feelings, intentions and desires to others. **Language links interlocutors in a dynamic, reflective process.** We learn about people through what they say and how they say it; we learn about ourselves through the ways the other people react to what we say; and we learn about our relationships with others through the give and take of communicative interactions (2003: 1).

6.2.5 Language as an Expression of Identity

Much of our identity is reflected in our language. As Samovar and Porter argue, **language is the major mechanism through which our culturally individual and group identities are constructed** (2009: 168); Language functions to express and maintain people's group, social, ethnic, gender, national and cultural identities. For instance, in terms of these identities, Edwards believes that language holds the role of maintaining national or cultural identity, and he regards language as "a core symbol" as well as "a rallying point" of

expressing ethnic and nationalist sentiment (1985: 15). The famous French writer Daudet in his short story *The Last Class* expresses a similar view by stating, "When a people falls into servitude, so long as it clings to its language, it is as if it held the key to its prison." **Like nationalism and religion, language can be an exceptional cultural unifier as well as a castrostrophic divider,** and many cultures have broken apart because of language and linguistic policies, for example, Belgium with a French language community in the south and a Flemish language community in the North.

6.2.6 Meaning, Thought and Culture

Words are the basic units of sentences, and **sentences, particularly in Western cultures, are the basis of language.** Thus, understanding the meanings of words is therefore crucial in verbal communication. **Lexical meaning can largely be classified into two types: denotational and connotational meanings. Denotational meaning is the conceptual, definitional meaning of the words.** However, **the connotational meaning refers to the extended meaning in which some implied associations that a word or phrase might suggest.** Thus the denotative meaning of the word "mother" is "the female parent," and its connotative meaning is the associations we usually have with the word "maternal love," "care," "nurturing," and "tenderness." So we can have the simile "the young teacher is like a mother to the children." **The meaning of words is personal as well as cultural and meaning resides in the mind.** Each individual has his or her own sphere of experience, and his or her connotations of certain words may well be based on his unique experience with the referent. The word "sea" may suggest very different emotional and perceptual meanings to someone who has lived on the seaside all his or her life and less emotionally to one that has only seen the sea by traveling or in the media. **Meanings are also culture specific.** Since people of the same culture share a lot in the physical environment, customs, traditions and other cultural heritage, they tend to have the same or similar understandings of what a word means and associative meanings derived from it. People from the Arctic area, East Asia and South Africa would have a different understanding of the word "snow" as the Sapir-Whorf hypothesis suggests. The children from India or in much of the West can never imagine the taste of "moon cakes" or "jiaozi" and the feeling of warmth and reunion they can bring to the Chinese, young and old. Therefore, each culture creates certain vocabulary to describe its unique physical and social environment as well as the activities its people engage in from those contexts. This can explain the phenomenon that in some cultures, some vocabularies may be absent. For example, words like "炕," (pronounced as "Kang", a heatable brick bed in North China), "节气," (pronounced as "Jie qi", solar term), "经络," ,"(pronounced as "Jing luo", main and collateral channels), and "玉皇大帝", ,"(pronounced as "Yu huang da di", the Jade Emperor and the Supreme Deity of Taoism), can only make sense to the Chinese but it would make people from other cultures feel confused; consequently, words like "privacy," "Thanksgiving Day," "the house of representatives," and "motel" are more familiar terms to the western people, particularly in North America.

In addition to the absence of equivalents in denoting certain referents between different cultures, **cultures also overlap in the denotation of certain vocabulary.** For instance, the English connotation of some kinship terms such as "uncle," "aunt," "sister" or "brother" can hardly cover the complex relations reflected in Chinese kinship vocabularies. Without mentioning the exact reference of the terms being used, these words cannot be translated into proper Chinese at all, since it is always necessary in Chinese to make a clear distinction about the relationships of the relative to the persons being concerned. Whether the relative is from one's mother's side or one's father's side, or whether he or she is younger or older than one's parents or oneself, all influence the exact term the Chinese uses in addressing him. What's more, **there are some words with the same denotations but different connotations in different cultures.** A typical example is the meaning of "dog." Although nowadays dogs have been kept as pets by more and more Chinese people, and often have the connotation "you are a lucky dog," however, dogs in Chinese language have some negative connotations and are used in a derogatory way. During the Beijing Olympics, Beijing restaurants were required to remove "the magnificent meat" from their menus so as not to offend western visitors. Unlike Chinese, in English, "dog" has the positive connotations of luck, faithfulness, and "man's best friend." Thus, there appear expressions like "A man has his hour, and a dog has his day," and "love me, love my dog."

6.2.7 Taoism's and Confucianism's Interpretations of Language

According to Taoism's and Confucianism's interpretations of language, the power of the words was quite limited, and truth was not found within the words or speech. "Dao" is a crucial concept in Lao Tzu's *Dao De Jing*; it provides the basic principle for the universe, and Lao Tzu believed that the real "Dao" could not be expressed in words by stating "The Dao that can be told is not the eternal Dao; the name that can be named is not the eternal name." He further illustrated the intrinsic connotation of "Dao" from the following famous metaphors: "The loudest sound can't be heard, the largest form can't be seen, and the Dao is invisible and nameless, only the Dao excels at creating the myriad things and bringing them to maturity." In a word, in Lao Tzu's interpretation, "Dao" represents the fundamental force in the universe, yet it operates silently and namelessly in the universe which denies any verbal explanation." Based on the interpretation of the universe, both Lao Tzu and Chuang Tzu deprecated outward expression and speech. As Jensen (1987) points out: "Eloquence, and even speaking in general, is deprecated and is associated with highly negative connotations. Eloquence is spoken of as glibness, quickness of speech, noise making and clap-trap, and is identified with shallowness, superficiality, untrustworthy cleverness, pretentiousness, pride, hypocrisy, and flattery" (1987 : 219–229).

When Confucius was asked: "If you were to administer a country, what would be your first measure?" Confucius answered: "It certainly would be to correct language" (*The Analects*, Book XIII). Confucius shared the same view by expressing his dislike of the people "speaking flattering words." Confucius also gave some advice on how to behave properly in one's life by stressing the prudent use of words in suitable occasions and avoid talking too much: "A gentleman, when things he doesn't understand are mentioned, should maintain an attitude of reserve. If language is incorrect, then what is said does not concord with what was meant, what is to be done cannot be effected."

6.2.8 A Review of Some Theories on Language and Culture

6.2.8.1 Sapir-Whorf Hypothesis

In terms of thought and culture, we can see that language is more than just a means of communication, it influences our culture and even our thought processes. As the Sapir-Whorf hypothesis has suggested, as language is one of the important components of culture, **it always influences how people perceive their reality as well as their categories or patterns of thought**. Sapir's hypothesis can be summarized: "Language is a self-contained, creative, sym-bolic organization, which not only refers to experiences largely acquired without its help but actually defines experience for us both by its structure and by our unconscious acceptance of the language's ability to influence all of our experience by shaping symbolic meanings for us…. Language is a guide to social reality…. Our reality is determined by our own language" (Prosser, 1985: 101). Although the Sapir-Whorf hypothesis which places language in such an important position remains controversial, it has revealed the fact that language has played a very important role in influencing our culture and thought processes. As Crystal underscores: "There is the closest of relationships between language and thought…. Language may not determine the way we think, but it does influence the way we perceive and remember, and it affects the ease with which we perform mental tasks" (1997: 10). Therefore, if we can consider that **there is a close relation between language and patterns of thought where our experience shapes our language which shapes our perceptions**, then the following is a good instance. For example, in English it is necessary to mark the verb to indicate the time of occurrence of an event one is speaking about: "It's raining; It rained; it will rain." While in Chinese, it is totally another picture. The Chinese verb does not have any tenses at all. It only uses the specific time referents such as yesterday, today or tomorrow to indicate the time of occurrence of an event. Sometimes even the time referent has been omitted. For instance, in the Chinese expression "下雨了" ("It's raining" or "It rained" in English), there is no subject "It" as in English, no verb tense alterations. It can mean either "It's raining now" or "It rained yesterday" but in English, it depends on the different situations about which the speaker is speaking. From this example, we can see that the Chinese ways of thinking appear to be more holistic and make little use of formal logic, and seem to be more sensitive to the environment context, while Westerners are more likely to make differentiations, and pay more attention to the proper use of rules and formal logic.

The Sapir-Whorf Hypothesis is also called linguistic determinism, and **linguistic determinism is the assumption that a person's view of reality stems mainly from his or her language**. Even though two languages may be similar, they can't represent the same social reality; the worlds of the people who speak the two languages are different. So even though languages often do have equivalencies in other language, the social reality can't be fully conveyed to a person who does not speak the language. For example, in Hopi, the language of an Indian tribe in North America, they don't make distinction between an airplane, a dragonfly, or a pilot. They just use one word for anything that flies. It seems absurd to us, but it is quite natural to them. Similarily in Chinese, there is no clear gender distinction, which leads many who speak or write in English to confuse "he" and "she."

6.2.8.2 Basil Bernstein's Interpretation

The Bernstein hypothesis explains how social structure affects language and is an extension of the Sapir-Whorf Hypothesis. Bernstein considers culture, subculture, social context, and social system to be part of social structure. According to the Bernstein Hypothesis, **speech emerges in one of two restricted and elaborated codes. Restricted codes include highly predictable messages** for those who share a common interest or experience and know one another quite well. Because of this shared experience and identity, elaborating on the verbal message is unnecessary. We may, for example find that our best friend sometimes finishes our sentences or knows what we are going to say before we finish speaking because of shared experiences. The restricted codes are quite similar to the high context messages articulated by Edward T. Hall. **Elaborated codes are more direct and low context**, favored by Western societies and are used with strangers; **they involve messages that are low in predictability**. We would need to give very explicit information to ensure that the message is understood. **The verbal channel is important in elaborated codes, while restricted codes make more use of nonverbal and paralinguistic clues.** Jia and Jia (2007: 138–140) indicate that "Differences in the speech behavior of requests between Chinese and American cultures lie in the semantic sequence or order of the components that make up a request…. The indirect style in the Chinese culture and the direct style in the American culture may differ in the extent to which the communicators reveal their intention through the implicitness or explicitness of their content messages…. The implicit request is often used in the Chinese culture between people who are friends and acquaintances, or at least, who have had a personal contact with each other for a long time." Hall gives a personal example of the difference between implicit and explicit language and meanings. He was in a Japanese hotel where shoes placed outside the door at night are shined and ready the next morning. Not thinking to give explicit directions, Hall found that the shoe shiner had shined his brown shoes black.

6.2.8.3 Noam Chomsky's Transformational or Generative Grammar

Chomsky argues in discussing transformational or generative grammar that **all natural languages have universally similar grammatical systems**, which in a practical way we can at least apply broadly to the Indo-European language family, with its romance and Germanic languages, or with the ideographic characters in Chinese, Korean and Japanese, as examples. He notes that there are two main problems to consider: in the descriptive study of a language, **the primary concern is to discover simple and revealing grammars**, and also to **develop a general theory of language structures cross-culturally**. For example, if an individual language has an oral usage, but no written expression, such as in a number of the African languages until almost the last half century, by applying general theories related to other African languages, we can establish the written language. In contrast, the Irish Gaelic language had lost its oral usage, but still existed in writing. Thus, an oral language was developed from the written form. **Descriptive grammar simply describes "what exists" in particular languages, while prescriptive grammar recommends "what should exist."** Joseph DeVito (1970: 45–46) defines language in this context (as opposed to language in general) as an infinite set of grammatical sentences and defines grammar as the device for specifying or describing this infinite set of sentences. He distinguishes between **linguistic competence** and **prescriptive rules** for the use of grammar and language, and argues that **it is more profitable to understand what linguistic competence is in a particular language than to worry so much about prescribing rules.** For many years, this was a specific problem in teaching Chinese learners English. The Chinese learners understood the English grammar and had a sizable vocabulary, but could not carry on competent communication in English. In the US, where by 2020 40% of the population will be speaking Spanish, students are now beginning to learn Spanish early, with the grammar and vocabulary, but are unable to communicate competently, or to have intercultural communication competence as we have discussed in Chapter Two. To sum up the concept of generative or transformational grammar briefly, **the theory argues that there are linguistic universals**, just as there are cultural universals, and by knowing correct and incorrect grammar usage within at least one language family, one can then establish a new grammar and lexicon (vocabulary) in other languages which either have no oral or written language by applying consistent grammar and vocabulary rules from a similar language, at least in the same language families.

A Scotchman Is Playing Bagpipe in Edinburgh Castle

6.3 Intercultural Nonverbal Communication

6.3.1 Defining Nonverbal Communication

In the early 1920s, *Physics and Character* was published, and perhaps was the first book on nonverbal communication. In 1952, *Introduction to Kinesics* was published, which is regarded as a classic book on nonverbal communication. In 1959, Edward Hall published his famous book *The Silent Language*, and later his equally famous 1966 book, *The Hidden Dimension* (relating to proxemics or the use of space). Other early important books on nonverbal communication include: Ralph Eisenberg and Ralph Smith's 1971 *Nonverbal Communication*; Ashley Montague's 1971 *Touching: The Human Significance of the Skin*; Mark Knapp's 1972 *Nonverbal Communication in Human Interaction* (which has been republished with coauthor Mary A. Hall also in 2009). More recent books include: Paul Ekman and Wallace V. Friesen's 2003 *Unmasking the Face: A Guide to Recognizing Emotions from Facial Expressions*; Carol K. Goman's 2008 *The Nonverbal Advantage: Secrets and Science of Body Language at Work*; Judee K. Burgoon, Laura K. Guerreo, and Kory Floyd's 2009 *Nonverbal Communication*; and Janet

Verbal and Nonverbal Communication

A Busker in Amsterdam, Netherlands

The relationship of man to his extensions is simply a continuation and a specialized form of the relationship of organisms in general to their environment (1966: 188–189). **"Nonverbal communication cannot be seen out of the context of its primary linkages with language"** (Prosser, 1985). Eisenberg and Smith argue that verbal expressions are self-reflexive, meaning that all languages can be used to analyze languages, but that nonverbal acts are less likely to be self-reflexive and therefore are substantively different than linguistic symbols (1971: 21). Samovar and Porter propose that "nonverbal communication involves all the nonverbal communication setting that is generated by both the source and his or her use of the environment and that has potential message value for the source or receiver" (2004: 169).

6.3.2 The Importance of Nonverbal Communication

Nonverbal communication is an important sphere in intercultural communication. Some researchers estimate that 70% of the information is transmitted through nonverbal means. Barnlund underscores the importance of nonverbal communication by expressing the following statement: Many, and sometimes most, of the critical meanings generated in human encounters are elicited by touch, glance, vocal nuance, gestures, or facial expression with or without the aid of words. From the moment of recognition until the moment of separation, people observe each other with all their senses, hearing pauses and intonations, attending to dress and carriage, observing glance and facial

Driver and Mauska van Aaist's 2010 *You Say More than You Think: Use the New Body.* All these books have laid foundations for nonverbal communication. When we consider nonverbal communication, however, we have to recognize that often these generalizations can be stereotypical, without any solid research to prove the concepts or examples being provided.

Hall thought highly of nonverbal communication, and referred it to "metacommunication," "paralinguistics," "second-order message," "the silent language," and "the hidden dimension of communication." In *The Hidden Dimension*, Hall states that "people cannot act or interact at all in any meaningful way except through the medium of culture. Man and his extensions constitute one interrelated system…

tension, as well as noting word choice and syntax. Every harmony or disharmony of signals guides the interpretation of passing moods or enduring attributes. Out of the evaluation of kinetics, vocal and verbal cues, decisions are made to argue or agree, to laugh or blush, to relax or resist, to continue or cut off conversations (1968: 536–537).

Therefore, **nonverbal communication is important because people use the message system to make observations, judgments and evaluations**. Furthermore, people also use the nonverbal communication system to express attitudes and emotions to create and manage impressions. As Samovar and Porter state: "If you observe someone with a clenched fist and grim expression, we do not need words to tell us that this person is not happy. If you hear someone's voice quaver, and see his or her hands tremble, you may infer that the person is fearful or anxious, despite what he or she might say. Your emotions are reflected in your posture, face and eyes—be it fear, joy, anger, or sadness—so you can express them without even uttering a word" (2004: 168).

The Belgium Student Is Performing the Chinese Dance

6.3.3 Nonverbal Communication Classifications

Samovar and Porter divide nonverbal messages into two comprehensive categories: those that are primarily produced by body (appearance, movement, facial expression, eye contact, touch, smell, and paralanguage); and those that the individual combines with the setting (space, time, and silence) (2004: 173) . Ruesch and Kees (1956) classify nonverbal communication into sign language (gestures), action language (all movements that are not used exclusively as signals), and object language (all intentional and nonintentional display of material things and the human body, clothing or tattoos).

6.3.3.1 Body movement

Body movement is not confined to hand or arm gestures. It covers a much larger area, referring to any little movement of any part of the body. Here we will discuss the commonly used body movements, such as posture, gesture, facial expression, and touch.

6.3.3.2 Posture

Posture is the way people hold their bodies when they sit, stand or walk, and it can send positive or negative nonverbal messages. As Chaney and Martin believe, "Posture can convey self-confidence, status and interest" (2002: 118). Based on Julius Fast's research (1971), they illustrate that "Confident people generally have a relaxed posture, yet stand

Verbal and Nonverbal Communication

erect, and walk with assurance. Walking with stooped shoulders and a slow, hesitating gait projects such negative messages as lack of assurance and confidence. Walking rapidly and swinging the arms indicates that the person is goal-oriented. A preoccupied walk, with hands clasped behind and head lowered, is thoughtful. Men who walk with hands on hips convey the message of wanting to get to their destination as quickly as possible. The posture of persons of higher status is usually more relaxed than that of their subordinates. Interest is demonstrated by leaning forward toward the person you are conversing with, while sitting back communicates a lack of interest. The posture of people in the United States tends to be casual; they sit in a relaxed manner and may slouch when they stand. This behavior in Germany would often be considered rude" (2002: 118). Fast further points out that "Posture when seated also varies with the culture. Many people in the United States often cross their legs while seated, women cross at the ankle and men cross with ankle on the knee. Crossing the leg with ankle on the knee would be considered inappropriate by most people in the Middle East. In the Arabic world, correct posture while seated is important; one should avoid showing the sole of his shoe or pointing his foot at someone as the lowest part of the body is considered unclean" (2002: 119). There is the famous example of a journalist throwing a shoe at President George W. Bush in Baghdad at a press conference, intended as a very strong nonverbal sign of disrespect. Later, when there were demonstrations in Egypt against President Hosni Mubarak, the disrespectful gesture expanded with many people throwing their shoes at his portrait.

6.3.3.3 Gesture

Gestures are another important aspect of body languages. Some gestures are more widely used. Here are some examples of types of gestures that an international business person is likely to come across. Hand gestures include the "thumb-up sign" which often means good or great. In some countries, it is also used for hitch-hiking, asking for a free ride. These gesture signals are approved in China, the USA, Russia, and Britain and many other countries. But in the Persian culture, it is highly offensive. However, the "thumb down," originally used by the crowds in the Roman coliseum during gladiator contests, and now popular in North America and other cultures, shows disapproval. In Greece it is still considered a rude sign and is often used by motorists to signal their anger over someone's crazy driving. The "V-sign," originally used by Winston Churchill in World War II, remains a signal for victory in many countries. People taking photos with other friends often use this sign behind their friends' backs as a humorous gesture. It also signals the number "two" in China and Bulgaria. But in England and South Africa, it has a rude connotation when used with the palm in.

Gestural head movements often indicate that in most cultures nodding one's head as a gesture is seen as agreeing and shaking one's head is seen as rejecting. But head movements convey "yes" or "no" in different cultures. In Bulgaria, for example, people may nod their heads to signify "no" and shake their heads to signify "yes," Gestural arm movements take up space and thereby enlarge the size of the speaker. A speaker who uses big arm movements can intimidate the listeners and appear more

A Smile Is the Most Inviting of All Gestures

powerful. In most cultures men tend to use larger gestures than women. Desmond Morris's famous European study on male gestures demonstrated that the closer the middle aged men in the study lived to the Mediterranean, they were far more likely to use huge gestures, often with obscene intentions, while those from Scandinavia often used much smaller gestures and without much intention for obscenity. For instance, also, when a businessman from the United States wants to emphasize a point in a discussion, he may very occasionally pound his fist on the table and underline his statements with staccato-like drumming on the table. Hopefully, as executives become more culturally sensitive, this disrespectful gesture is diminishing. President Obama often points his right index finger in a professorial manner to punctuate his persuasive messages. Businesswomen in the United States in the same situation typically use far fewer arm and hand movements. However, the Japanese use still far fewer arm movements than Americans. Arabian and Latin American men use their arms expressively even more than men from the United States and English speaking Canadians.

However, those from the romance language cultures tend to use their gestures more broadly than those from the germanic language cultures.

6.3.3.4 Facial Expressions

We usually use facial expression to express our emotions, often unintentionally. In many countries, when people are surprised, they may open their eyes wide and open their mouth. When they like something, their eyes may beam, or raise up, and they may smile. When they are angry, they may frown and narrow their eyes and brows. Often when people find a statement unbelievable, they may roll their eyes and lift their brows. Smiling occurs in all countries at times; however, the meaning of a smile may vary in an attempt to appear open and friendly. People in the United States and Africans tend to smile a lot. To the people of other countries, the American smile often appears insincere and frozen. McDonalds had a hard time early teaching employees in Moscow the importance of the smile and the proper type of "McDonalds' smile." Germans smile, but not nearly as much as people in the United States, sometimes recognizing earlier that "life is severe and there is very little to smile about." The East Asian smile can be used to mask an emotion, or to avoid answering a question, or even to hide embarrassment and to save "face." For example, when one's husband has just died, the widow might smile to cover her sadness. Actually, in Japan, Korea, and China, one doesn't so freely show his or her feeling, hiding emotions.

The expression of showing anger also varies from culture to culture. In addition, cultural varieties often indicate who can show anger. It is a power concept. Old people, men, and people in authority may show anger on their faces and by their bodily gestures more readily than younger people, women, and subordinates. One of the milder forms of showing anger in western cultures is frowning and knitting one's brows. In countries like Japan, Korea, and China where the open expression of one's feeling is not as appreciated, frowning may be much more subdued.

Another way of showing anger is shouting and making gestures. Germans, some Canadians, Arabs, and Latin Americans often raise their voices when angry. The Japanese, Chinese, and Koreans seldom raise their voices when angry. However, street arguments in China can often become very intense, with the women shouting, pushing, and shoving as much as the men who are involved.

6.3.3.5 Eye Contact

We often say that the eyes are the window of the soul. So, eye contact is an important aspect of nonverbal communication. All cultures have their unique rules governing their eye contacts. In North America and northern European cultures, eye contact is considered to show openness, trustworthiness, and integrity since one doesn't have anything to hide. However, the eye contact is not steady; it is maintained for a second or two, and then moved away quickly. One is not supposed to look at one's eyes for too long. Staring at someone while talking is not considered polite. Hispanic children in American schools tend to lower their eyes when talking to the Anglo teacher, while the teacher

may insist that the children look them in the eyes. Two different cultural learned patterns are at work in that case.

In China, Japan, and Korea, people generally believe that sustained and direct eye contact would be a sign of bad manners and impoliteness and they tend to look at someone's nose or mouth instead of directly into his or her eyes. The Japanese may sit close together in an office, but they seldom look at each other in the eyes. The Arab culture, even more than western cultures, uses very intense eye contact and concentrate on the eye movement to read real intentions. Often, all five senses are united in active nonverbal behavior. Additionally, such cultures that are more high-context tend to stand close to feel the other's breath.

6.3.3.6 Touch and Tactility

According to Chaney and Martin, touch and tactility "refer to communicating through the use of bodily contact. When used properly, touch can create feelings of warmth and thrust; when used improperly, touch can betray trust and cause annoyance" (2002: 113). Axtell (1998) has classified the following cultures as "touch" and "don't touch." Based on Axtell's study, Chaney and Martin illustrate, "In touch-oriented cultures such as those of much of Africa, Italy, Greece, Spain and Portugal, both males and females may be seen walking along the street holding hands or arm-in-arm" (2002: 113). Latin American, many African, and Middle Eastern males will stand close to a male colleague and even hold him by the lapel or shoulder. In the Middle East and Northern Africa, as well as in India or Pakistan, one would avoid touching the person with the left hand because it is considered unclean and reserved for personal hygiene. Food is eaten or shared with the right hand. In other countries, such as in the United States, intimate touching between men may be considered as an indication of homosexuality. However, in sports in the US and other cultures, there is a great deal of intimate touching, especially when a goal has been achieved, which is considered acceptable. In China, Japan, and Korea, young boys and men often have their arms around others' shoulders, and girls and women walk arm in arm. Hugging is becoming more and more popular in many cultures throughout the world. The "high five" handshake is increasingly popular. Kissing as friends is very common in many cultures, including Latin American, Arab, and southern European cultures, often with the double cheek kiss or two kisses on the left cheek and one on the right cheek. In the American south, it is very common for people to brush a woman's cheek as a simulated kiss of greeting. Even interculturally, close friends often provide each other a cheek kiss when they meet or depart.

People from various cultures have very different attitudes toward body odors. "Most people of the United States respond negatively to what they consider bad odors such as body odor, breath odor or clothes that emit unpleasant aromas such as perspiration. They place great importance on personal hygiene and consider it normal for people to remove body odors by bathing, or showering daily and by brushing teeth to remove mouth odors" (Chaney&Martin,2002: 112). As many people are becoming upset about tobacco odors, often there are subtle facial negative gestures aimed at the smokers. However, as Chaney and Martin point out, "Other cultures have quite different concepts of natural odors; they consider them as normal and think attitudes of people in the United States are unnatural. Arabs are quite comfortable with natural odors and typically breathe on people when they talk" (2002: 112). In Japan, the Philippines, Samoa, smells also play an important role. Of course, they do also in every culture, but their impact varies from culture to culture. Often all five senses are at play nonverbally: sight, sound, smell, taste, and touch.

6.3.3.7 Paralanguage

Paralanguage involves both the linguistic and nonverbal aspects of oral communication, how something is said and not the actual meaning of the spoken words, such as volume of voice, laughing and giggling, or markers of paying attention to someone else ("uh huh, mmm, ah, er, eh, oooo! ai"). Internet usage internationally has many nonverbal markers to display emotion, such as smiley faces. Often Arabs speak with a greater volume and regard it as strength and sincerity, while Thai people perceive "a loud voice" as impolite and Japanese people believe that a gentle and soft voice reflects good manners and helps maintain social harmony. In terms of laughing and giggling, Americans often interpret laughing and giggling as expressions of enjoyment and they are the signs to show that people are relaxed and having a good time, while Southeast Asians may regard the same behavior as a sign of extreme embarrassment or discomfort. Typing all in capital letters on the Internet is seen usually as an emotional expression of anger.

6.3.3.8 Silence as a Nonverbal Factor

Silence is an important topic which can be perceived either in a positive or a negative approach. As Bruneau (2009) has expounded: "for thousands of years, wise people have commented on the virtues and negativities of silence. There have been hundreds of quotations, sayings, and maxims about silence for thousands of years in Western groupings. For example: around 280 BC we find Epicuris the Stoic saying that, God gave people two ears, but only one mouth, that they may hear twice as much as they speak; around 53 BC, we find Cicero, the Roman statesman/orator, commenting that there is an eloquence of silence to be found in conversations; and, around 42 B.C., we find Publius Syrus noting that a person who does not know when to speak does not know when to be silent." Here Bruneau states how silence is perceived in the western tradition, though the western world has a long history of valuing speech and rhetoric from the ancient Greek period, the virtues of silence are also greatly accentuated. When an important person has died, or various people have died tragically, there is often announced "a moment of silence."

6.3.3.9 A General Survey of Silence in Different Cultures

It is generally acknowledged that it is in the Eastern tradition that silence is interpreted as a positive issue. For instance, the Japanese view of silence can be observed from the following proverbs: "It is the duck that squawks that gets shot," "A flower does not speak" and "The mouth is to eat not to speak with." Thus in Japanese culture, silence is highly preferred while talking is regarded as a negative issue. As Jawoeski (2006) notes: "Reticent individuals are trusted as honest, sincere, and straightforward. Thus silence is an active state, while speech is an excuse for delaying activity." Buddhism also holds a negative attitude towards speech by stressing "What real is, and when it is spoken it becomes unreal." It is the same case with Hinduism, and it holds the view that "self-realization, salvation, wisdom, peace, and bliss are all achieved in a state of meditation and introspection when the individual is communicating with himself or herself in silence" (Jain and Matukumalli, 1993). Therefore, Hinduism stresses self-realization rather than outward expression and regards that the inner peace and wisdom can only be obtained through silence. As the famous Indian leader Chief Joseph states: "It does not require many words to speak the truth."

Nevertheless, in some other cultures, talk instead of silence is greatly valued. A famous Greek idiom says "Nothing done with silence is done without speech;" obviously it emphasizes the importance of talk as a means of communication. A similar Arabic saying is "A man's tongue is his sword." With this saying, a man's tongue is compared to his sword, and the Arabs are taught to value words, to use them as a powerful tool. Mexican culture also enjoys the value of conversation, there is a famous Mexican idiom: "Conversation is the food for the soul." From the Mexican proverb we see their preference for talking, in Mexican people's daily lives they value talking with their friends and the family, and it has been one part of their tradition.

Many scholars think that silence is not interpreted as a meaningful part of life in the dominant American culture, "numerous studies have pointed out that most Americans believe that talking is an important activity and actually enjoy talking." (Wisemann, Chen, and Giles,1986) Most people in the United States spend their spare time talking, watching TV, listening to the radio and taking part in other sound-producing activities in order to keep them from silence; thus, American people prefer talking to silence in most cases, as Bruneau (1997) notes, "Many people especially in some Asian societies, feel that Americans talk too much, clarifying and explaining and trying to make their meanings more and more certain. But, such talk often happens because these Americans feel that it is only through talk that meanings are conveyed and silences do not imply communication for them." Althen offers a similar remark of American people's preference with language in the statement: "Americans depend more on spoken words than on nonverbal behavior to convey messages. They think it is important to 'speak up' and 'say what is on their mind.' They admire a person who has a moderately large vocabulary and who can express herself clearly and shrewdly." Therefore, in the dominant American culture, talk is often regarded as a positive attitude and manner. While silence is interpreted as a negative issue, to most American people, silence means lack of attention and lack of initiative. Jandt (2004: 138) even thinks that "To most people in the United States, silence can mean one is fearful of

communicating" and he further uses the term "communication apprehension" to refer to "an individual's fear or anxiety associated with either real or anticipated communication with another person or persons."

From the general survey of the different perceptions of silence and talk in various cultures mentioned above, here we notice there are two different views towards the virtues and negativities of silence. One view holds the belief that silence is a positive issue which possesses the rich connotations of credibility, thoughtfulness, meditation and truth. While another view regards talk as a powerful part of life and perceive silence as a negative element. Then, what is the case in traditional Chinese culture?

6.3.3.10 Perception of Silence in Chinese Traditional Culture

Generally speaking, in traditional Chinese culture, silence is often perceived as a positive issue while talk is deprecated. In Lao Tzu's interpretation of the beginning of the universe, "There was something formless yet complete, / That existed before the creation of heaven and earth. / Without sound, without substance, / Dependent on nothing, unchanging, / All pervading, unfailing. / One may think of it as the mother of all things under heaven. / Its true name we do not know; 'way' is the by-name that I give it." (Lao Tzu, 1999: 53) "Way" is the equivalent word of "Dao" discussed above, which is interpreted as "invisible," "inaudible" and "intangible" by Lao Tzu .

This traditional Chinese philosophy has exerted a far-reaching influence on Chinese traditional arts, such as Chinese painting and ancient poems. For instance, the Chinese "landscape painting" lays great emphasis on the empty space which provides the readers with much room for contemplation, and the Chinese poems contain rich and profound connotations beyond the words. The Chinese traditional culture also affects the Chinese people's thoughts and behaviors. The saying "Silence is gold" is still very popular in Chinese people's minds and offers a guidance in their daily life.

In short, in traditional Chinese culture, silence has been endowed with positive connotations of thoughtfulness, productivity and profoundness.

However, with the passage of time, Chinese people's interpretation of silence has changed a lot. Verbal communication has been attached greater importance in Chinese contemporary culture, while silence is not necessarily perceived as a positive issue among Chinese people, especially among Chinese young people.

6.4   The Role of English in Chinese Education

6.4.1   Chinese Children and Youth Learning English

Chinese children in the strongest schools in China often begin to learn English at about the third grade level. In the increasing number of foreign language primary and middle schools, they are often learning simple English as early as kindergarten. Many Chinese kindergarten children can recite the ABCs, count to 100 in English, and know the days of the week and sometimes also the months in English. If Chinese children do not begin learning English earlier in rural areas or smaller cities, at least by the age of about twelve they will have begun the process of learning it. Many of the 350,000,000 Chinese learning English (more than the total populations of the United States, Canada, Australia, and New Zealand), most as students at various levels may just be marginally competent. Fortunately, they

only have to begin by learning a romanized alphabet of 24–26 characters, a little more than a dozen punctuation marks, and how to count reasonably in Arabic numbers.

Typically, when students enter the university, they often shift to American English, perhaps because many of their foreign teachers, and the foreign teachers of their teachers, have been Americans. For example, at the Beijing Language and Culture University, there are usually nine to ten native speaking foreign teachers in the English Department, most of whom are Americans, teaching a wide range of subjects to the Chinese English majors. Additionally, among the 1,500 foreign students coming to learn Chinese at BLCU (the largest number of international students in the world), many are Americans and thus constantly are modeling for the 4,000 Chinese students enrolled there. One hundred thousand foreign teachers are hired annually in China, most of whom teach English. Gregory Mavides and Ken Hayes provide an excellent and lengthy "Foreign Teachers' Guide to Living and Working in China," focusing especially on the opportunities and problems affecting English teachers at both the secondary and tertiary levels (2007).

Every Chinese college and university has an English department or college, and usually the English major represents the largest institutional major even if the college or university is a science or technology college. At Shanghai International Studies University, for instance, there are now twelve classes of undergraduate students each with 30 students at the freshman and sophomore grade levels in the College of English. SISU's College of International Education has still more English majors who become teachers of English after graduation. Often, the women's English proficiency as beginning undergraduates was stronger than that of the men. In contrast, in scientific, engineering and technology colleges and universities, the men students are likely to surpass the women students by the same ratio, and conversely, their English tends to be at a lower level than that of the women. All Chinese applicants for China's university admission or postgraduate programs must pass at least a written exam in English.

6.4.2 English Language Companies and Tests

Besides pupils and students studying English who are enrolled in all levels of formal education, companies teaching English in China are among its most prosperous educational businesses. The New Oriental School (New Oriental Education and Technology Group), the largest private education company in China, founded by Michael Yu in 1993 is a primary example. Before the end of 2009, 7 million students were enrolled, including 1.5 million in 2009, with 270 learning centers, including 48 schools, 23 New Oriental bookstores, plus 5,000 third party book stores, and approximately 5,200 teachers in 40 cities, and an online network of 5 million registered users. Nearly 100,000 copies of *New Oriental Magazine* are sold monthly (www.NewOrientalSchool.com, 2010).

World-wide, 1.2 million take the IELTS (International English Language Test System) annually, which is accepted in 6,000 secondary and tertiary institutions in most countries, but less often in the United States colleges and universities. In China there are 9 centers in the East, 15 in the North and central areas, 8 in south China, and 5 in the southwest. Cambridge English provides ESOL (English as a Second Language) certificates for learners and teachers at various educational levels, with 6 centers in China: 3 in Beijing, 2 in Shanghai, and 1 in Shi Jiazhuang. Various other English exams are available in different parts of China, for example, the Cambridge TOEFL (Test of English as a Foreign Language) which is the usual standard for American colleges and universities and is accepted by some Canadian universities. The Cambridge English language tests also include the SAT (Standard Admissions Test) for admission to colleges and universities in the US, GRE (Graduate Required Exam), GMAT (Graduate MBA programs), TOEIC (Test of English for International Communication), MCAT (Medical College

Admission Test) which is computer based for Canada and the US, and Grammar (www. cambridgeenglish.com).

6.4.3   English and Bilingual Teaching Reforms in Chinese Higher Education

China's former Minister of Education, Zhou Ji, has identified three major proposals for the reform in the teaching of English, noting that "The Ministry of Education and the universities have always attached great importance to the teaching of English to enable Chinese students to communicate in the language and develop a global vision" (Zhou Ji, 2006: 95–96). Thus, the Ministry has provided three major proposals:

First, *the Ministry of Education has set new basic requirements for teaching English, with practicality and the students' comprehensive ability to use the language as the guideline. According to the new requirements, the teaching of English should shift its focus on reading to comprehension, and the traditional curriculum should be reformed to give universities autonomy and space for development.*

The second proposal *is to establish a campus-based English teaching network. The traditional reading mode of a blackboard, a piece of chalk and a textbook should be replaced by modern education technology to improve the students' self-learning ability.*

The third proposal *is to develop a new evaluation system to assess the teaching*

of English in colleges at different levels, from different angles, and during different processes. For example, evaluation should be the students' learning process as well as their final examination. The teachers' work should be evaluated with reference to the students' progress. The Band Four and Band Six college English tests should also be further reformed to help students improve their ability to use the language. (Zhou Ji, 2006: 96).

All college and university students in China must take and pass the CET-4 band test in English, usually in their second year of study. Many others take the CET-6 band test to provide themselves this credential for later study or employment, especially for international trade companies, most of which require a written test and often an oral English test before candidates are employed. Among the large number of texts preparing students to take either the CET-4 or -6 exams, typically on a formulaic framework (title, topic sentence or paragraph, a main paragraph with pros and cons on the topic, a final summary paragraph, expressions of one's own views or most likely solutions to a stated problem. Zhou Ji also noted the Chinese Ministry of Education's 2001 reforms in bilingual education among China's colleges and universities which were intended to actively promote the use of English and some other foreign languages in the teaching of such fields as biotechnology, information technology, law, and finance and other specialty courses for undergraduates. In 2001, China began to send faculty of basic subjects to English native language countries to improve their English and subject-based training. By 2004, university and other presses had greatly expanded their

English language text books, with more than 1,400 computer science texts alone (Zhou J., 2006: 96).

6.4.4 Social, Cultural, and Economic Boundaries in Learning English

Jia Xuxin and Jia Xuerui stress that it is not enough simply to say that Chinese are learning English, but that the symbols which are a part of the social processes have meaning only in the context of cultural and social settings, thus requiring an understanding of the social, cultural, political and ethnic boundaries through the communicative processes that inform them: "The situation at present is that Anglo-American English has been considered as Standard English … and as a lingua franca in the Chinese cultural context. … This variety of English used by the Chinese is generally called China English, which develops from both internationalization and indigenization of Anglo-American English. It has the native-speaker based world of English as its core system but integrates with Chinese symbolic systems, underpinned with Chinese cultural values." They argue that "English is used for every aspect of life in China. This is of great significance for both China and the international community, because China and the world need to enter one another's world in their pursuit of peace and further development. Without China-English, communication between China and the world is almost impossible today" (2007).

Nobleza Asuncion-Lande notes that while there are a variety of Englishes, including "new Englishes," "The ascendance of American English as the world's lingua franca means the dominance of American cultural values that clash with a country's native cultures." However, she replies that there is really no such thing as 'cultural purity' except in the minds of those who in search of the perfect culture…. As we move forward in the information age, the prospects for English as the dominant language of intercultural communication at least in the early part of the twenty-first century remains undiminished. It has become an international property that no one country can claim as its own" (1998).

6.4.5 Chinese Students Studying in the United States

Robin K. Cooper writes that in 2009 there were 671,616 international students studying in the US, spending $17 billion for tuition, travel, and living expenses, with 98,500 Chinese undergraduates studying in American colleges and universities (plus the postgraduates), a 21% increase over 2008 (Facebox, Education in China, 2010, January 15, see also Internet Reuters, 2008, December 12; UN Human Development Report, 2009). A comment about Chinese students enrolled in universities in California is often made that there no longer are just a few Chinatowns but that California's university system can now be called China-universities. Chinese students tend to do very well in the math portion of the Graduate Record Exam, and are increasingly stronger in the GRE and TOEFL written English tests. Many universities in the US are now holding phone interviews for promising Chinese students to determine if their oral English is satisfactory.

Verbal and Nonverbal Communication

Both the IELTS English exam for universities in the British Commonwealth system, and TOEFL now also have oral components (See Prosser, 2009).

6.4.6 Li Yang: A Crazy Talker

An anonymous author writes: "There's nothing in traditional Chinese philosophy about a man—Li Yang—whose greatest success in life was abject failure. In fact, there is nothing traditional whatsoever in a man who isn't afraid to tell you, 'I love losing face.'" His approach to inspire China's *laobaixing* (ordinary folk) into speaking English is to stand up in front of tens of thousands, "shouting and gesticulating slogans and catchphrases." We learn from the article that he has an almost cult following in Asia of more than 20 million people, that he lectures to crowds of 20,000 to 30,000, perhaps as often as 15 times a month in different locations. His goal is to introduce English to more than 300 million people in what he calls "crazy English" and he wants to develop a global program to teach "crazy Chinese" to Westerners, with offices being set up in the US and Europe.

Li Yang says:

"Any language is easy if you learn it with your mouth. You cannot learn to be a successful swimmer in the classroom." The writer continues: *"In what Li refers to as 'tongue muscle training,' (a self-devised combination of listening, reading, speaking, writing, and translation, with grammar books put aside), he … founded what is today the best known*

English language program in China. … Crazy English is today run by a staff of 140 in Greater China, Korea, and Japan." Li Yang gets average Chinese to stand up in front of thousands and shout: "On a bus! In a car," "I want to be somebody someday," or "You need a vacation?" "Don't take me as China." Li says. "Take me as Asia." because Crazy English isn't just for the Chinese [but also for all the East Asians whose English is often terrible]. Among his expressions which he teaches his audiences are: "If you are strong enough, you are your own god," "Get up every morning believing it's going to be a nice day," "The best preparation for tomorrow is doing your best today," "Don't admire Li Yang borrow from Li Yang."

Li intensely dislikes Zhang Yuan, the director behind the documentary style film *Crazy English* (2000), "in which a camera crew escorted Li around the country filming him at his height. The film itself gained international recognition, and was the first of Zhang Yuan's films to be screened in China, 'But,' says Li, "the movie was stupid.' It was not a real documentary because its intention was to please a Western audience." Zhang's film portrayed Li as a pseudo-religious buffoon, cavorting across the stage spouting phrases to all and sundry. The portrayal, Li feels, was harsh, to say the least: 'I hate people who pretend to be noble—to be god.'" The writer concludes: "His prediction that in the 21st century, people with a mastery of both English and Chinese will be in great demand around the world has prompted Li Yang to believe Crazy Chinese can look forward to the same successes as its English counterpart. 'It's about the right attitude, and good publicity. 'I never promote shortcuts,' 'learning a language is a lifelong process. It's about the right direction and the right way to do things."

6.5   Case Study: "English is a Crazy Language"

By *Richard Lederer*

English is the most widely spoken language in the history of our planet, used in some way by at least one out of every seven human beings around the globe. Half of the world's books are written in English, and the majority of international telephone calls are made in English. Sixty percent of the world's radio programs are beamed in English, and more than 70 percent of international mail is written and addressed in English. Eighty percent of all computer texts, including all websites, are stored in English.

English has acquired the largest vocabulary of all the world's languages, perhaps as many as two million words, and has generated one of the noblest bodies of literature in the annals of the human race. Nonetheless, it is now time to face the fact that English is a crazy language—the most loopy and wiggy of all tongues.

In what other language do people drive in a parkway and park in a driveway?

In what other language do people play at a recital and recite at a play?

Why does night *fall* but never break and day *break* but never fall?

Why is it that when we transport something by car, it's called *a shipment*, but when we transport something by ship, it's called *cargo*?

Why does a man get a *hernia* and a woman a *hysterectomy*?

Why do we pack suits in a *garment bag* and garments in a *suitcase*?

Why do privates eat in the *general mess* and generals eat in the *private mess*?

Why do we call it *newsprint* when it contains no printing, but when we put print on it, we call it a *newspaper*?

Why are people who ride motorcycles called *bikers* and people who ride bikes called *cyclists*?

Why—in our crazy language—can your nose *run* and your feet *smell*?

---

*   Lederer, R. (1996). Crazy English: The ultimate joy ride through our language. New York, NY: Pocket Books. [Excerpt used with permission of Richard Lederer.]

Verbal and Nonverbal Communication

Language is like the air we breathe. It's invisible, inescapable, and indispensable, and we take it for granted. But when we take the time to step back and listen to the sounds that escape from the holes in people's faces and to explore the paradoxes and vagaries of English, we find that hot dogs can be cold, darkrooms can be lit, homework can be done in school, nightmares can take place in broad daylight while morning sickness and daydreaming can take place at night, tomboys are girls and midwives can be men, hours—especially happy hours and rush hours—often last longer than sixty minutes, quicksand works very slowly, boxing rings are square, silverware and glasses can be made of plastic and tablecloths of paper, most telephones are dialed by being punched (or pushed?), and most bathrooms don't have any baths in them. In fact, a dog can go to the bathroom under a tree—no bath, no room; it's still going to the bathroom. And doesn't it seem a little bizarre that we go to the bathroom in order to go to the bathroom?

Why is it that a woman can man a station but a man can't woman one, that a man can father a movement but a woman can't mother one, and that a king rules a kingdom but a queen doesn't rule a queendom? How did all those Renaissance men reproduce when there don't seem to have been any Renaissance women?

Sometimes you have to believe that all English speakers should be committed to an asylum for the verbally insane:

In what other language do they call *the third hand* on the clock *the second hand*?

Why do they call them *apartments* when they're all together?

Why do we call them *buildings* when they're already built?

Why it is called a *TV set* when you get only one?

Why do they call food servers *waiters*, when it's the customers who do the waiting?

Why is *phonetic* not spelled phonetically? Why is it so hard to remember how to spell *mnemonic*? Why doesn't *onomatopoeia* sound like what it is? Why is the word *abbreviation* so long? Why is *diminutive* so undiminutive? Why does the word *monosyllabic* consist of five syllables? Why is there no synonym for *synonym* or *thesaurus*? And why, pray tell, does *lisp* have an *s* in it?

English is crazy.

If adults commit *adultery*, do infants commit *infantry*? If olive oil is made from olives and vegetable oil from vegetables, what do they make baby oil from? If a vegetarian eats vegetables, what does a humanitarian consume? If a television is a TV, shouldn't a telephone be a TP? If a pronoun replaces a noun, does a proverb replace a verb? If *pro* and *con* are opposites, is *congress* the opposite of *progress*?

Why can you call a woman a mouse but not a rat—a kitten but not a cat? Why is it that a woman can be a vision, but not a sight—unless your eyes hurt? Then she can be "a sight for sore eyes."

A writer is someone who writes, and a stinger is something that stings. But fingers don't fing, grocers don't groce, hammers don't ham, humdingers don't humding, ushers don't ush, and haberdashers do not haberdash.

If the plural of *tooth* is *teeth*, shouldn't the plural of *booth* be *beeth*? One *goose*, two *geese*— so one *moose*, two *meese*? One *index*, two *indices*—one *Kleenex*, two *Kleenices*? If people ring a bell today and rang a bell yesterday, why don't we say that they flang a ball? If they wrote a letter, perhaps they also bote their tongue. If the teacher taught, why isn't it also true that the preacher praught? Why is it that the sun shone yesterday while I shined my shoes, that I treaded water and then trod on the beach, and that I flew out to see a World Series game in which my favorite player flied out?

Why do people say that they *slept like a baby* when babies wake up every two hours and cry?

Why do we *watch* television but *see* a movie. Why are we *on* television but *in* a movie?

If we conceive a conception and receive at a reception, why don't we grieve a greption and believe a beleption? If a firefighter fights fire, what does a freedom fighter fight? If a horsehair mat is made from the hair of horses, from what is a mohair coat made?

A slim chance and *a fat chance* are the same, as are *a caregiver* and *a caretaker*, *a bad licking* and *a good licking*, and "What's going on?" and "What's coming off?" But *a wise man* and *a wise guy* are opposites. How can *sharp speech* and *blunt speech* be the same and *quite a lot* and *quite a few* the same, while *overlook* and *oversee* are opposites? How can the weather be *hot as hell* one day and *cold as hell* the next?

If *button* and *unbutton* and *tie* and *untie* are opposites, why are *loosen* and *unloosen* and *ravel* and *unravel* the same? If *bad* is the opposite of *good*, *hard* the opposite of *soft*, and *up* the opposite of *down*, why are *badly* and *goodly*, *hardly* and *softly*, and *upright* and *downright* not opposing pairs? If *harmless actions* are the opposite of *harmful actions*, why are *shameful* and *shameless behavior* the same and *pricey objects* less expensive than *priceless ones*? If *appropriate* and *inappropriate remarks* and *passable* and *impassable mountain trails* are opposites, why are *flammable* and *inflammable*

materials, *heritable* and *inheritable property*, and *passive* and *impassive people* the same? How can *valuable objects* be less valuable than *invaluable ones*? If *uplift* is the same as *lift up*, why are *upset* and *set up* opposite in meaning? Why are *pertinent* and *impertinent*, *canny* and *uncanny*, and *famous* and *infamous* neither opposites nor the same? How can *raise* and *raze* and *reckless* and *wreckless* be opposites when the words in each pair contain the same sound?

Why is it that when *the sun* or *the moon* or *the stars* are out, they are visible, but when *the lights* are out, they are invisible; that when I clip a coupon *from* a newspaper, I separate it, but when I clip a coupon *to* a newspaper, I fasten it; and that when I *wind up* my watch, I start it, but when I *wind up* this essay, I shall end it?

English is a crazy language.

How can expressions like "I'm mad about my flat," "No football coaches allowed," "I'll come by in the morning and knock you up," and "Keep your pecker up" convey such different messages in two countries that purport to speak the same English?

How can it be easier to assent than to dissent but harder to ascend than to descend? Why is it that a man with hair on his head has more hair than a man with hairs on his head; that if you decide to be bad forever, you choose to be bad for good; and that if you choose to wear only your left shoe, then your left one is right and your right one is left? Right?

Small wonder that we English users are constantly standing meaning on its head. Let's look at a number of familiar English words and phrases that turn out to mean the opposite or something very different from what we think they mean:

Verbal and Nonverbal Communication

I really miss not seeing you. Whenever people say this to me, I feel like responding, "All right, I'll leave!" Here speakers throw in a gratuitous negative, *not*, even though *I really miss seeing you* is what they want to say.

The movie kept me literally glued to my seat. The chances of our buttocks being literally epoxied to a seat are about as small as the chances of our literally rolling in the aisles while watching a funny movie or literally drowning in tears while watching a sad one. We actually mean *The movie kept me figuratively glued to my seat*—but who needs figuratively, anyway?

A non-stop flight. Never get on one of these. You'll never get down.

A near miss. *A near miss* is, in reality, a collision. A close call is actually *a near hit*.

My idea fell between the cracks. If something *fell between the cracks*, didn't it land smack on the planks or the concrete? Shouldn't that be *my idea fell into the cracks (or between the boards)*?

Pick up the phone. When someone rings you up, you pick up the receiver, not the entire telephone.

A hot water heater. Who heats hot water? This is similar to garbage disposal. Actually, the stuff isn't garbage until after you dispose of it.

A hot cup of coffee. Here again the English language gets us in hot water. Who cares if the cup is hot? Surely we mean *a cup of hot coffee*.

Doughnut holes. Aren't those little treats really *doughnut balls*? The hole is what's left in the original doughnut. (And if a candy cane is shaped like a cane, why isn't a doughnut shaped like a nut?)

I want to have my cake and eat it too. Shouldn't this timeworn cliché be *I want to eat my cake and have it too*? Isn't the logical sequence that one hopes to eat the cake and then still possess it?

A one-night stand. So who's standing? Similarly, **to sleep with someone.** Who's sleeping?

Operators are standing by to take your call. Who's standing? They're sitting.

I'll follow you to the ends of the earth. Let the word go out to the four corners of the earth that ever since Columbus we have known that the earth doesn't have any ends.

It's neither here nor there. Then where is it?

Extraordinary. If *extra-fine* means "even finer than fine" and *extra-large* "even larger than large," why doesn't *extraordinary* mean "even more ordinary than ordinary"?

The first century BC. These hundred years occurred much longer ago than people imagined. What we call *the first century BC.* was, in fact *the last century BC.*

Daylight saving time. Not a single second of daylight is saved by this ploy.

Twenty degrees below freezing. Isn't that still freezing?

The announcement was made by a nameless official. Just about everyone has a name, even officials. Surely what is meant is "The announcement was made by an unnamed official."

Preplan, preboard, preheat, and prerecord. Aren't people who do this simply planning, boarding, heating, and recording? Who needs the pretentious prefix? I have even seen shows "prerecorded before a live audience," certainly preferable to prerecording before a dead audience.

Pull up a chair. We don't really pull a chair up; we pull it along the ground. We don't pick up the phone; we pick up the receiver. And we don't really throw up; we throw out.

Put on your shoes and socks. This is an exceedingly difficult maneuver. Most of us put on our socks first, then our shoes.

A hit-and-run play. If you know your baseball, you know that the sequence constitutes "a run-and-hit play."

The bus goes back and forth between the terminal and the airport. Again we find mass confusion about the order of events. You have to go forth before you can go back.

I got caught in one of the biggest traffic bottlenecks of the year. The bigger the bottleneck, the more freely the contents of the bottle flow through it. To be true to the metaphor, we should say, *I got caught in one of the smallest traffic bottlenecks of the year.*

Underwater and underground. Things that we claim are *underwater* and *underground* are obviously surrounded by, not under the water and ground.

I lucked out. *To luck out* sounds as if you're out of luck. Don't you mean *I lucked in*?

Because we speakers and writers of English seem to have our heads screwed on backwards, we constantly misperceive our bodies, often saying just the opposite of what we mean:

Watch your head. I keep seeing this sign on low doorways, but I haven't figured out how to follow the instructions. Trying to watch your head is like trying to bite your teeth.

They're head over heels in love. That's nice, but all of us do almost everything *head over heels*. If we are trying to create an image of people doing cartwheels and somersaults, why don't we say, *They're heels over head in love*?

He's got a good head on his shoulders. What? He doesn't have a neck?

Put your best foot forward. Now let's see. … We have a good foot and a better foot—but we don't have a third—and best—foot. It's our better foot we want to put forward. This grammar atrocity is akin to **May the best team win.** Usually there are only two teams in the contest. Similarly, in any list of **bestsellers**, only the most popular book is genuinely a bestseller. All the rest are bettersellers.

Keep a stiff upper lip. When we are disappointed or afraid, which lip do we try to control? The lower lip, of course, is the one we are trying to keep from quivering.

I'm speaking tongue in cheek. So how can anyone understand you?

Skinny. If *fatty* means "full of fat," shouldn't *skinny* mean "full of skin"?

They do things behind my back. You want they should do things in front of your back?

They did it ass backwards. What's wrong with that? We do *everything* ass backwards.

English is weird.

In the rigid expressions that wear tonal grooves in the record of our language, *beck* can appear only with *call*, *cranny* with *nook*, *hue* with *cry*, *main* with *might*, *fettle* only with *fine*, *aback* with *taken*, *caboodle* with *kit*, and *spick* and *span* only with each other. Why must all shrifts be short, all lucre filthy, all bystanders innocent, and all bedfellows strange? I'm convinced that some shrifts are lengthy and that some lucre is squeaky-clean, and I've certainly met guilty bystanders and perfectly normal bedfellows.

Why is it that only swoops are fell? Sure, the verbivorous William Shakespeare invented the expression "one fell swoop," but why can't strokes, swings, acts, and the like also be fell? Why are we allowed to vent our spleens but never our kidneys or livers? Why must it be only our minds that are boggled and never our eyes or our hearts? Why can't eyes and jars be ajar, as well as doors? Why must aspersions always be cast and never hurled or lobbed?

Doesn't it seem just a little wifty that we can make amends but never just one amend; that no matter how carefully we comb through the annals of history, we can never discover just one annal; that we can never pull a shenanigan, be in a doldrum, eat an egg Benedict, or get just one jitter, a willy, a delirium tremen, or a heebie-jeebie? Why, sifting through the wreckage of a disaster, can we never find just one smithereen?

Indeed, this whole business of plurals that don't have matching singulars reminds me to ask this burning question, one that has puzzled scholars for decades: If you have a bunch of odds and ends and you get rid of or sell off all but one of them, what do you call that doohickey with which you're left?

What do you make of the fact that we can talk about certain things and ideas only when they are absent? Once they appear, our blessed English doesn't allow us to describe them. Have you ever seen a horseful carriage or a strapful gown? Have you ever run into someone who was combobulated, sheveled, gruntled, chalant, plussed, ruly, gainly, maculate, pecunious, or peccable? Have you ever met a sung hero or experienced requited love? I know people who are no spring chickens, but where, pray tell, are the people who are spring chickens? Where are the people who actually would hurt a fly? All the time I meet people who are great shakes, who can cut the mustard, who can fight City Hall, who are my cup of tea, who would lift a finger to help, who would give you the time of day, and whom I would touch with a ten-foot pole, but I can't talk about them in English—and that is a laughing matter.

If the truth be told, all languages are a little crazy. As Walt Whitman might proclaim, they contradict themselves. That's because language is invented, not discovered, by boys and girls and men and women, not computers. As such, language reflects the creative and fearful asymmetry of the human race, which, of course, isn't really a race at all.

That's why we wear a pair of pants but, except on very cold days, not a pair of shirts. That's why men wear a bathing suit and bathing trunks at the same time. That's why brassiere is singular but panties is plural. That's why there's a team in Toronto called the Maple Leafs and another in Minnesota called the Timberwolves.

That's why six, seven, eight, and nine change to sixty, seventy, eighty, and ninety, but two, three, four, and five do not become twoty, threety, fourty, and fivety. That's why first-degree murder is more serious than third-degree murder, but a third-degree burn is more serious than a first-degree burn. That's why we can open up the floor, climb the walls, raise the roof, pick up the house, and bring down the house.

In his essay *The Awful German Language*, Mark Twain spoofs the confusion engendered by German gender by translating literally from a conversation in a German Sunday school book: "Gretchen. Wilhelm, where is the turnip? Wilhelm. She has gone to the kitchen. Gretchen. Where is the accomplished and beautiful English maiden? Wilhelm. It has gone to the opera." Twain continues: "A tree is male, its buds are female, its leaves are neuter; horses are sexless, dogs are male, cats are female—tomcats included."

Still, you have to marvel at the unique lunacy of the English language, in which you can turn a light on and you can turn a light off and you can turn a light out, but you can't turn a light in; in which the sun comes up and goes down, but prices go up and come down—a gloriously wiggy tongue in which your house can simultaneously burn up and burn down and your car can slow up and slow down, in which you fill in a form by filling out a form, in which your alarm clock goes off by going on, in which you are inoculated for measles by being inoculated against measles, in which you add up a column of figures by adding them down, and in which you first chop a tree down—and then you chop it up.

6.6   Summary

In this chapter, we have a very long and rich dialogue, with the class members, Professor Zhang, and Michael discussing varied elements of language. If we recognize that each dialogue includes not only light, but culturally descriptive conversation, and also often important informal discussions relating to the chapter itself, then we can see the comments of Professor Zhang and Michael as well as class members as providing very useful information about the content of the chapter. In this dialogue comments are made both about Chinese and English, the difficulties in learning these and other languages, the metaphor, puns, Michael's monolingusalism, writing simple poetry like the Japanese haiku, and even briefly mentioning Li Yang's "Crazy English" which then may be discussed more deeply in the chapter. Professor Zhang offers the idea that "Language is the soul of culture, and metaphor is the soul of language." In the major part of the chapter, we have discussed the nature and characterization of language, the intercultural, Chinese, and English aspects of language in China, plus nonverbal communication. By understanding the major content of this chapter, we can see differences between Chinese and English within the context of Chinese society, and the importance that English has in Chinese learning, including goals of the Ministry of Education, Li Yang's influence in teaching "crazy English." We note that nonverbal communication is often considered 90% of the information provided while the spoken language only accounts for about 10%. The case study by Richard Lederer in which he calls English a crazy language gives us many examples of English idioms which make no practical sense if considered in a literal context.

Verbal and Nonverbal Communication

6.7 Questions for Discussion

6.7.1 We notice in this chapter's dialogue that the class members continue to become more and more confident in responding to Professor Zhang's and Michael's comments, with more and more humor developing. If you were to analyze the humor occurring in this dialogue as a critical thinker, what is its contribution to the total development of the chapter on cultural linguistic and nonverbal cultural aspects? Why?

6.7.2 The class, Professor Zhang, and Michael discuss various types of writing, including poetry. As Chinese students, has writing poetry been a key point in your development as a student before and during your university experience? If so, how has it enriched your learning? If not, what can you do to develop an interest in understanding, appreciating and writing poetry? Can you produce a number of the standard format Japanese haikus and share them with your classmates?

6.7.3 Professor Zhang in the dialogue identifies several considerations for good writing. Also, several books about writing are noted in the suggested additional readings below. Do you think that these are useful for your own development as a writer? If so, how has learning to write well been beneficial to your own maturation? A good class assignment in an intercultural communication class would be to write in English in a journal about any intercultural experiences that you are having, and then analyze them regularly to see how your own intercultural competence is developing. If you haven't been writing such entries into a journal, are there career goals that you have that would benefit from such writing? Why?

6.7.4 In the chapter's discussion about defining language and its importance to the study of intercultural communication, we can note the saying: "Language is the soul of culture and the metaphor is the soul of language." If this is true, how can we describe the role of language and the metaphor in prose, poetry, drama, cinema, animation, and the media? Would we have different characteristics for each category? Why? Why not?

6.7.5 Confucian views of language as expressed in *The Analects* have a very important place in the overall study of language for you as Chinese students. What are the major Confucian concepts of language that are important for you to appreciate as a contemporary young Chinese? Why?

6.7.6 Cultural orientations as discussed in Chapter Five have an interlinking relationship with the nature of language. Can you compare two of these cultural orientations and illustrate how language is an important aspect of these orientations?

6.7.7 In the chapter's discussion about the role of English for Chinese, we see that the Ministry of Education has made both English and bilingual learning important priorities. Many Chinese students grumble about having to learn English, or for English majors, still another language. Still, such learning must have some important benefits individually and for the Chinese society. How would you describe these benefits for the society and for yourself individually?

6.7.8 If you decide that you wish to study overseas, either as undergraduates or postgraduates, you will need to study for and take such tests as SAT, GRE, IELTS, TOEFL, GMAT, MCAT, TOEIC, ESOL, and others to gain admission into these overseas institutions. What are the best ways to prepare carefully for such tests and how will they be beneficial to your success in passing the tests and for your future career? What resources are available to assist you in preparing for these exams and being successful?

6.7.9 Many writers describe English as THE global language because of its international scope. As critical thinkers, consider this argument and its opposite that Chinese is destined to be THE global language. What are the benefits of each opposing argument? Which one would you agree with and why?

6.7.10 When we discuss the importance of nonverbal behaviors as an aspect of communication, we argue that it often constitutes about 90% of the time, while verbal language represents only 10%. Would you agree with this assumption or not? If you agree, what are the major elements of nonverbal behavior that are most important in communication? If you disagree, then how would you frame your argument in favor of verbal communication as more important than nonverbal communication?

6.8 Suggested Readings

Carroll, D. W. (2000). *The psychology of language.* Beijing, China: Foreign Language Teaching and Research Press.

Chaney L. H. (2002). *Intercultural Business Communication.* Beijing, China: Higher Education Press.

Chang, H-c. (2010). *Clever, creative, modest: The Chinese language practice.* Shanghai, China: Shanghai Foreign Language Education Press.

DeVoss, D. N., Eidman-Aadahl, E., & Hicks, T. (2010). *Because digital writing matters. National writing project.* New York, NY: Jossey-Bas.

Gillie, J. W., Ingle, S., & Mumford, H. (1996). *Read to write: An interactive course for non-native speakers of English.* New York, NY: McGraw Hill.

Hiederman, S. (1991). *Bridging cultural barriers for corporate success.* New York, NY: Lexington Books.

Huckin, T. N. & Olsen, L. A. (1991). *Technical writing and professional communication for non-native speakers.* New York, NY: Mc Graw Hill International Editions.

McKay, S. L. & Bokhorst-Heng, W. D. (2008). *International English in its sociolinguistic contexts: Towards a socially sensitive context EIL pedagogy (ESL & applied linguistics professional series.* New York, NY: Routledge.

O'Conner, P.T. (2003). *Woe is I: The grammaphobe's guide to better English in plain English.* New York, NY: Riverside.

Strunk, W. Jr., White, E.B., & Angell, R. (2000). *Elements of style: Fourth edition.* New York, NY: Longman.

Toyomasu, K.G. (2001: January 10). *Haiku for people.* www.toyomasu.dot.com

Trudgill, P. & Nahan, J. (2008). *International English: A guide to the varieties of standard English, Fifth Edition.* London, England: Hachette UK Co.

Walsh, W. (2004). *The elephants of style: A trunkload of tips on the big issues and gray areas of contemporary American English.* New York, NY: McGraw Hill.

Wardhaugh, R. (1998). *An introduction to sociolinguistics.* London, England: Blackwell Publishers Ltd.

Chapter SEVEN

Contemporary Youth

7.1 Dialogue

Professor Zhang: Class, we have a very special treat for you today. Several foreign students have agreed to meet with us so that we can have a multicultural dialogue. Today, we have Gleb from St. Petersburg, Russia; Rasid from Morroco; Bernard from near Durban, South Africa; Pablo from Santiago, Chile; Yoshiko from Kyoto, Japan; and Pierre from Montreal, Canada. Welcome to the class.

Pierre: Bonjour. Ça va? Montreal has many Chinese secondary and university students. This is what made me decide to come to China to learn Chinese. I speak French as my native language, but also English and Spanish, and I think it is very important also to learn Chinese as the Chinese language is very important in the world.

Bernard: As you can see, I am an Indian, but I have never been to India, nor have my parents been there. My father has two wives, and therefore I have an older brother and a younger sister, and half-brothers and half-sisters. I spent a year in high school in the US. On the first day of class, the English teacher said that she would speak slowly since the foreign students would not be so strong in speaking English. I didn't say anything, but several days later when she slowly asked me a question, naturally I spoke in perfect English as I started taking English in the first grade. She was very surprised.

Contemporary Youth

Pablo: Como esstas, amigos. I am a computer science major from Chile. I was having dinner at an outside restaurant with my friend Elvino and Michael in Santiago two days before the 8.8 magnitude earth quake hit Chile in 2010. It was quite terrible, even worse than your 2008 Sichuan earthquake, and Michael was lucky to leave as the quake did a lot of damage to the Santiago airport. I have a girlfriend named Angela. She is intelligent and beautiful, but Elvino and I still like to watch the beautiful Chilean young women go by. It makes Angela jealous.

Jason: Wow! You and your family were fortunate to not get hurt in your quake. Several thousand people from Sichuan were killed, including many students and children.

Lucky: Bernard you are very dark and Gleb, you have blue eyes and blond hair. Are all Indians dark and all Russians blond and blue eyed?

Michael: Lucky, we have to be careful about stereotypes. Remember you asked me once that since all the American teachers at our university have beards, do most white American teachers have beards? A lot do, but many other American men don't have beards. There are various skin colors among Americans, South Americans, Chinese, Russians, and South Africans, including Chinese, Indians, whites, and the native Africans.

Angel: I get jealous when my boyfriend looks too hard at other girls. Pablo, your girlfriend Angela must feel resentful when you are looking at other girls passing by. What does she think about you studying Chinese here at our university?

Pablo: It's my life. She is a good sport. I let her look at other handsome young men too. There are lots of pretty young Chinese women at this university, so I can look as they pass by, but Angela will be waiting for me when I come home to Santiago. In Chile, we young couples are very romantic even out in public. Chinese and English are both hard languages for me but I am enjoying my experience here.

Lucky: Not too long ago, I heard that Han Han was interviewed in a celebrity interview by The China News Agency and he was asked how many girlfriends he had at one time, and he responded, "Five." I'm waiting for my first one. Pablo, tell me what romance and love are?

Laughter

Catherine: Buenos Dias, Pablo. I am studying Spanish here as my second foreign language. All of us girls would like to have Han Han as a boy friend. You would be OK too!

Gleb: Young Russians are very romantic too. I have a lovely Chinese girlfriend and it is very charming being in an intercultural dating relationship. She is much shyer than the Russian women. We make lots of people stare at us—a blond, blue eyed Russian man and a black haired, black eyed Chinese girl arm in arm.

Peter: I am twenty-two, but I am sorry to say that I don't have a girlfriend and I have never been in a romance.

Yoshiko: We Japanese girls are very shy and modest just like many of the Chinese and Korean girls. But the Japanese boys are quite different from us, spending a lot of time on computer games, especially Pachinkoo.

Fiona: Well, Peter, I am younger than you, and I don't have a boyfriend either, so I don't know much about romance, love, or marriage. But I dream like being one of the romantic women characters in Jane Austen's novels. John Gray's book, *Men Are from Mars, Women are from Venus* which I bought from a street book cart seller says a lot about gender differences for us here in China.

Michael: Some like to call it "the poverty of romance." I have an American friend who was in China in the early 1980s, Thomas Bruneau (who taught my son intercultural communication) and he said then it was unusual to see young Chinese couples together romantically. But at night, in the countryside young men would hide outside and sing lovely romantic songs to young women up inside their houses.

Gloria: Oh! Just like Romeo and Juliet!

Laughter

Rashid: Assalamu alaikum. May you all remain safe from pain, sorrow or harm. I grew up in Rabat, Morocco where my father was an aide to a government official. When I was a teenager, I had a one year exchange student experience in the US, and then I attended a university in Virginia. As an exchange teenager, I had to change families, as I am Muslim and my host family wanted me to attend their church with them. It made me feel uncomfortable, and then I got another Christian family who were very tolerant that I came from a different religion. Now, I work in Cairo, but as our company wants to make more financial connections with China, I have come here to spend a year learning Chinese. So far, it has been a good experience although I am older than a lot of foreign students here and I am more traditional than students like Pablo, Pierre, and Gleb.

Ali: Wakaikum as salaam! As the Prophet Mohammad, peace and blessing be upon him, says, "Those who are nearest Allah are they who are first to give a salutation." So, though I am probably not so close to Allah as you, I am giving you greetings first. I am glad to meet another Muslim, Yolanda and I are the only Muslims in this class, I think.

Ivy: Rashid, you say that your father was an aide to a government official. What did the government official do?

Rashid: Oh, he was the Prime Minister.

Gloria: How wonderful! Your family must have been very rich.

Rashid: We managed all right, aided by Allah's will.

Gleb: Rashid, I know that you have a wife and little son and that his name is also Rashid Ali. I would like to go to Egypt some day. Perhaps, then I will come to see you and your family.

Rashid: That would be wonderful!

Ali: Maybe, Rashid, you named your son after me? When you come to Xi'an, you can see our Muslim quarter and the Grand Mosque.

Professor Zhang: Class, let's spend some time now with cross-cultural observations about contemporary youth in several different cultures as examples of what it means to be young in different times and places. I wonder what Professor Prosser has to say about American contemporary youth. Professor Li Mengyu has written an essay for us about Chinese contemporary youth. We can discuss if you agree with these observations or not. We also have several others writing about youth in their own countries so that you can make cross-cultural comparisons.

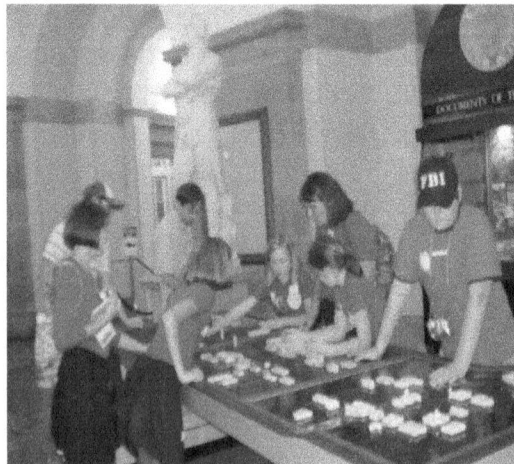

American Youth

7.2 Selected Examples of Contemporary Youth

7.2.1 American Contemporary Youth: The Millennials (Michael H. Prosser)

Always a multicultural country, like a "salad bowl" rather than the old description of a "melting pot," in the not too distant future for the United States, several states such as California, and major cities will have the white population in the minority, while those from Latin America will represent 40% and African Americans 14–15% of the population. Frank Rich, writing in *The New York Times*, said that in 2010 births to Asian, African American, and Hispanic women in the United States consisted of 40% of the children being born (2010: March 27). African Americans represent about 14% of the American population. Jaques Martin writes that there are 3,376,000 Chinese in the US Chinese disaspora, following Indonesia (7, 566,000), Thailand (7,153,000), Malaysia (7,070,000), and Singapore where the Chinese represent more than half of the population. Even Canada has 1,612,000 Chinese residents (2010: 437).

Neil Howe and William Strauss' article, *The New Generation Gap*, in *The Atlantic Monthly* (1992: December), provided a very insightful look at various American generations: the "Silent Generation" (born from about 1925 to about 1942) the : "Boomers" (born after the end of World War II: 1943–1969), the "Thirteeners," or sometimes labeled "Generation Xers," born around 1961, representing the thirteenth generation since the founding of the United States and about 80 million in the population, and those born after the early 1980s whom the authors called "The Millennials," because of the then coming Third Mellennium (since the birth of Christ). In China they are called the "Post 1980s Generation." Henry Luce, the creator of *Time*, in 1941 stressed that "American jazz, Hollywood movies, American slang, American machines and patented products are in fact the only things that every community in the world, from Zanzibar to Hamburg, recognizes in common" (Martinez, 2010: March 22, 41). Howe and Strauss identify two contrasting generations: in the 1960s the young generation claimed the high moral and cultural ground, attacking their elders, but the baby-boomers representing 69 million Americans, at the time of Howe and Strauss's writing and ranging in age from 32 to 49, now were attacking their juniors (67).

The 1960s and first half of the 1970s in the United States were the periods of flower children, hippies, the Civil Rights movement, the Gay Rights movement, the Feminist movement, the anti-Vietnam war movement, and the assassinations of President John F. Kennedy, Martin Luther King, Jr., Malcolm X, and Senator Robert Kennedy. In the late 1960s, young Americans, and many others around the world denounced the Vietnam War, chanting "Hey, Hey, LBJ [President Lyndon B. Johnson] how many kids have you killed today?" and "Hell, no, we won't go" (CNN Cold War Series: *The Sixties*, 1998). Peter M. Hall and John P. Hewitt (1973: 530) wrote that during the Nixon

White House period in 1970, with the war in South East Asia heating up, many young people were protesting in the streets, having "speak ins" about the Vietnam war and the American bombing of Cambodia. Some, however, were becoming violent. President Nixon called for "communication, not violence." On May 1, 1970, the relatively quiet anti-war movement was filled, as Hall and Hewitt explained it, with renewed "rallies, demonstrations, bitter rhetoric, anger, frustration, and outrage.... Strikes, confrontations, building burnings, tear gas battles, and arrests, and law enforcement agencies were mobilized on numerous campuses" (Hall & Hewitt, 530). On that same day at the Pentagon, the President contrasted the heroic action of the American military in Vietnam with the violent dissenters whom he characterized as "bums." However, on May 4, young national guardsmen opened fire on peacefully demonstrating students at Kent State University, killing five and wounding others. It was widely reported in the American and world press, and also for several days on the front page in *People's Daily*. President Nixon held a press conference in which he adopted what appeared to be a conciliatory attitude toward the protesters, and during the dawn hours of May 9, he came to the Lincoln memorial in Washington, D.C. to talk to young demonstrators assembled there. On May 9, 75,000 to 100,000 protesters came to Washington, many of whom were students, for an anti-war rally. Hall and Hewitt stress that some members of Nixon's own cabinet had criticized the US administration for its insensitivity toward the young Americans, and that "the main response of the administration was to cool its own rhetoric, establish lines of

communication … and lend verbal support to the right of [peaceful] dissent" (531). Hall and Hewitt note that "Underlying the emphasis upon communication as a tool for conflict resolution is an American myth of common values" (531).

Howe and Strauss suggest that the "Boomers" started as the most indulged and self-indulged young people in the US, and for middle class youth, poverty, disease, and crime seemed invisible. In 1965, *Time* claimed them to be on the edge of a "golden era," but that all that they found was a cultural "generation gap" and many of them began to sing the Beatles' song, *Let it be*. The term "yuppie" was coined to describe the "young upwardly mobile professionals" as they moved past their teens and twenties. Later, the *New York Times* called them the "grumpies" ("grown up mature professionals"), more value-oriented, involved in various spiritual movements from evangelical Christianity to Asian or New Age humanism, and even creating an "American cultural civil war" and moving conservatively to the right politically (Howe and Strauss, 74).

However, Howe and Strauss claim that the cynical "Thirteeners" were youth in the suburbs, often children in divorced marriages, as the ethnically and racially more inclusive school education often found them later in low-paying jobs, while in the inner cities, there were more and more unwed teenage mothers and unconcerned and uninterested teen aged fathers (75). At the same time, these young people had to be "pragmatic, quick, sharp-eyed, able to step outside themselves and understand how the world really works" facing, however, "a rising tide of mediocrity" (75). Mark Bauerlein's book *The Dumbest Generation*, details this continuing tide of mediocrity among American youth (1999). Inner-city high schools were often called "the blackboard jungle." Many high schools had signs, "The largest reason for teenage poverty is teenage pregnancy," The Charlottesville, Virginia High School during the "millennials" generation, with a mix of students who were the children of highly educated parents in a small town with the prestigious University of Virginia and many others from inner city poverty had 47 young unwed pregnant women in 1994, and some for the second time. The school needed a baby-care center so that these young unwed mothers could complete their high school education. On the other hand, many "Thirteeners" and later "millennials" students competed vigorously to enter the best American private and public universities. For example, at the University of Virginia, between the mid 1980s and 2009, 20,000 high school students applied annually for approximately 2,000–2,500 freshmen seats and 500 transferring students from other colleges and universities. More and more college and university educated graduates were entering such fields as computer and information science, but often entering science and engineering students from the US were far outmatched by bright Chinese and Indian students.

Reihan Salam notes that three of every ten students in American high schools as recently as 2006 were graduating and less than a third of young people in the US have finished college or university. He calls it the "cusp of a dropout revolution, one that will spark an era of experimentation in new ways to learn and new ways to live." Nonetheless, "the millennial generation could prove to be more resilient and creative than its predecessors, abandoning old,

familiar and broken institutions in favor of new, strange and flourishing ones … many of the young embrace a new underground economy, a largely untaxed archipelago of communes, co-ops, and kibbutzim that passively resist the power of the granny state while building their own little utopias…. This new individualism on the left and the right will begin in the spirit of cynicism and distrust that we see now, the sense that we as a society are incapable of solving pressing problems. It will evolve into a new confidence that citizens working in common can change their lives and in doing so can change the world around them" (Salam, 2010: March 22, 46–47).

Tim Wu writes: "Face it: Americans love their smart phones and Internet television as much as they love their cars and air conditioners…. The bottom line is that if everyone keeps using the Internet and other services as much as they like, something will have to give. It is unlikely that the American appetite for bandwidth will diminish anytime soon, nor it is even clear that we want it to" (2010: March 22, 45–46). Salam concludes his *Time* essay with the words: "Somewhere in the suburbs there is an unemployed 23-year-old who is plotting a cultural insurrection, one that will resonate with existing demographic, cultural and economic trends so powerfully that it will knock American society off its axis" (47).

In practical terms, the UCLA's "American Freshman National Norms Fall 2009" survey was administered to 219,864 entering students at 297 bachelor-awarding colleges and universities in the US, as it has been annually since 1966, the largest annual study of American higher education. The 2007–2009 recession caused the largest financial concerns for first year college students in nine years, with more than half of the incoming students reporting "some concern" about financing their college expenses, and 53% having to take out loans. Only 63% of the incoming students reported having worked as high school seniors, compared to 69% in 2007. "Being well off financially" was a top goal in 2008 and at 78% in 2009, the highest since 1996.

A new recognition of the importance of developing "excellence, integrity and civic responsibility" was noted by 31% saying that there was "a very good chance" that they would take part in civic engagement and volunteer work, with 57% of those who had volunteered in high school, expecting to do so. However, only 33% said that they discussed politics frequently, down from 36% in 2008, and only 33% said that they would seek to promote racial and ethnic understanding, down from 38% in 2008. Among the entering classes, 65% said that they had taken at least one or more high school Advanced Placement courses, which could be used for college or university credit, and thus speeding up their college or university graduation. At the same time, 21.2% of the entering college classes had had special tutoring or remedial work in high school, the largest number reported since the surveys began, and 38.7% indicated that they probably would need such tutoring or remedial work in their college or university study (Prior, et al, 2009: Fall).

Mark Bauerlein in his book, *The Dumbest Generation* (2008), argues that American students make excellent "Jaywalking" targets because their ignorance is so widespread; they don't read books and don't want to read them either. He says that with the computer, they do not need to spell. Even when they have original thought and good writing, their peers ridicule them and they spend too many hours playing with computer games. He states that they do not memorize or store the information which they receive, since their teachers don't tell them to do it or test them on it. A final problem is that they are still young and immature. Bauerlein's arguments are plausible, but at the same time the serious students are very serious as noted above. Sharon Begley (2008, May 24) counters his arguments by reminding us that young people who play computer games have to be cognitively active and demanding, requiring players to create "elaborate fantasy" narratives, use deductive reasoning, identify causes and effects, test hypotheses, and become problem solvers: "Writing off any generation before it's 30 is what's dumb."

In an informal and unscientific survey of teenagers from around the US, Shine from Yahoo *Ten Things your [American] Teenager Won't Tell You* (2010: December 1), gives the teenagers' own advice to American parents: Teenagers may want: (1) having more privacy; (2) parents listening to their own views without nagging them; (3) dating even if the parents say that they can't date; (4) sometimes not getting good grades on every assignment; (5) not talking to their parents about sex; (6) hating it when parents don't hold their brothers or sisters accountable for their own actions; (7) giving them some slack or leeway without always criticizing them; (8) sometimes lying to their parents to stay out of trouble; (9) getting frustrated when parents use their young age against them as a parental advantage in an argument; (10) wanting their parents to trust them.

Recently, I had a 45 minute interview with three young male teenagers, Stephen, Jordan, and Brennan, and earlier with another 16-year-old boy, Alexander (the post 1990s generation) to find out about their lives in a suburban setting near where the University of Virginia is located. All four are juniors in high school. The three white teens, aged 16, are all on their high school honor roll and the African American, aged 17, said that he is a bit above average in his grades, All four have been senior leaders in a local Boy Scout Troop. They gave me these responses to my dialogue questions: all four are happy and respect their parents; one's parents are divorced; all four go to church with their families on most Sundays. Two of them have a brother or sister; all three study about three hours daily on week nights, watch television and play some computer games; the three on the honor roll expect to go to an elite university; the African American whose grades are more average hopes to go to an in-state university with a less difficult admission rate. Three of the four are in the high school band and one of them is a section leader for the band. Only one plays school sports; one of the three has had a girlfriend for about a year; and one works about 15 hours a week. They each give their Monday nights to assist the younger boys in the Scout Troop, and all four participate in weekend Scout camping trips about once a month. As many high school students are indeed divided between those taking honors and advanced placement classes so that they can get into good colleges and universities, and those for whom school is an irritant who are waiting until they are sixteen to leave school legally, thus my sample is not representative of young American high school students, nor of those

living in urban settings. Their high school is named Monticello High School, after the home of Thomas Jefferson a short distance away.

While teaching in Chinese universities from 2001 to 2009, I saw each of my three children and their three children about a week and a half in the summer. Now living back in the US with my daughter, Michelle, and her three children (Darya, 13, Sanders, 12, and Sophia, 9), I am learning again to be an involved grandfather and to bond more closely with my grandchildren. All 9 of my grandchildren (6 girls and 3 boys): Michelle's children; Conner 12, Jordan 10, and Luke, children of my son Leo and his wife Hope; and Christine 18, Elizabeth 17, and Mary Catherine 14, daughters of my own youngest son, Louis and his wife Bernadette, have their own unique personalities, even within the same families. They are also very closely linked, often hugging each other and sharing enjoyable experiences together. The three sets of children share genetic characteristics of their parents (for example, three already tall, and three others are expected to be tall), while having their own individualities. All are Christians. Five of the six children aged twelve and above are honor role students, 3 of whom are in private religious secondary schools. The grandchildren's political interest tends to follow those of their parents. One house receives *The Washington Post Daily*, *Time*, *Newsweek*, and *People Magazine*. All three homes have at least two computers and are linked to the Internet. The six oldest grandchildren have Facebook accounts and read frequently. The two oldest girls work in the summer holidays. Most of the five who are twelve or older are involved in some sort of sports (swimming or soccer for four of the girls; baseball, basketball and swimming for one of the boys, and previously Taekwondo for two of the boys). One says that he would like to go to a university on an [American] football scholarship. The three boys have been in the Cub Scouts or Boy Scouts and two of the girls are in Girl Scouts. Two are in their school choral groups, band, or orchestra. One is a ballet dancer. All nine children expect to go to college or university. We should note that our family has had two great grandparents and one grandmother with an MA degree, one grandfather with a PhD degree, three mothers with masters' degrees (one in psychology, one in nursing, and one in communication), one divorced father with an MA degree in communication, and two fathers with BA degrees (one in psychology and one in communication) and one of whom has advanced certificates in financial planning and insurance. My sons and daughter have been to Europe several times, one son also had a semester abroad in Denmark, and my daughter has also been to Central and Latin America. My daughter and her three children have been to China, Michelle for a second time. Thus our family is also not representative of American youth in general.

7.2.2 Argentine Contemporary Youth (Daniel Fernando Alonso, Magister, Universidad Austral, Argentina)

Approaching their respective bicentennials (among others, Haiti 1804, Argentina 1810, Venezuela 1811, Paraguay 1811, Chile 1818,

Peru, Guatemala, Costa Rica, El Salvador, Honduras, Nicaragua, Mexico 1821, and Brazil 1822), Latin American countries face the challenge of educating their twenty-first century generations to adapt to democracy and globalization. Since their independences, Latin American countries have struggled to strike an elaborate balance between the growing demands of affirming native traditions, European ancestry—which usually included the Catholic faith, Spanish language, and certain other cultural traits imported from noticeably England or France, and the growing North American influence coming from the US.

Demographic diversity is noticeable throughout the continent. Indigenous descendants, called Amerindians, constitute majorities in Andean countries such as Bolivia and Peru, while white European descendants constitute substantive majorities in other former Spanish colonies, such as Argentina and Uruguay. An African population is noticeable in some Northern South American countries, particularly in Brazil, while mestizos—the mixture of White and Amerindians and mulattoes—the mixture of Africans and Amerindians have spread around the continent. Twentieth century immigration has been led by Italians, with contributions of several other European nationalities (Encyclopedia Britannica Online retrieved on April 30th, 2010).

Sharing such a cosmopolitan composite, younger generations have merged into the common tendency to keep closer ties with (North) American culture, by being influenced by the American way of life, pop culture, and Hollywood cinema. Nevertheless, this has sometimes been in tension with more rebellious groups who have yielded towards active social involvement, more leftist political—or even Cuban-friendly—preferences, and non-alignment.

In spite of being quite similar in these previous attitudes and traditions, educational backgrounds have been quite different. The fight against illiteracy has been a fundamental one throughout the continent, with results being diverse. Some countries have dropped illiteracy to seemingly developed countries rates, while others still stand afar from such coveted standard. On the one hand, Argentina (according to the 2001 National Census, illiteracy in people under 30 was 2.3 %), Uruguay and Chile enjoy a less than 3% illiteracy rate, while others (Guatemala, Bolivia and Brazil) suffer illiteracy rates of over 10%. However, the region as a whole has the lowest illiteracy rates among developing regional groups (UNESCO, World Adult Literacy Rates, 2000).

Some countries, particularly Argentina, Colombia, and perhaps Mexico, have enjoyed a profound leadership among their neighbors in formal education, editorial work, and—very particularly—in university studies. According to Argentina's 2001 National Census, over 26% of the working population (población ocupada) over 15 years of age have undergone some university studies and another 19% have completed secondary school studies). Most recently, other countries have significantly improved their university prospects in order to catch up with their neighbors. Meanwhile, others continue to have their upper classes educated in US universities, with a lesser number of students pursuing postgraduate studies in Europe.

Though many times Latin American university studies have been reserved for the elite, a wider social base for university education has been growing. This is essentially the case for Argentina where the number of university graduates has increased. In addition, there is a tendency to enlarge the number of post-graduate studies for students leading to masters or PhD degrees. With comparatively high unemployment levels, job opportunities and salaries for people not pursuing university studies are less attractive than for those holding a degree. For poorer classes, the risk of governmental dependency and populism arises.

Exchange programs, including semesters abroad, have been gaining popularity both at university and at secondary school levels. Once again, though many students prefer the North-South America exchange, some choose European placements. Argentina's cosmopolitan background and ethnical compound have fostered intercultural dialogue at university level with many European countries, particularly, Spain, Italy, France, Germany, and England.

As for foreign language studies, English continues being the most popular foreign language to learn throughout Latin America. American English has always been the most popular choice, though Argentines learn both British and American English on a similar basis. For South American countries, Brazilian Portuguese is lately enjoying some momentum. With Brazil's leadership blooming and GNP in consistent growth, most neighbors' youth perceive some benefit from learning the Brazilian language. Vice versa, many Brazilians choose to master Spanish in order to nurture liaisons with their fellow countries. Foreign language study of French, Italian and German have some stronghold in areas where these countries' culture has exerted influence.

Asian culture has expanded in very diverse ways in the different countries. To begin with, Chinatowns and the like are not so common in Latin America. And though most large urban conglomerates have their share of Chinese, Japanese and Korean immigrants, they usually have not become a power of their own. Chinese and Japanese immigrants are more numerous in Brazil and Peru. Exposure to Chinese culture has increased lately. First, there is the undeniable presence of Chinese products which range from the simplest to the more complex that include electronics and cars. Needless to say, the youth are particularly acquainted with this phenomenon. Second, the Beijing Olympic Games have been widely seen and opened a window of interest in China's geographical, historical as well as present traits; this factor again has had an influence on Argentine youth. Finally, Sino-Argentinean bilateral relationships as well as with other Latin American countries have thrived during the last decade, this due to tourism as well as commercial ties, and some investment interests of Chinese companies in Argentina.

While fostering intercultural dialogue, global awareness has sprung cultural change in areas such as human rights, and the environment. It has simultaneously triggered Pan American understanding and cooperation, and, in some cases, reciprocal acquaintance has developed the sense of a common nation: Latin America, with common roots and traits bringing populations closer, but yet distant from political or economic union.

7.2.3 Belgian Youth: A Free Person with Rights and Responsibility (Helene Dislaire, Malmedy, Belgium)

(Translated from French by Jean-Louis Dislaire)

A Belgian teenager is a person between thirteen and nineteen years old. The teenager is a free person with rights and rules, under the supervision of his or her parents. During this period, we young Belgians will seek our limits, like most Europeans. We will experience life, like me, and will get autonomy little by little. The young Belgians are not only young persons who like to watch TV eating snacks; we are also young persons who test the others. We set for ourselves our own limits and rules. Thus many young people like to cross the rules: it is like a game. When we know the limits, we will have to decide on our way. Then several choices are given to us. For me, the choice was quickly done. The situation of my family was not always marvellous. I have a sister and a father but an empty space will always remain with no mother at home. My current relation with my sister is rather good; she left the house and lives with her boyfriend. She works as a manager in a nursing home. The relation with my father is the only parental relation I have. It was not always easy but we work on it every day.

The young Belgian, in the best situation, has a mother and a father, and even sometimes brothers and sisters. This is what we call a "close family" with blood ties. But for some time, marriages here are breaking up. In this case, most of the young Belgians have a mother and a father but that they see them only at a regular interval (this week with mom, and the next week with dad). It is what is called in Belgium a family "with shared guardian." Many families are recomposed; a Belgian thus finds himself or herself sometimes with three sisters and two brothers whereas he or she had only one sister in his or her own family. It is what is called a recomposed family. Sometimes we have a family with one parent, because the other died or left. We call this a "single-parent" family. It is actually my situation. I think that in Europe and everywhere in the world, we will find this type of families. We are not the only ones in this situation. Unfortunately, the "adults" forget sometimes that they have children.

When I grew up, I have made grow with my imagination and my eccentricity (which I entirely assume). I always wanted to draw and create in order to share my feelings with others. In compensation of my mother and our wound from her leaving us, my father sent me to a painting class which I took for seven years. We young Belgians must often carry our sufferings with us. Either we decide to accept them and to make our richness out of them, or we mope and get rid of them only with difficulty. However, every choice we will make during our adolescence will influence the rest of our lives. The relations we will have with our parents can depend on our lives and our parent's lives and experiences. It is possible that there is no communication; in this case, we young people are often left to our own devices. We test our limits without comments or restriction given by our parents. Often, some young Belgians come to a bad end as drug dealers, convicts, or racketeers. It is not a job; it is sad and lamentable to be there at the end.

My values are peace, serenity, frankness, respect and love. I am not a believer in a religious faith but I hope to give this love that I did not receive as I would like to be the one I did not have and I would like to stay free. I have received these values from my close relations, but for some of them, I have built them from my experiments and research of myself. Young Belgians who want to be successful in life, will seek values from their experiments, good or bad, but in their own way. We can always find positive things in bad situations. I think that young Belgians stay in a continual conflict with themselves. We try to find our goals in life.

I want to be a drawing teacher; I want to see my children growing, to have a husband and to love him for what he is. Cannabis looks old fashioned and like a pain-killer these days but just try it and you will understand. Drugs are also included in our adolescence. There are a few people who did not try to smoke. But a lot of people will continue. In my country, the law says that people cannot take drugs before 16–18 years old and when we are 18 years old, we can have only three grams of cannabis. The cannabis is considered as a soft drug, which is not the case for heroin, coke and other drugs which are hard drugs. Cigarettes are prohibited for teenagers who are not 16 years old. It is not allowed to smoke in restaurants, schools, buses and other public places. I do not deny smoking sometimes, but always reasonably, once in a while. Alcohol is easier to find and to buy. It is the subject of many ethylic comas and serious car accidents for our young people. But each of us wants to know our limits. I drink and I smoke. I am disgusted and disappointed to see the way in which the young people consider love and romance. Of course, love is not presented as "dirty" but it becomes dirty romance in the ways it is practiced. We receive a lot of information from the media against the transmissible diseases and the dangers of pregnancy. It is not in our practice to be mothers at 14 years old but it happens nevertheless. All these topics can bring problems, incomprehension and questions from the young Belgians and Europeans. Faced with this problem, we can find answers thanks to our parents, our close relations, doctors and psychologists. Personally, I had to receive help from those people and for many reasons.

The media attack us everywhere, that is through television, Internet, cell phones, people magazines or others, and, of course, the newspapers. We know what happens in the world (for the young people who are interested) and we have the right to make our own opinions. Personally, I always like to listen to the radio and I appreciate medical information, news and the newspapers. I like to know in which world I live, the position I have in my country and what are my rights as a citizen. We do not all have the chance to travel. When I was six, I stayed for six weeks in Morocco. This experience opened my mind. When I was eight, I came to the United States. Also, I learned a lot of new things but also the sonority of the English language. When I was 12 years old I had another opportunity to go to Morocco; at 14 I went to Senegal and last year, I spent three weeks again in the States. I had the chance to travel quite a lot when I was young. Every Belgian is not that lucky.

As I have said, my values are peace, serenity, frankness, respect and love and I want to be free.

7.2.4   Chinese Contemporary Youth: The Post 1980s Generation (Li Mengyu)

China has the largest youth population in the world. The generation has been shaped by a strong traditional culture as well as the global world culture. Nowadays in China, when we mention Chinese youth, we mainly refer to the post-1980s and post-1990s young people whose ways of living, values and even communication styles are quite different from those of their parents' and grandparents' generations. Since China keeps opening up to the outside world, the Chinese youth are under the influence of various foreign cultures. First, they are greatly influenced by the western cultures and they hold a more positive view towards the western developed countries and their cultures, such as the United States as well as the European countries. As one student in the Ocean University of China says: "We are more Westernized. For example, we watch more American movies, TV series, we listen to BBC and VOA, and celebrate Western holidays." They also show much interest in Western style fast food such as KFC, McDonalds and Pizza Hut, and like wearing Nike or Addidas clothes. Many of them choose to go abroad to pursue further study and experience a new life. Next, they are also under the influence of their neighboring countries, such as Japan and Republic of Korea; they like to watch the Japanese cartoons and Korean's TV series, and some girls like to follow the dressing trend of the Japanese and Korean women. In short, nowadays, under the influence of various cultures, the Chinese youth now have diversified ways of living; their eye views have been broadened and most of them want to live a more interesting and colorful life. They spend more time on traveling, sports, music as well as watching movies, TV series and go shopping in their spare time.

In terms of the value aspect, the Chinese youth display some complex and mixed value dimensions; on the one hand, the traditional Chinese culture still exerts a far-reaching influence on them; they still adhere to collectivism and group unity as well as the Confucian values of benevolence, good conduct, practical wisdom, and proper social relationships. On the other hand, they appear to be more individualistic. They cherish the value of self-confidence, self-independence and self-esteem, and try to be different from others by seeking their unique personalities. Besides, there is more emphasis on personal choice, freedom, and more equality of the sexes among the present Chinese young generation. Even some Chinese university girls speak quite frankly that they believe that they are the center of the world. But as a coin has two sides, the tendency of individualism also has its negative effects as many of them turn out to be self-interested and self-centered which has given rise to many communication problems.

The communication style of Chinese youth has also changed dramatically. Particularly, for the urban young people, they prefer to communicate with their friends by the means of QQ, MSN on the Internet, or sending short messages instead of face-to-face communication. It seems to them that the Internet has become a more real world. It has become a fashion or lifestyle for the Chinese youth to have their cyberspace on Renren Network or QQ Network, on which they can upload their photos, blogs and other material they would like to share with others. As Zhaojing from the College of Liberal Arts and Journalism and Communication in the Ocean University of China says: "Nowadays, writing micro blogs is popular with netizens, and as the college students are in a large proportion, we can express our personal views on hot issues. If these netizens can draw much attention and have some fans, they will become the 'opinion leaders,' and their view will be transmitted from person to person. But different students have different purposes; some are willing to be the opinion leaders while others just want to get more information from their concerned celebrities." In short, the Chinese youth, particularly the young Chinese urban people spend more and more time on the Internet and cyberspace has become a public place for their personal communication.

However, there are many problems which the Chinese youth are facing, among them, one common problem is the pressure. For students, they are under enormous pressure to get excellent grades, to get into university and then compete for good jobs. For those educated urban professionals, they also work under great pressure and intense competition for high social positions, good salaries and house issues. For those in the rural population, they have to go to cities and towns to work even harder for the purpose of earning money to support their families back in the rural areas.

Anyway, the Chinese youth are generations who have dreams. The Chinese youth are now still on their way of pursuing the "Chinese dream," that they want to enjoy life and have a life with meaning and value.

African Youth in China

7.2.5 Egyptian Youth: Past, Present, and Future

7.2.5.1 Growing Up in Egypt (Aliaa A. Khidr, M.D., Ph.D., Professor of Phoniatrics, University of Virginia)

Growing up in Egypt provided me with a sense of community, respect of elders, and independence. Both of my parents were born in the 1930s and by 1960, when I was born, they both had finished their higher education in Cairo University, the leading Egyptian Higher institute of education. Both of my parents came from middle class families, my father from a rural village in Egypt, and my mother from Cairo. At that time, higher education was only a privilege for the elite rich and a handful of high achievers who were able to earn scholarships that granted them a free university education. Both my parents were among that group.

Not only that but right after their graduation they worked for a few years then started their master's degrees in education, becoming junior faculty at the university. As I was finishing my elementary education, they were finishing their doctoral education.

Life during that period had a soothing rhythm. Winter, spring and fall were school time, while summer was vacation time. School days were mostly the same: wake in the morning to the radio with the music of a famous program called "kelmeteen we bas " (only two words) that discussed social issues, followed by morning news and excerpts of famous Egyptian songs. I can still hear my dad's voice singing along and holding my hands in dance like steps, and smell dates, eggs and butter from the kitchen as mom was preparing our daily breakfast and school sandwiches. We each had two home-made sandwiches, the first was always cheese and the second varied from "halawa" (a type of sweet spread) to jam or dates spread. "Belila" (organic wheat and milk) was another daily item for breakfast, which is a totally organic based cereal.

In elementary school years, dad used to drive us to school, but as soon as we started middle school we started taking the metro on our own. Every day my brother and I would walk to the metro accompanied by all the kids in our neighborhood, each going to a different school. We could tell schools by the uniforms: public schools had overall brown uniforms, while each private school had suit uniforms for girls or pants, shirts and ties for boys. Inside the metro all of us bundled up standing waiting for our station to come and get out because the seats were always reserved for the grown ups. So even if we found an empty seat, we would sit in it untill a grown up came by, where we would usually get up saying "tafadal" (please have this) and the grown up would accept and reward us by a huge smile, a pat on our backs and a lengthy prayer for our happiness, success and health. It almost felt like reserving the seat for the morning good-luck prayer. The conductor would come by calling on us "Ebney " (my son) or "binty" (my daughter); we usually would give him ticket money or show him our seasonal pass addressing him as "amou" (uncle). Once each group arrived at its station the doors would open and tens of short and tall kids would get out and start running in different directions to their schools.

Afternoons on school days started with a short nap, followed by an hour or more of playing with neighborhood kids on our street. We had to make up new games to keep ourselves engaged. Not only that but we had to keep modifying the rules of the games to get everyone engaged. We also made up plays and took our roles very seriously. We almost never had adults sit down to watch our plays, but they would come by every now and then give us homemade cookies or drinks. Looking back, that must be part of why were happy to see them come out. Sunset was the official time to come back to dinner followed by homework until bed time. Television had little role in our lives at that time; the radio was our main source of news and entertainment.

Summer vacations were always luscious and long. We spent two months in Cairo and one month on one of Egypt's fascinating beaches. Most of the middle class families did the same. It was always the most anticipated adventure of the year. We had a whole month to spend with our family as well as a lot of new people of all ages. Those usually ended up being our new group of friends.

Nowadays the middle class majority has disappeared and is being replaced by economically sound families or economically challenged families. The former group is more and more visible on the streets, in the sport clubs, in the malls and in the media. Public schools that were a respectable choice in the past are only selected by those who cannot afford a private school. Private schools in turn range from "affordable ones" to "totally outrageous ones" where tuition is paid in US dollars. Obviously those who graduate from the latter schools tend to attend one of the many foreign universities in Egypt. Accordingly the youth experience growing up in Egypt now totally depends on their economical level. The metro and the buses are no longer used by everyone. Most of the "well to do" youth have never experienced using any public transportation. Private cars and personal drivers would be the only transportation they would be willing to try. Kids waiting for the metro today are no more taking pride in being independent and part of a "nationwide family like community." And most kids waiting for their private school's buses have never had a chance to meet, greet, or do any activity with other kids less privileged than themselves. Their community is limited to their socio economic compatible peers. Even food choices differ along those lines; homemade sandwiches and healthy whole grain "affordable" meals become an unwelcomed destiny of the poor, while unhealthy snack style meals and fast food become the norm for those who can afford it and the dream for those who can't. Playing on the street with the neighbors is only reserved for the poor, while private sports clubs and malls are mainly populated by the rich. Kids end up not knowing their peers from their own neighborhood and having no contact whatsoever with anyone outside their family and parents' network. Similarly, summer vacations which now have been shortened to one week depend on the family's income. The rich spend their vacation in expensive private resorts where their kids complain about what they are not enjoying, and the poor spend it on one of the many beautiful public beaches wondering how would it feel like being in a resort.

But one very positive feature of Egyptian youth today, is that regardless of their socio economic status, they all thrive on technology; they make it their job to understand every new gadget inside out, whether they are cell phones, desktop computers, laptops, satellite dishes, a motor cycle, a fully equipped car, truck or airplane. They discuss and analyze the differences between different technologies as if this were their field of expertise. It doesn't matter whether they own one or not and it doesn't matter if they could even afford one in the future or not. Not only that but they follow up closely all global developments of different products, and brag about whichever nation or company has become the new leader in the technology discussed. This can be linked directly to the nationwide affordable access to the Internet through phone lines and Internet cafés as well as international and local satellite channels. The youth have become the experts on using technology for communication, research, and networking and even have gone a step further. Many active young Egyptians are finding a new way to express their opinions

and report uncensored live events. They have become experts in using video streaming and uploading to different blogs and face book networks to rally public support on different issues as well as to expose corruption.

These advantages have made Egyptian youth more bold than before, more trusting in their own opinion, and more daring in the way they are expressing themselves. They are feeling more connected to the outside world and keep sizing themselves up against other nations' youth hoping they can use different experiences to help them deal with their own challenges.

7.2.5.2 Egyptian Youth Nowadays Are a Mystery (Edmaad M.O. Abdel Rahman, M.D., Ph.D., Associate Professor of Nephrology, University of Virginia)

Though I am not considered a youth any longer, I still remember those days. Things were different. There are things that changed to the better, others took a nose dive! My teenage years were in the early 1970s. Egypt was witnessing a major change in directions. After being ruled by President Gamul Nasser for close to two decades, President Anwar Sadat came to power. The major shift from the socialist regime led by Nasser to the open market regime led by Sadat was affecting every aspect of our lives. In the late 1960s and early 1970s, we had television, black and white, with only two channels. Programs started at 5: 00 PM and ended by 11: 00 PM. It was only on during our weekend days. On Fridays, programs would go on until after midnight, with a late night movie. Only three newspapers were available. While this limited our source of information as well as entertainments, it allowed us more family time. Another benefit was that we shared with our peers the same entertainment. A new movie would be seen by everyone, and would be the topic of our next day discussions.

Our days were simple. Coming from a family where both my parents were working parents, my brother, my sister and I would go to school in the morning and return around 2:30 PM. By 3:00 PM my parents would be back from work and we, as a family, would sit together for our main midday meal. A couple of hours of napping would freshen us up. If the weather permitted, my brother and I would go down to the street and play soccer. No traffic was there, with limited cars in Cairo at that time. After sunset came homework time, followed by a 30 minutes of watching television with the family. Days were simple with no worries. Weekends were the days to go to the sporting club and occasionally a movie theater.

By the mid to late 1970s, changes were apparent. Now the television had color with more channels and longer hours of programming. The Cairo streets were seeing more cars. Working opportunities were opening in the rich gulf countries and families were starting to separate. Progress continues! This was then. Things have changed dramatically now, and I can see that just by looking at my nieces and nephews. The information technology explosion had its toll on everything. Satellite dishes, cable, Internet, cell phones, while adding a lot, took away a lot. Youth nowadays are more informed and more entertained. This came at a price. The family fabric was shattered. Playing in the streets in Cairo is no longer an option. Just crossing the street has become an adventure. On the positive side, the youth are becoming more independent and "free" as well as computer and technology savvy.

Youth nowadays are a mystery. They are a heterogeneous bunch of people. They range along the rainbow colors, mirroring the huge spectrum that Egypt now is witnessing. The division that occurred in the community has been happening at many levels; maybe the most evident cutting line, though by no means the only dividing line, is the line that separates the "have" and the "have nots." The youth in Egypt nowadays can encompass the teenagers who just are old enough to get a driver's licenses who are roaming the streets of big cities driving recklessly in the car that their parents bought them, without the least concern for their safety or the safety of others. It also can encompass those who stand for hours waiting for the public transportation, to go to work to support their families at a very young age. Youth can be highly educated, mastering more than two foreign languages to illiterate young men and women unable to read and write.

Whether then or now, youth is youth; the vibrant time of our lives. The mixture of the illusion of one's own immortality with the uncertainty of what the future has in store. During my youth, the solidarity of family and community ties was our main support system. For today's youth, this has been replaced by the confidence of knowledge and the ability to connect to the outside world through modern technology.

7.2.5.3 Life as a Teenager in Egypt (Ali E. Abdul Rahman, seventh grade, Charlottesville, Virginia)

Nowadays in Egypt we have more and more youngsters and teens conforming to Western (American) life. Westernizing, they eat fast food such as KFC, McDonalds, Taco Bell, and Pizza Hut instead of what they used to eat; traditional Egyptian/Arabian food and fresh fruits and vegetables. The new generation of Egypt is also listening to mostly all American music and watching western television instead of famous all time Egyptian singers like, Umm Kalthum or Abdel Halim Hafez. If you asked them their favorite food/song/television show, over half of them would say American/western things. And yes, that means that almost all of them speak some English. The rich kids in private English schools can hold conversations in English, and the not so rich still learn English as a second language starting in elementary school and can say many meaningful phrases.

I personally think that Egyptian youth are feeling down because of the current limitations in job positions and resources. They dream about enjoying a highly paid job in a rich society like the United States, and think that by dressing, eating and acting like Americans; they are a step closer to living like them. With that said, there are still a lot of youth who live by old fashioned Egyptian principles and really want to be good people; they are willing to lend a helping hand even to people they have never met before; they will go out of their way to have a nice conversation with you to make you feel good, and will show a lot of respect to their parents, grandparents as well as any elders.

7.2.6 Indian Contemporary Youth (The Hindustan Times Survey, January 25, 2006)

The *Hindustan Times*, January 25, 2006, in a survey of 15,000 Indians on their values reported the following: 72% said that parents should have the final say over their children's marriage; 65% said that young Indians should not date; 74% said that inter-cast marriage was unacceptable; 56% said that interreligious marriages, for example between Hindus and Muslims, should be opposed; and 75% said that young Indian men should live with their parents after their marriage and that the bride should move in with her parents-in-law; and 77% said that young Indian men and women should have equal inheritance rights. In terms of the demographics in the survey, 17% reported themselves as liberal, including 26% of the young urban women; 24% of the young urban men; 13% of the elderly rural men and 15% of the elderly rural women. 38% of those completing the survey labeled themselves as conservative, including 26% of the young urban women 24% of the young urban men, 47% of the elderly rural men, and 44% of the elderly rural women. 69% of the educated urban respondents indicated that they prayed daily, and 43% of the uneducated rural respondents indicated that they prayed daily, for a total of 55%.

7.2.7 Japanese Youth Today: The Global Generation (Judy Yeonoka, Kumamoto Gakuen University, Kumamoto, Japan)

Japan conjures up an image of young salary men all dressed alike, jostling for space in a crowded commuter train or on a busy Tokyo street. However, young people have been facing new challenges—and can be found more often at home with their parents, still in school, living in net cafés, or even on the streets. From ages 3 to 33 and beyond, "what these groups have in common, for all their diversity, is that they have not yet become full-fledged members of 'the adult social order'" (Matthews & White 2004: 6).

The young people of Japan today may be best described as "lost"—or perhaps more appropriately, they have (been) derailed. The "adult social order" was supposed to be the end station of a track of "best schools," laid for them by education mamas and papas and teachers and jukus (cram schools). All the children had to do was sit tight and hold on for the ride, and they would be rewarded with a fine adult life at the end. However, nowadays their end station is no longer clearly in sight, and their train is generally seen to be going nowhere.

The causes for this derailment can be summed up in three words: *demographics*, *economics* and *technology*. First, a top-heavy generational displacement means that for the first time in Japan's history, there are more older people than younger ones. The *dangai no sedai*, Japanese equivalent of baby-boomers born after World War II, are nearing the end of their careers and running out of steam. Moreover, they have fewer children and grandchildren

than previous generations: the Japanese birth rate has been under 1.5 since the 1990s and currently stands at 1.21. This presents the young generation with a double whammy. First, their fathers are in a bottleneck at the top of most major companies, allowing fewer of their children to be hired; and second, these same children must look forward to being financially and physically responsible for aging parents (and their friends) down the road. This demographic dilemma is coupled with an economic one; since the burst of the bubble in 1991, the lucrative jobs that were supposed to be at the end of their education have been absent. This produced the first generation of freeters—full time part-timers who are now in their 30s. They should be married by now, with children of their own; instead, they are living at home as "parasite singles," and working at jobs meant to supplement college students' incomes. Finally, advances in technology have followed the younger generation throughout their lives, bringing them video games, cell phones, and Mixi (the Japanese version of Facebook). Like their counterparts around the world, many young Japanese find it easier to relate to a LCD screen than to a human face.

The results of these changes have manifested themselves in many ways. Some young people withdraw, becoming *hikikomori* (hide-at-home) and *futoko* (playing truant). Others rebel, creating *gakkyu houkai* (class destruction) even in traditional schools that have prided themselves on having "perfect" students. In March 2010, when 7-year-old Princess Aiko, granddaughter of the present Emperor, could not attend her elementary school because of bullies, it made national news, and the country was shocked that even the ultra-elite Gakushuin could have such mundane problems.

On the other hand, the current generation is more globally-oriented than any generation before them. Many have been abroad, even on school trips, and all have studied several years of English. They have grown up with the Internet, and are aware of what the net revolution means to the world today. They are more connected with more people in more different ways than ever before, and they relate to their peers less as fellow Japanese and more as global teenagers. In this sense they are very much like students their same age around the world.

However, they face the dilemma of harmonizing a past in which they were simply expected to "stay on track" with a future for which they must be the trailblazers. The world has changed around them, and they will have to find new ways of coping to get where they want to go. In other words, they will have to develop independence and inner strength to survive the sink-or-swim situation they are facing today.

7.2.8 Youth in Modern Russia (Sergei A. Samoilenko, MA, George Mason University)

In modern Russia, young people (age group 17–26 years) are more individualistic, self-dependent and feeling responsible for their own destiny than their former Soviet youth peers. They are experienced gamers and Internet users, less concerned about money making compared to the youth from the 1990s, but more eager to get a high-quality education and follow their life goals and professional calling.

According to the analytical report *Youth in new Russia: Values and Priorities*, Russian youth think of life in their country more positively than their parents or earlier generations did. This fact can be explained by their growing financial stability and increasing job placement for Russian youth. According to this research, about 87 percent of young Russians are satisfied with their financial status and life overall.

Although young Russians consider financial well-being among the most important criteria for success, they believe that a good education, strong family and interesting/challenging work are equally important. When looking for work, young Russians are not only interested in how much it pays, but also whether this job is interesting and what kind of social status it represents.

A large family represents another important criterion of success for many young Russians. Since young people prefer to rely mostly on themselves, they start working early to assure their financial independence and stability by a certain age. These goals dictate their motivational behaviors and life decisions, including their choices for education and career.

Similar to the generation of the 1990s, young Russians nowadays prefer occupations related to law and finance. However, the popularity of professions, such as managers, scientists, computer specialists and doctors is increasing. Many young Russians consider Gasprom, the largest extractor of natural gas in the world, and the administration of the Russian president as top employers.

In today's Russia the political preferences show (Milyukova, 2002) contradictory political consciousness of the Russian youth. Numerous political youth groups in Russia include: Pro-

Kremlin movements (e.g, Nashi or "Ours", Youth Democratic Anti-Fascist Movement); Democratic Oppositional movements (e.g., Oborona), and Oppositional Youth movements (e.g., National Bolsheviks). Although the majority of young Russians mainly believe in democratic changes supported by the ruling and largest political party United Russia (or Yedinaya Rossiya), chaired by Prime Minister Vladimir Putin, studies show (Institute of Sociology RAN, 2007) a correlation between socioeconomic status and party preferences in this country. Young people supporting Pro-Kremlin organizations are usually satisfied with their financial standing, as opposed to those who support liberal national-patriotic and left-wing parties. According to sociologists (Pautova, 2009), Russian youth are less critical of the government than older generations and consider work for local or federal authorities among other top career options. The popularity of the Russian government can be explained by the relative economic growth and stability that allowed many of young Russians to find new ways for self-actualization.

Despite the apparent popularity of political youth movements, only 14 percent of young Russians are actively interested in politics. It could be explained by other aspects of life that young Russians consider important. Besides typical hobbies and traditional interests, such as sports, music, and reading, Russian youth combine the customary ways for rest and recreation with new opportunities introduced by globalization and technological innovations. For example, now more Russians spend their leisure time in chat rooms, forums and on social networking sites. The most important resources include Vkontakte (Russian version of Facebook), Moi Mir (My World), Odnoklassniki (Russian version of Classmates. com) and instant messaging services. The Internet has become a trustworthy news channel for many young Russians that is only second to television. (Pautova & Lebedev, 2008)

Traditionally, Russians highly appreciate the value of interpersonal communication and call interaction with friends and relatives among the most important ways to spend their leisure time. Besides its primary communication purpose, human interaction with friends and family members is also used as a strategy for bonding, establishing new connections and maintaining good relationships with the community to assure their help and support in times of need.

Unlike their parents, who believe in a slow but sure strategy for life planning and career building, Russian youth are more ambitious, goal-oriented, and aggressive. They aspire to integrate into the international youth scene, and to participate in global economic, political and humanitarian developments.

The new generation is not afraid to take risks, believe that success implies playing for high stakes, and have no doubts that they will become more successful than the generation of their parents.

7.2.9 Togo: Corridor and Smile of Western Africa (Yves Assidenou, MA: Shanghai University of Finance and Economics)

Togo is a small country located in western Africa. With an estimated 5.2 million inhabitants among whom 43% are less than 15 years old, Togo is a multicultural and multiethnic state. The official language is French and the most spoken national languages are Ewe (in the south) and Kabye (in the north). At least 40 ethnic groups live within boundaries of this land which historically was a refuge for those who were escaping from wars and persecutions of ancient Kingdoms of Ashanti (now a part of Ghana), Abomey (Benin) or Ife (Nigeria) among others. German and French colonization brought Togo into modernity but ancestors' culture is still in practice in rural areas while Christianity is almost always practiced in cities.

Togolese youth are then influenced by all these ethnic, with many cultural and linguistic differences that observers consider as a great advantage. Meanwhile, Togolese young people are very open-minded like their parents because they desire to establish a common society in peace with multicultural characteristics. Although political factors influence the behavior of people from different regions, it is easily noticed that mixed marriage in Togo is becoming more and more a lifestyle. Togolese people generally believe that marriage between two persons from different ethnic groups is a factor that would eliminate regionalism and promote better understanding among the population. That's why for a long period, the country has never experienced ethnic conflict even if there were political troubles and instability during the last decade 1993–2005 of democratic process.

One policy that all Togolese governments undertook since 1960 was to send public servants from their origins to another region in order to promote Togo's multiculturalism and make people know more about others. I was personally involved in such an experience as my parents were public servants. I know almost the southern and northern part of Togo and their ethnic groups. Much more, I have a lot of friends from different regions of Togo as well as my parents. This situation is not a unique one because other persons also experience this kind of life. But I think that much improvement in multicultural integration has to be done because there is still existing some kind of conservatism in some areas or ethnic groups. The conservatism factor is due to the lack of education and sometimes to religious fanatics. The wrong interpretation of religion prescriptions leads to such exaggerations and conflicts.

At regional levels, African youth culture differs across countries that are either French or English speaking. The colonization heritage plays a central role in these differences. A Nigerian or a Ghanaian would not be easily understood certain cultural behaviors by a Togolese or Senegalese. This captures the fact that a vertical cultural relationship originating from Europe is still influencing young people's behavior across the countries in western Africa. Even when some ethnic groups are dispatched across countries, the horizontal cultural relationship that might exist between western Africa countries is not so deep. For example, the Ewe-Mina ethnic group is present in Togo,

Ghana and Benin. Even when those people can speak a common language, their belonging to different national entities makes them more influenced by either French or English taste. However, such differences were more pronounced in the early 1960s but with the current regional economic integration process, there is a hope that in the future, intercultural distortions will be eliminated.

About the Youth's Future in West Africa

Youth experience in West Africa has been impacted by some armed conflicts and political instability that restrain their hope about the future. Young people seem less optimistic about the political leaders' will, especially concerning the building of a society of peace and justice. They believe that political leaders are so linked to corruption that the dilapidation of common resources by a few people in-power is the main cause of the streaming state of poverty within the population. There is less confidence in political leaders in western Africa than in other regions like southern Africa. This fact might be an explanation of high emigration rates in that region towards Europe. However, some countries undertake a huge battle against corruption and injustice, among which is Ghana the best example of democracy and governance in the region. Non-governmental organizations also are making great efforts to enhance young peoples' daily life by providing relief programs in rural and post-conflict areas. Despite the current situation, there is still a hope among young intellectual leaders about the future of West African youth, since multicultural settings play an important role in melting people in the region. The regional economic integration project must be the leading enterprise for the consolidation of hope about the future among young people in West Africa.

Personal Experience in China

As an international student, my personal experience about intercultural communication in Asia and China is related to some facts that capture differences with my country of origin. I experience a lot of differences with Chinese but less with European students. I think a lack of knowledge about Chinese traditions and Chinese peoples' behavior made me sad the first days of my arrival in this great country. I find Chinese students so silent that I could not imagine making friends. But later I discovered that people here are friendly in ways that are not ours in Africa. This finding is not especially true for Chinese but also for those originating from other Asian countries as well. There are other simple facts that can illustrate such differences in culture with Chinese people. For example, red color means positive things in China while in Togo this almost means negative things or a perception of a danger. Young people in West Africa are accustomed to shake hands in ordinary greetings but here it not a very common habit. Broadly speaking, it is not easy for one coming from outside to feel well in his or her first days in China but the more time passes the more one complies with Asian and China specificities.

7.3   Case Study: Making the World Your Classroom

Bob   Gibson*,   Sorenson   Institute,   University of Virginia

[Reprinted with permission, Bob Gibson, Daily Progress, Charlottesville, Virginia, USA, Published: 2010: April 18]

I feel like one of the luckiest students at the University of Virginia. Every semester for the past two years, I take a graduate course in the education school. This spring's academic adventure is a fascinating study of schooling around the world in a new era of economic, cultural and political globalization. The class is all the more enlightening with its delightful foreign-born cohort of grad students from China, Republic of Korea, Haiti, Colombia, Kenya, Cameroon, Egypt and elsewhere. Even discussion of food is mouth-watering, as are Haitian curried chicken dinners shared together. Twice in one month we meet through the Internet on a real time basis talking with a university class in Seoul.

A Market of Ideas

If Americans could learn Korean and Chinese languages as well as these students learn English, the US would be better off for the next century. Korea is engaged in mass study of English as a means to get ahead in the world economy. We are exporting democratic ideals born here in Virginia more than 200 years ago and we are offering top-quality higher education. Asian nations are exporting the 21st century equivalent of gold: the products and prodigies of science, technology and, increasingly, liberal arts. In the past 10 years, China has become the world's leader in sending students abroad for higher education. Ever higher numbers of foreign degree holders return to China each year, fueling a growing economy and creating a brain gain that is heavily promoted by that nation's government while it hugely enriches top American and British universities. Leaving China for study abroad is seen by Chinese families as a way to provide a leg up in fierce competition for massively unequal distribution of resources.

China rolls out the red carpet and increasing incentives to win the return of those who spend and send their children abroad for top educations. Chinese and Korean students in our Comparative Education class say they do intend to return to their homelands once their graduate studies at UVa [University of Virginia] are completed and wonder how "Americanized"

---

*   Bob Gibson is Executive Director of the Sorensen Institute for Political Leadership at the University of Virginia. The opinions expressed here are his own and not necessarily those of the Institute.

they must sound to their friends and families back home.

Assimilate, Individualize

Foreign students' identities change as they spend time here. "My style is so American," said a fellow student from Cameroon who wonders if those in her West African nation even understand exactly what she means in her postings on Cameroonian Websites. "You are so American," a Korean student in the class said she has been told by Korean friends. "There are so many layers to this," she said of the identity she sees herself gaining. That's not a bad thing in the new globalized economy. It can add cultural capital to the Asian students who seek higher education in the US and at UVa. Another Korean student said so many Koreans are gaining valued degrees at American universities that alumni groups in Korea from the University of Wisconsin and the University of Texas have become major social and professional networks for their many alumni there.

While many foreign students can gain prestige from having an American degree and appreciate the academic freedom found here, life isn't always easy for these students as they cope with long separations, often from spouses or children. This separation has a name. A "wild goose" is someone split apart from immediate family members, one said. American students also study abroad, but not as much in the ways that many Asian and African students do.

American college students prefer shorter stays such as a semester, or even an eight-week term abroad in a foreign country. They soak up the cultural and social opportunities in addition to the studies abroad but not the same long periods of isolation. And, American students do not see as much benefit in attaining a degree from a foreign university in many fields. China, India and Korea are racing past the United States in terms of understanding and attaining keys to economic success through globalization. More of their residents gain social and cultural capital through more intensive study abroad.

The University of Virginia is a big beneficiary of this growing international trend, sending more of its students abroad and collecting more foreign scholars and their dollars and yens, yuan and wen, as well as the cultural transfer and good will of many people. The numbers of foreign students attending UVa continue to climb, jumping from about 630 in 1991 to more than 1,730 in 2008. The numbers of Chinese students studying at UVa has risen by about 60 students a year for several years, to a total of 600 as of this spring. More than 250 students from Korea attend UVa, and India also has more than 250 students attending. One trend that China and America seem to share is the production and reproduction of growing economic disparity. The rich on each side of the Pacific now grow richer faster than the common citizen's chances to climb up the ladder in a global market where trained brains reign. UVa's students, myself included, learn more about the world by sharing experiences with the smart foreign students earning graduate degrees. Having friends and fellow alumni on various continents feeds a quest for understanding.

7.4 Summary

Chapter Three: "Creating Our Own Cultural Stories," and Chapter Seven: "Contemporary Youth," are very different in content from all of the other chapters in *Communicating Interculturally* in that the brief essays in these chapters represent different realities than the academic information provided in the content of all the other chapters. In the first case, with cultural stories by both authors of the book, Professors Li Mengyu and Michael Prosser, as Chinese students you can get a clearer understanding of their own backgrounds that have led them to teach courses in intercultural communication and to co-author this book as intercultural collaborators, and then illustrative stories of young people, all Chinese but one, a young Russian university student living with her parents in the US. In the present chapter, we have a mix of academic ideas about young people in several different cultures and more personal information about the youth in these societies. Ali E. Abdul Rahman and Helene Dislaire from Belgium are our youngest writers. This chapter has provided examples from the US, South America, China, India (by a survey), Japan, Russia, and Africa. We are of course limited to only a selection of several countries rather than much more broadly, but the chapter adds to the understanding of cultural, intercultural, and multicultural dimensions of society and contemporary youth.

We can ask how do these illustrative examples in Chapters Three and Seven correlate not only with the dialogues introducing each chapter earlier, but also the academic content of these chapters? In Chapters One: "Culture" and Two: "Communication," we have learned how intertwined both concepts are to each other. Now, what implications are apparent as we introduce both real examples of self-disclosures by the young people in Chapter Three and the understandings, in Chapter Seven, of mostly well-educated adults (except for Helene Dislaire, speaking as a Belgian youth, and Ali E. Abdul Rahman, an Egyptian twin growing up in the US but of Egyptian background). As the chapters have continued to this point, we have learned academically about such concepts as perceptions, beliefs, attitudes, world views, values, culture patterns and value orientations in Chapters Four and Five and cultural language and nonverbal communication in Chapter Six.

As emerging critical thinkers, besides simply memorizing material for an upcoming test, how do the earlier chapters linked with Chapters Three and Seven, help you to think creatively and critically about intercultural communication in general and more specifically about aspects that you might not have considered at an earlier time in your education? In the context of Chapter Seven, you can make cross-cultural comparisons among the cultures represented and even among the cultural voices that we have now experienced. Both the dialogue for this chapter and Bob Gibson's case study return us to the concept of positive multicultural, international and global communication. Evelin Lindner (2010: 9) asserts that "equality in dignity is the new hoped-for future" and that the ideal global society fosters "respect, mutuality, and balance." It is "dialogue among partners considering each others as equal in dignity." She calls the most serious human challenges "a global culture of trust and cooperation." There needs to be a "bottom-up movement" that "calls on each global citizen to participate." Chapters One, Two, Four, Five, and Six have provided an academic background; the dialogues, though imaginary, have offered an informal approach to the issues; and Chapters Three and Seven have given us specific views of both young people and mature adults toward the creation of a global society of mutuality, trust, and dignity.

7.5   Questions for Discussion

7.5.1 In this chapter's dialogue, for the first time, we have a multicultural classroom, quite typical in many American universities, but rare in Chinese universities. What similarities and differences are apparent in considering an intercultural classroom, with only a couple of cultures represented, and this one in which there are several cultures in the dialogue? Why?

7.5.2 In the dialogue, we note that the Chilean student, Pablo, and Russian student, Gleb, freely discuss romantic topics; Yoshiko from Japan is very shy and modest; and Rashid and Ali demonstrate their devout Muslim beliefs. If we are noting how their identities are expressed differently, we might tend toward stereotypes about the different cultures. How can we use these examples as starting points to understand their cultures, rather than as stereotypes of all young people from their cultures?

7.5.3 In Michael Prosser's description of young Americans as "millennials," what differences emerge between the Americans called the "boomers" and the "millennials?" How can we see the relationships between the more academic descriptions of the millennials and his more personal view of a small group of Contemporary American youth, including the four high school students whom he interviewed and his own grandchildren? It is worth noting too that the four teenagers that Michael Prosser interviewed had never heard of the term "millennials." What then is the difference between the term given current young Americans as millennials and the real lives that these young students are living?

7.5.4 In Prosser's essay on American youth, he cites Mark Bauerlein's book, *The Dumbest Generation*, where Bauerlein is exceptionally harsh toward the recent American youth, and a contrasting argument by Sharon

Contemporary Youth

Begley who argues that being involved in computer games requires great skills of logic and rapid thinking. If you have met young Americans studying Chinese in your university, which view seems more reliable to you? Why?

7.5.5 Daniel Alonso, an Argentinian professor of law, discusses not only young people from Argentina, but also more broadly in Latin America where several bicentenarial independence celebrations have been taking place. Cross-culturally, what similarities and contrasts do we recognize between youth in the different countries in Latin America that he comments on?

7.5.6 The youngest writer of a short essay for *Communicating Interculturally*, Helene Dislaire (19 at the time of her writing) is decidedly more direct in her description of Belgian youth, and by extension, those in countries nearby, and about her own life than most of the young Chinese writing their cultural stories in Chapter Three. She seems very independent and somewhat rebellious, while at the same time aware of her own responsibility as a unique individual. Several of the writers in this chapter are mature adults and teaching in universities, while she is herself a student. Her comments relate to her own life situation, rather than the views of academics about the youth in their cultures. What are the major contributions that Helene makes in our understanding of her personal views about being young in northwestern Europe today? As young people yourselves, how would you compare your lives as young Chinese with Helene's life or Anya's life as she describes it in Chapter Three?

7.5.7 As young Chinese university students, "the post 1980s generation" and more likely the "post 1990s generation," how do you see your family's recent past and present situations, in comparison with Professor Li Mengyu's description of young Chinese? What are the challenges, opportunities, and problems that you face both collectively and individually as you plan your own future?

7.5.8 Egyptian society and its youth are very different than Chinese society and its youth. What are the major comparisons and contrasts that can be made between Egyptian, or other Middle Eastern youth and Chinese youth? What are the influences of a Muslim society on Middle Eastern youth versus the influences in an essentially atheistic society such as that in China on Chinese youth?

7.5.9 In the Hindustan Times survey results, we see that the lack of romance developing before marriage and the typical arranged marriage are very much the norm in the Indian society. Both China and India are the two largest Asian countries. How can Chinese society, which for the most part now allows romance before marriage and individual choices for marriage partners, compare with Indian society on these matters? Both societies and their young people believe that their patterns are wise and correct. What does this tell us about the major characteristics identified in Chapters Four and Five about Asian societies in general?

7.5.10 Professor Judy Yeonoka in describing Japanese youth as "the glocal generation" indicates that many young Japanese still live with their parents until their thirties, and may be identified as "lost" or "derailed." At the same time, they are often very globalized. How can we explain a generation of young Japanese who seems very parochial on one hand, and at the same time as globally oriented? Japan and China have often had a tumultuous relationship. What contributions are possible for reconciliation between the two societies that both young Chinese and young Japanese can make toward each other?

7.6 Suggested Readings

Chang, I. (2003). *The Chinese in America: A narrative history*. New York, NY: Viking.

Condon, J. C. & Saito, M. (Eds.) (1974). *Intercultural encounters with Japan: Communication, contact, and conflict*. Tokyo, Japan. Simul.

Donahue, R. T. (Ed.) (2002). *Exploring Japaneseness: On Japanese enactments of culture and consciousness*. Westport, CT: Ablex.

Farrer, J. (2002). *Opening up: Youth, sex, culture, and market reform in Shanghai*. Chicago, IL: University of Chicago Press.

Mathews, G. & White, B. (2006). *Japan's Changing Generations: Are Young People Creating a New Society*? Routledge. Japan Anthropology Workshop Series.

Chapter EIGHT

Cultural Media

8.1 Dialogue

Professor Zhang: Class, today we will discuss media of various sorts, and especially media that are intercultural or international such as newspapers, magazines, books, radio, television, cinema and the Internet. You may read *The People's Daily* in Chinese, English, Arabic, French, Russian, or Spanish; *China Daily*, *Inside China Today*, *Shanghai Daily*, *South China Morning Post*, *The Economic Observer*, or *Twenty-First Century* all in English.

Sunny: My father got me a subscription to *Twenty-first Century* and each week I had to read to him from the paper to practice my English. Once I entered the *Twenty-first Cup* competition and I gave a very good speech on the general topic *Never Give Up*. I talked about why I never gave up learning English. I really liked the paper's advice columns, and I sent in a question that got included and answered in the paper.

Joy: I also used to read *Twenty-first Century* and I was in the *Twenty-first Century Cup Competition* too. Perhaps we were in the finals at the same time as the general topic was also *Never give up*.

Michael: At two Chinese universities where I taught, I received *China Daily* six times a week and it was very useful for me to know what was going on in China. *China Daily* is one of the top ten online newspapers in the world. I have read *The Shanghai*

Cultural Media

Daily and *The South China Morning Post* as well. I also used to read *Twenty-First Century* to check to see what topics my students were writing about in my advanced writing classes and to be sure that I wasn't receiving plagiarized articles from issues of the paper. Except in 3 to 5 star hotels, or on newsstands near universities, it is often hard to find the English language newspapers like *China Daily*, and even *Twenty-first Century*.

Professor Zhang: Among the top circulation English newspapers in the world five are published in the UK: *The Sun*, *The Daily Mail*, *The Mirror*, *The Daily Telegraph*, and *The Daily Express*. Fleet Street in London is known world-wide as the center of the British newspaper industry. Only four are published in the US, *USA Today*, *The Wall Street Journal*, *The New York Times*, and *The Los Angeles Times*. Rupert Murdoch owns *The Wall Street Journal* which is very conservative. *The Times of India* is the only one outside of the UK or US among the top ten English newspapers in the world. But, among the top world online newspapers, as Michael mentioned, *The China Daily* is one of the top ones, number six I think. *The New York Times*, *The Washington Post*, and *The Los Angeles Times* are the top three. Another California online newspaper, *The San Jose Mercury News*, is number four. *The Financial Times* out of London is the fifth. Then after these six, there are four others, one in Tokyo; one in Munich; one in Sydney; and one in Buenos Aires.

Maria: I read an article during the 2008 US election about Sarah Palin who was running for Vice President with Senator McCain that when she was asked which newspapers she read, she couldn't mention any. Which newspapers do you read, Michael?

Michael: I read articles online from the three top online American newspapers and *The Daily Telegraph* almost every day. I usually start the day checking emails and also reading headlines or full articles from these online newspapers. I have a subscription to *Time Magazine* and read it online too. In December 2010, *Time* featured Sarah Palin on the cover with the title: "Palin in Progress: Does she want to be President? Or just rich and famous?" She is certainly one of the most popular women today in America.

Catherine: Being rich and famous would be quite nice!

Fiona: I have taken Spanish. Maybe I can read *The Clarion* from Argentina or another Spanish speaking country online. My teacher had some copies of *La Pais* from Spain and *La Vanguardia* from Argentina which I found very interesting. I couldn't read too much as my Spanish vocabulary is not strong enough. I was really happy a few classes ago when Pablo joined us from Chile.

Professor Zhang: Fiona, you might try www.clarion.com for the Argentine online newspaper.

Ava: I have studied French, and I have read some newspaper articles from *Le Monde* and *La Figoro* from France. I read *Victor Hugo's Hunchback of Notre Dame*, but in Chinese.

Peter: I have studied German, and we read some of the issues of *Der Spiegel Magazine*.

Professor Zhang: Some of you might read the fashion magazines or life style magazines like *Woman*, *WomanFriend*, *Mercury Digest*, *Trends Magazine*, the literary magazine *Tian Ya*, the e magazine *Qi Meng* (Enlightenment Monthly), *Modern Weekly*, or *Live Fun*. The boys might like sports magazines like *Sports Weekly* or *Titan Sports*, or for style *Men's Style*. You may all like news weeklies such as *Outlook*, *Oriental Outlook* or *Phoenix Weekly* from Hong Kong. Of course, you can all listen to China Radio International or music stations. On TV, there are a lot of game shows and romance shows, plus Channel V and MTV. The classic Chinese books, *Journey to the West* and *The Dream of the Red Chamber* have been popularized as a Chinese TV series here in China. CCTV Channel 4 is a world-wide Mandarin Chinese network, and the Channel of CCTV *News* has been a world-wide English network. Those of you who like sports will probably watch CCTV 5, or ESPN for those who live close to Hong Kong. Phoenix TV is all in Chinese but it has good news coverage, and its sister channel, Star, has some very good movies. CCTV has an Arabic, French, Portuguese, Spanish and Russian network as well, and even a classical music station.

Jasmine: Professor Zhang, you know a lot more about Chinese media than we do, but my favorite life style magazine is *Live Fun*. It is one of the best of the magazines for us. I like the music on MTV and Channel V. Sometimes MTV also has very fascinating black rapper singers too. I am trying to learn to do rap music too in English.

Peter: I am interested in a business career, so I read *Business Beijing* which is a bi-monthly magazine.

Lucky: South Park is supposed to be an adult animated TV show, but I like it too. Personally, I also like The Simpsons. It has been on the air 20 years and Bart never gets any older. Some people say that I look like him.

Laughter

Joy: Why, come to think of it, Lucky, you do look like Bart Simpson!

Laughter

Cultural Media

Mike: I watched all 10 years of *Friends* and I have learned a lot of English. Since I own the whole set, I can watch a program and then watch it again to catch some of the phrases of Chandler, Joey, or Ross, and then practice them. "How ya doin' Rachel?" "What'up, Ross?" My favorite character is Phoebe and her evil twin Ursula. She plays both parts, you know.

Summer: My twin sister, Spring and I like that part too, but especially when Phoebe had triplets. Since we are identical twins, perhaps each of us will have twins as well.

Michael: Would you say then that *Friends* is not just entertainment, but also is teaching you more English? I have had a lot of students who own the entire ten years set, and practice their American English that way. I watched all ten seasons with students. Often though, there are a lot of puns that are hard for Chinese audiences to understand, even though the American audiences are laughing loudly. Or perhaps it is just a laugh sound track?

Ivy: I watch movies which I download on my computer. One of my favorites was *The Chronicles of Narnia: The Voyage of the Dawn Treader*.

Tony: My favorite movie was *Harry Potter and the Deathly Hallows*, but when they broke it into two movies, I got tired of how long Harry and his friends were wandering around the forest in the first part. I have heard that now there is a boxed set of all seven books in English. I wish they would do the same in Chinese. Now Harry Potter is about our age. I am watching *The Vampire Diaries* on my computer.

Jason: Besides my favorite movies *Harry Potter and the Deathly Hallows*, *2012*, and *Tron*, I also liked *Brokeback Mountain* directed by the Chinese director Ang Lee.

Michael: Before, some of you talked about your favorite movies. Catherine, you said that you really enjoyed *Tangled* in which Disney retells the Rapunzel story, and Sunny, you said that you liked *Kungfu Panda*. Lucky, you told us that *Avatar* was your favorite movie. My grandchildren said the same thing. What impressed you the most?

Lucky: Jake was my favorite character, and before the movie ended, he returned to life and got his legs back. He helped the Na'vi people a lot. The Na'vi people were really brave.

Ava: I liked the mixing of the humans and the animation for the characters on the Na'vi home tree. I think that the great animation was done in New Zealand. I was surprised that *Avatar* lost out to *Hurt Locker* in the Oscar awards.

Jade: There was an important moral lesson in the movie. The general told the main character, Jake, that he could have his legs back and healthy, but he had to betray the Na'vi people in the giant Home Tree. He didn't do it, and in the end he was returned to life while Grace did not return. Why did she die and he lived?

Jason: James Cameron was a terrific and imaginative director. The Americans made *Kungfu Panda*, but I think that Chinese animators could have made it even better. Some of the best animators are from Japan. China could have animators as good as in Japan and the US if we tried. Maybe some of us now in university will make big breakthroughs in animation.

Michael: My Chinese webmaster Wing is very good in creating animation. In the 2004 Ultima series, *Avatar* represents a set of ethical guidelines called the Virtues. James Cameron's 2009 *Avatar* is not only the highest grossing movie in the US, China, and more broadly, even surpassing *Titanic*. It is a very challenging epic science fiction movie for us to discuss in an intercultural communication class. James Cameron said that the movie about the Na'vi (or native) people on Pandora, the fictional extraterrestrial moon universe which the technologically superior former marines wanted to destroy to obtain the precious uobtanium, really was the contrast between those who believe that humans should have total control over nature, and those who want to preserve nature and those civilizations which do not wish to be so technologically advanced. Some critics called it a remake of James Fenimore Cooper's *The Noble Savage*, or "an all purpose allegory."

True Nation: I read in *Twenty-First Century* that Cameron may have made the destruction of "Home Tree" as a metaphor about the 2001 destruction of the twin towers in the World Trade Towers, or as the American and British invasion of Iraq in 2003. What do you think? Some people believe that it did not receive an Oscar in 2010 because of what was seen as an anti-American theme. In any case, there are themes and subthemes of cultural and societal imperialism, racism, militarism, excessive patriotism, and corporate greed versus citizens' rights. Since so many of us saw it in the cinemas or online, I agree that it's worth talking about in our study of intercultural communication.

Robin: I loved all three of the *Toy Story* movies because of their great animation, but I also liked the different versions of *Shrek*. *Avatar* was my favorite movie with both the humans and the animated scenes on the Na'vi home tree.

Tony: I am not surprised that *Hurt Locker* won the Oscar award for the best movie. Cameron's former wife, Kathryn Bigelow's *Hurt Locker* was a really awesome Iraq war movie. *Inception* was very pschologically interesting, placing a dream inside a dream in the characters' minds, but it was very violent too. I also liked *Matrix* when we were young which was also a psychological drama. One of the great old psychological movies was Alfred Hitchcock's *Psycho*. I also liked the Coen brother's movie *Intolerable Cruelty*.

Michael: Peter W. Singer's 2009 book, *Wired for War: The Robotics Revolution and Conflict in the 21st Century*, which was a *New York Times* bestseller, talks about how not only computer games but now more and more real battles are being fought using robotics instead of humans. Japan and Republic of Korea both had an important part in the development of game theory and robotics as friendly household helpers, but nowadays both China and the US are developing very fast technology to use even small robotics to send out missiles, or to set off a bomb or incendiary device, or to stop a missile launch in mid-air. Pakistan and Afghanistan leaders are both concerned about the hundreds of drone attacks that the US is launching with near pin prick precision against enemy bases in their countries and killing lots of innocent civilians.

Jade: As we learned before, the more that we increase our intercultural communication competence, and have actual experiences with foreigners, then we see less of a threat. Even when I meet the Japanese students I now realize that what their grandparents did in China in the 1930s and 1940s is not the fault of the young Japanese nor their responsibility.

Professor Zhang: Class, if we were talking about your favorite English novels, what would they be?

Jasmine: I don't like to read unpleasant books about international relations, wars, or threats. I like Jane Austen's *Pride and Prejudice* and *Sense and Sensibility*. Austen promotes the importance of women long before other English novelists.

Michelle: I have read all of the Harry Potter books. I really liked *Harry Potter and the Half Blood Prince*. I have also watched all of the Harry Potter movies that have been available in China. I want to read *Harry Potter and the Deathly Hallows*.

Michael: Three of my granddaughters, Christine, Elizabeth, and Mary Catherine Rose and I went to a giant book store to get copies of *Harry Potter and the Half Blood Prince* at midnight the day it became available. There were long lines of people dressed like Harry Potter characters.

Tiger: I like action movies, like *Saving Private Ryan* or *Hurt Locker*. I told you already that I took my name from *Crouching Tiger, Hidden Dragon*. I hear that the

Americans loved that Chinese movie, but it was very ordinary for us. For books, I like suspense books like Dan Brown's *The Da Vinci Code* and *The Digital Fortress*. Recently I downloaded the 2010 movie *2012*. When the world is falling apart, where do you think that everyone wants to come? China!

Class applause

Forest: You all know that I took my English name, Forest, from *Forrest Gump*!

Vivian: We know Forest, and how you like boxes of chocolate because you never know what you are going to get! Have you ever watched any other movies?

Laughter

Forest: Yes, *Back to the Future* was one that I liked because it was like Forrest Gump. But, as I said, I also liked *Brokeback Mountain*, Vivian. I also liked the movie, *Charlie and the Chocolate Factory*!

Vivian: Naturally, you would like that movie, Forest. You would like to be "Charlie in the chocolate factory."

Laughter

Forest: Why not? Then I could have all of the chocolate that I want.

Laughter

Michael: One of the few movies that I have seen in a Chinese cinema besides the Harry Potter movies, *Titanic*, and *Pearl Harbor*, was Zhang Yimou's 2002 *Hero* which I heard was China's most expensive film up to that time. I liked Jet Li's role. There didn't seem to be much plot, but of course I was seeing it in Chinese rather than English, and it was filled with beautiful colors.

Gloria: Yes it was a wonderful story of the Qin Dynasty. It made us all proud. And Zhang Yimou designed the entire opening ceremony for the Beijing Olympics which I was proud to see as an Olympics volunteer. He is considered today China's best mainland film director, but don't forget the Hong Kong film director too, Wong Kar-Wu. His *Mood for Love* movie was very exciting.

Echo: What do you think are favorite books in American literature, Michael?

Michael: Probably *Tom Sawyer* and *Huckleberry Finn* by Mark Twain. I read them when I was about 12 or 13. There is a new Autobiography of Mark Twain published recently. He said that these materials couldn't be published until 100 years after his death. Now that's happened.

Cultural Media

Cindy: I have read both *Tom Sawyer* and *Huckleberry Finn* and also his *Life on the Mississippi*.

Echo: My favorite American novel was Herman Melville's *Moby Dick*.

Ava: Emily Dickinson is my favorite American woman poet. My favorite British woman poet is Elizabeth Barrett Browning. I liked Mian Mian's novel *Candy*.

Michael: When I was your age, I read a lot of the novels by William Faulkner, Ernest Hemmingway, John Dos Pasos, and John Steinbeck. I have given Hemingway's *Old Man and the Sea* to teenagers who are learning English as the English is simple but powerful. I wrote my MA thesis on solitude in the writings of Nathaniel Hawthorne. He was writing more than 100 years after the Puritan period that his novels and short stories depict. Perhaps among the British literature, I liked Charles Dickens as an author best with his *Oliver Twist*, *Great Expectations*, and *Tale of Two Cities*. These books are popular again in the US.

Michelle: I particularly liked *Oliver Twist* and I saw the musical *Oliver*. I also liked Victor Hugo's *Les Miserables* and I have also have seen that musical, both of them in the US when I was there. Both were very moving to me.

Michael: Oh, Michelle, that's great. I have seen both musicals too. On the other hand, in my own case, in terms of poetry, I especially like Edgar Allen Poe's *The Raven*, Walt Whitman's *Leaves of Grass*, Carl Sandburg's Chicago poems or those of Toni Morrison and her book *The Color Purple* which later became an excellent movie, Maya Angelou with her autobiographical *I Know Why the Caged Bird Sings*, and the authors James Baldwin's *Go Tell It on the Mountain* and Ralph Ellison's *Invisible Man* both impressed me. I read a lot of biographies like James Boswell's famous biography of Samuel Johnson and historical and political works too, and of course a lot about culture and communication. I have read a number of books about contemporary Chinese culture, some of which are not available in China. I try to read two books a month on average.

Jenny: That's a lot of books, Michael. If I read one book a month, it is like one of Han Han's light novels, especially *His Life*.

Professor Zhang: I read a lot of books professionally about social and cross-cultural psychology. My life is teaching, teaching, teaching, and grading, grading, grading! When I have time, I read and write professionally as much as possible about intercultural communication.

Cherry: You told us, Michael, that you have read some of the major Chinese classics in English.

Michael: Yes of course in English, Cherry. I would have to start with Confucius' *Analects*, which I have read several times, plus Lao Tsu's *The Art of War*. I have enjoyed also in English some of Lu Xun's works like *Diary of a Mad Man* and *The True Story of Ah Q*. I have a four volume set of his selected works. I also liked *Moment in Peking* by Lin Yutang, as well as his book, *My Country and My People*, and his philosophical book, *The Importance of Living* which was a gift to me from Professor Li Mengyu. Lin Yutang and Pearl Buck, who wrote *The Good Earth*, were close friends. I have read some of *Dream of Red Mansions*, *Romance of the Three Kingdoms*, *The Outlaws of the Marsh*, and *Journey to the West*, all in English. Another earlier book about China that I found very interesting was Edgar Snow's *Red Star Over China*.

Coco: You know, Michael, Edgar Snow's mausoleum is near Nameless Lake at Peking University? It's a lovely and quiet setting. There is a beautiful pagoda nearby.

Michael: Yes, I have visited there several times. Nowadays, we can do almost everything through the Internet, get Amazon's Kindle, read major articles in the world's best newspapers, see streaming TV shows or movies, search for materials through Bing or Google, and have instant translations, be involved in chat rooms, and meet old and new friends almost all on line. I have even remet some of my former Chinese students who are living outside of China on Facebook or Linked In. Even though Mark Bauerlein's book, *The Dumbest Generation*, decries the American youth's lack of interest in intellectual endeavors, a lot can be learned by absorbing popular culture too.

Sophia: I saw Han Han's t blog about being in the top ten of *Time*'s list of the world's most influential people. His final sentence in the blog said: "And those of us on this stage, even those who built this theater in the past, should make efforts to gradually take down those high walls and light bulbs. Let the sunshine in. That kind of light, no one can extinguish it again." I really like that sentence, "Let the sunshine in." He really is the voice of Chinese youth. It reminds me of Shakespeare's quote from "As You Like It," "All the world's a stage, and all the men and women merely players."

Tiger: Michael, have you heard the mythical story about the ancient Chinese dove, Gu Ge? It used to live in mainland China, but in March 2010, it decided to fly from the mainland to Hong Kong, as the giant river crab decided that they could no

Cultural Media

longer live together. Because of the change in the climate, the ancient voracious bird species Pidu ate all of food that Gu Ge used to eat, and became bigger and bigger and increased the population of the Pidu in the mainland. the river crab which always walks sideways had to work hard to keep moving harmoniously without his friend Gu Ge to help point out the way.

Laughter

Michael: Yes, Tiger, I have heard that myth, promoted I think by Han Han. It is a very interesting one. The Chinese also used to have the myth that the Great Wall and the Egyptian pyramids were the only man-made structures that could be seen from outer space. However, when the Chinese technonauts reported on their explorations of space, they said that they could not see any man-made structures from space. Each culture has its own myths. For example, in the US, as children we learned that our first president, George Washington, as a boy had cut down his father's cherry tree, and said to his father, "Father, I cannot tell a lie. I have cut down the cherry tree." The only problem with that story was that it was a myth that was created in the 1880s about 90 years after Washington died.

Laughter

Professor Zhang: Chinatoday.com recently indicated that in 1978 there were 186 newspapers and 93 magazines, but in 2010 there were 2,081 magazines and 9,363 newspapers. That's a phenomenal growth, don't you think? Some critics say that Han Han's 14 novels are really only one novel about disaffected youth in China. What is his magazine supposed to be about?

Lucky: Han Han said that his magazine, *Solo Party*, would not be a very literary magazine, but like a Zhiyin magazine, or like *Reader's Digest* for Chinese young people. His magazine has presently been shelved, as Han Han has said, "The flight is delayed, not due to mechanical troubles, but poor weather conditions."

Laughter

Robin: I went to the World Expo in 2010, but there were so many lines that I could hardly get into any pavilions. I did not see the Chinese Pavilion. Han Han was answering questions in April 2010 on his blog: "Come quickly. Leave quickly!" about the Expo crowds and the Expo's mascot, "Haibao," and he said: "Haibao makes my head hurt." He made some funny and sarcastic comments about the shape of Haibao which a lot of young people liked. Haibao was really sort of silly as a mascot! But I got a little Haibao when I was at the Expo.

Ivy: Yes, I read that blog too, when he said that the Expo would be a big spectacle, and Chinese love spectacles, like the CCTV Lunar New Year Eve giant four hour show, mostly for older people. But many million people watch it.

Professor Zhang: I visited the Expo and liked very much the German high-tech pavilion. I couldn't get in the China Pavilion after the Expo closed and I have heard that there are still thousands of people going to see that exhibit, mostly Chinese of course.

Forest: I went too, and I had some delicious chocolates at the Belgian Pavilion. After the Expo ended on October 31, 2010, most of the pavilions were torn down, but not the Chinese pavilion which continued to have 35,000 Chinese coming in every day for a long time.

Professor Zhang: There are still a lot more challenging things we could talk about in terms of the media, but today, in our class lesson, we are going to focus primarily on Chinese and also international and global media. We have started a good discussion about the importance for intercultural and cross-cultural communication in the TV programs, books, magazine, cinema, the Internet and blogs. There are now 384 million Internet users in China and 181 million blogs. Cooper Wakefield has a very good essay on how to assess intercultural and international cinema and Cui Litang has a good case study for us, "Wrangling the Media Market Place."

Tony: Ok. Let's do it!

8.2   Media and Mass Communication Theories

Kevin J. Pearce (2009: 623–627) reminds us that until rather recently there were only eight traditional media types: **books, newspapers, magazines, recordings, movies, radio, television**, and **the Internet**. He defines mass communication as "the process by which a person, group of people, or large organization creates a message and transmits it through some type of medium to a large, anonymous, heterogeneous audience. In mass communication, the source is typically a professional communicator or a complex organization that incurs at a great cost. The message is typically rapid and public." However, Pearce says that in computer mediated communication today "with a good computer and basic computer skills, a single individual can publish his or her own professional looking magazine." He notes that some scholars see that even cell phones with their text messaging, Internet and web connection capacity can often be considered aspects of mass media. Many more traditional media scholars and teachers would disagree with this idea. We would agree that both mobile phones, with cameras, text messaging, gaming, email, and news reception are indeed aspects of the media. Indeed, ipods, kindle, gaming stations, Wii, and robotics are also parts of the media, deserving to be studied. Even the vast entertainment empire of Disney is a medium itself, as is advertising. Surely, the 2008 Beijing Olympics, the Shanghai Expo in 2010, the 16th Asian Games in Guangzhou, and the 2010 World Cup in South Africa were also important examples of mass media.

Pearce believes that print media wereot the force that caused mass media to be studied but the introduction of film, radio, and TV, as the first films were made at the end of the 1800s and the early 1900s; the first radio station was inaugurated on November 2, 1920. He suggests three paradigms in considering mass media: (1) **the powerful effects paradigm** (with the audience considered as passive: 1920s–1940s); (2) **minimalist effects or limited effects paradigm** (mass media having little direct influence on voting behavior: Paul Lazarsfeld and others promoted this paradigm); and (3) **cumulative effects paradigm** (developing influence over a long period and powerful). The last paradigm is often considered the most influential. American children certainly see far more television before they are twelve years old than all of the time spent learning in school, and thus longitudinal studies are frequently conducted by media scholars.

Among the several media and mass communication theories discussed by Pearce, of particular importance for you as intercultural communication students are the **cultural and societal theories**, and he argues that most of these theories are involved more with the macrolevel of culture and society, for example, **the media dependency theory** (a systems based theory that examines the mutual dependence between the media system, the political system and the general public). In this case, the political and media systems need each other. In the Western countries, Japan, and India, with a libertarian media system, the media have a great deal of leeway in investigative journalism and in criticizing the government; plus they are often considered the "watchdog" of the government or "fourth estate" with the executive, legislative and judicial bodies. In the United States' first amendment to the Constitution, besides the freedoms of speech, press, religion, and assembly, the fifth aspect is that citizens have the right to petition their government for redress of grievances. There are several European countries which allow groups of citizens to control aspects of the press or electronic media based on the number of members in their group.

Four other media theories relate to culture and society according to Pearce. **The agenda-setting theory** indicates whether the social and political agenda can be set by the government (top down) the media itself, or individuals acting together or on their own (bottom-up). When individuals or groups of individuals act on their own (grassroots), sometimes this forces either the government or the media to make changes that would not otherwise happen. **The spiral of silence theory** is a theory of public opinion or suppression against those with deviant behavior or novel ideas. **The knowledge gap hypothesis** relates to the role and use of communication technology in society, with the information **haves** (information-rich) and **have-nots** (information-poor) leading to faster adoption of new technologies more quickly for the information-rich members

of the society than for those who are information-poor. Governments often try to assist the latter group through **development communication**, whether it is related to domestic situations, agriculture, business or education. For example, in China, by the simplification of the Chinese ideograph system of language and the introduction of *pinyin*, more than 100,000 million rural Chinese have become literate and moved out of poverty—a remarkable feat in modern China. **The cultural imperialism theory** stresses mostly on how Western nations, including the US and European Union, seek to dominate all aspects of the media with potentially powerful negative effects around the world. In Chapter Nine, our case study considers the concept of the McDonaldization of society, with both its positive and negative cultural and societal effects. We will see implicitly the effects on society that McDonaldization has in making its citizens culturally dependent on fast food, and representing Westernization or even Americanization. Pearce identifies the last of the cultural and societal theories as **the critical cultural studies theories**, considering how the media relate to "matters of ideology, race, social class, and gender." This theory developed initially in Germany and the UK.

Another category of theories related to the media which Pearce introduces are the **theories of influence and persuasion**. In Chapter Two, we gave an extended example of President Obama's use of a "personalized" three-step persuasive media message through the Internet to Michael Prosser on laws which he wished to have Congress enact against Wall Street financiers. Pearce notes that such theories are the most researched theories with effective studies, and he cites four theories in this class: **social cognitive theory** (researching how and why people tend to model what they see in the media without having direct experience); **the cultivation theory** (where earlier researchers believed that TV was the major force and story-teller, convincing people to take certain actions); **the elaboration likelihood model** (examining the ways in which people are persuaded), and **the desensitization theory** (where repeated exposure to violent or sexual images reduces their initial negative reactions and makes people comfortable with seeing, hearing or reading about such images). The Vietnam War was the first war that was delivered to American TVs, and the theory would suggest that these violent images had the effect of desensitizing those who watched it to other types of violence.

Finally, Pearce offers the **media use theory** which studies the uses and gratification concept, focusing on why we choose to expose ourselves to specific forms of media. **We can**

question if images produced by McDonald's Golden Arches, KFC's Colonel Sanders, and Disney products, movies, and theme parks are more and more successful in China because many Chinese want to associate themselves with personal images that are Western.

Pearce says that if users need information, there are many different media, individual, or organizational sources to choose from. Why do we choose one media outlet over others? In the current period, computer mediated communication, ipods, Blackberries, mobile phones, and other media producing devices, including even robotic communication, make it easy to gain such information, or to seek pleasurable entertainment, especially when we can carry such small media sources with us wherever we go. Pearce concludes that with definitions of media and mass communication in a constant state of flux, "new communication technologies are blurring the lines and altering the definitions. New theories are being developed to address the changing nature of the media" (627).

8.3   Broadcasting Theory

James Shanahan (2009: 79–83) recalls that **broadcasting theory** was the most important media theory development in the twentieth century, but that such theories are far fewer than we might expect, as most media theories deal with **media effects**. In terms of **broadcasting theories**, he notes first that the **media effects theory** was applied to newspapers and other print media, with the

hypothesis for broadcasting "that mass media had relatively powerful effects in terms of forming and changing beliefs and that the audience was relatively passive in terms of processing messages and accepting them." He identifies Harold Lasswell's **communication model** "Who says what to whom in what channel with what effect?" This **"powerful effects" theory** was discounted as early as the

1940s, and the model changed to the **personal influence** or **limited effects paradigm** because studies began to show that the media were no more powerful than those individuals who were closest to those receiving the messages. As late as the 1950s, Shanahan claims, there were few reasonably tested **broadcasting theories**, particularly in terms of radio which had been the dominant electronic medium up to that time. Some scholars coming out of the Frankfurt School in Germany conceived of mass media, especially the electronic media as a **culture industry**. Shananan recalls that after the claim of "the death of communication research" by Bernard Berelson, media scholars began to test theories that were in the middle of the **limited effects theory** and the **powerful effects theory**.

George Gerbner and his colleagues at the Annenberg School at the University of Pennsylvania began to consider the **cultivation theory** as it related to **broadcast media**, especially television. Gerbner hypothesized that because television produced a lot of violent images, then the viewers would tend to see the world as a violent place. As has already been noted above in our discussion of **media and mass communication theories, the agenda-setting theory** was developed: "media might tell people, not what to think, but what to think about." A third theory which Shanahan discusses is the **spiral of silence**, also discussed in the previous section of this chapter. Shanahan suggests that all of the theories were a response to the continuing development of **television as a power medium**. Then as other media developed, more and more social critics concerned themselves with building **additional media theories**. The impact of **television violence** (and by extension, **cinematic violence** and others, became a major focus in the development of **broadcast theories**. Since the 1972 US Surgeon General's report, later updated to 1982, **linking television violence to societal violence**, "the dominant view has been that television violence does result in negative outcomes such as **desensitization to violence**, **imitation of violence** seen, and **acceptance of violence** as a way to solve problems." Shanahan claims that "there is little doubt that television has been viewed within society as **the most powerful mass medium** ever devised, at least since the 1960s." He does admit that television's importance in developing **broadcast theories** has declined since the growing influence of the Internet.

However, the December, 2010, decision by *Time* Magazine to name Mark Zuckerberg, the founder of Facebook, which now has a billion subscribers world-wide as its "Person of the Year" certainly challenges this statement by Shanahan. He discusses theories of **modernization** and **technological determinism** with the media being shaped by its form as articulated by Marshall McLuhan, saying that all of these theories have led more and more to the broader concept of **globalization**. Shanahan concludes his essay by noting that Raymond Williams' 2003 book, *Television, Technology and Cultural Form* theorizes that political, social, and cultural decisions always affect how the **media technology** develops and is utilized (83).

8.4 International and Global Media Theories

In contrast to the cross-cultural national characteristics or dimensions, when we discuss **international** and **global communication**, Thomas L. McPhail, in his book, *Global Communication* (2010) defines it as referring "to the cultural, economic, political, social, and technical analysis of communication and media patterns and effects across and between nation-states. International communication focuses more on global aspects of media and communication systems and technologies and, as a result, less on local or even national aspects or issues" (2010: 2). McPhail believes that "What is significant, then, is that international communication is no longer solely focused on the role of the print press and the newsgathering habits of the international news agencies, such as AP or Reuters.It is growing to encompass a broad range of issues that arose from the emergence of global broadcasting, global advertising, and the global economy" (34).

Noting a number of critical issues relating to **international communication**, he argues that they can be explained through three major theories or movements: **NWICO (New World Information and Communication Order)**, **electronic colonialism**, and **world system theories**: "International communication will have a greater impact on the future of the planet than exploration and transportation combined" (35). McPhail identifies the debate about the **NWICO** as dominating **the international communication agenda** for about two decades in the twentieth century,

with its final objective to restructure the system of media and telecommunication priorities so that lesser developed countries could "obtain greater influence over their media, information, economic, cultural, and political systems" and represents:

> *(1) An evolutionary process seeking a more just and equitable balance in the free flow and content of information;*
> *(2) A right to national self-determination of domestic communication policies;*
> *(3) And at the international level, a two-way information flow reflecting more accurately the aspirations and activities of less developed countries (12–13).*

McPhail identifies the **Electronic Colonialism Theory** (ECT) as passing through four epochs of **empire-building**: the Greco-Roman period; the Crusades of the Middle Ages, also called Christian colonialism; the mercantile colonialism in the seventeenth and eighteenth centuries of the British, French, Spanish, Belgians, Italians, Dutch, and Portuguese conquests of the Americas, Africa, Asia, and the Middle East; and finally, with the rise of nationalism and decolonization, the recent and current **electronic colonialism** represents the dependent relationship of poorer regions on the post-industrial nations, especially in the area of **communication transfer**. This has resulted in a **new global culture** created by "the large multimedia conglomerates." "ECT focuses on how global media, including advertising, influence how people look, think, and act…. Just as the era of the Industrial Revolution focused on manual labor, raw materials, and then finished products, so also the Information Revolution now seeks to focus on the role and consequences concerning the mind and global consumer behavior" (16–24).

McPhail labels what he considers the third major aspect in considering both the **international and global communication revolution** as the **World System Theory (WST)**, which identifies the **core**, **periphery**, and **semiperiphery zones** in today's global setting. He defines the **core zone** as "Capital intensive, high-wage, high-technology production, involving lower labor exploitation and coercion"; the **semi-periphery zone** as "Core-like activities, Peripheral-like activities" and the **periphery zone** as "Labor-intensive, low-wage, low-technology production involving high labor exploitation and coercion." He contends that the "World system theory states that global economic expansion takes place from a relatively small group of core-zone nation-states [the industrialized West] out to two other zones of nation-states, these being in the semi-peripheral and peripheral zones." He identifies China as among the **semi-peripheral nations**, along with Brazil and India, all of which can expect in the near future to become **core nation-states**, rivaling both the US and European Union's initial ten nation-states. McPhail sees both the recent **Electronic Colonialism Theory** and the **World System Theory** as being closely linked (24–30).

In this sense, we can also see the merger of both **international and global communication** through what McPhail calls "three new strong hegemonic communication forces stemming from: (1) expansion of cable and satellite broadcasting systems; (2) An avalanche of Western, primarily American, television and movie programming, and (3) The collective rules of the World Trade Organization, the World Bank, and the International Monetary Fund." McPhail notes that issues facing both **international and global communication** are explained through the three major theories or movements which he has proposed: "Collectively, they help organize or frame the trends, economics, technologies, and stakeholders involved in the dynamic, globally significant, and expanding role of international communication" (31–35).

8.5 Media Diplomacy

(**Michael H. Prosser, published originally in Stephen Littlejohn and Karen Foss (Eds.) (2009). The Encyclopedia of Communication Theory 2. Los Angeles: Sage, reprinted with permission**).

William R. Slomanson writes that the study of international relations began after WWI and increased considerably after WWII, but especially in the 1970s. He argues that it assesses good and bad relations, initially between sovereign states, and now more recently between states and other international actors, with a polarity between law, especially international law, power, and interests. It consists of rules governing the conduct of states, international organizations, non governmental organizations, individuals, and corporations in certain instances. Slomanson indicates that the monist approach assumes that international law and national laws form a unified, universal legal system while the dualist approach says that they are distinct systems, allowing states to accept or ignore international law if it conflicts with their national law. International law, according to Slomanson is the body of laws by which nations are bound in their mutual relations, based on conventions, treaties, customs, general principles of law, judicial decisions, and scholarly writings.

Diplomacy may be defined as the official conduct of international relations between national leaders, conducted privately and often in secret, or through public diplomacy. Diplomacy includes the establishment of foreign missions, ambassadors, envoys and consular services. Diplomatic efforts require nations to develop ministries of foreign affairs, the creation of national and international policies, and the establishment of missions abroad accredited by the host governments to carry out the policies and necessary personnel to make the systems work efficiently. The foreign ministry negotiates for the home government and reports on important events in the foreign country. It deals with many other activities, including exchanges at the level of specialized members of societies, public and media diplomacy, consular services for its citizens in other countries and visas for foreign citizens and residents.

Public diplomacy, a term coined in **1965 by Dean Edmund Gullion of the Fletcher School of Law and Diplomacy at Tufts University**, is all international diplomacy other than the direct official interactions between national governments, and includes the ways in which a country or an organization such as the United Nations communicates with citizens in other societies. It deals with the influence of public attitudes and opinion on the formation and execution of foreign policies, encompassing the cultivation by governments of public opinion in other countries; interactions of private groups and interests in one country with those of another; reporting foreign affairs and its impact on policy; and communication between diplomats and foreign correspondents. Central to public diplomacy is the transnational flow of information and ideas. Typically, considerable diplomatic media report addresses and meetings at the United Nations, often with as many as 1,000 or more journalists present during the annual General Assembly meetings. Currently, as many as 130 heads of state and government are present for the General Debates annually, with journalists reporting on the activities and debates on a global, regional, or national basis. Many other international and regional governmental and nongovernmental agencies and organizations exchange diplomats and utilize public and media diplomacy, such as the African Union, Arab League, ASEAN, European Union, Organization of American States, UNESCO, WHO and WTO. **Government-sponsored programs inform or influence public opinion in other countries; through publications, cinema, cultural exchanges, radio, television, the Internet, art, music, drama, sports, and public exhibitions**. In this sense, it is a dialogical two-way exchange between diplomats and citizens of other countries, or between citizens of various countries. Public diplomacy is thus people centric. Public diplomacy is also called cultural diplomacy, media diplomacy, public information, internal and external broadcasting and print media, transnational news, and political influence. Increasingly, public diplomatic media also include the internet, websites, chat rooms, and blogs which rapidly cross cultural, national, and regional borders.

Two public and media diplomacy case studies are illustrative. One of the most successful public and media diplomacy initiatives was the creation by international treaty in the 1950s of the European Coal and Steel Community which later became the European Union. Supporters of European integration believed that the Union has the benefit of creating greater international understanding and dialogue among European countries and as outreach to other countries. The European Union in 1994 identified three joint aims in developing media diplomacy for the contemporary information society: (1) A world perspective, encouraging international alliance strategies of companies and operators. (2) Awareness of European characteristics: multilingualism, cultural diversity, economic divergence, and preservation of its social model. (3) An open and competitive international system, and adequate development of basic information technologies. Another example that exemplifies public and media diplomacy is the US Office of Public Diplomacy and Public Affairs whose stated goal is to promote mutual understanding between the United States and other nations by conducting public educational, informational and cultural activities and explaining American foreign policy and US national interests abroad, primarily through its open and transparent media diplomacy.

Cinema

Among its media diplomacy endeavors are the shortwave Voice of America (VOA), its satellite 24 hour WORLDNET Television channel, as well as surrogate international broadcast services such as Radio Free Europe/Radio Liberty, Radio Marti, and Radio Free Asia. VOA presents more than 660 hours of programming weekly in more than 53 languages. The US Bureau of Public Affairs and International Information Programs provides electronic

and printed materials to TV and radio stations throughout the world, as well as regular position papers to foreign governments and media outlets. Cultural programs connected to the US embassies and consulates abroad often have an extensive paper, book, magazine and electronic information resource center for use by the foreign citizens.

Thus, official diplomacy is almost always supplemented by public and media diplomacy.

8.6 Cinema

8.6.1 Assessing Intercultural and International Cinema (Cooper Wakefield, MA, University of Kansas)

Films represent a great opportunity for IC students because moving pictures provide such vivid representations of people and cultures, stories and symbols. Through sight, sound, and narrative, films can engage both our emotions and our minds. This is why we love movies— they move us and cause us to be moved, whether it is fear, joy, excitement, sadness, or mirth, and spur us to imagine new things.

One of the possible positive results of this affective-cognitive experience is the potential to develop empathy— if we take the time to reflect on the cultural context that frames a film and allow ourselves to identify with the characters. While strange at first, or perhaps "unrealistic," an in-depth viewing and reflection can lead to deeper understanding of the systems at work in

a society and circumstances faced by the people. This can happen while watching a film from our own country, or a foreign film.

Take the film, "Tsotsi" (Hood, 2005) for example. The story of a teenaged gangster living in the shantytown of Soweto, South Africa, it is a brutal tale of crime and violence. The title character can easily be written off as no more than a thug (the meaning of tsotsi), but when one explores the societal systems, specifically the history of Apartheid, and the AIDS epidemic, the meaning of Tsotsi evolves. The movie "makes sense," and is no longer a film about gang violence, but about a boy's journey of transformation, and identifying, empathizing with the main character becomes possible, even desirable.

While films have great potential to be used for good, and to affect us in positive ways, there are also dangers. Stereotyping easily happens because films tend to depict exciting, novel, or unusual stories, and many viewers are unaware that pictures (moving or not) are not objective, neutral media, but rather complex constructions. People usually do not think that they believe films are "real" depictions of people but films may leave residue on our minds that resurfaces as truth if we do not critically examine them. An example of this is the violence prevalent in mainstream American films. Many who do not live in the United States assume that almost everyone must carry guns in the United States—far from the truth! Other much more destructive generalizations are the film portrayals of African Americans or other minorities, or the tendency for viewers of ethnographic films to adopt or strengthen stereotypes of "uncivilized" people groups (Martinez 2008). This can happen even to well-intentioned viewers hoping to learn about other cultures and is not helped by the fact that films often objectify groups of people, including women or minorities.

So, if we want to avoid the dangers and achieve the benefits, how should we go about it? First, develop a critical, reflective film watching habit. I suggest students take notes as they watch, asking questions or noting strange or unusual aspects of a film (props, dialogue, setting, narrative, etc). After the film, talk about it with others and write about it and your thoughts and feelings. Talking and writing about the film will keep your brain engaged with the problems of the film, and will help you reflect on it (Zoreda, 2006). Next, develop an understanding of how images in films, commercials or advertisements are used to create messages. Skill in "reading images" will serve you well in all areas of communication.

8.6.2   Chinese Cinema: A Challenging Chinese Film: "Nanjing! Nanjing! City of Life and Death:" Directed by Lu Chuan (Michael H. Prosser)

Iris Chang's 1998 *Rape of Nanking* claimed that upward towards 300,000 of Nanjing's citizens were brutally killed and 20,000–80,000 women and girls were raped by Japanese soldiers in the six weeks 1937–1938 period following the fall of the then capital of the Republic of China on December 13, 1937. It was an immediate sensation in the United States, receiving both widespread media commendation and severe criticism for possible exaggerations and inaccuracies. Chang later committed suicide.

On April 22, 2009, with a 2007 permit by the Chinese government and support of Politburo member and Head of the Chinese Propaganda Department, Li Changchun, Chinese Director Lu Chuang released his third feature film in Chinese, "Nanjing! Nanjing!" ("City of Life and Death"). Lu shot the film over eight months on the outskirts of Changchun with a cast of 100. It was in Chinese cinemas for nearly three weeks, viewed by three million people, and making Lu only one of five Chinese film directors to earn more than 100 million rmb at the box office. After a warm reception at the Cannes Film Festival, it was purchased for screening in British cinemas beginning in April 2010 (Moore, 2010: April 16). Lu received the "Achievement in Directing Award" and his colleague, Ye Cao received the "Achievement in Cinematography" award at the November 27, 2009 UNESCO endorsed Queensland, Australia Gold Coast Asia Pacific Screen Awards (Dwyer, 2009: November 27). It was well received at the

Toronto and Mar del Plata film festivals. The Chinese government pulled it and another Chinese film, Ye Kai's short "Quick Quick Slow Slow," from the January 2010 Palm Springs (Florida) International Film Festival because of other films about China that were displeasing to the government (Zhao, K, 2009) .

Writing in *The New York Times*, Edward Wong noted that Lu was enthusiastic about cinema as a senior middle school student, particularly about the works of Fifth Generation Chinese film directors, Zhang Yimou and Chen Kaige, and that his favorite American film was "Apocalypse Now." Though he wanted to go to a film university, his father required him to enroll at a PLA university. Later, however, he wrote his MA thesis on the directing of the famous American director, Francis Ford Cappola. His first two feature movies were "Missing Gun" in 2002, and a low budget film, "Kekexli" which cost 12 times less to make than "Nanjing! Nanjing!" (Wong, 2009: May 23).

Synopsis, International Media Data Base (2009), posted by Zhao Kaiyu:

> *"'City of Life and Death' takes place in 1937, during the height of the Second Sino-Japanese War. The Imperial Japanese Army has just captured the then-capital of the Republic of China, Nanjing. What followed was known as the Nanking Massacre, or the Rape of Nanking, a period of several weeks wherein tens of thousands of Chinese soldiers and civilians were killed. The film tells the story of several figures, both historical and fictional, including a Chinese soldier, a schoolteacher, a Japanese soldier, a foreign missionary, and John Rabe, a Nazi businessman who would ultimately save thousands of Chinese civilians."*

Writing in The Telegraph, Malcolm Moore entitled his article,"Nanjing: A Journey to Hell!" which had been a quote made by Lu after the film was released. Lu said that "The very fact that the movie got a permit shows that the Chinese government has made baby steps in tolerating and embracing the different, the controversial and the other." Many Chinese viewers and bloggers condemned the movie and him because "They basically could not accept that I tried to portray Japanese soldiers as humans, rather than as beasts" and "That war crushes even the victors." He cast the well-known Japanese actor Hideo Nakeuzumi as Kaokawa, who was tortured by his requirement to kill so many people; the famous Chinese actress, Yuanyuan Gao as Miss Jing, who was brutalized by the Japanese soldiers, and Ye Liu as Liu Nianxiong. Some of the Japanese actors in the movie were reviled both by the Japanese and Chinese and two lead actors moved to China because of their ill treatment in Japan. Gao as Miss Jing became so depressed that she hid often in her dressing room, and was so emotionally distraught that sometimes a single brutal scene had to be redone 20 times. One half of the cast of 100 left before the final scenes were shot. Lu, himself, and his family received death threats and warnings that he would be dismembered or castrated for showing the Japanese soldiers, including Nakeuzumi as conflicted and tortured killers and rapists. Moore quotes Lu as saying: "I thought I could deliver a new message and perhaps persuade some people who had mistaken ideas about the war. Japanese soldiers also paid a price during the war, and that theme got me the most criticism" (Lu quoted by Moore). When the movie was accepted for the British screen in April, 2010, Lu stated: "I feel that the movie must be a success overseas. I am hoping that a good reception overseas will change the minds of the domestic audience" (quoted by Moore).

8.7   Chinese Computer-Mediated Communication

On September 20, 1987, China's first Internet connection outside of China was sent to Germany with the message "Across the Great Wall, we can reach every corner of the world." In June 2007, the China Internet Network Information Center (CINIC which was founded in 1997) indicated that more than half of the Internet users were male, unmarried, and under 25, most of whom had a college or university education. www.Sina.com with more than 100 million subscribers, www.Sohu.com, and www.163.com remain the most popular Chinese websites. There are three free online Chinese encyclopedias: Hudong, Biadu Baike, and the Chinese Wikipedia (Statistical Survey Report: 2010: June 30).

In "The Internet Timeline of China" published by the China Internet Network Information Center, we find the following information (2010: January):

Until December 31st, 2009, it is shown according to the statistical data of China Internet Network Information Center (CNNIC), the net citizens in China has reached 384 million; the popularity of internet reached 28.9%; net citizens of wide band reached 346 million; users of web shopping reached 108 million and transaction of web shopping market reached 25 million yuan; mobile net citizens reached 233 million, with 120 million added in a year. There are 232 million IPv4 addresses, with 16.82 million domain names. There include 13.46 million domain names and 3.23 million websites. And International band width has reached 866,367Mbps.

More recently, however, in June 2010, 420 million Chinese Internet users were identified, with the expectation that by the end of 2010 the number would reach 469 million (35% of China's population, and that by 2013, there would be 718 million (53% of the total population), Chinese Internet users spend two billion hours weekly on the Internet, while the US has 129 million hours weekly. Most Chinese users were online 20 hours a week. More than 227 million were using the Internet by their cellphones, and there were 323 million websites by the end of 2009 (Statistical Survey Report: 2010: June). Brian Womack and Katrina Nicholas (2010: February 26) report that China "may have 840 million Internet users or 61% of the population, by 2013, according to E-Marketers, Inc. in New York."

In Cui Litang's Case Study below, he discusses the wrangling over China's media market, extending our understanding of Chinese media in general, and Google in China as a part of its internet. In Chapter Nine, we will discuss China's media billionaires.

China Media Factoid
(approximate figures from various sources)

Media Type	Offerings	Users (million)	Revenues (million Yuan)
Newspapers	1,943 titles	44.4	57
Magazines	9,549 titles	310.5	19.8
Books	250,000 titles	7,400 million copies	42.0
Radio	673 stations	120	496.8
TV	3240 stations	110.15	500
Cable TV	250 networks	>126	33.4
Internet	16.8 million domains	475	3,500
Fixed phones		274 million households	7,840
Mobile phones		1.2 billion contracts	2,000
Cinema	456/4,723 screens	150	6,200

8.8 Case Study: Wrangling the Media Market Place

(Cui Litang, Shanghai, Industry and Commerce Foreign Language College)

At the height of the Google/China row over censorship in China in January 2010, over 80% of Wall Street Journal English readers voted yes for Google to leave China, and nearly as many, over 70% WSJ Chinese readers voted no and would like Google to stay, according to a WSJ survey respectively done among its English and Chinese readers.

These strikingly polarized opinions over Google's fate in China unmistakably pointed to

two different watersheds and value orientations on which the differentiating opinions had shaped, serving to either highlight an intriguing Google story, or spell a Google dilemma, as a media operation, in and across two different media systems, that of the decentralized media in the US, and that of the centralized media in China.

All media in China are centralized in the sense that they are controlled in ideology by the state government under the banner and framework of China's socialist market economy, despite increasing social and cultural multi-polarization, emerging interest groups and numerous attempts in pushing the envelope. Manifestation of media centralization in practice is cross-media censorship, the latest incidences of which include the imposed Google China censorship, the flunked Green Dam Youth Escort web filter bundled with computers and the Great China Firewall still in place that reportedly is blocking access in China to the social media sites like Facebook, Myspace, Twitter and Youtube.

State media are heavily but discrepantly subsidized by the central government and the sponsorship is also significantly endorsed in circulation and advertising avenues where a media market has emerged and is being redefined, as media convergence continues to improve and alternative media become accessible to wider and better educated mass audiences. This has put to test the media's ideological loyalty and professionalism. If there is no disillusion about the party line the media are still to toe, there have been plenty of fancies and exercises for media power and miracles, as well as numerous adventures in pursuit of the media market place. As a result, commercial and entrepreneurial practices in media are common and have become important, and the party color fades in or out in the rhetoric according to policy and circumstances, and to some extent, vox populi are heard, addressed and answered, which is no longer culminated in what the term propaganda is adequate to define.

Over the past decades, China has emerged as an economic power in sheer general GDP and a well-wired country with over 457 million web users (January 2011), translating into a media consumption power that the market mix of capped annual exhibition of 20 foreign movies per cinema could hardly satisfy, a tip of the iceberg of China's inadequacy in its media industry and a far cry from vast tangible industries where China has done so well. If China is to sustain development and growth out of this prominent market discrepancy between the tangible and intangible industries, China may want to get rid of any possible and potential non-tariff barrier like censorship, and at the same time, seek more media investments and opportunities for joint ventures by opening up its media market, embracing and engaging the mainstream media in the world.

Unfortunately, this has seemed to become difficult and a high-profile issue when the Google China rift eventually ended up in Google leaving China upon its unilateral cease of censorship on March 23rd despite its "5,000–year patience " with China, as China continued to trumpet up its anti-Google rhetoric to the point of accusation of Google's political agenda "to impose its own value and yardsticks on Internet regulation to China that has its own time-honored tradition, culture and value." While it is hard to predict what developments are to roll out in "the brave new world" of media, the media scene remains a window on China for scrutiny in time to come.

8.9   Summary

This has been a long chapter on the cultural media including one of the longest but richest dialogues in *Communicating Interculturally*. Now as the book moves toward a conclusion, we can note that the class members have gotten very active in their dialogue, identifying various media that they like, including American TV shows and movies. The chapter's length precludes further study of additional important media such as music, theme parks, advertising (which will be included in Chapter Nine), gaming, mobile phone technology, ipods, Blackberries, and robotics, to name only a few of the emerging media. The major brief articles by name have included a description of **media and mass communication theories** articulated by Kevin J. Pearce; broadcast theories articulated by James Shanahan; Thomas McPhail's **international and global media theories**; Prosser's "**Media Diplomacy**"; Cooper Wakefield's essay, "Cinema: Assessing Intercultural and International Cinema"; Prosser's "Chinese Cinema: A Challenging Chinese Film: "Nanjing! Nanjing! (City of Life and Death) Directed by Lu Chuan"; and Cui Litang's case study: "Wrangling the Media Market Place."

The chapter also includes some brief essays, complemented by a media list of the sort typically favored by Time Magazine. Both our brief essays and the list should be seen only as illustrative, but potentially instructive for you to get a sense of all of the possibilities that the study of media theories, international and global media theories, and practical aspects of international and global media and Chinese media provide.

8.10 Questions for Discussion

8.10.1 We can see in this dialogue that several students are becoming increasingly good critical thinkers and that considerable analysis is occurring, for example in their discussion with Professor Zhang and Michael Prosser on Avatar. What are the clearest examples of this development of their critical thinking and analytic skills in this dialogue? Why?

8.10.2 In this dialogue, we already have a very rich discussion about the media. As we can see, the dialogues are not just intended to entertain you as students in this intercultural communication class, but more importantly are significant but informal teaching methods about the subject of the chapter, in this case, "Cultural Media." What are the most important contributions that this dialogue has provided in relation to learning the topic information? If you were to compare two or more aspects of the dialogue in terms of the media, which would you select as the most important? Why?

8.10.3 In the dialogues beginning the chapters, a great deal of humor and satire is employed. What are the major ways that humor and satire have been utilized in this and other introductory dialogues to teach the course material effectively? How do you see yourself in terms of this dialogical humor and satire as co-teachers of the course if you were members of the imaginary class? Is it an innovative technique for an intercultural communication text book? Which would you prefer, this style in the dialogues or more emphasis on straight textual materials? Can humor and satire provide elements of effective analysis? Why? Why not?

8.10.4 If you have an exam over the topic areas of this chapter, you could be required to memorize various facts about Chinese and international and global media. If these are major facts to remember, then such an exam might be very appropriate. However, if your teacher asks you to help design the exam which would provide you with the best long term understanding of the chapter's main ideas, how would you proceed? How can you use your critical thinking and analytic development to create the most effective exam for long time understanding?

8.10.5 Pearce, Shanahan, and McPhail offer us several theories related to a study of media and mass communication in general, and also on international and global media. Comparing the brief description of such theories, which do you consider the most important ones related in general and also on international and global media theories? For the study of intercultural communication, which theories do you consider to have the most promise? Why?

8.10.6 How does Prosser's earlier published essay on media diplomacy assist us in understanding more specifically about the key elements of such diplomacy in studying international and intercultural communication theories? What would you consider the specific contributions of this essay?

8.10.7 Cooper Wakefield, an expert on intercultural and international cinema, offers us a very useful way to assess such cinema. What are the contributions of this essay for us to understand its relationship to cultural, international and global media studies? Why?

8.10.8 Under our study of cultural, international, and global media, as we have noted, the chapter's length does not easily lend itself to still more studies of unconventional media, not typically included under traditional studies of media and mass communication. If you were going to add a brief section about these media, which would you choose to emphasize and why?

8.10.9 After you have read Wakefield's essay assessing intercultural and international cinema, does Prosser's essay about Lu Chuan's film, "Nanjing! Nanjing!" give you any practical applications of the concepts that Wakefield introduces? If so, what are they? If not, what new ideas should Prosser have introduced in studying this particular Chinese film? If you were to write an essay, for example, on "Hero," how would you use your critical thinking skills to make your assessment of it?

8.10.10 There are various lists in this chapter, both about international and global media and about Chinese media. Which ones are especially helpful in understanding the concept of the chapter as cultural media? Which are the least helpful? Why?

8.11   Suggested Readings

Ebrey, P. B., Walthall, A., & Palas, J. B. (2006). East Asia: A cultural, social and political history. Boston, MA: Houghton Mifflin.

Hui, C-c (2010). Clever, creative, modest: The Chinese language practice. Shanghai: Shanghai Foreign Language Education Press.

Raghatta, C. (2008: July). Bollywood in Hollywood. The Times of India.

Raj A. (2007). Indian cinema and Indian disapora. In D. Dicispora and S. Steinberg (Eds.) Media Literacy: A Reader. New York,, NY: Peter Lang.

Shanahan, J., & Morgan, M. (1999). Television and its viewers: Cultivation theory and research. London, England: Cambridge University Press.

Williams, R. (2003). Television, technology, and cultural form. 3rd edition. New York, NY: Routledge.

Xu, G. G. (2007). Sinacape: Contemporary Chinese cinema. Oxford, England: Rowman and Litchfield.

Chapter
NINE

Intercultural Communication in Business, Training and Education

9.1 Dialogue

Professor Zhang: Most of you are looking for careers in intercultural business and international trade. Some of you are interested in going into education, and a few might be interested in becoming intercultural trainers. You might wonder how all three of these topics are important for the study of intercultural communication. There are a number of text books in China concentrating on intercultural business, but this is a more general course on intercultural communication, and we therefore thought it might be useful to give you an overview of intercultural business and international trade. Several of you will become teachers, with more and more of the fifty-six Chinese nationalities in your classes, and thus it is also important to have some sense of intercultural education. In your careers, you might do intercultural training, whether you are in business or international trade or teaching. Therefore it is useful also that we have a brief overview of all three of the major topics developed in this chapter.

Amelia: This is very practical for me, Professor Zhang, as I want to be a teacher, probably in English at a senior middle school. I am interested in knowing more intercultural theories and practice that will help me be a good teacher. Even if all of my students will be Chinese, I need to show them that they live in an intercultural world even here in China.

Intercultural Communication in Business, Training and Education

Jason: Premier Wen has encouraged us young Chinese to consider becoming entrepreneurs and to start our own businesses. I have a friend, Calvin, who decided to start his own company teaching English to primary children in his hometown near Wenzhou. He started off small, hiring only two regular teachers of English to give classes after school and on the weekends, but like Michael Yu, who started the New Oriental School, perhaps he will become a great success.

Michael: When I first came to teach in China, a small group of entrepreneurs were trying to start an English training company, and they thought that they could teach *Crazy English* and become very successful. I recommended that they not do that as they would have had a very different reputation than if they had a more traditional English training company. Unfortunately, as undergraduate business majors, none of them personally had the educational background to start an English training company and it failed. Perhaps seeing how many people have learned some English through *Crazy English* and how many hundreds of thousands that Li Yang encouraged to learn English, and how many *Crazy English* books are in the book stores, I should have encouraged them in that direction.

Professor Zhang: Yes, but Michael, we know, and even Li Yang agrees on this principle, learning a language is a long-time process. We would prefer that our Chinese citizens not only can communicate in English well, but also in the proper style, which people don't always learn in Li Yang's lectures to thousands of people at a time, and in teaching them to shout out, sometimes meaningless slogans. So perhaps many people know these meaningless slogans, but not how to communicate in real conversations with others.

Angel: I have a former teacher in Kunming who was part of a new English training company which did very well. All of the teachers had a background both in English and in intercultural communication. That company is making a big influence in Kunming. My boyfriend took some courses from the company and learned a lot of good English.

Forest: You will all be happy to know that my career goal is either to work for Hersey's Chocolates or a Belgian or Swiss chocolate company.

Laughter

Maria: I would like to work in an international trade company and so I am very glad to be learning about intercultural business communication. Some of my friends in the business school don't have a good background in English or the intercultural communication competence to work well with managers from foreign countries.

Also, some of the managers from other countries don't seem to know how to deal with their Chinese skilled or unskilled workers.

Gloria: When I was training to be a volunteer at the Beijing Olympics, we had a lot of intercultural training since we were going to be assisting people from many different countries coming to see the games. I even met President Bush briefly when he was there, and he and his family seemed very kind to me. So, I agree that we all should have some background in intercultural training if we are going to be involved in international business and trade.

Joy: When volunteers were being trained for working at the World Expo, I took some good training, but like Gloria, I couldn't give up six months for volunteering and I missed the chance to use the training that I received. Still, it was good.

Professor Zhang: Perhaps, Joy, you and Gloria will be able to use the skills you learned in becoming interculturally competent in other situations.

Tiger: Since I come from Hong Kong, I would have liked to be a part of the volunteers for the Sixteenth Asian games in Guangzhou, but I couldn't take so much time off from classes here.

Sunny: I really do want to have a career working in international business and trade, perhaps working in an international company in Nanjing or Shanghai. I think that my strong English will be an asset for me, but I am glad to learn more information about getting ready for such a career opportunity. As I have said before, my father, a university English teacher, started teaching me English when I was starting to learn Chinese. So I definitely think that a bilingual education is good to become a professional in an international company.

Professor Zhang: Sunny, it is true that you speak English so well that you will be a real asset in an international trade company. With the intercultural information which you are learning in this class, we hope that you will be a great success for a future in international commerce.

Michelle: Like Michelle in Chapter Three who is a trading manager in Chicago, and since I lived in the west coast of the US as a teenager, I hope that I too can become a trading manager overseas, perhaps also in the US.

Spring: Michelle, your book in Chinese about your experience in the US was so good, that now that I am fluent in English, I wish I could read it in English too.

Summer: Though we are getting more independence since we have come to the university, Spring and I both hope that we could be employed in the same company if

Intercultural Communication in Business, Training and Education

possible. We could be like the two identical twins in the Disney TV show *Suite Times* about them both being on a student exchange program on a ship at sea. It would be a good show to be developed by CCTV and we could be the stars. In that show, there are students from several different cultures, so it gives us an idea of a multicultural setting with all of its good and bad parts. It is exaggerated in terms of the cultural differences, with lots of stereotypes, but it is a very funny show. Then we could show Chinese teenagers how to become more multicultural and to solve the cultural problems between the groups.

Michael: My grandchildren that I live with like that show. They have all been to China with their mother to see me. Right now, Darya is in a high school girls' choir, and they are singing musical songs from several different countries and in different languages. Sanders has wanted to become a film director since he was little, and maybe he will include interesting cultural and international stories if he becomes one. Sophia who is nine and a little friend are composing some simple songs with upbeat melodies. They are all very creative, which should help them as adults if they choose their own intercultural careers.

True Nation: Michael, when they are older, you need to send them back to China for a year to study Chinese. Then they can be involved with international trade with China.

Mike: Then like you Michael, perhaps they will become "Chiamericans."

Laughter

Michael: When we think about the importance in intercultural business and international trade that the media, the Internet, and social networks like MySpace, Youtube, LinkedIn, Twitter, and others have today.

Mike: Since I want to have a career in an international information technology firm, I have already joined LinkedIn.

Fiona: So have I joined LinkedIn. I have worked in a bank some time, and I would like to be an expert in international finance. Do you have ideas for me, Professor Zhang and Michael?

Robin: I would like to be in a public relations or advertising business, especially in real estate. Do you have any materials about these subjects?

Professor Zhang: Yes, we do have some information in *Chinese Communicating Interculturally* on the role of communication in international fianance with an essay by Hugo Rocha, and discussions about advertising theories and corporate communication. We also have essays about intercultural education by two Chinese teachers who work with minorities in China, and Don Rutherford's discussion about the major elements of intercultural training. Professor Li Mengyu's and Michael's book *Chinese Communicating Interculturally* opens a door for further explanation on many of these topics. Shall we being the lesson now?

Tony: Ok. Let's do it, shall we?

9.2 Intercultural Business and International Trade

9.2.1 The Importance of Intercultural Communication in Global Financial Relations (Dr. Hugo Rodrigo Rocha, Senior Network Manager, The Bank of New York Mellon, Madrid, Spain)

I was born in the 60's of the twentieth century in Lisbon, and I was lucky enough to grow up within a social and economic environment that was evolving at a somehow rapid path, yet as challenging and attractive as it could. In my youthful years, the desire to better understand other peoples' thoughts and behaviors, as well as the interest for international affairs, took me to another country for almost a year, the US, an experience that—I have often realized—has strongly influenced my personal and professional life.

In these past 15 years of activity in a very specific area of the quickly developing financial industry, the need to work with people from various different national and cultural backgrounds—many of them colleagues, many others representing a diverse universe of institutions domiciled in the most varied countries—has been a day-to-day reality that I have been faced with. A rewarding one, I must say.

We recognize that two of the main features of today's financial sector are its sophisticated technological developments and the fact that it is very strongly interconnected.

Nonetheless, regardless of how technologically advanced banks and other financial institutions are, this is a sector where people still make the difference! As a matter of fact, it is probably one of the most important aspects in the relationship between international financial institutions and between them and their customers, precisely due to the high technical standards that have been reached. Many of the issues and problems that we face on a daily basis in most circumstances can be resolved only if dialogue and understanding supersede. Luckily, machines are still incapable of interacting emotionally and developing intercultural relationships based on mutual trust and understanding; just like humans do.

In this industry, it is also most relevant for one to recognize that a given behavior may seem to be illogical and absurd in a given country, but absolutely normal and well accepted in another one.

In fact, the ability to understand, comprehend and accept the differences is most probably the starting point to achieve a high level of mutual trust, and the best way to develop a relationship that, at the end of the day, can bring the most positive results for those involved.

As I mentioned before, financial markets around the globe are extremely interconnected, with all the advantages—and disadvantages— that they bring to us, individuals. The financial sector is, therefore, not much different from many others which, due to their international nature, suggest a high level of intercultural communication in order to function properly.

Today, we are regrettably living in the midst of a worldwide crisis with serious impacts at various levels of the society in every region of the world. The financial sector is in the center of the storm and it will certainly take much time for confidence to be reinstalled.

So, considering the extreme importance that the roles played by financial institutions have on the lives of each and every one of us—wherever we may be—the financial sector possibly is the area of activity where soft skills and an excellent capacity of intercultural communication are absolutely required.

With those factors in mind, we can at least work towards ensuring that the most positive outcome for all of us is achieved and, eventually, we may also be playing an important part, no matter how small it may seem, in the efforts to try and avoid future crises as harmful as the one we have been witnessing.

Be it in the global financial relations, or any other activity with international impact, the beauty of intercultural communication, when well used and further developed, is that it gives us the tools that can change our lives.... and those around us.

9.2.2 Intercultural Business Communication and International Trade (David Henry, Shanghai International Studies University)

Intercultural Business Communication (IBC) deals with how culture can help organizations achieve their business goals. In this age of rapid globalization, organizations are likely to include diverse people from many cultures. The manager of a multinational organization with employees and suppliers and customers from differing cultures must communicate organizational goals and implement strategies in a way that keeps all these diverse people working together.

When managers make decisions about who to hire and how to train them, how to organize work to get the best result and how to motivate employees to do their best, how to reward workers fairly and who to promote to more responsible position, they must be aware of how their decisions will be perceived through the various cultural lenses of their employees.

A German production manager trying to impose German standards of promptness, individual rewards, and impersonal relationships finds himself frustrated in the company's Latin American subsidiary where workers value personal relationships, collective rewards and a flexible attitude toward time. He is likely to be seen as cold and mean-spirited by the Latin American employees.

Outside the company, managers work with suppliers and customers on a world-wide scope. They are constantly building relationships with people from other cultures and negotiating with them over price and quality and delivery schedules. If they assume all people see the world in the same way, they are liable to fall short of their goals.

People have cultural preferences for how messages are organized and delivered. A comparison of Chinese and English sales letters showed Chinese letters employed both logical and emotional appeals to initiate the long-term goal of building relationships, stressing politeness and respect and mutual cooperation. In contrast, the English letters used logical appeals only to achieve a short-term goal of moving the individual reader to action, emphasizing offers and incentives proposed in personal terms. (Zhu, 2005) Clearly, the cultural expectations of how to write a sales letter are very different and business people trying to sell across cultures would be well advised to know this.

The medium used to deliver a message can also be affected by culture. A study of hotel workers in international hotels in Thailand found that lower level Thai workers put more trust in oral messages conveyed by their co-workers than formal written messages from their supervisors or even from the top managers. These managers might be well-advised to check the news in the "grapevine" to be sure their communications are being accurately received.

Managers have to decide if they can sell their standard product in a given market or if they have to differentiate it to suit local tastes. Disney learned a hard lesson when it tried to open an exact copy of its American theme parks in France. American park-goers like to "graze" their way through the park, eating small amounts throughout the day; but French visitors expect to sit down to a full lunch at lunch time. As a result, Disney had not built enough dining capacity to accommodate the French practice. The American parks prohibit alcoholic beverages to create a family environment; but French families expect to have a glass of wine with their meal. Disney's failure to consider local tastes and habits nearly spelled disaster for their first foreign venture.

Cultural issues in business are not always easy to see. A Chinese manufacturer that had been successfully selling its products overseas for many years, ran into trouble when it tried to sell a new high-tech, state-of-the-art product. His customer complained that the price was too high. Yet the manufacturer knew the advanced product should command a premium price. Most IBC issues are intrinsically bound to other business strategy issues. In this case, the business pricing strategy has to be implemented with a communication strategy meant to change the foreign customers perception of the manufacturer from a low cost supplier to a high quality provider. These two issues cannot be separated.

Managing across cultures is no simple task. Cultures are always changing; people adapt to differing circumstances. The Chinese salesman is working as hard to adapt to his American buyer's culture as the American buyer is trying to adapt to the Chinese supplier's world. There is no manual to teach us how to do business in each and every intercultural situation.

So IBC competence is a skill, not a knowledge set; a skill that future business leaders will have to posess. Knowledge of specific cultural differences can make us aware of the role culture plays in achieving business goals, but it doesn't provide a "how to" formula for all future decisions. Instead, managers need the openness to recognize the cultural context of their decisions and the flexibility to adjust strategies and their implementation in ways that respond sensitivly to these constantly changing cultural contexts.

(Zhu Y. (2005). Written communication across cultures. Amsterdam, The Netherlands: John Benjamins Publishing Co.)

9.2.3 Organizational Culture

It is defined by Sarah J. Tracy (2009: 713–716) as "the shared assumptions, values, beliefs, language, symbols, and meanings systems in an organization." She indicates that there are two basic approaches to understand this aspect of culture: the management approach by which managers and organizations "can control and improve their corporate culture," with managers noticing that organizations with strong cultures—such as Disneyland, Coca-Cola, IBM and Japanese car manufacturers—were extremely successful. This spurred the notion that by being able to engineer an appropriate corporate culture, managers could increase productivity" and several groundbreaking management books, such as Tom Peter's and Robert Waterman's *In Search of Excellence* found that organizations that were extremely successful "had in common strong cultures with close customer relations, employee empowerment, clear missions, and a flat organizational hierarchy."

Tracy identifies the second approach as **the interpretative approach** based on Clifford Geertz's book, *The Interpretation of Cultures*, which "examines organization as tribes and views the familiar as strange, wondrous, and exotic." "Such an approach," Tracy claims "is socially constructed through organizational values, folk tales, rituals, and practices." Tracy suggests that there are several cultural levels in each organization such as national or regional cultures, professional cultures, and various emerging subcultures. The **organizational culture** may be power-related as we discussed in Chapter Five about low and high power distance; **role cultures** which emphasize "logic, rationality, achievement, and efficiency"; **achievement cultures**, in which the task is the primary focus of the organization; and **person-support cultures** that are "egalitarian, emphasizing personal growth and development as equally important as business objectives." In **strong organizational cultures**, the leaders have a vision for the organization and seek to lead the members toward that vision, and frame certain goals and objectives as more important than others, often using **unobtrusive cultural control** methods by which, "through idenfication, employees adopt the core values of the organization," considered to be loyalty, commitment, feeling of belonging, and pride in a certain group" (715).

Eric M. Eisenberg, in his essay, *Organizational Communication Theories* (2009: 2, 700–705) identifies them as "the process by which language and social interaction promote coordinated action toward a common goal." Eisenberg distinguishes this concept as studying the practical and effective communicative aspects of organizations. Eisenberg proposes two metaphors to address **communication in an organization: the systems theories**, which describes **organizational communication** not simply as something that happens within systems, but as "the very process by which organizing happens" and **cultural theories of organizational communication**, for example in the considerable success of Japanese auto makers in establishing prominence over the American auto makers in the 1970s which scholars attributed to the unique Japanese culture.

While Eisenberg doesn't note one aspect of this phenomenon, Prosser speculates that part of their success resulted from an "unobtrusive control" of selling the autos. That is, in Prosser's experience, there was never a Japanese salesperson in the auto showrooms, thus avoiding the American fear of the "Japan economic threat" that was prevalent in American society then and for a long time after, even as recently as the late 1990s. In Prosser's viewpoint, the Chinese Haier Company has had much the same success as many Americans who buy Haier products are not aware that its products are coming from China. On the other hand, since Chinese labels adorn many smaller items produced in China, Americans tend to feel that these items are indicative of the "Chinese economic threat." Recently on a winter day, Prosser was questioned on what he might be wearing at the time that was made in China. His answer was: "Everything I have on, except my socks, was made in China."

Eisenberg concludes his essay by identifying the future directions of **the organizational communication theory**: "Organization com-munication theories mirror the flow of society … societal interest has expanded from an isolated view of organizations to a more situated perspective that takes into account the importance of not-for-profit organizations and the quality of life in communities … [and the commitment of many organizational scholars] to conduct more problem-centered research focused on persistent social challenges such as justice, safety and security."

"Finally," Eisenberg argues, "It is quite likely that future theories of organizational communication will take a broader view of nonhuman agency.… Human-machine interactions will be a key focus of **organizational communication theory** in the 21st century" (705).

9.2.4 Advertising Theories

Olaf H. Werder (2009: 1, 18–22) discusses several **advertising theories** and notes that as late as 2007 in the US, advertising expenditures were more than $149 billion for the year, making the industry a very important aspect of the economy. In 2010, advertising costs for the US midterm election (senators, congressmen and women, governors, and state legislatures) were at their highest level ever, and advertising expenses for the losing gubernatorial candidate in California, Meg Ryan ($142 million of her own wealth), were the most expensive since records have been kept. Werder notes that developing theories about **advertising** have mixed together business and social science theories. Except now in the political elections in the US, most advertising there "seems to occur in the area of consumer perception of a brand." He argues that culture "fills a product with meaning based on biological, social, and psychic needs the product fulfills…. The function of advertising is to create subcategories of values and needs within the social structure to connect these with the product" (18). Werder comments: "The different social histories of Europe, Asia, and other parts of the world produce consumers who exhibit unique cultural characteristics that influence their needs and wants, their methods of satisfying them, and the messages to which they are most likely to respond [as has been noted above with several examples by David Henry]." Werder continues: "Advertising studies now include the analyses of the meaning of verbal and nonverbal language, concepts of time and space, and cultural-value indicators such as individualism-collectivism, masculinity-femininity, uncertainty avoidance, and long-term versus short-term orientation [as we have discussed in Chapter Five]."

Werder proposes that studies about advertising might be categorized as **functional advertising, advertising processes, advertising outcomes**, and **advertising as popular culture**. He identifies five specific theories related to the studying of advertising: the first is **the hierarchy of effects model** (theoretically weak, with several different models developing over time, but with a core factor being the active or passive involvement both by the advertisers and the consumers). Second, **the audience involvement theory** in which "people can internalize a message soley on the fact that it is socially and emotionally satisfying; that is, persuasion relies not necessarily on information and logic alone but also on social and affective factors." The third indicates that there are **theories of personality and motivation** (finding out whether motivational advertising causes changes in

behavior by "principles of environmental influences, perception, memory, cognitive development, and emotion, or are concepts unique to motivation more pertinent?" [such as we saw in Chapter Two with the personalized message to many by President Obama]. The fourth relates to **association theories** (with four principles defining the theory "

(1) All ideas are associated together in the mind through experience;

(2) all ideas can be reduced to a basic stock of simple ideas;

(3) these simple ideas are elementary, unstructured sensations; and

(4) simple, additive rules are sufficient to predict the properties of complex ideas from the properties of the underlying simple ideas."

The fifth is **the reversal theory**, a theory of motivation and emotion, which "focuses on flexibility and what spurs reversals from one psychological state to another…. An individual reverses between states as situations—and the meaning that one attributes to them—change. A person's emotions result from whether one's motives are being fulfilled or not." Werder concludes by saying that with the development of the Internet, online advertising, and newer media "the long-held notion of the mass market has given way to that of a more individualized consumer as digital consumers are no longer 'passive' receivers of the advertiser's message but will actively select the advertising message or completely disregard it" (Werder, p. 22).

9.3 Intercultural Training for Global Business People

Don Rutherford. President, Culture Connect, Calgary, Canada

Intercultural training is intended to help participants become more successful in their business relationships and, ultimately, achieve their business objectives. A quality training program builds competence, curiosity and confidence. Intercultural competence can be seen as a continuum of knowledge, attitudes and skills. Training will move the participant along the continuum to greater effectiveness in doing business across cultures. The learner gains insight, not just into the target culture, but also into his or her own cultural and personal values. Curiosity about the target culture is stimulated, as is the motivation to learn more. One's confidence to engage successfully with people of another culture expands. Quiet confidence is a significant success factor for international business people.

Components of an intercultural program can include:

(1)   Culture concepts (culture defined and why it matters)

(2)   Country/region background (history, geography, population, ethnicity, religion, politics, economics, sports, and recent news stories in context …)

(3)   Cultural value comparisons—home vs. target culture (hierarchy, individualism, status, time …)

(4)   Business culture (applying the values to communication styles, relationship-building, persuasion, negotiation, manager/subordinate relations, decision-making, teamwork, workplace etiquette….)

(5)   Guided question and answer time with target country national business person. Guided question and answer time with expatriate who has lived and worked in target country

(6)   Culture shock and adjustment (if going expatriate or on rotation)

(7)   Formulating a personal action plan (strategies on how success will be achieved in an intercultural environment).

The theoretical basis of value comparison material typically comes from the work of Geert Hofstede, Fons Trompenaars, Charles Hampden-Turner, Edward T. Hall, and others.

If the training program is intended to be culture-general rather than specific to a country/region, the agenda can be easily modified. In some cases, various nationalities may already be functioning together in a workgroup, a joint venture or a supplier relationship. The training required in these instances also requires modification. The trainer, rather than acting as a presenter, is more of a discussion facilitator amongst the culturally diverse people in the program. Exercises are introduced that allow participants to share their behavior preferences in various business scenarios with culturally different colleagues. Examples might include manager/subordinate relations, decision-making, teamwork and so on. The facilitator's role is to build trust and to help learners see the cultural roots of their perceptions. The business people learn to build bridges crossing the cultural divide and

School Children in Xinjiang, China

to devise common strategies and practices, in order to function more successfully together.

Having a variety of methods in any training program breathes life into the program. Minimizing the use of presentation slides and maximizing interactive exercises is vital. Cultural competence is best gained by challenging participants with discussion, interactive exercises, case studies and role plays, as culturally appropriate.

The most successful business programs also tend to be specific. Knowing the reason an organization wants intercultural training, their expectations, what their intercultural challenges have been in the past, and their international business plans going forward are all valuable insights for the development of a program.

9.4 Intercultural Education in Urumqi

Dilhara Turdi, Urumqi Technical College

Intercultural education exists when one teaches a class which is full of different ethnic groups or one has lesson in a class which is taught by a different ethnic person. This environment provides a wide range of cultures to cope with. Language teaching comes alongside with cultures. One cannot use an acquired language well unless he or she understands the culture of that language.

Teaching in an ethnic classroom, one might find it will be difficult to communicate with the students because of not understanding their native language or their cultural background. The important elements in teaching the

minority group are: first, it would be a good idea for the teacher to know their students' native language as well as Chinese, because they can communicate with the students well and when it comes across in the grammar, it would be easy to explain it in both languages by giving related sentences. Secondly, the teacher should have the general cultural knowledge of each specific minority group—it might not only be one ethnic group in one class. It helps the teacher to have intimate relationship with each student and inspires the students' eagerness of learning English. Last but not least, for teaching in a minority class, one should bear in mind that the behaviors or the questions of the students are not usually wrong but different.

Being an English teacher, I have been teaching English majored Uyghur students for many years. I found out that there are some interesting issues related to the cultural differences within the Han-Chinese students and Uyghur students. While I was teaching in an Uyghur class, I found it is very easy for the students to grasp the words and pronunciations. They are very active and cooperative in the classroom. They like to share their ideas with others. While in a Han-Chinese class, I found it is difficult for the students to grasp the pronunciations. They are shy to express their ideas and indifferent in classroom activities.

Minority groups who get bilingual education are sure to be bicultural. They learn the dominant language, and with that language they understand the culture of that certain dominant group. Gradually, they become a part of that dominant culture. A person who is bicultural or multicultural has more respect for other people and other cultures than the monocultural person does. In learning English,

specifically with my students, I find that one who is bilingual can accept another language better than one who is monolingual. "There is a cultural difference," one of my students said as I asked her whether she found any difference between the English culture and our own. "But I can accept it. Because every place has its unique characteristic; otherwise there would be not places like China or the USA." She is a bilingual student. But when I told one of my monolingual students that some Americans call their parents by their name, he was shocked and said, "Won't their parents beat them? It's disrespectable."

The Uyghur language is written in a modified Arabic script which helps to identify its speakers as Muslims. The sentence structure of the Uyghur language is subject, object and verb, not like Chinese which is subject, verb and object. The Uyghur language and Chinese are not related in any way and Uyghurs have to learn Chinese as a foreign language. Because of this, most monolingual students would prefer that English teachers explain the grammar with their native language, while most bilingual students prefer using Chinese.

9.5 Practical Applications

9.5.1 Global Knowledge and Local Wisdom (Zhang Wei, Shanghai)

In April 2006, a few days after the first round written test, I received a phone call from "Charlie," my first boss and, who, besides setting the venue and date for a second round interview, also requested me to, as a condition

for potential employment, submit an essay on a real estate subject, together with a recommendation letter from two professors in my field of studies. I was the first among my classmates to be requested to do so, which was not a common practice for a Chinese company. Charlie, a Taiwan-born American, spent several

Intercultural Communication in Business, Training and Education

years in the US, mostly handling China-related cases.

At our first meal, we talked about things with little relevance to the job, like a book detailing the lives and ordeals of democratic officials during the Cultural Revolution, which was published in mainland China but later banned. He smiled and said, "You are lucky, because I can lend the Hong Kong version book to you." We also talked about topics like China as a rising power and some underlying problems in the Chinese society. I remember clearly that he said "God bless China." I didn't ask whether the "God" he meant was western or Chinese. In this case, the usual rule of no politics in work place didn't work.

With the spring festival of 2007 approaching, Charlie talked of visiting my family during the festival holidays. I didn't take it seriously and thought he was merely showing his kindness. But on one afternoon during the spring festival, he called and informed me that his plane would arrive the next day. That was truly a big surprise! He talked about how many efforts parents take to bring up a child and he wanted to show his gratitude to my parents for raising me, sending me for a university education and now, I was working for him. Another reason for his visit, I guess, would be that he hoped to foster a kind of relationship beyond that established on basis of a one year or two years labor contract.

Once during our discussions of the English translations of laws published by a prestigious mainland law press, he asked what a market economy with socialist characteristics is. I recited to him what I learned from the textbook while I was still a child. He noted, "It's nonsense. Market economy is capitalist-oriented. What

does it have to do with socialism?" Another time he noted that it would serve me well to study in the US someday for one year or two, one advantage being to enlarge my horizon and think from different perspectives. Maybe this was one of his long term plans. He still made the same statement during our recent conversation, the only difference being that I am working for another foreign company now.

The French firm I am currently working for is far more international and culturally diverse than the first one. When I was first interviewed, I expected it to be in English, but it turned out all in Mandarin. I introduced myself to the foreign colleagues in English, but later learned that most of them could either understand or speak Mandarin Chinese, and some could speak the Shanghai dialect. Here, the bosses, male or female, took their naps sitting in their chairs, legs crossed on the desks. One partner used to smoke in his office before the smoking ban in certain public areas in Shanghai. Smoke sensor? Don't worry, he unplugged it! Once during our annual dinner, he handed out cigarettes to those who smoked and lit them for the others. The food for annual dinners always is western-style. Here I am no longer called by my English name, but my Chinese name. When a staff meeting is held, we all stand! Though we provide legal services, blue jeans and shirts are allowed, as long as we don't wear them to meet a client. One consensus shared among my Chinese colleagues is that the French managers are really sloppy in efficiency. They complicate things and are slow to take action. From June to August, business is slack, because all the French managers have flown to beach areas to get suntanned. Or, maybe they think their Chinese colleagues are difficult to understand, just like a

Chinese colleague stationed a long term in Paris would ask questions that we consider matter of course.

If you ask me which one I like better, the commonplace answer is that they both have their merits. It's not absolutely one way to the exclusion of the other. While still carrying their own cultural brands, people from different cultural backgrounds learn and adapt to a local culture. In an age of globalization and free flow information, a person with global knowledge and local wisdom will strike better chances of winning.

9.5.2   The Rules of My Brazilian Manager—Or Brazilian Culture? (Clare Li, Former Junior Associate in a Brazilian Law Firm's Shanghai office, Hangzhou)

Having studied English and law for the bachelor degrees at Shanghai University and intercultural communication for the master degree at Shanghai International Studies University, it seems quite reasonable for me to find a job in an international law firm, yet working for a Brazilian law firm was indeed beyond my expectation. Despite knowing little about what a Brazilian workplace would be like, looking back, I seemed to have little fear when I accepted the offer. This may be largely attributed to my exposure to intercultural communication studies. I might not be familiar with the Brazilian culture, but I was open-minded and prepared to understand and appreciate any uncertainty and culture difference.

After working in the Brazilian law firm for over one year, I find that what matters more in our workplace may not be the Brazilian culture, but the rules of our Brazilian manager. Brazil is famous for its football, barbecue, coffee and samba dance, which are all good and proper reflections of the entertaining and enthusiastic Brazilians. When a Brazilian female is greeted, it is common that she is kissed beside both cheeks of the woman. However, our Brazilian manager in the workplace is anything but being entertaining or enthusiastic. He is a serious manager and strict lawyer, and even does not allow loud conversations in the office. Like many Latin Americans, it is true that the Brazilians tend to be casual with time and work. From my experience, I also find that it is not uncommon that a previously confirmed important meeting may be cancelled at the last minute and the deadline of a project may be delayed several times. Of course, being punctual is always appreciated. Besides learning the rules of our Brazilian manager, I am also learning the basic greetings in Portuguese and for example, "Bom dia" means "good morning" and "Chao" means "good bye". Just like we surely appreciate it when a foreigner tries to say "*Nihao*" and "*Xiexie*", I believe even if I do not speak Portuguese, it is always appreciated to know a couple of words in Portuguese.

To me, the adjustment to the workplace is not difficult because I am lucky to work closely with an experienced and intelligent Chinese lawyer. She knows how to play safe. Although she sometimes complains with us in private how unreasonable that a project is taking a lot more time in Brazil or how rude that an appointment is cancelled at the last minute, she knows what the Brazilian manager expects and how to avoid direct confrontations. However, if she is wronged or disrespected, she would speak it out, which actually brings more respect from the Brazilian manager. In other words, she knows how to play the game according to the rules of our boss, the Brazilian manager. This is quite useful because in the context of our workplace, the rules of the Brazilian manager may often be more powerful and even outweigh the influence of Brazilian culture in general.

9.5.3 Touching the Tiger's Tail (Maxwell May, Suzhou)

For most of my working experience, I have cared most about focusing on "colleagues," as I consider this the main part of communication or cooperation. Also since 2005, I have already been reinforced by the acknowledgement that "Once you work, you gain your upper position and promotion by good communication with people." That is for sure.

I thought I was quite popular, as I felt quite strongly confident that I can cope with everyone (I seem to be boasting), because I work hard, I am easy to cooperate with, willing to accept ideas anytime, have my cell-phone open 24 hours, am considerate to any other departments, and give a quick response to customer complaints. When I resigned in late August, 2009, nearly every level of company management tried to lure me or ask me to stay. But they failed, as other personal reasons motivated me to leave. I joined this Italian company very soon after I left the Hong Kongese company. The Italian invested brand seemed more shining or glittering in my eyes. I really

loved it, until one day when we had guests from the Italian headquarters.

Unfortunately, in November, 2009, I was down in the dumps, for there was a severe quality issue that happened in which we had to scrap more than 130,000 PCs finished products. I was the key person to control it but it was too late to find the problem. One afternoon, an Italian specialist GM and I were in the lab altogether. We were doing a "Defect Rate and Problem Finding Test," which is quite common to define the problem or to try every means to rescue the lost product. I was very careful to watch the Italian, waiting and cooperating with him. He did the test totally out of my imagination, which I felt should be corrected. Then I came up and said in English immediately "Sorry, maybe you don't understand." He stopped and looked at me with a weird gesture. Then I repeated again with same words which I thought were quite acceptable. He put everything down and then angrily shouted with his face filled with indignity to me in Italian. "How long you staying in here?" His English was very bad, I thought, and I replied, "three months." I didn't know what happened. "I staying in company 14 years three months, I know the problem, I know! Don't speak I don't understand!" Now I came to realize that I touched the tiger's tail. After five minutes I said to him "sorry," then, "I appreciate your job," and I tried to make it back to being quiet. He accepted my apology.

After this, I spent some time in finding historical and social characteristics of the Italians for reference as I think that is the basis of understanding. Then I came to realize it. The managers from Italy, as they don't care about systems, don't like to accept numbers and lines.

They are proud of shoes, clothing and bags, and even cars. Different from the Japanese, whose working to them is their life only, for our Italian managers, once working time was finished, everyone vanished in a second. We would send email for questions for weeks, until they finished their holiday and would tell us that their PC was broken during passing the Alps. Most of them would take a taxi 40 minutes every day to eat pizza and drink espresso coffee and then come back to work. Of course, this behavior is not completely right to everyone.

To me, the real idea is to respect the others. As that accident exposed my shortcoming, I had excessively expressed my ideas without consideration of the Italian communicating method. I cared mostly about the impression by others, as they would like to accept "Will you please help to review the findings during the incoming inspection from your side? There is non-conformity with standards which you mentioned before" rather than "Hi, let's go to see the problems." Once again learning from the Italians, before we talk to some foreigners, we should wait a second to find what is their country like, what their history is, what they don't like, what would humiliate them. Then we can decide, what is our counter-action, being honest, kind, cooperative, and punctual. Even for some people, they would like to see us sacrificing long hours of extra working or no pay.

9.5.4   Multicultural Training and Teaching Business English (Anthea Yang Sha, Purdue University)

When pursuing my graduate study in intercultural communication, I had considerable contact with my two American professors, which was rather valuable intercultural experience in China. I further experienced the power of this field when participating in the 2007 annual workshops on intercultural communication in Portland, Oregon. Since this field integrated well with the field of business, the workshops were generally business-oriented. Most of the participants were Americans from diverse racial, ethnic, social class and cultural groups, while a few of us were from the other parts of the world. Two of us were from China, one from Northeast China and I from Anhui Province.

I benefited greatly from the instructors' inspiring pedagogies and cultural diversity within the workshops. The instructors used examples, case studies, group discussions, games and intriguing questions to activate our mind, bring us together and encourage different ideas. In the "Personal Leadership" workshop, we analyzed how a German counselor wisely handled the challenges faced by the American expatriate manager in the company. This case study guided us to be more tolerant of other cultures and other people as well as to deal with intercultural problems appropriately. In the "Teaching Intercultural Communication" workshop, instructors used a game to make us realize how we unconsciously accepted people who looked like ourselves and excluded people who looked different. After the game, we listened to the feelings of the "excluded" participants. Furthermore, self-reflection practices, which were viewed as significant for the intercultural training program, progressed throughout each workshop. In the multicultural surroundings, I heard different voices speaking of different values, life stories and spirits. All these broadened my horizon and encouraged me to explore more of myself and the world.

When I began to teach in a business college after receiving my MA, my previous experiences provided useful for me in teaching several business courses in which I had no specific educational background. My three new challenging courses were "International Business Culture," "Negotiation Strategies," and "Public Relations and Etiquette." The first two courses shared some similarities, and the third course would become more pragmatic and interesting by integrating knowledge of business. In addition to learning new knowledge in each course by myself, I applied what I had learned in my graduate study and at Portland to my own courses, including case studies, games, dialogues and group discussions. When I was in the training workshops in Portland, Oregon, I was impressed with the very positive effects of videos on learning. When it came to my teaching, I searched for videos online when necessary, such as advertisements of different countries on the same product. Those activities not only impressed upon students the fresh and interesting aspects of business culture, but also taught them to understand and respect personal and cultural diversity.

Although I tried my best to organize the new courses, I felt that it would be more beneficial for students to have teachers who were equipped with both professional knowledge and work experience in the specific field. It is not unusual that in many Chinese universities, teachers of "business English" were English majors and did not have specific educational background in business. Take my school for example. In 2009, I did a survey among the sophomores and juniors in the Department of English who had taken some business English courses. I found that about 80% of the students were interested in studying business English to prepare themselves for the Chinese societal needs. However, the conditions of teachers could not well satisfy students' needs. Students also thought that the most effective mode of business English training at college was a combination of English language and business knowledge acquisition plus opportunities of practice. Effective opportunities of practice such as internships are also a challenge for many Chinese colleges and universities to develop.

9.5.5 Abstract for an MA Thesis as an Illustration of Research Related to Business Communication: On Managing Cultural Integration in Cross-border Acquisitions from the Perspective of China's IT Industry (Hu Guowei (2009), Shanghai: Shanghai International Studies University)

Globalization and the rapid development of China's economy ushered in a new era, an era when many companies in China now are actively engaged in cross-border acquisitions to expand their operations and increase their competitive advantage. Cross-border acquisitions, however, are still a new field. Despite their optimistic expectations, these cross-border acquisitions have typically failed to achieve the targeted results, partly due to the failure of culture integration.

Based on the current status of the Chinese IT industry and its industry characteristics, this thesis proposes a framework for managing cultural integration in cross-border acquisitions by exploring two cases: BenQ's acquisition of Mobile Devices from Siemens and Lenovo's acquisition of IBM's PC division.

The thesis consists of six chapters: Chapter One provides information about the research background, significance of the study, and the structure of the thesis. Chapter Two examines the existing theories about culture,

corporate culture, acquisitions, and the cultural integration model. Chapter Three illustrates the research method and case studies used in this thesis, offering information about the case study approach, data collection, data analysis, and criteria for case selections. Chapter Four gives an overview of the Chinese IT industry, including its current situation and recent cross-border acquisitions. Chapter Five points out the problems and proposes the framework for managing cultural integration by scrutinizing the two high-profile cross-border acquisitions that took place in the IT industry. Chapter Six summarizes the main findings of this thesis, namely pointing out the directions for further research in the future.

9.6   Case Study: The McDonaldization of Society

(Michael H. Prosser)

George Ritzer's book, *The McDonaldization of Society* (1996) offers the following four major characteristics of McDonald restaurants in many parts of the world: efficiency, calculable measurement factors, predictability over time and space, and the substitution of nonhuman technology instead of human labor. Ritzer calls this phenomenon a process where fast food dominates not only the US, but many parts of the world. It affects not only fast food, and its indigenous clones, but also fast education, health care, law, travel and tourism, leisure, politics, the family, religion, media, sports,

and even pornography and death. What is called "The McDonald Factor" suggests that when McDonalds, KFC, Taco Bell or other Western fast food franchises enter a market in an emerging country, others will follow, and when they leave, others will leave as well. Thomas Friedman argues that when countries have McDonalds or other Western fast food restaurants, they appear less likely to go to war with each other as there is a certain element of westernization there. When natives of a particular country are angry at another nation's leaders, they not only hang the leaders in effigy, burn the flag, boycott the nations' symbolic restaurants or stores, as in the case in China

Intercultural Communication in Business, Training and Education

with protests and boycotts of Carrefour over the French protests against the Olympic torch relays in 2008, and often smash the windows of the symbolic restaurants or stores. Sometimes, the perpetrators of violence against such restaurants like KFC or McDonalds, or against Carrefour forget that 99% of the employees are natives of the host country, and that nearly all of the food or other products may come from that country.

The first McDonalds Restaurant in the US was created in 1967, but by 1988, there were 2,000 restaurants outside the US, with $1.8 billion in income, and by 1994, there were 4,700 international franchises, with a revenue base of $3.4 billion. The first McDonalds in Russia was in Moscow, only a few blocks from Red Square. It attracted 30,000 customers the first day. However, in 1992, the new McDonalds in Beijing (now demolished) had 700 seats, 40,000 customers the first day and 850 Chinese employees, making it for a time the winner over McDonalds in Moscow, and thus temporarily the largest restaurant in the world. In 1987, KFC had entered the Chinese market, so even today, it has more restaurants than McDonalds (2008: KFC—China, 2,200 restaurants; McDonalds—China, 950; Japan, 3,500; Malaysia, 300; Pizza Hut—China, 140 (Jacques, 2009: 128)).

We can identify the following advantages of McDonaldization [or other western fast food restaurants] in a culture or society: It is predictable; there are international standards applied; the restaurants are clean; the technology and techniques are easily transferable; the food and service are fast; entertainment is provided; there are gifts for children; it is a good informal gathering place; and there is a clear feeling of Westernization. However, there are also a number of disadvantages such as negative environmental factors; the dehumanization and robotization of both workers and customers; a superficial concern for a happy quality of life; it is a fast food factory; it provides the illusion of quality, quantity and intimacy; there is a loss of traditional culture; it is more expensive than traditional foods; people in societies where no such fast food restaurants exist feel deprived of the benefits of Westernization; and it is likely to have negative effects on the future.

In Morgan Spurlock's two hour movie, *Super Size Me: A Film of Epic Portions*, the promotional description of the movie is as follows: "In *Super Size Me*, filmmaker Morgan Spurlock unravels the American obesity epidemic by interviewing experts nationwide, by subjecting himself to a 'McDonald's only'

Brand	Global Locations	Countries	US Market Share
KFC	15,580	109	44%
Pizza Hut	13,175	97	15%
Taco Bell	5,833	17	54%
Long John Silver's	1,060	7	35%

Date as of 12/31/2008

diet for thirty days straight. His Sundance award-winning feature is as entertaining as it is horrifying as it dives into corporate responsibility, nutritional education, school lunch programs and how we as a nation are eating ourselves to death" (2004). Eating three meals daily for 30 days at McDonalds, he not only gained more than 25 pounds, but he also came near to seriously damaging his health and was urged on day 21 to stop the experiment. "Ain't it cool news" called the movie: "Amazing! This movie will blow you away." Rolling Stone Magazine exclaimed: "I'm lovin it!"

However, now a serious fast-food competitor Yum has become the world's largest fast food restaurant, overseeing 36,000 KFC, Taco Bell, Pizza Hut, Long John Silvers, A&W, and East Dawning restaurants spread across 110 countries. Yum's locations exceed McDonald's restaurants three to one. *The Economist* (2009: October 29) says that "Yum is the most successful foreign fast-food firm in China" and presently Yum is investing $1 billion in its China's operations from 2010–2012 in opening 1,500 new stores (Motley Fool Stock Report, 2010: April).

Yum has the following stores, among others (cf. table on previous page).

So, perhaps, this case study should be called "The Yumization of Society" rather than "The McDonaldization of Society."

9.7 Summary

In the dialogue for this chapter, several students indicate their interest in joining an international trade company, and thus their interest in learning more about intercultural business communication. Throughout various parts of Chinese Communicating Interculturally, you will notice various references to business. It is an important subject and there are quite a few books now related to the topic of intercultural business communication which you can obtain for a further understanding of the topic. Here, we are simply introducing this topic, with essays by Hugo Rocha and David Henry, and returning to the topic again with Rutherford's essay on intercultural training. As some of you will become teachers here in China, we have also included an essay on intercultural education by Dilhara Turdi who teaches minority students in their universities in China.

Areas which we have not discussed because of space limits have been translation and interpretation, also important considerations for you in an intercultural communication class. Some of you will find that your intercultural business and international trade careers will involve these aspects of communication, as Zhang Wei notes in his own essay in the section on practical aspects.

We can see clearly from several of these practical essays that there are significant problems developing for young Chinese

Intercultural Communication in Business, Training and Education

professionals in dealing with managers from other cultures, such as those expressed by Zhang Wei, Maxwell May, and Clare Li. Anthea Yang Sha has had intercultural training at the Portland, Oregon Summer Institute for Intercultural Communication (as has Zizi Zhao Zhao, among the writers of cultural stories in Chapter Three). Anthea found herself teaching three new courses in intercultural business without any specific education addressing these subjects. She relates the problems for new teachers in such a situation. Now she is a Ph D student in international education at Purdue University in the United States.

9.8 Questions for Discussion

9.8.1 In the dialogue for this chapter and other chapters recently, we see that Professor Zhang is becoming more relaxed and humerous with the students than in the early chapter dialogues. Are there intercultural implications for a more relaxed and humorous feeling for Professor Zhang as a co-teacher with Michael who has been fairly humorous with the students from the beginning? Is this the result of sharing intercultural communication and teaching, or just individual personality aspects of the two co-teachers of the course?

9.8.2 Hugo Rocha's father was very international in his outlook; Dr. Rocha was an exchange high school student in the US; and he has been involved in Lisbon with the implementation of the Euro currency for Portugal. Additionally, he has been involved with banking in Lisbon, Luxembourg, and Madrid, thus having a very intercultural view since he was young. Though he does not claim to be an expert academically in intercultural communication competence, in his practical life and career, it has been an important aspect of his development. What insights about communication, intercultural communication, and communication competence do we find from his essay that are useful for studying intercultural communication in terms of business and international trade?

9.8.3 David Henry, a long time university teacher in China, was involved in several businesses before coming to teach in China. He has also been a trainer of many Chinese in English proficiency who wish to study abroad. He provides several fairly well known tips both from his own experiences and calling upon the writing of Zhu's Written Communication across Cultures. Among all of the tips that Henry has offered, which ones do you consider the most important ones? Why?

9.8.4 In the discussion on organizational culture and organizational communication theories in this chapter, cultural media theories are also implied. What is the specific nature of organizational culture and its application in organizational communication theories? In our discussions about practical applications, what are the ways that these case studies and Hu Guowei's MA thesis abstract can be utilized as examples of organizational culture and organizational communication theories?

9.8.5 In the discussion on advertising theories, Werder suggests that such theories have a mixture of business and communication aspects, but that such theories are often weaker than other communication theories. Noting the extraordinary role of advertising in the media, why is it that these theories have not developed as strongly as other communication theories? Is it possible to suggest that public relations and advertising theories have less content to explore or that the field of business has not effectively been linked to mainstream communication studies?

9.8.6 Compare the major similarities and differences between the process of intercultural training and education. If you join an international trade company, and are asked to upgrade your cultural and intercultural background, and then conduct training programs for Chinese professionals, how would you approach both tasks to be most beneficial to your international company?

9.8.7 Don Rutherford, President of Culture Connect in Calgarary, Canada, provides us a very clear and practical discussion about the major elements of intercultural training. His training recommendations tie in closely to intercultural business communication. What correlations do we see among the elements that he discusses with the earlier essays by Rocha and Henry, and with the practical examples that are offered in this chapter?

9.8.8 Zhang Wei, Maxwell May, and Clare Li indicate that they have faced serious intercultural problems with their foreign company managers. Zhang Wei's managers are French; Maxwell May's managers are Italian; and Clare Li's managers have been Brazilian. What are the similar intercultural problem trends that these three young Chinese professional employees have faced in the three firms? How have each of these young Chinese attempted to solve these intercultural problems? Have they been successful? How would you seek to help in such a situation if you were working in one of these foreign owned enterprises? Would American managers be more or less successful than the European managers in working with a Chinese workforce?

9.8.9 Assume that you are going to be posted in an English speaking country in Africa for two years as an interpreter and translator for your Chinese supervisors whose English is much less strong than yours. You have a brief time before departure to prepare for this assignment. What would be the major tasks that you would want to undertake to prepare yourself for this assignment? Why?

9.8.10 Anthea Yang Sha, now a PhD student at Purdue University, has an MA in intercultural communication, has undertaken intercultural training at the Portland, Oregon Summer Intercultural Communication Institute, and has also taught in a business college in Shanghai, setting up new intercultural business courses for her students. These three developments in her career so far have blended well for her. What does she consider the most important aspects of her intercultural communication education, training, and teaching to make her and her students effective in intercultural communication competence? Why?

Intercultural Communication in Business, Training and Education

9.9 Suggested Readings

Brislin, R. W. & Yoshada, T. (1994). *Intercultural training: An introduction.* Thousand Oaks, CA: Sage.

Cooren, F., Taylor, J., & Van Every, F. (2006). *Communication as organizing.* Mahwah, NJ: Lawrence Earlbaum.

Dong, S. (2006). *Chinese and American corporate culture and its application in cross-cultural management.* Unpublished MA thesis. Shanghai: Shanghai International Studies University.

Dou, W. (2005). *Intercultural business communication.* Beijing: Higher Education Press.

Eisenberg, E. M. (2006). *Strategic ambiguities.* Thousand Oaks, CA: Sage.

Feng, T. (1999). *Chinese culture and Chinese business negotiation style.* Thousand Oaks, CA: Sage.

Gallo, F. T. (2011). *Business leadership in China: How to blend best western practices with Chinese Wisdom.* Singapore: John Wiley.

Haley, G. T., Haley, U. C. V., & Tan, C. T. (2009). *New Asian emperors: The business strategies of the overseas Chinese.* Singapore: John Wiley.

Hutton, W. (2006). *Writing on the wall: Why we must embrace China as a partner or face it as an enemy.* New York, NY: The Free Press.

Laroche, L. & Rutherford, D. (2007). *Recruiting, retaining and promoting culturally different employees.* Amsterdam, The Netherlands: Elsevier.

Martin, J. (2002). *Organizational culture: Mapping the terrain.* Thousand Oaks, CA: Sage.

Ritzer, G. (1996). *The McDonaldization of society. Revised.* London, England: Sage.

Tan, Y. (2011). *Chinnovation: How Chinese innovators are changing the world.* Singapore: John Wiley.

Wang, H. (2010: December 8). The Chinese dream: The rise of the world's largest middle class and what it means to you. *Forbes Magazine.*

Chapter TEN

Intercultural Theories and Research

10.1 Dialogue

Professor Zhang: We recognize that many of you are more interested in the practical dimensions of intercultural communication than being involved in research on the topic.

However, it is important that you have a competence in understanding the nature of such theories and research and the ability to conduct reasonable research yourselves if you need or wish to do so now or at a later date. Both undergraduates and postgraduates will usually be called on at some point to do either qualitative or empirical quantitative research, for example in conducting a field study either in a group or by yourselves. This is especially important since many of you wish to undertake postgraduate study in China or abroad.

Michael: Many universities abroad request that you identify your proposed research topic as a part of your personal statement and application for admission to their postgraduate programs. The GRE exams in the United States test basic knowledge in English, logic, and math. Many Chinese students do very well in math, because of serious earlier study of it, but may not do as well in the English or logical analysis of the test, since English is your second language, and Western and Asian logical patterns are often quite different. In fact, adapting Western logical patterns is very important if you are going to be a student in Western universities. Even

Intercultural Theories and Research

though you speak very good English, sometimes the TOEFL and IELTS exams do cause problems.

Tulip: I have taken the GRE and TOEFL exams already and got very good scores. I have to write a thesis in my program here at this university, so I am glad to know more about how to do good research. I would like to study for a PhD in the US after I get my MA in China.

Jason: I have taken the IELTS exam and did well and hope to be admitted to a postgraduate program in one of the English speaking countries besides America, perhaps the UK, Canada, Australia, or New Zealand.

Michelle: I have been accepted in an American university in a combined master's program relating to communication and technology. After I finish that program, I want to earn an MBA so that I can use it as a leader in business first in the US and later back here in China.

Ben: Presently, I am writing a thesis on *Structural Equivalence of Values Domains in China: Values among Migrant workers and permanent residents in Shanghai*. It won't be an easy task, but the topic is of great interest to me as I am from Shanghai, and there are many migrant workers coming all the time into Shanghai. So I would like to know what they consider important in their own lives. Perhaps if I pass the Shanghai Civil Service exams, then I can help them in a practical way to develop better lives for themselves and their families in the future. I have read Chu and Yu's field study, The Great Wall in Ruins and also James Farrer's study *Opening Up: Youth, Sex, Culture, and Market Reform in Shanghai*. They have helped me in a general way. I read Frederick Williams' *Reasoning with Statistics*, which will help me in my study and later if I should apply for a PhD program.

Professor Zhang: We hope that some of you in this course will seriously consider advanced postgraduate degrees. China needs more and more educated citizens and even if you study overseas, we are eager to welcome back returning talents.

Echo: Ben, you are older than we are, and more mature. I wouldn't know where to start with research.

Ben: The first thing you have to do is to read a lot about the topic that you want to do research on. I have read Chu and Yu's field study, The Great Wall in Ruins and also James Farrer's study, Opening Up: Youth, Sex, Culture, and Market Reform in Shanghai. They have helped me to get some general knowledge, especially Farrer's book, although his research was done several years ago. He also has a Chinese wife from Shanghai, and she was able to give him a lot of advice.

Jason: Then I should marry a Shanghai wife before I begin serious research?

Laughter

Professor Zhang: Whether you are writing a research paper, an article for a journal, a BA or MA thesis, or even a PhD dissertation, there is a standard pattern that is generally followed in writing the paper. As Aristotle said, every message needs a head, a body, and feet, or at least a thesis or claim supported by evidence. The higher level the degree is, the more detail and evidence is required, 20–25 pages for a good journal article in a reputable journal or for a BA thesis; then 60–70 pages for an MA thesis; and 200 or more pages for a doctoral dissertation. A very early thesis at Harvard University was only six pages, but a recent dissertation in Humboldt University in Berlin by an American professor took two full volumes with hundreds of reference citations. As Professor Li and Michael have demonstrated in this text book, the references should be generous, as others will stand on your shoulders in later research.

Jasmine: I would like the early thesis at Harvard rather than the very long dissertation in Berlin.

Robin: I want to study in London. I would like to explore how Chinese students there adapt to the British culture. Earlier, we saw that Lili has adapted fairly well to a British husband.

Michael: We have several examples to give you about intercultural research, including applying intercultural theories, cross-cultural research, a brief essay by Zhang Rui at the University of Alberta, Canada, who used intercultural conflict constructs and theories for his own MA thesis here in China. We will help you learn how to develop your own intercultural study, and we have eight MA thesis abstracts as brief examples of intercultural communication research concluding this chapter.

Professor Zhang: Some of you who are interested in research on cinema may be interested to know that a large number of doctoral dissertations have been written about "StarTrek." A good way to learn about the process of intercultural communication is to see how other successful studies have been done by some Chinese postgraduates. We hope that several of you will become professional researchers or college or university teachers.

Intercultural Theories and Research

Gloria: Professor Zhang and Michael, the semester will soon end. This has been a very good class, and I am sure that we have learned a lot about intercultural communication. We want to thank you for your good cultural dialogues with us, your serious advice, and your humor. It made the class interesting to attend. We are proud to be Chinese students here at our university..

Grace: The class text book, *Chinese Communicating Interculturally*, has been an interesting experience too, with a lot of interesting information that we didn't know and humor in it. Also, I learned a lot. Professor Zhang, I really appreciated all of the wisdom that you gave to us. I think that both you and Michael gave us a lot to think about to make us more culturally competent and sensitive to other cultures and our own Chinese culture.

Professor Zhang: We have enjoyed having you all in class for our course, "Intercultural Communication." There has been a lot more dialogue between Michael, me, and class members and between class members themselves than sometimes happens in our Chinese classes. There certainly are some unique characters among members of this class!

Michael: Remember that your goal should be to become world citizens.

True Nation: I wonder what Han Han would say about the class? Maybe he would say that "the ship sailed smoothly and the weather was quite favorable."

Laughter

Mike: Michael, I am glad that we shared the same name.

Michael: Yes, I am glad too, but I know that your family name is also Hu. Which Hu are you? President Hu or Mike Hu? Or maybe he is your uncle?

Amelia: Really, Michael, you are more like my grandpa, and Professor Zhang, since I am also a Zhang, perhaps we are related too.

Professor Zhang: Since there are about 100 million Zhangs in China, we probably have been related in the distant past history! There are a lot of students in this class with the family name Zhang. It has been our pleasure to co-teach this class, but we don't want to forget to praise Professor Li Mengyu, the first author of our text book. Thanks then to Professor Li and Michael. We will send Professor Li a copy of our class photo and here is a special present for Michael, a laughing Buddha!

Michael: Wah! Ha. Ha. He does look like me.

Applause

10.2 Theorizing about Intercultural Communication

In his 2005 edited book, *Theorizing about Intercultural Communication*, published after his death, William B. Gudykunst asked the authors whose essays were included the following questions:

(1) What got you interested in developing your theory?

(2) What is the scope of your theory? What is it designed to describe and/or explain?

(3) What are the metatheoretical assumptions underlying your theory (including assumptions about communication and culture?

(4) How did you develop your theory (i.e. a historical overview of the development of the theory)?

(5) What are the theoretical propositions of the theory?

(6) What research has been conducted testing the theory?

(7) How can your theory be applied (i.e. to improve the effectiveness of communication? (2005: vii).

These are all good questions to consider in your own research that you may undertake either as a research paper or a thesis.

10.2.1 Intercultural Identity Theories

In his article, *Obama's Culturally Trans-formational Identities and Accommodations toward the Middle East and Islam,* Prosser adapts Gudykunst's three intercultural theories related to identity: **identity** *management theory (IMT) as proposed by W.R.Cupach and T. Imahori*, **identity negotiation theory**, developed in large part by Stella Ting-Toomey, and **cultural identity theory**, presented by M. J. Collier and M. Thomas. Gudykunst states that the **identity management theory** is based on the concept of interpersonal communication competence, which naturally also relates to intercultural communication competence (ICC). Identity theories can provide expectations for behavior and motivate individuals' behavior. Cultural and relational identities can be seen as central to the **identity management theory**. The Chinese concept of "face" can be applied to this theory as dialectical tension develops, which incorporates three phases; (1) fellowship versus autonomy face; (2)competence versus autonomy face; (3) autonomy versus either fellowship or competence face. Because outside forces develop positive or negative stereotypes in intercultural communication competence and face, individuals must work diligently to utilize the positive stereotypes and overcome the negative ones.

Gudykunst notes that **identity negotiation theory** demonstrates that individuals negotiate their concept of identity with their own perceptions of their multiple identities and those perceptions of others with whom they communicate. Again, individuals' resourcefulness in negotiating the identity or identities which they see for themselves and those which others see for them helps them to manage their own security-vulnerability and inclusion-differentiation. The more secure the individuals' positive self identification, the greater is their own identity coherence and global self-esteem, and the greater their membership in collective esteem, the more resourceful they are when interacting with strangers, who may be positive or negative in their perceptions of the individuals under consideration. The specific motivations to communicate with strangers, whether positive or negative in their perceptions of the individuals lead them to be resourceful in communication with the strangers.

As explained by Gudykunst, the **cultural identity theory** includes Collier and Thomas' five axioms: (1) the more that norms and meanings differ in discourse, the more intercultural the contact; (2) the more individuals have intercultural communication competence, the better they are able to develop and maintain intercultural relationships; (3) the more that cultural identities differ in the discourse, the more intercultural the contact; (4) the more one person's ascribed cultural identity for the other person matches the other person's avowed cultural identity, the more the intercultural communication competence; (5) linguistic references to cultural identity systematically have important contacts with sociocontextual factors such as participants, type of communication episodes, and topics.

10.2.2 Intercultural Accommodation or Adaptation Theories

Three theories in intercultural communication, as identified by Gudykunst, focus on accommodation or adaptation, including (1) **communication accommodation theory (CAT)**; (2) **intercultural adaptation theory**, and (3) **co-cultural theory**. CAT has four key aspects:

(1) sociohistorical context incorporating relations between the groups having contact and the social norms regarding contact;

(2) the communicator's accommodative orientation which tends to perceive encounters with outgroup members in interpersonal terms, intergroup terms, or a combination of the two;

(3) the immediacy situation with five interrelated situations organized around the communicators' interpersonal or intergroup orientation goals and addressee focus, discourse management, behavior and tactics, and labeling and attributions;

(4) evaluation and future intentions, focusing on the communicators' perceptions of their interlocutors' behavior in the interaction.

Intercultural adaptation theory is designed to understand how communicators adapt to each other in "purpose-related encounters"; the extent to which the setting affects the invocation of culture-based belief differences, and how the setting favors one or other participants. **The co-cultural theory** is based on how social hierachy privileges some groups over others and specific positions in society which provide subjective, rather than objective ways that individuals look at the world. (Gudykunst, 2005: 3–32).

These illustrative intercultural communication theories can be tested in a qualitative (subjective), quantitative (objectively and empirically tested) or a mixed qualitative and quantitative method. In addition to these theories, Gudykunst notes others, such as theories in which culture and communication are integrated; cultural variability in communication; theories focusing on effective outcomes; theories focusing on acculturation and adjustment. Gudykunst concludes his introductory chapter in his edited book, *Theorizing about Intercultural Communication*, by noting five issues still needing to be addressed in future development of theories on intercultural communication: (1) There is a need for more subjectivistic (human action/interpretative) theories and for integrating subjectivistic and objectivistitic (causal process) theories; (2) The vast majority of the theorists were born in the United States with a lack of indigenous theories developing; (3) The issue of power is not incorporated into many of the theories so far; (4) Many of the theories developed so far are compatible and overlapping; (5) There is little or no published research supporting most of the intercultural communication theories which he has identified as the leading ones (25–26).

10.3   Cross-Cultural Communication

10.3.1 Defining Intercultural and Cross-Cultural Communication Research*

The most intracultural communication may be between identical twins, then fraternal twins, followed by brothers and sisters. If the twins meet twins from a different culture and converse and interact, whether unintentionally or purposefully, then intercultural communication occurs as in the presence of another, all behavior is communicative. Most intercultural communication occurs within an interpersonal setting. In this way, both intercultural and interpersonal communication is complementary. When researchers want to compare or contrast how the twins from different cultures interact interculturally, then a cross-cultural communication study occurs. While one definition of cross-cultural communication informs the theoretical study of comparative and contrastive cultures and cultural variables, an alternative definition states cross-cultural communication is communication which takes place between members of whole cultures in contact, or between their cultural spokespersons or representatives. William B. Gudykunst identifies both the study of intercultural communication and

---

*   Michael H. Prosser (published originally in Stephen W. Littlejohn and Karen A. Foss (Eds.) (2009), Encyclopedia of Communication Theory. I Thousand Oaks, CA: Sage (reprinted with permission) Numbering added to essay.

cross-cultural communication as segments of intergroup communication. Academic fields with a special interest in cross-cultural communication research include anthropology, communication, international relations, psychology and sociology.

Intercultural and cross-cultural investigations may include such areas as attitudes, beliefs, cognition, cross-cultural business and training, journalism, language and linguistics, mass media, nonverbal cues, organizational culture, perceptions, stereotypes, thought-patterning and values, Gudykunst and Carmen M. Lee argue that among the following elements of communication several can be accurately considered cross-culturally as theoretical constructs for current investigation: (1) cultural variability including the spectrum of similarities and differences, plus horizontal versus vertical national cultural dimensions, as identified by scholars such as Geert Hofstede, Michael Harris Bond, Robert Ingelhart, and Shalom Schwartz; (2) individualism-collectivism with the study of ingroups and outgroups, as well as individualistic versus collectivistic values and (3) self-construals or the ways that people see themselves.

Additionally, Gudykunst and Lee propose other theoretical dimensions of cultural variability such as low and high context culture, initially introduced by Edward T. Hall in his 1976 book *Beyond Culture*; face-negotiation theory, proposed by Stella Ting-Toomey in 1985, which illustrates how members of cultures manage high or low face and conflicts; the conversational constraints theory, developed by Young Yun Kim in 1993 as goal or task oriented and coordinated conversations in relationships; the expectancy violations theory, proposed by J. K. Burgoon in 1978, by which

guidelines are delineated for appropriately expected behavior in communicative situations; the anxiety/uncertainty management theory (AIM), developed by Gudykunst in 1995, which focuses on effective interpersonal and intergroup communication as it incorporates how communicators manage anxiety and uncertainty processes; and the communication accommodation theory (CAT) which Gudykunst also includes in theoretical intercultural communication studies, occurring between people of different ingroups and outgroups by assessing their language, nonverbal behavior, and paralanguage in communicative situations.

10.3.2 Principles or Criteria Guiding Cross-Cultural Communication Research

Stephen McDowell stipulates that a field of inquiry is not just a series of substantive topics, but a set of core problems, concepts, theories, and methods and an ongoing discussion among practitioners. Various principles or criteria guide researchers in studying intercultural and cross-cultural communication. Among these are the cultural principles identified by Michael H. Prosser in his 1978 book, *The Cultural Dialogue*, of similarities and differences, the role of conflict and conflict resolution, communicative cultural control and power, the impact of technology and especially information technology, cultural stability and cultural change, cultural imperialism and cultural dependency or interdependency.

Steve J. Kulich recommends a nine-level analysis of culture for future cross-cultural research: (1) culture as propagated mythic ideals; (2) as mainstream promotion or mass trends; (3) as model-citizen norms; (4) as expected behavior mechanics; (5) as integrated meshworks; (6) as mediated metaphors; (7) as mindless personal responses to familiarity; (8) as personal matrix options; and (9) as personalized meaning. In the context of social science research, Kulich proposes that an integrated grid can be developed in the cross-cultural study of culture and communication and they can be studied at the cultural, subcultural, co-cultural, contextual, and individual levels of culture. An integrated grid could include historically transmitted socialization, socially constructed perceptions within the context of cultural groups and personally, and reflective and relative senses of meaning.

Gudykunst and Lee offer five approaches to incorporate culture into communication theories: Culture can be viewed as (1) a part of the communication process in theories or (2) as creating culture; (3) Theories designed in one culture can be generalized to other cultures; (4) can be generated to explain communication between people from different cultures; (5) or to explain how communication varies across cultures. For cross-cultural theory construction and analysis, they believe that in addition to standard social science requirements such as logical consistency, explanatory power, and parsimony, the following should also be added: including more than one dimension of cultural variability, linking dimensions of cultural variability directly with the cultural norms and rules that influence the communication behavior being explained, and avoiding oversimplifying the process or inappropriately coupling the way that the cultural variables

influence cultural norms and rules or the reverse.

10.3.3 Illustrative Examples of Effective Cross-Cultural Communication Research

An early and longitudinal example of major cross-cultural research efforts include Charles E. Osgood's Cross-Cultural Universals of Affective Meaning Project to develop near cultural and language universal theories in approximately fifty cultures In this multinational study, 100 teenaged boys in each culture were chosen to assess 100 terms for their understanding of goodness or badness, power or lack of power, and swiftness or slowness through a seven point semantic differential scale. This study tested and confirmed the hypotheses that regardless of language or culture, human beings use the same qualifying and descriptive framework in allocating affective meanings of concepts which involve attitudes, feelings, stereotypes and values.

Desmond Morris's study of middle-aged male usage of nonverbal gesture cues in twenty-five European cultures, described in his 1980 book *Gestures*, hypothesized and confirmed that middle-aged men living closer to the Mediterranean Sea, and already strongly fixed in their own national culture behaviors, would utilize far more exaggerated and bolder gestures than would those middle-aged men living in the northern European or Scandinavian countries. Also, the hypothesis that the former group would have more gestures with sexual implications than the northern European or Scandinavian cultures was generally confirmed. Later, in his 1994 book,

Bodytalk: A World Guide to Gestures, more cross-cultural nonverbal studies were significantly explored in a much wider geographical range.

In the 1974 bicultural research conference in Japan, it was hypothesized that Japanese participants would be more task-oriented and the Americans would be more process-oriented. Perhaps, not surprisingly, it was found that the younger Japanese and American participants were more process-oriented, while the older Japanese and Americans were more task-oriented.

One of the most important cross-cultural studies of national attitudes and values has been Dutch sociologist Geert Hofstede's analysis of 116,000 responses to his earlier IBM questionnaire, first reported in his 1980 book *Culture's Consequences* and later modified in a second edition in 2001. Based on this study, he initially proposed the development of four national cultural dimensions, uncertainty avoidance, power distance, individualism versus collectivism, and masculinity versus femininity, with a fifth dimension incorporated by Michael Harris Bond, in 1987, called Confucian dynamism or later short-term versus long-term orientation. Uncertainty avoidance specifies the level to which members of a national culture avoid or accept uncertainty; power distance is the extent to which less powerful members of organizations and institutions accept unequal distributions of power. Masculinity versus femininity, more recently described as aggressiveness versus nurturing, emphasizes how a national culture manages its gender issues. Individualism versus collectivism, initially proposed by cross-cultural psychologist Harry C. Triandis, focuses on whether members of a national culture are more oriented to individual versus collective or communitarian values. *The Chinese Culture Connection* in 1987 proposed that Hofstede's western bias needs to be supplemented by a Chinese methodological bias of Confucianism. This cultural variability dimension has three aspects: status relationships, integration or harmony with others, and moral discipline. In 2008, Hofstede has added two new dimensions: indulgence versus restraint and monumentalism versus flexible humility.

10.3.4 Illustrative Problems in Western versus Non-Western Cross-Cultural Communication Research

Many early cross-cultural studies focused on comparisons between Americans/Japanese, Americans/Europeans, or between American/Soviet cultural patterns. More recently considerable research has emphasized bipolar cultural aspects between the Americans/Chinese or Chinese and other Westerners. Bond recommends that while these bicultural studies are useful, including those by cross-cultural psychologists, they are primarily descriptive as they use Western research methods to deal with indigenous cultural patterns. He urges cross-cultural researchers to move toward more pan-cultural studies, as Hofstede's studies have done, and that for serious reliability, at least ten cultural groups are needed when using standard social science statistics.

Hwaang Kwang-Kuo also argues that the development of social scientific cross-cultural research in the indigenous Asian setting is problematic because Western social science methods are not always appropriate to study indigenous Asian cultural factors. He believes that western social science theories, or the scientific micro-world versus the indigenous Asian life-world for intellectuals in non-Western countries has serious limitations as the philosophy of science for constructing a scientific microworld is essentially a product of alien cultures which is inconsistent with practical Asian cultural traditions. Thus, a cross-cultural communication researcher must construct a tentative theory to solve scientific problems caused by (1) inconsistencies between western theories and the observed phenomena or results of experiments in more traditional Asian societies; (2) contradictions within a system or a theory; and (3) conflicts between the two types of theories. For example, formal justice in western scientific cross-cultural studies includes such basic elements as authority in an unequal relationship but does not practically consider the notion of Confucian respect for the superior in determining what is justice.

Referring to cross-cultural communication studies for Chinese scholars as illustrative, Guan Shijie of Peking University notes several problems for China, and by implication for other Asian cultures: (1) More dialectical research is conducted than empirical studies; (2) Too much research is conducted in individual disciplines rather than on an interdisciplinary basis; (3) More general introductions are provided than on specific topics with Chinese characteristics; (4) More Sino-US research is done than comparing China with other countries studies than domestic cross-cultural research of different Chinese communities. He argues that this Chinese unitariness of research methodology has been a bottleneck in restraining further in-depth cross-cultural Chinese and Asian communication research.

10.4   A Researcher's Journey: Some Issues in Intercultural Communication

(Zhang Rui, University of Alberta)

10.4.1 Theoretical and Methodological Diversity

Being interdisciplinary, intercultural communication is marked by theoretical and methodological diversity. Whereas diversity is considered a sign of academic productivity, I want to outline a number of issues that pertain to the further development of the field by using my Master's thesis as a humble illustration below. **First**, although culture is a shared interest that unites the field, no widespread consensus has been established on how to define culture and how it affects psychological and communication processes. For example, cross-cultural psychology champions an approach that examines if the effects of culture are mediated by the extent to which people report themselves as being independent or interdependent on a scale. **Second**, paralleling the theoretical issues are research methods that can be used to study culture empirically. Given the complexity of the subject matter, the qualitative-quantitative distinction seems inadequate to capture the particularities of methodological preference. Some of the common methods include experiments, survey, interviews, and textual analysis of cultural products (discourse and media analysis). Consumers of the intercultural literature should bear in mind the choice of methodology and be aware of their trade-offs. **Third**, intercultural research also differs in its willingness to apply universally meaningful concepts (etic or comparative) or to construct local interpretations through in-depth understanding (emic or indigenous). One example is the continued debate on the usefulness of the individualism/collectivism construct as an overarching framework to illuminating cultural differences. **Fourth**, there is a need to move toward a more nuanced understanding of culture, especially how it interacts with macro-structural changes and individual experience. No one will doubt that when studying cultures in the globalizing world we live in now, we encounter changes, for better or worse, as a result of compressed distance, dismantled obstacles, and increased opportunity for intercultural contact. These dynamic changes need to be accounted for both theoretically and empirically.

10.4.2 Interpersonal Conflict: A Brief Demonstration

For my master's thesis, I settled on interpersonal conflict to make sense of how it is managed in a rapidly changing environment of mainland China. In two studies using surveys and follow-up interviews, I examined the extent to which interpersonal conflict styles vary from one situation to another in a Chinese student sample in Shanghai and compared with those of an American sample in California. They provided some interesting, albeit tentative, clues to the broad issues noted above.

The stereotypical view that Chinese, or East Asians in general, are more avoiding and accommodating in handling conflict was not supported. Instead, the data bore out a complex picture depicted from a more contextual approach that the target involved in a given episode of conflict matters. What stood out, among others, is that contemporary university students are as open and expressive with their parents as their American counterparts. Cultural differences on other conflict styles such as avoiding, if any, were not overwhelming. When I compared responses to how independent or interdependent people think they are between the Chinese and American sample, the differences were again practically small, even if statistically significant. More importantly, this self-concept measure, derived directly from the universal framework of individualism/collectivism, offered relatively limited information on how those students decided to use a particular conflict style with their parents and fellow classmates.

10.4.3 Some Implications

What did the combined results imply? The etic framework seems too coarse to be useful in understanding specific conflict behavior in culturally rich contexts or illuminating why differences occur if cultures are compared.

Moreover, the assumption that cultures are immune from innovation that comes from within or without seems problematic as well. Cultural stereotypes, which are often expressed in simplistic and timeless terms, cannot explain the coexistence of individualism and collectivism or modernity and traditionality, or the emergence of some degree of interculturality in the era of globalization.

10.5 Intercultural and Cross-Cultural Research in China

Guan Shijie writes that in China since the intercultural communication discipline began to develop seriously in 1995 a number of contributions have been made to its study. These include the expansion of research groups, research centers, more exchanges with foreign scholars, more frequent symposia, the increase of colleges and universities that have begun to offer intercultural communication courses, and the recruitment of postgraduate and PhD students. He points out that the opening up of Chinese scholars' vision for the field includes: (1) The study of interpersonal communication across different cultures has been integrated with the reality of China. (2) Intercultural communication between different countries has become an important topic in communication study. (3) Research on IC between China and foreign countries has gone beyond the range of intercultural communication between China and the United States. (4) Intercultural communication between Chinese ethnic groups has become a focus of research as well. (5) Interdisciplinary study containing IC theories with other disciplines has also become a research interest.

However, Guan notes that there have been several weaknesses to date in Chinese intercultural research. He calls them as "the five more-thans: " (1) More dialectical research than empirical studies. (2) More research on individual disciplines than on interdisciplinary research. (3) More on general introductions than on specific topics with Chinese characteristics. (4) More on Sino-US IC than on IC between China and other societies. (5) More on international IC studies than on domestic IC problems. He argues that the unitarianess of research methodology has proven to create a "bottleneck" holding back further and more in-depth research in IC studies (Guan, 2007: i-xiii).

10.6 Developing Your Own Intercultural Research

When we write research papers, if possible, we should have a genuine, and perhaps even passionate interest in the chosen topic. There are simple rules for undertaking intercultural or cross-cultural research: immerse yourself as deeply as possible in the subject; be openminded, become as culturally aware as possible, and have passion for your topic. For postgraduate research, theses, or Ph.D. dissertations, our research becomes an important aspect of our reputation. Thomas Bruneau, an intercultural expert on silence and also on the brain, chose the first topic for an early postgraduate research paper, and dedicated himself to discover everything that he could learn about silence cross-culturally. The paper was published in a noted communication journal, and since then he has frequently been recognized as an expert on silence culturally. Later, he began to develop a considerable interest in the working of the brain, both physiologically and psychologically, and then increasingly across cultures. Even now as an emeritus professor, he remains wildly considered as a scholar for these two areas of expertise.

Intercultural, cross-cultural, or multicultural research typically includes research questions and may be of a qualitative, quantitative, or mixed method nature. A field study initially utilizes the library, internet-retrieved materials, human resources, or a laboratory but moves into "the field" to conduct the actual study. Deductively, a theory, or set of research questions, or common assumptions or inductively (often called "grounded" research) with selected individual cases is tested, incorporating hypotheses and subhypotheses, which are "educated guesses," including justifications for why the hypotheses or subhypotheses have been chosen. The study's goal is to determine or not if they are confirmed, and testing both the validity and reliability of the study. The SPSS system is very useful in determining the validity and reliability of the study. The study may include both synthesis (the result of combining elements and creating a new unified whole) and/or analysis (separation into components to discover what it contains, or to examine individual parts, or to study the structure of the whole, World English Dictionary, 1999). Field studies may include a literature review, questionnaire surveys, interviews, focused group panels, observations of verbal or nonverbal communication, and participant observations, among others.

10.6.1 Front Matter: Title Page, Abstract and Table of Contents

The **title** itself is important as it precisely identifies the focus of your paper. Often, it has to be narrowly stated to avoid unreasonable generalization. For example, in Chen Jie's abstract below, she indicates that the study is being done about the education of farmer migrant workers' children in Yangzhou City. We understand immediately that she will consider their psychological adjustment and that they are facing an identity conflict. We have included eight case study abstracts. The topics selected are quite varied and have cross-cultural dimensions either within Chinese society, in other cultural contexts or in the case of Zhang Yangfan's theoretical value types of Shalom Schwartz and their implications for young people. The **abstract** is written last (often actually written early but reformatted when finishing the study), but presented first as it briefly covers all of the major aspects of the research topic. A few **keywords** allow those who only can read the abstracts to know what the author considers most important in the paper.

As an article abstract for an academic journal, let us consider Prosser's abstract for the essay, "Obama's Culturally Transformational Identities and Accommodations toward the Middle East and Islam" published in the 2010 Journal of Middle Eastern and Islamic Studies (in Asia) 3 1. It reads as follows:

This paper uses intercultural identification and accommodation theories. Since Obama became US President on January 20, 2009, he has widely demonstrated a considerable cultural transformation in his thinking toward the East and Islam. Chinese Middle Eastern scholars' perspectives on US policies toward the Middle East and Islam include likely future positive developments by Obama. This paper assesses this transformation during his campaign, in the 2008–09 Gaza crisis bridge issue between the Bush and Obama administrations, with events occurring later, and his June 4, 2009 address in Cairo, Egypt.

Keywords: *Gaza, Islam, Israel, Intercultural theories, Middle East, Obama, Palestine*

Although the specific dimensions of the theories being used for application are not yet clarified, we know that a theoretical base will be utilized. We can see that Chinese scholars are cited relating to Obama's emerging views toward the Middle East, which is a sort of brief literature review, and that three major subtopics are considered in the article: Obama's views toward the Middle East and Islam, the 2008-09 Gaza crisis and later as a bridge between the Bush and Obama administrations, and his speech at Cairo University on June 4, 2009. The keywords list is expansive, considerably more than those seen in the eight abstracts in the case studies below. However, missing from Prosser's abstract is the precise **methodology** which he uses in making his assessments and a discussion of the **results of his study**. Based on the abstract, we can assume that his study is of a **qualitative** (or **subjective**) nature as opposed to a **quantitative** (or **objective**) research method. Yang Xiaoting's thesis about experiential learning in intercultural communication courses is very **qualitative** in its approach. We note, however, in the abstract by Zhang Yangfan, that her **quantitative methodology** includes the information that: "210 postgraduates and undergraduates (104 males and 106 females) from Shanghai and Beijing are asked to pick out 10 items they value most from Schwartz's 57 value items. Respondents' results are compared with 1997 and 2003 results and males are compared with females." Thus, it is not only quantitative, but also somewhat

longitudinal in its approach. Dilhara Turdi's thesis abstract provides an explicit **quantitative methodology** too, including earlier precise social scientific measurements with validity and reliability: "Two survey questionnaires (Schwartz's PVQ and Phinney's MEIM) containing items on values as well as items on ethnic identity were administered to 250 college students from different cultural and educational backgrounds." Although less explicitly, Chen Jie's abstract also identifies a **quantitative methodology**: "This thesis describes, based on investigation (questionnaires, interviews, and homework analysis), the psychological status of the farmer laborers' children living in Yangzhou City as well as those studying in a government school and additionally a self-established school special for farmer laborers' children." Additionally, we see that Wang Xiaoling's **abstract** notes a **quantitative survey study**, also less explicitly than Zhang Yangfan's study, for example: "Then, the thesis develops a survey study at a university for Chinese ethnic minorities to examine the influence of ethnic identity and intercultural contact on anxiety/uncertainty management and communication satisfaction." Yu Wei's thesis about Chinese students' acculturation and their use of Xiaonei in the UK identifies her use of **mixed qualitative and quantitative** research methods as well as four variables to be tested:

A sequential mixed methods design was adopted so as to get a better understanding of the phenomenon. At the first phase of qualitative study, initial observation was followed up by face-to-face interviews to approach the research questions.... Based upon qualitative findings, five hypotheses were posited, which predicted association between ethnic SNS Xiaonei use and psychological acculturation in particular. A web survey was used in the second quantitative study phase to measure 4 major variables: sociodemographics, Xiaonei use intensity, perceived social support from Xiaonei, and psychological acculturation. Data analysis of 175 Chinese students in the U.K. suggested that age, length of stay in the U.K. and perceived social support from Xiaonei were closely associated with Xiaonei use intensity.

The **table of contents** should include all headings and subheadings in a balanced fashion. Every heading or sub heading in the Table of Contents should also appear in the text of the paper. Where you are using capitals or lower case, they should be consistently used. Likewise, if sentences, noun phrases, or participles ending in "ing," are being used, there should be consistency in their usage. Approximately 10% of the text of the paper should be devoted each to the introduction and conclusion; 30% each to the literature review and the discussion of results of the study, and about 20% to the methodology section.

The next pages show an example of an effective table of contents from Zhong Min's 2010 MA thesis.

10.6.2 The Introduction

You should indicate why you have chosen this particular study, its purpose, a thesis statement, one or more research questions and their justification for inclusion. Ideally, if the paper relates to intercultural communication, you will want to indicate how your particular study relates to the broad topic. You may identify the most important resources which have been helpful in your study. You can briefly introduce major hypotheses and subhypotheses, and the justification for choosing them. Additionally, you can briefly identify what each major section or, if it is a thesis, what each chapter will include. Remember that all sources cited in the introduction, literature review, or other parts of the paper must also be included in the references. Unless your supervisor requests a different citation and reference pattern, you should always use APA citation and reference patterns, sixth edition (used in this text book), to match the international social science standards.

10.6.3 The Literature Review

The **literature review**, **citations**, and the **references** should all demonstrate your competence in undertaking your research and should be rich, rather than parsimonious. What has been discovered previously about your topic? You may be standing "on the shoulders" of previous researchers on the topic. There are often two or three major subtopics,

for which additional resources are available. Note for Zhong Min's outline above, for the **literature review**, he is discussing values, their significance, the nature of value studies, levels of analysis, and cross-cultural value studies which have been conducted previously.

Perhaps in a research paper of twelve double-spaced pages or even an MA thesis of 60+pages, the **literature review** and **discussion of your findings or results** would each take up about a third of the text of the paper. This would leave 10% each for the introduction and conclusion, and 20% for the methodology section. The following is an example of the literature review for a brief article or conference paper.

ANCIENT ASIAN AND CONTEMPORARY APPROACHES TO INTERCULTURAL COMMUNICATION (Michael H. Prosser)

Through Confucianism, Taoism, Buddhism, and Hinduism in ancient Asia, many implicit approaches to an understanding of intercultural communication developed very early, as Robert T. Oliver (1971), K.S. Sitaram and Roy Cogsdale (1976), K.S. Sitaram (1995), G. Gao and Stella Ting-Toomey (1998), Wenshan Jia (1999), Hui-ching Chang (2007) Guo-ming Chen and William J. Starosta (1998), and K.K. Hwang (1988), and others have articulated. Many contemporary explicit Asian theories and concepts of intercultural communication have made significant linkages to their roots in ancient Asian societies, including such illustrative factors as have been discussed, for example, by K.K. Hwang (2007) as the face and favor model, Confucian ethics for ordinary people, S. T. Fei's social network of differential orders, Francis L.K. Hsu's psychosociogram, D.Y.F. Ho's relational orientation, methodological relationism, the individual, self, and person, and the relational self, or Wenshan Jia's and Stella Ting-Toomey's face practices, Ringo Ma and Guo-Ming Chen's Chinese conflict resolution, or Michael Harris Bond's Chinese value studies, or K.S. Sitaram's Asian responsibility concepts versus Western individualism and freedom concepts. . Edward T. Hall, perhaps the American grandfather of intercultural communication, considered culture and communication interchangeably: "culture is communication and communication is culture" (1959: 186).

10.6.4 The Methodology

If you have developed a **thesis sentence** and **research questions** for the paper, then you may have a set of very precise **hypotheses** and **subhypotheses** which you want to test to see whether they can be confirmed or not. Many **field studies**, even with excellent research questions, hypotheses and testing, do not confirm the "educated guesses" that you may have made. In fact, many hypotheses and subhypotheses are not confirmed or are only partially confirmed. They should not be so general that you have learned very little from your study. It is important that you provide a **justification** for choosing each hypothesis or

subhypothesis. Ask yourself if another person wishes to validate or determine the reliability of your study, or if you wish to validate the study of already published or unpublished work, how useful your research questions and how precise your own hypotheses are.

Zhang Yangfan utilized Schwartz's 10 motivational value types: self direction, stimulation, hedonism, achievement, power, security, conformity, tradition, benevolence, and universalism as Schwartz investigated them in 1995–97, 2003, and 2007, where he found as the core of Chinese values: benevolence, conformity, tradition, security and achievement. Zhang Yangfan adapted Schwartz' study as the basis for her own thesis and she offers three research questions for her thesis on values (but no hypotheses):

RQ 1: Did the items of the SVS [Schwartz Values Survey] instrument take on new or distinct connotations when they are applied in the China's culture context?

RQ 2: Could the 10 value types be further classified according to the personal focus and social focus dynamic principle?

RQ 3: What values are changing and what are enduring during the past 10 years?

In his study on values, Zhong Min utilizes the same 10 Schwartz values adapting his **Portrait Values Questionnaire** as part of his own research, and offers several hypotheses:

H1: The emerged projection of the value structures of the two Chinese samples confirms the value model predicted in Schwartz's value theory, though with slight deviations.

H2: The value structures projected on the two-dimensional space of the two samples differ from each other.

H3: The value structure of the representative sample of the rural-to-urban migrant workers appears less clear on the SSA projection than do that of the Shanghai urban residents.

H4: There is no observable systematic pattern presented by the two sample-specific data in their deviations from the ideal value structure which suggests an alternative value structure exists in the Chinese culture.

H5: In the Chinese context, self-transcendence values rank higher [than] self-enhancement equivalence of values domains in China. [In Zhou Min's MA Thesis, among 31 values selected he hypothesizes that openness to change values rank higher than the conservation values.]

H6: The value priority of the sample of migrant workers differs substantially from that of the urban Shanghai residents.

H7: Along the conservation—openness to change dimension, the migrant population values conservatism higher, while the Shanghai urban population values openness to change higher.

H8: Along the self-enhancement—self-transcendence dimension, the Shanghai urban population puts more value on the self-enhancement

(power and achievement) than do the migrant workers.

Although without the full context in these brief examples, we can ask if Zhang Hangfen's research questions and Zhong Min's hypotheses clearly articulate what the two authors intend as the starting point for their own methodologies, and later data analysis. Both have used reasonable sample populations for their studies. Eight hypotheses in an MA thesis are probably too many.

10.6.5 The Discussion of Results

In both theses, these two authors provide strong discussions of their results. Both Zhang Yangtang and Zhong Min provide effective synthesis and analysis in their discussions on their findings in their theses.

10.6.6 The Conclusion, References and Appendices

In some ways, the paper's **conclusions** are a longer version of the initial abstract. The conclusion generally includes a **summary of the thesis**, a **self evaluation**, or **limitations for the study** and **recommendations for future research**. If the data analysis has been strong, then the concluding chapter is easy to write. Zhong Min has done an effective **cross-cultural study** of migrant workers and his concluding chapter includes the following: a summary, practical implications, limitations, and future directions.

10.7 Honesty and Integrity: The Hallmark of an Ethical University Education and Research

An issue of critical importance in writing research papers is the researcher's honesty and integrity. Plagiarism has become a very serious problem in many countries, including the United States and China. At the University of Virginia, founded by President Thomas Jefferson and one of the most prestigious public American universities, and certain other private and public American universities, for example, the US military academies, the students must follow an honor code, often regulated by a student honor committee, signing a pledge for every assignment and test, "On my honor as a student, I have neither given nor received unauthorized assistance on this assignment, paper, or test." Plagiarism has intensified immeasurably because of frequently unverified resources on the Internet, through such search engines as Baidu, Bing, Google, Wikipedia China, 163, and Yahoo, as well as many other international or Chinese search engines. Except when writing from your own generalized knowledge, all directly quoted or paraphrased materials must credit the source. The citations and references in this book give evidence to the requirement to give proper credit to all sources that have been included in the book as far as is reasonable. In the cases where we have included long articles from published sources, we have sought and received permissions to reprint them here. It is your ethical responsibility to treat the ideas and statements of experts and writers with a recognition that intellectual property rights should be respected in your own course papers and research. In teaching in American, Canadian, and Chinese universities, Michael Prosser has found many students engaged in plagiarism and cheating. His respect for the honest students is always enhanced, and for those who have acted dishonestly, his respect for them has been diminished.

In 2010, former President George W. Bush's presidential memoir, *Decision Points* was published. Ryan Grim called it "a mash-up of worn-out anecdotes from previously published memoirs of his subordinates. "Grim writes that Bush "lifts quotes word for word, passing them off as his own recollections," borrowing from "non-fiction books about his presidency or newspaper or magazine articles from the time." Grim calls it an indictment of Bush's character: "He's too lazy to write his own memoirs." (Grim, 2010: November 15). If this accusation is reasonable, **you may say**, "important people like the American president use ghostwriters all the time. If President Bush is charged with plagiarism, borrowing and lifting materials from other sources, why should we as Chinese students be put to a different standard?"

The answer is clear: because you should live lives of honesty, decency, respect and integrity! If you want others to respect you, you must respect yourselves!

10.8 Case Studies: MA Thesis Abstracts and Keywords Related to Youth

(Shanghai International Studies University)

10.8.1 Reconsidering Schwartz's 10 Basic Human Value Types and Locating Chinese Young People
(Zhang Yangfan)

Based on previous studies on values, culture, and human needs, Schwartz concluded that there are three kinds of basic human needs which include: (1) Needs of individuals as biological organisms, (2) Requisites of coordinated social interaction, and (3) Survival and welfare needs of groups. From these three needs, Schwartz derived 57 value items across cultures, which in turn statistically and consistently fall into 10 motivational types. The 10 types are further ideally divided into four axial dimensions: openness to change, v.s. conservation, self-enhancement, v.s. self-transcendence. More research and applications of these 10 motivational value types continued to be conducted to get a more in-depth understanding.

As a part of the Shanghai Chinese Values Project (SCVP), this paper will study these 10 value types in China's context for two purposes: to find out how the 10 value types and the corresponding 57 value items fit the Chinese culture and what the changing trend of Chinese young people's values. 210 postgraduates and undergraduates (104 males and 106 females) from Shanghai and Beijing are asked to pick out 10 items they value most from Schwartz's 57 value items. Respondents' results are compared with 1997 and 2003 results and males are compared with females. Among the 10 most chosen items, the meaning of several items appears to be ambiguous in the Chinese context, so further interviews were conducted. The research results show that in China's current context, 5 of the 10 value types could be further categorized and part of the 57 value items in Schwartz's SVS instrument bear new connotations; at the same time, changing trends have been detected among Chinese young people.

The significance of the paper lies in three aspects: first, it gives insights for the further study in the application of SVS instrument and Schwartz's value theory in the China's context; secondly, it shows important changes in Chinese young people. Thirdly, this thesis will encourage further studies on Schwartz's basic human value set to make it serve better as a global value measurement instrument in the future.

Keywords: China's context, SVS instrument, value change, value study

10.8.2 Psychological Adjustment of Farmer Laborers' Children in Yangzhou City: The Identity Conflict of Migrant Children under the Background of the Urban-Rural Dualistic Social System (Chen Jie)

The problem of farmer laborers' children in cities has become the focus of social attention. Academics have emphasized these children's problems of entering school to be educated. With the society developing, the physical and mental health of these children comes to attention too. This thesis chooses the psychological status of farmer laborers' children in Yangzhou City as its research point and probes the similarities and differences among farmer laborers' children in a self-established school, farmer laborers' children in a government school and urban children in a government school. On the one hand, there are not many essays from this point of view.

On the other hand, as migrant into cities these children show their unique features on psychological status with the change of living surroundings. They differ from the children living in the countryside all the time, also from the native children in cities. This dissociating condition brings great negative influence on their physical and mental development. With investigative collection of data, this thesis explores objectively the psychological status of these farm laborers' children, and makes attributions to improve their mental health and future growth.

This thesis describes, based on investigation (questionnaires, interviews, and homework analysis), the psychological status of the farmer laborers' children living in Yangzhou City as well as those studying in a government school and additionally a self-established school special for farmer laborers' children. Then it considers the status with the urban children together to figure out the differences between them on these dimensions of mental health, environmental adjustment, communication with others, study conditions, and self-evaluations. Then the author further probes the influence of communication with generalized others on the identity construction process of farmer laborers' children in Yangzhou City, how those children recognize themselves and construct their identity on such a basis and how the urban-rural dualistic social structure influences this process. In the communication with generalized others, farmer laborers' children take urban citizens as a reference and construct a marginal identity just as their parents do. The duties are often overemphasized while lawful rights are frequently ignored. However, identity is an ever-changing process rather than a fixed entity. Active communication can have active influences on the remediation of negative identity.

Keywords: Farmer laborers' children in city, identity construction, Marginal people in Yangzhou City, Psychological status

10.8.3 Integrating Experiential Learning Techniques into Intercultural Communication Courses (Liao Yuan)

Multicultural and global educators agree that students need experiential learning with people different from themselves if they are to develop cross-cultural skills, knowledge, and competence. However, students have little access to chances of experiencing cross-cultural differences, though they are often exposed to various theories through classroom learning and after-class reading. Experiential learning has already gained prominent success in adult education and has been applied to many other contexts and areas. In all likelihood, what is lacking in the regular intercultural communication (IC) course curriculum can be supplemented with experiential learning. Thus, by integrating experiential learning techniques into IC course, the author designs a supplementary experiential training program for MA IC students.

Taking into consideration IC MA students' learning capability and research needs, traditional or regular IC courses give priority to the study of IC theories and the training of cognitive awareness. Affective and behavioral components of cross-cultural communication competence are equally important, yet have been neglected. The thesis designs a training program for intercultural communication MA students based on experiential learning theory, stressing affective and behavioral factors concerning cross-cultural communication.

In the literature review, an extensive description has been included on the power of face-to-face cross-cultural experience in developing the knowledge, skills, and dispositions of world-mindedness (Brislin, 1989; Brislin & Yoshida, 1994; Gochenour, 1993; Gudykunst & Kim, 2003). The thesis adopts a combination of qualitative and quantitative methodology. The descriptive analysis of the training design, including

training objectives, content and activities, constitute the main body. Prior to the training design, a questionnaire is designed and used to investigate the needs of the prospective trainees. After the training implementation, another survey is done to examine whether or how the proposed training program helps improve the trainees' attitude and competence.

Chapter I introduces the background and significance of the study as well as the thesis structure.

Chapter II reviews the key points concerning experiential learning and intercultural communication training (ICT), and examines the necessity of synthesizing experiential learning activities and ICT program.

Chapter III puts forward research questions and hypotheses, and explains the questionnaire design and data collection procedure.

As the central part of the thesis, Chapter IV is devoted to the development of an experiential training program for intercultural communication MA students, following the procedure of assessing the needs, setting the goals, specifying objectives, determining contents, selecting methods, planning sequencing and pacing, implementing and evaluating the training.

The concluding chapter summarizes the thesis and points out its limitations and the directions for future studies.

Keywords: experiential learning, intercultural communication competence, intercultural training design

10.8.4 The Influence of Ethnic Identity and Intergroup Contact on Intercultural Communication: A Study at a Chinese University for Minorities (Wang Xiaoling)

Ethnic identity and intergroup contact are mostly studied from the perspective of social psychology. Their roles in intercultural communication have not received sufficient attention either in emic (localized) or etic (universalized) study.

This thesis examines the influence of ethnic identity and intercultural contact on the perceived communication effectiveness of three groups in China: the Uygur, Mongolian and Tibetan minorities. The inclusion of Chinese samples in the present thesis is intended to fill in a research gap, since there are few studies using Chinese ethnic groups to study intercultural communication effectiveness.

The context of the study will be addressed at the beginning of the present thesis. Then relevant theories and studies both in social psychology and the intercultural communication field will be identified: namely, ethnic identity intercultural contact, Anxiety/Uncertainty Management Theory (AUM) and communication satisfaction. Based on the discussion of the eminent studies in these fields, several hypotheses and a research question have been developed. Then, the thesis develops a survey study at a university for Chinese ethnic minorities to examine the influence of ethnic identity and intercultural contact on anxiety/uncertainty management and communication satisfaction. Next, subjects, procedures and measures have been illustrated in detail. The research results lead to a discussion on the dual purposes of the present thesis: the universality of AUM in the Chinese context, and findings in regarding to the role of ethnic identity and intergroup anxiety in intercultural communication. The thesis ends with a summary, the limitations and implications of the present study, and suggestions for future study.

Keywords: anxiety/uncertainty management, communication satisfaction, ethnic identity, intergroup contact

10.8.5 Bilingual Education and Intercultural Communication Among Uyghurs in Xinjiang, China (Turdi Dilhara)

There has been a lack of research on the relationship between bilingual education and intercultural communication in Xinjiang, China. By reviewing the history and reality of bilingual education in the Peoples' Republic of China, the author shows the importance of conducting research in this area. With an introduction of some key concepts and theories about bilingual education and intercultural communication, this thesis reports the results of a survey conducted among students from different ethnic backgrounds in Xinjiang, a region with multi-ethnic groups. The aims of the survey were to identify the influence of bilingual education on students of different educational and cultural backgrounds and to explore the relationships between bilingual education and intercultural communication. Two survey questionnaires (Schwartz's PVQ and Phinney's MEIM) containing items on values as well as items on ethnic identity were administered to 250 college students from different cultural and educational backgrounds. Findings indicate that bilingual education does influence the values and both bilingual and monolingual Uyghur students have a clear understanding of their own ethnic identity. As for intercultural communication, the survey results show the positive influence of bilingual education on students from ethnic groups other than Han Chinese in lowering their anxiety level, and boosting their confidence in communication with Han students. Besides, it also enhances the mutual understanding between different ethnic groups. All these findings confirm that bilingual education and intercultural communication are closely related to each other, and can benefit each other in their interaction.

Keywords: bilingual education in China, ethnic identity, intercultural communication, positive influence, Uyghur, values, Xinjiang

10.8.6 Chinese Students' Acculturation in the UK and Their Use of Xiaonei (Yu Wei)

Previous studies have been conducted to explore the relationship between sojourners' mass media appropriation habit and social-cultural as well as psychological adaptation in a new country, but little attention is paid upon the role of the Internet in acculturation studies. The Internet is wielding an immense influence nowadays, especially upon youth transcending time and space boundaries. The popularity of social networking sites (SNS) like Facebook.com and Xiaonei.com in recent years have caught the eyeballs from both social and academic venues. While numerous studies of SNS largely centers around self-presentation, privacy, friendship, etc., very few touch upon what part SNS plays in sojourners' acculturation process and helping them adapt to the new environment. To address the limitations of literature, motivated by personal experience in the United Kingdom, this study investigates the relationship between Chinese students' acculturation process in the United Kingdom and their use of the ethnic social networking site Xiaonei. A sequential mixed methods design was adopted so as to get a better understanding of the phenomenon. At the first phase of qualitative study, initial observation was followed up by face-to-face interviews to approach the research questions. Several themes regarding difficulties met in acculturation process, motives for Xiaonei use as well as relation between Xiaonei use and life in the UK emerged in the in-depth analysis of the twelve interview transcripts. Based upon qualitative findings, five hypotheses were posited, which predicted association between ethnic SNS Xiaonei use and psychological acculturation in particular. A web survey was used in the second quantitative study phase to measure four major variables—sociodemographics, Xiaonei use intensity, perceived social support from Xiaonei, and psychological acculturation. Data analysis of 175 Chinese students in the UK suggested that age, length of stay in the UK and perceived social support from Xiaonei were closely associated with Xiaonei use intensity. Among the individual types of support, emotional and companionship support were found to be significant predictors for level of engagement on Xiaonei. Besides, the positive relationship between perceived social support from Xiaonei and psychological acculturation level was also detected even when taking sociodemographic variables into account. These findings highlight the potential of SNS in aiding cross-cultural adaptation process, raise new directions and avenues connecting new media and acculturation research.

Keywords: acculturation, Internet, social networking sites (SNS), sociodemographics, UK Xiaonei

10.8.7 Styles of Managing Interpersonal Conflicts Between American and Chinese University Students (Zhang Rui)

My thesis research constitutes an interdisciplinary attempt to study how interpersonal conflicts are handled among contemporary university students in coastal China from both an emic (local) and etic (universal) approach. I was mainly driven by two probing questions of interest: (1) Is the overarching framework of individualism/collectivism prevalent in the cross-cultural research the conceptual toolkit with which one can make sense of the Chinese psychology and conflict communication? (2) How does the tension between modernity and traditionality play out among the adult cohort extensively exposed to modernization?

In the first study, over-reliance upon individualism/collectivism was critiqued from the perspective of social psychology and communication; antecedents of Chinese way of handling conflicts endemic to the Chinese culture were reviewed. In conjunction with the use of interviews, data from self-report questionnaires revealed variation of conflict styles that ranged from situation to situation. The stereotypical view of Chinese being obliging and avoiding was not supported.

The second study built upon the first one by drawing a cross-cultural comparison with a student sample in the United States and incorporating measures of self-construals. For both samples, self-construals were found to have poor power in predicting facework behaviors. Convergence and divergence between American and Chinese samples were analyzed by taking a more contextual approach and taking into account the dynamic interplay of modernity and traditionality.

Implications for cross-cultural research were noted. I called for moving beyond the simplistically cross-national comparisons based upon unwarranted assumptions and enunciated the concept of multiple modernities.

Keywords: interpersonal conflict, individualism/collectivism, modernity/tradi--tionality, culture

10.8.8 Structural Equivalence of Value Domains in China: Values Among Migrant Workers and Local Permanent Residents in Shanghai (Zhong Min)

Values, the most central feature of culture (Schwartz, 1999; Hofstede, 1980; Weber, 1958; Williams, 1968), have been one of the core concepts in explaining cultural differences.

Among various theorizing attempts of values, Schwartz's comprehensive values framework is gaining acceptance from an increasing number of social psychologists. As Bond (1996, p 218) noted: „It appears that Schwartz's value survey will become the standard measure against which other value instruments will be examined … a value map for the world's cultures, a map which will empirically anchor discussions of value similarities and differences."

However, a comparison between individuals (and samples) from two countries should only be undertaken if structural equivalence at the individual level has been demonstrated for those countries (Fischer et al., 2010). Given the diversity of the Chinese society, validations of the fit of the value structure of the Chinese individuals to the common structure on a variety of samples are needed.

By employing two samples, migrant workers (N=208) and local permanent residents (N=174) in Shanghai, which enables discriminating within-country from between-country difference, the current study examines the cross-cultural equivalence of the internal structure of the values domains in China to the theorized universal model, as measured by the Portrait Values Questionnaire (PVQ). This study also examines the similarities and differences in the value priorities of the two sample groups in seeking to distinguish the hierarchy of their values, hoping that it might lead to behavior prediction which would promote the harmonious social contact of the two groups.

This study has the following findings: (a) the observed structure of the Chinese individuals fitted to the individual level universal structure of human values as postulated a priori by Schwartz. (b) Certain deviations from the ideal model were observed, which did not reveal reliable and meaningful patterns proposing an alternative structure of values in the *Chinese Equivalence of Value Domains in China* (Zhong Min, MA thesis, Shanghai International Studies University). (c) Conformity ranked at number one for both groups. (d) The two groups attributed equal importance to conformity, achievement, security and tradition. (e) Shanghai local permanent residents put more emphasis on self-enhancement and openness to change values while the migrant workers emphasize more on the transcendence values. (f) Power was the least important value for the migrant workers. (g) The migrant workers tended to be more social-focused while the Shanghai permanent resident tended to be more person-focused.

Practical implications of the present study of values in China from the cross-cultural perspective are noted and directions for future research are also proposed at the end of the thesis.

Keywords: Chinese values, migrant workers values, Shanghai residents values, the PVQ

10.9 Summary

This chapter has moved beyond topics discussed in earlier chapters by emphasizing the nature of actual **intercultural theories**, using as specific examples **intercultural identity theories** and **intercultural adaptation or accommodation theories** as illustrations. A previously published essay by Michael, *Cross-cultural Communication* broadens the topic of **cross-cultural research**. University of Alberta Ph D student Zhang Rui has offered his own contributions to a further understanding of intercultural communication issues using his conflict resolution study as his own example. We have provided a step by step process to write an intercultural research paper or thesis with a number of specific examples. Analysis has been provided to understand more fully the eight Shanghai International Studies University MA abstracts which have been included as Case Studies for the Chapter.

10.10 Questions for Discussion

10.10.1 For the first time in the dialogues, it becomes obvious that despite the more complicated topic in this chapter than in earlier chapters, some students wish to further their own academic careers by additional study, either in China or abroad. In 2009/2010, there were 690,923 international students studying in the US, of whom 128,000 were from China, with 39,921 being undergraduates (Lewin, 2010: November 15). What are the basic steps that individual students must consider to take the national postgraduate exams in China, or for study in a country where English is the standard educational language?

10.10.2 How can the intercultural identity theories and intercultural accommodation theories be compared in terms of their usefulness in conducting intercultural research? How does a theory differ from a concept? How can it be tested most efficiently?

10.10.3 In Michael Prosser's reprinted article, Cross-cultural Communication, he defines both intercultural and cross-cultural communication. How are these terms both similar and different? Can intercultural communication be also international and global, and at the same time cross-cultral? Why? Why not?

10.10.4 Zhang Rui devotes time discussing issues in intercultural or cross-cultural research. How do these issues relate more broadly both toward culture and communication? His study is related to conflict resolution among Chinese students. How can this be applied more broadly?

10.10.5 If you wanted to develop one of the studies among the eight abstracts into a multicultural study, what additional information and resources would you need to develop in order to do a reasonable, valid, and replicable study. Why?

10.10.6 In the step by step process of conducting intercultural or cross-cultural research which we have provided, which step is the most difficult, the literature review, the methodology, or the discussion of findings? Why do you understand this step as the most difficult?

10.10.7 Which pattern do you consider the best method of research, the qualitative, quantitative, or the mixed method? When the study is completed, how are the results likely to be similar or different by using these three different patterns?

10.10.8 What is the value of doing a pilot study as Zhang Rui has done, before undertaking the main study? This was not the pattern followed by the other researchers at least as we can determine from their abstracts. What extra benefits could Zhang Rui have achieved by moving directly to the full study, instead of adding the extra time and effort to do the pilot study?

10.10.9 Ben, in the imaginary dialogue for this chapter, is seen as getting ready to write a thesis, and later, Zhong Min's thesis outline appears, as well as his actual abstract. Based on this information, what would you consider to be the most important characteristics of his plan comparatively to do the study, and the actual conduct of the study itself?

10.10.10 Among the eight MA thesis topics, which is the strongest one in terms of providing you enough information to have a brief understanding of the research topic? Why? At least 3 of them were award-winners in the SISU MA intercultural communication program. What characteristics helped them to become outstanding theses? Why?

Intercultural Theories and Research

10.11 Suggested Readings

American Psychological Association (2002). *Publication manual of the American Psychological Association, fifth edition.* Washington, D.C.: The American Psychological Association.

American Psychological Association (2011) *Publication manual of the American Psychological Association, sixth edition.* Washington, D.C.: The American Psychological Association.

Dissertations and theses: Full text. (annual)

Dissertations in progress (annual). American Historical Association Directory of Dissertations. xxx

Dissertations of China (annual).

Heisey, D. R. (2000). *Chinese perspectives in rhetoric and communication.* Westport, CT: Ablex.

Jia, W. , Lu, X, & Heisey, D. R. (2002). *Chinese communication and research: Reflections, new frontiers and new directions.* Westport: CT: Ablex.

Lu, X., Jia, W., & Heisey, D. R. (2002). *Chinese communication studies: Contexts and comparisons.* Westport, CT: Ablex.

Reynolds, M. M. (1985). *Guide to theses and dissertations: An international bibliography of bibliographies, Revised and enlarged.* Phoenix, AZ: Oryx.

EPILOGUE

A Final Conversation:
Think Globally and Act Locally

Professor Zhang: Shall we do a brief evaluation of our Intercultural Communication class this semester? What were some of our strong points?

Tony: Sure, let's start.

Gloria: I learned a lot about how to think globally and act locally. I think that I did it by volunteering for the Beijing Olympics, which brought 10,000 athletes together, and was seen in Beijing by thousands, and on television and downloading on the Internet by millions. I had a lot of personal local contact with our international visitors. I met President Bush and his family too. I told him that we Chinese are all very proud of our country, and we were glad to welcome him and the other leaders, athletes, and guests to China.

True Nation: You all know that I am very nationalistic. But, you will be happy to know, Professor Zhang and Michael, that I have learned how to become more conscious of the beliefs, attitudes, and values of people from other cultures, and to be more tolerant of other points of view.

Catherine: On the first day of the class, I told you, Professor Zhang and Michael, that so far we hadn't learned anything about intercultural communication.

Michael: How do you feel now, Catherine?

Catherine: I really appreciated that you both kept encouraging us to be creative and to become critical thinkers.

Forest: I decided during this class that I really want to work for an international chocolate company.

Laughter

Forest: But seriously, the class did help me to decide that I would like to work in an international trade company.

Ali: It was a special blessing to have Rashid from Morocco come to our class and to meet him as a fellow Muslim. He was the first Muslim I have met from outside of China. I felt like he was my older brother. I liked the whole multicultural class that we had, the cultural stories of other young Chinese, and the class on contemporary youth.

Spring: Summer and I always know that as identical twins we have a very special relationship, but I was glad also to know that the two of us are at one end of the cultural spectrum and that perhaps, you Michael, are at the opposite end of the spectrum as an American. Still, we had many common traits that made us appreciate even more our similarities and finding ways to overcome our cultural differences.

Summer: I agree with Spring. But we both are becoming more independent from each other.

Grace: As the Holy Bible says, "As for me and my house, I follow the Lord."

Michelle: I had already spent a year in the US when I was a teenager, but I feel sure that I would now like to get a Master's degree in the US, and then to work there for a while. Zhang Jing who told her story from the little UN at Beijing Language and Culture University to working at the real UN and I were classmates. I am proud to have her representing China at the UN.

Michael: She is my first student that I know of who has worked at the United Nations. Now she is an assistant in the Office of the Spokesperson for Secretary General Ban-ki Moon.

Tulip: The discussions about studying overseas and learning to do some serious research were new to me. I hope that I can study later in an overseas university.

Ben: I feel the same way, and would like to do research on migrant workers in the urban settings in China for my MA degree.

Jason: Perhaps I can also study overseas and then bring back my knowledge to help China develop more and more.

Vivian: Professor Zhang, several of us have the same family name. That makes us all part of a great big family, and we can learn to treat each other with equal dignity and respect.

Peter: Perhaps from this class I have learned that it would be good to spend a couple of years as an educator in the western part of China or in a developing African or Asian country.

Yolanda: Peter, you would be welcome to come and teach in Xinjiang. We need more good teachers. It would be wonderful if several members of the class would come to Xinjiang.

Cindy: My favorite parts of the class were the very interesting and often very humorous dialogues and the many short essays that we found throughout the book, *Chinese Communicating Interculturally*. It made me feel that a class like this one is really a good way to learn both serious and humorous ideas about culture and intercultural communication.

Lucky: Michael, in this class, who was more humorous, you or I? Maybe should I be a comedian for my future career? I was in a Shakespeare class and I remember the quote from *Loves' Labor Lost* that "A jest's prosperity lies in the ear of him that hears it, never in the tongue of him that makes it." Afterall, a good comedian knows what jokes work best to make an audience laugh. Forest and his obsession on chocolate have taught us that. So, perhaps I will become prosperous by making others laugh!

Laughter

Forest: And I will become famous working for a chocolate factory!

Mike: Yes, Lucky, I feel lucky (a pun) to have been in this class with you. Perhaps because of this class I will become an AmeriChinese and then I can meet our ChiAmerican friend Michael in his own country. I have a haiku for Michael: "Today it's over. / Come outdoors with us to play. / So sunny and warm!"

Laughter

Professor Zhang: Thank you for your comments, class. Don't forget the slogan: "Think globally and act locally." *Zaijian.*

Michael: And remember the goal so that you can say with Socrates, "I am neither a citizen of Athens, nor of Greece, but of the world." Or, "I am neither a citizen of Beijing, Shanghai, Guangzhou, nor Xi'an, nor of China, but of the world!" *Xiexie. Duoxie*!

Tony: Let's take a class photo, shall we?

Class applause and dismissal

Joy: Professor Zhang and Michael, is that a tear I see in your eyes?

Professor Zhang: Meo, Meo. I have had much joy having all of you in class.

Michael: I hear Beethoven's *Ode to Joy* about to begin! And who are the most beautiful young women and most handsome young men here in China?

Class: It's us! Michael and you are our best grandpa!

References

Adler, P. (1974: August). Beyond cultural identity: Reflections on cultural and multicultural man. *Topics in Learning*. 23–40.

Afifi, W. (2009). Uncertainty management theories. In S. W. Littlejohn and K.A Foss (Eds) *Encyclopedia of Communication Theory 1*. Los Angeles, CA. Sage.

Agranovich, M., Korolyova, N., Poletaev, A., Sundiev, I., Seliverstova, I., & Fateeva, A (2007). *Youth Development Report: Condition of Russian Youth*. Retrieved May 20, 2010, from http://unesdoc.unesco.org/images/0014/001431/143147e.pdf

Alleyne, M. D. (1995). *International power and international communication*. New York, NY: St. Martin's Press.

Alleyne, M. (2009). International communication theories. In S. W, Littlejohn and K.A. Foss (Eds.) *Encyclopedia of Communication Theory 1*. Los Angeles, CA: Sage.

American Psychological Association (2011). *Publication manual of the American Psychological Association, sixth edition*. Washington, D.C.: The American Psychological Association.

Asante, M. K. Miike, Y. & Yin, J. (2008). *The global intercultural communication reader*. London, UK: Routledge.

Asuncion-Lande, N. (1998). English as the dominant language for intercultural communication: Prospects for the next century. In K. S. Sitaram and M.H. Prosser (Eds.), *Civic Discourse: Multiculturalism, Cultural Diversity and Global Communication*. Stamford, CT: Ablex.

Barboza, D. (2010 : January 13). Baidu's gain from departure could be China's loss. *New York Times*.

Barnlund, D. C. (1968). *Interpersonal communication: Survey and studies*. Boston, MA: Houghton Mifflin.

Barnlund, D. C. (1975). *The public self and the private self in Japan and United States*. Tokyo, Japan: Simul.

Barnes and Noble (2010: December). *Top ten best sellers, December, 2010*. www.barnesandnoble.com.

Barnes and Noble (2010: December). *Ten greatest American writers: 2009*. www.barnesandnoble.com.

Barry W. T., Chen W. T., & Watson, B. (1960). *Sources of Chinese tradition*. New York, NY: Columbia University Press.

Bauerlein, M. (2009). *The dumbest generation: How the digital age stupefies young Americans and jeopardizes our future (or don't trust anyone under 30)*. New York, NY: Jeremy P. Tarcher/Penguin.

Begley, S. (2008: May 24). The dumbest generation? Don't be dumb. *Newsweek*.

Benedict, R. (1934). *Patterns of culture*. Boston, MA: Houghton Mifflin.

Benedict, R. (1946). *The chrysanthemum and the sword: Patterns of Japanese Culture*. Boston, MA: Houghton Mifflin.

Berry, M. & Scorsese, M. (2005). *Speaking in images: Interviews with contemporary Chinese Filmmakers*. New York: Columbia University Press.

Bonvillain, N. (2003). *Language, culture, and communication: The meaning of messages, fourth edition*. Upper Saddle River, NJ: Prentice Hall.

Brahm, E. (2006). Public diplomacy. In: G. Burgess and H. Burgess (Eds.), *Beyond intractability*. Conflict Research Consortium. Boulder, CO: University of Colorado

Bridges, J. A. (2009). Corporate campaign theories. In S.W. Littlejohn and K. A. Foss. The Encyclopedia of Communication Theory 1. Los Angeles, CA: Sage.

Brislin, R. W. & Yoshida, T. (1994). *Intercultural training: An introduction*. Newberry Park, CA: Sage.

Bruneau, T. J. (1990). Chronemic: The study of time in human interaction. In J. A. Devito and M. L. Hecht (Eds.), *The Nonverbal Communication Reader*. Prospect Heights, IL: Waveland Press.

Bruneau, T. (2007: June). Unpublished paper presented at the Sixth Biennial Conference of the Chinese Association for Intercultural Studies, Harbin, China.

Burgoon, J. K., Guerreo, L. K., & Floyd, K. (2009). Nonverbal communication. *Communication Monographs, 51*, 193–214.

Bush, G. W. (2010). *Decision Points*. New York, NY: Random House.

Carroll, D. W. (2000). *The psychology of language.* Beijing, China: Foreign Language Teaching and Research Press.

Casmir, F. (1998). *Ethics in intercultural and international communication.* Mahwah, NJ: Earlbaum.

Castells, M. (2000). *The rise of the network society, 2nd edition.* Malden, MA: Blackwell.

Chaney, L. H. & Martin, J. S. (2002). *Intercultural business communication.* Beijing, China: Higher Education Press.

Chang, H.-c. (2007). Interface between Chinese relational domains and language issues: A critical survey and analysis. In S. J. Kulich and M. H. Prosser (Eds.), *Intercultural Perspectives on Chinese Communication.* Shanghai, China: Shanghai Foreign Language Education Press.

Chang, K-i. S. & Owen, S. (Eds.). (2008). *The Cambridge history of Chinese literature. 2 Volumes.* Cambridge, England: Cambridge University Press.

Chang, I. (1997). *The rape of Nangking.* New York, NY: Viking.

Chant, S. & Jones, G. A. (2005). Youth, gender and livelihoods in West Africa: Perspectives from Ghana and Gambia. *Children's Geographies (3)*2, 185–199. London, England: London School of Economics.

Chen, G.-M. (2009). Intercultural communication competence. In S. W. Littlejohn and K. A. Foss (Eds.), *Encyclopedia of Communication Theory.1.* Los Angeles, CA: Sage.

Chen, G.-M. & Ma, R. (2002). *Chinese conflict management and resolutions.* Westport, CT: Ablex.

Chen, G.-M. & Starosta, W. J. (2005). *Foundations of intercultural communication.* Lanham, MD: UPA

Chen, J. (2009). *Psychological adjustment of farmer laborers' children in Yangzhou City. The identity conflict of migrant children under the background of the urban-rural dualistic social system.* Unpublished MA thesis [Abstract]. Shanghai: Shanghai International Studies University.

Chen, L. (2007). Is culture communication?—Considerations from Chinese communication studies. In S. J. Kulich and M. H. Prosser. (Eds.), *Intercultural Perspectives on Chinese Communication.* Shanghai, China: Shanghai Foreign Language Education Press.

Cherry, C. (1971). *World communication: Threat or promise.* New York, NY: Wiley.

Chinese classic novels. www.YellowBridge.com .

Crystal, D. (1997). *The Cambridge encyclopedia of language, 2nd edition.* Cambridge, NY: Cambridge University Press.

Chu, G. (Ed.) (1978). *Popular media in China: Shaping new cultural patterns.* Honolulu, HA: East- West Center Books,The University of Hawaii.

Chu, G. C. & Ju, Y. (1993). *The great wall in ruins: Communication and cultural change in China.* Albany, NY: State of New York Press.

Condon, J. C. & Yousef, F. (1975). *An introduction to intercultural communication.* Indianapolis, IN: Bobbs-Merrill.

Consulate General of the People's Republic of China in Houston (2003). Houston, TX: Consulate General of the People's Republic of China in Houston.

Cooren, F., Taylor, J., & Van Every, F. (2006). *Communication as organizing.* Mahwah, NJ: Lawrence Earlbaum.

Corliss, R. (1996: September 16). Hooray for Bollywood. *Time.*

Cribb, M. (2009). *Discourse and the non-native speakers.* Amherst, NY: Cambria Press.

Curtin, M. (2007). *Playing to the world's biggest audience: The globalization of Chinese film and tv.* Berkeley, CA: University of California Press.

Dai, X. D. & Kulich, S. J. (Eds.) (2010). *Identity and intercultural communication: Theoretical and contextual constructions. Intercultural research. Vol. 2.* Shanghai, China: Shanghai Foreign Language Education Press.

Dai, X. D. & Kulich, S. J. (Eds.) (2011). *Identity and intercultural communication: Contextual applications: Intercultural research, Vol. 3.* Shanghai, China: Shanghai Foreign Language Education Press.

Davis, L. (2001). *Doing culture: Cross-cultural communication in action.* Beijing, China: Foreign Language Teaching and Research Press.

Day, K. D. (1998). Ethics in intercultural communication. In K. S. Sitaram and M. H Prosser (Eds.), *Civic Discourse: Multiculturalism, Cultural Diversity and Global Communication.* Stamford, CT: Ablex.

Day, K. D. (1998). Fostering respect for other cultures in teaching intercultural communication. In K. S. Sitaram and M. H. Prosser (Eds.) *Civic Discourse: Multiculturalism, Cultural Diversity and Global Communication.* Stamford, CT: Ablex.

Deng, Y. (2005). *Ancient Chinese inventions. Trans. Wang Pingxing.* Beijing: Intercontinental Press.

De Vito, J. (1970). *The psychology of speech and language: An introduction to psycholinguistics.* New York, NY: Random House.

DeVoss, D. N., Eidman-Aadahl, E., & Hicks, T. (2010). *Because digital writing matters. National Writing Project.* New York: Jossey-Bas.

Dissertations and theses: Full text (annual). Westport, CT: Libraries Unlimited.

Dissertations in progress (annual). American Historical Association Directory of Dissertations. xxx

Dixon, D. (1993). *Your heritage: A sequence of thinking, reading and writing assignments. Foreword by S. Blau.* New York, NY: National Writing Project.

Donahue, R. T. (1998). *Japanese culture and communication: critical cultural analysis.* Washington, DC: University Press of America.

Donahue, R. T. (Ed.) (2002). *Exploring Japaneseness: On Japanese enactments of culture and consciousness.* Westport, CT: Ablex.

Donahue R. T. & Prosser, M. H. (1997). *Diplomatic discourse: International conflict at the United Nations.* Stamford, CT: Ablex.

Dong, S. (2006). *Chinese and American corporate culture and its application in cross-cultural management.* Unpublished MA thesis. Shanghai, China: Shanghai International Studies University.

Dou, W. (2005). *Intercultural business communication.* Beijing: Higher Education Press.

Drew, P. (2005). Conversation analysis. In K. L. Fitch and R. E. Sanders (Eds). *Handbook of language and social interaction.* Mahwah, NJ: Lawrence Erlbaum.

Diuke, N. (2006). *Pervoe svobodnoe pokolenie.* Retrieved, May 20, 2010, from http://www.ecsocman. edu.ru/images/pubs/2006/11/16/0000295102/07-dyuk-53-62.pdf

Driver, J. & van Aaist, M. (2010). *You say more than you think: Use the new body language to get what you want!* New York, NY: Three Rivers Press.

Ebrey, P. B., Walthall, A., & Palas, J. B. (2006). *East Asia: A cultural, social and political history.* Boston, MA: Houghton Mifflin.

Edmonson, M. S. (1973). The anthropology of values. In W. W. Taylor, J. L. Fischer, and E. Z. Vogt. (Eds), *Culture and Life: Essays in Honor of Clyde Kluckhohn.* Carbondale, IL: Southern Illinois University.

Eisenberg, E. M. (2006). *Strategic ambiguities.* Thousand Oaks, CA: Sage.

Eisenberg, E. M (2009). Organizational communicational theories. In S. W. Littlejohn & K. A. Foss. (Eds). *The Encyclopedia of Communication Theory 2.* Los Angeles, CA: Sage.

Eisenberg, R. & Smith, R. (1971). *Nonverbal communication.* Indianapolis, IN: Bobbs-Merrill.

Ekman, P. & Friesen, W. V. (2003). *Unmasking the face: A guide to recognizing emotions from facial Expressions.* Cambridge, MA: Malor Books.

Elegant, S. (2009: November 2). China's literary bad boy. *Time Asia.* 28.

Ellul, J. (1964). *The technological society.* New York, NY: Knopf.

English People's Daily Online (2009: September 23). *Han Han: Finding happiness by being different.*

Encarta World English Dictionary (1999).

Evans, K. (2001). *The lost daughters of China.* New York, NY: Jeremy P. Tarcher/ Putnam.

Evans, R. (1993). *Deng Xiaoping and the making of modern China.* New York, NY: Viking.

Everett, P., Williams, T., & Myers, M. (2004: August), *Evaluation of search for common ground activities in Sierra Leone.* http://www.sfcg.org/programmes/ westafrica/youth.pdf

Facebox (2010: January 15). *Education in China.*

Fang, T. (1999). *Chinese culture and Chinese business negotiation style.* Thousand Oaks, CA: Sage.

Flannery, R. (2010: November 26). China wealth: In search of China's new rich, Part I: The mainland. *Forbes Online.*

Fox, M. (1983/1996). *Original blessing: A primer on creation spirituality.* Rochester, VT: Bear & Company.

Friedman, T. L. (1999). *The Lexus and the olive tree: Understanding globalization.* New York, NY: Farrer, Straus and Giroux.

Friedman, T. L. (2007). *The world is flat: A brief history of the twenty-first century: Further updated and expanded.* New York, NY: Picador/Farrar, Straus and Giroux.

Fung, Y.-L. (2007). *A short history of Chinese philosophy.* New York, NY: Macmillan Company.

Fürst, J. (2001). *Cutting edge: Anti-Stalinist youth groups.* Retrieved, May 20, 2010, from http://www.timeshighereducation.co.uk/story.asp?storyCode=160227&se ctioncode=26

Gallo, F. T. (2011). *Business leadership in China: How to blend best western practices with Chinese wisdom. Revised edition.* Singapore: John Wiley & Sons.

Galvin, M., Prescott, D,. & Husman, R. (1992). *Business communication: Strategies and skills, fourth edition.* Sydney, Australia: Holt, Rinehart and Winston.

Gamble, T. & Gamble, M. (2002). *Communication works.* New York, NY: McGraw Hill.

Gao, G. (2009: December 4). The four modernizations. *English People's Daily.*

Gao, G. & Ting-Toomey, S. (1998). *Communicating effectively with the Chinese.* Thousand Oaks, CA: Sage.

Geertz, C. (Ed.) (1971). *Myth, symbol, and culture.* New York, NY: Basic Books.

Geertz, C. (1973). *The interpretation of cultures.* New York, NY: W.W. Norton..

General Administration of Press and Publications (GAPP) (2010). www.chinatoday.com.

Gibson, B. (2010: April 18). Making the world your classroom. *Daily Progress.*

Gillie, J. W., Ingle, S., & Mumford, H. (1996). *Read to write: An interactive course for non-native speakers of English.* New York, NY: ESL and Applied Linguistics Professional Series.

Giri, V. N. (2009). Intercultural communication theories. In S. W. Littlejohn and K. A. Foss (Eds.), *Encyclopedia of Communication Theory 1.* Los Angeles, CA: Sage.

Goman, C. K. (2008). *The nonverbal advantage: Secrets and science of body language at work.* San Francisco, CA: Berrett-Koehler Publishers, Inc.

Google mainland China service availability (2010: May 3). *Google China.*

Gostin, L. (2007: December 6). The journey of an intercultural/international communication scholar: Dr. Michael Prosser. *China Media Reports.*

Gray, J. (2005). *Men are from Mars, women are from Venus.* New York, NY: Vermillion.

Greenberg, J. H. (1971) *Language, culture, and communication: essays selected and introduced by Anwar S.Dill.* Stanford, CA: Stanford University.

Grossman, L. (2010: December 27). 2010 person of the year Mark Zuckerberg. *Time.*

Grumbine, R. E. (2010). *Where the dragon meets the angry river: Nature and power in the People's Republic of China.* Washington, DC: Island Press.

Guan, S. (2007). Foreword. In S. J. Kulich and M. H. Prosser. Eds. *Intercultural Perspectives on Chinese Communication.* Shanghai, China: Shanghai Foreign Language Education Press.

Gudykunst, W. B. (Ed.) (2003). *Cross-cultural and intercultural communication.* Thousand Oaks, CA: Sage.

Gudykunst, W. B. (Ed.) (2005). *Theorizing about intercultural communication.* Thousand Oaks, CA. Sage.

Gudykunst, W. B. & Kim, Y. Y. (2007). *Communicating with strangers: An approach to intercultural communication.* Shanghai, China: Shanghai Foreign Language Education Press.

Gudykunst, W. B. & Mody, B. (2002). *Communication in Japan and the United States.* Thousand Oaks, CA: Sage.

Guo , Z. Z. & Fu, H. S. (2004). *An anthology of popular ancient Chinese poems.* Wuhan, China: Wu Han University Press.

Haley, G. T., Haley, U. C. V., & Tan, C. T. (2009). *New Asian emperors: The business strategies of the overseas Chinese.* Singapore: John Wiley & Sons.

Hall, B. (2002). *Among cultures: The challenge of communication.* Belmont, CA: Wadsworth/Thompson Learning.

Hall, B. & Derryberry, W. P. (2010). *Are aversive racists distinguishable from those with high explicit racial prejudice? Beliefs and Values: Understanding the Global Implications of Human Nature.* New York, NY: Springer Publishing Company.

Hall, E. T. (1959). *The silent language.* New York, NY: Anchor Books.

Hall, E. T. (1959). *The silent language.* New York, NY: Fawcett.

Hall, E. T. (1966). *The hidden dimension.* New York, NY: Anchor Books.

Hall, E. T. (1976). *Beyond culture.* New York, NY: Anchor Books.

Hall, E. T. (1983). *The dance of life.* New York, NY: Anchor Books.

Hall, E. T. (1985). *Language, society and identity.* Oxford, England: Blackwell.

Hall, E. T. & Hall, R. H. (1990), *Understanding cultural differences: Germans, French, and Americans.* Yarmouth. ME: Intercultural Press.

Hall, P. M. & Hewitt, J. P. (1973). The quasi-theory of communication and the management of dissent. In M.H. Prosser (Ed.), *Intercommunication among Nations and peoples.* New York, NY: Harper and Row.

Hecht, M. L., Collier, M. J. & Ribeau, S. A. (1993). *African American communication: ethnic identity and cultural interpretation.* Newbury Park, CA: Sage Publications.

Heisey, D. R & Gong, W. (Eds.) (2000). *Chinese perspectives in rhetoric and communication.* Stamford, CT: Ablex.

Henry, J. (1963). *Culture against man.* Middlesex, England: Penguin.

Hindustan Times. (2006: January, 2006). *The Hindustan Times survey.*

Hofstede, G. (1980). *Culture's consequences.* Thousand Oaks, CA: Sage.

Hofstede, G. (1991). *Cultures and organizations: Software of the mind.* London, England: McGraw-Hill.

Hofstede, G. (2001). *Culture's consequences. 2nd edition.* Thousand Oaks, CA: Sage.

Hofstede, G. & Bond, M. (1984). Hofstede's culture dimensions. Journal of Cross-Cultural Psychology. 15: 417–433.

Hong, Y.-y., Morris, M. W., Chiu, C.-y., & Benet-Martínez, V. (2000). Multicultural minds: A dynamic constructivist approach to culture and cognition. *American Psychologist, 55*, 709–720.

Hood, G. (2005). *Tsotsi.* Johannesberg, South Africa, Miramax Home Entertainment.

Howe, N. & Strauss, W. (1992: December). The new generation gap. *Atlantic Monthly.*

Hu, G. (2010). *On managing cultural integration in cross-border acquisitions from the perspective of China's IT industry.* Unpublished MA thesis, Shanghai, China: Shanghai International Studies University.

Huckin, T. N. & Olsen, L. A. (1991). *Technical writing and professional communication for non-native speakers.* New York, NY: Educational Linguistics.

Hughes, C. R. (2006). *Chinese nationalism in the global era.* London, England: Routledge.

Hui, C.-c. (2010). *Clever, creative, modest: The Chinese language practice.* Shanghai: Shanghai Foreign Language Education Press.

Huntington, S. P. (1996). *The clash of civilizations and the remaking of world order.* New York, NY: Touchstone.

Hutton, W. (2006). *The writing on the wall: Why we must embrace China as a partner or face it as an enemy.* New York, NY: The Free Press.

Hwang, K. K. (2007). The development of indigenous social psychology in Confucian society. In S. J .Kulich and M. H. Prosser (Eds.), *Intercultural perspectives on Chinese communication.* Shanghai, China: Shanghai Foreign Language Education Press.

Inglehart, R. F., & Welzel, C. (2005). *Modernization, cultural change, and democracy: the human development sequence.* Cambridge, England: Cambridge University Press.

Institute of Sociology RAN (2007). *Molodyozh novoi Rossii: Tsennostnye prioritety. Youth in new Russia. Values and Priorities.* Retrieved May 20, 2010, from http://www.isras.ru/analytical_report_Youth.html

Internet Timeline of China (2010: March 24). China Internet Network Information Center.

Jandt, F. E. (1995). *Intercultural communication: An introduction.* Thousand Oaks, CA: Sage.

Japanese Center for Intercultural Communication Website (2008).

Jensen, J. V. (1987) Rhetorical emphasis of Taoism. *Rhetorica. 5,* 3.

Jia, W., Lu, X., & Heisey, D. R. (2002). *Chinese communication theory and research: Reflections, new frontiers, and new directions.* Stamford, CT: Ablex.

Jia, Y. & Jia, X. (2007). The study of Chinese language behavior cross-culturally: A sociolinguistic approach to intercultural communication. In S. J. Kulich and M. H. Prosser (Eds.), *Intercultural perspectives on Chinese communication.* Shanghai, China: Shanghai Foreign Language Education Press.

Kale, D. (1991). Ethics in intercultural communication. In L. A. Samovar and R. E. Porter (Eds.), *Intercultural communication: a reader.* Belmont, CA: Wadsworth.

Kelly, A. (2010: May 5). The great brain race: Review, *The American: The Journal of the American Enterprise Institute.*

Kim, E. Y. (2011). *The yin and yang of American culture: A paradox.* Yarmouth, ME: Intercutural Press.

Kim, K. S. (2002). *Non-western perspectives on human communication: Implications for theory and practice.* Thousand Oaks, CA: Sage.

Kincaid, L. D. (2009). Convergence theory. In S. W. Littlejohn and K. A. Foss (Eds.), *Encyclopedia of communication theory. 1.* Los Angeles, CA: Sage.

Kluckhohn, F. R. & Strodbeck, F. L. (1961). *Variations in value orientations.* Evanston, IL: Row, Peterson.

Klyukanov, I. E. (2005). *Principles of Intercultural Communication.* Boston, MA: Pearson.

Klyukanov, I. E. (2010). *A communication universe: Manifestations of meaning, stagings of significance.* Boulder, CO: Lexington Books.

Kluver, R. (1999). Elite-based discourse in Chinese civil society. In R. Kluver and J. H. Powers (Eds.), *Civic discourse, civil society and Chinese communities.* Stamford: CT: Ablex.

Knapp, M. L. (1972). *Nonverbal communication in human interaction.* New York, NY: Holt.

Knapp, M. L, & Hall, J. A. (2009). *Nonverbal communication in human interaction.* New York, NY: Holt.

Kroeber, A. (2010: April 11). Five myths about the Chinese economy. *The Washington Post.*

Kulich, S. J. (2007). Chapter 1: Introduction: Linking intercultural communication with China studies—Language and relationship perspectives. In S. J. Kulich and M. H. Prosser (Eds.), *Intercultural perspectives on Chinese communication.* Shanghai, China: Shanghai Foreign Language Education Press.

Kulich, S. J. (2009). Values theory: Sociocultural dimensions and frameworks. In S. W. Littlejohn and K. A. Foss (Eds), *Encyclopedia of communication theory 2.* Los Angeles, CA: Sage.

Kulich, S. J ., Prosser, M. H., & Weng, L. P. (Eds) (2011). *Value frameworks at the theoretical crossroads of culture.* Shanghai, China: Shanghai Foreign Language Education Press.

Kulich, S. J., Weng, L. P., & Prosser, M. H. (Eds.) (2011). *Value dimensions and dynamics across cultures.* Shanghai, China: Shanghai Foreign Language Education Press.

Kulich, S. J. & Zhang, R. (2010). The multiple frames of 'Chinese' values: From tradition to modernity and beyond. In M. H. Bond (Ed.), *The Oxford handbook of Chinese psychology* (pp. 241–278). New York, NY: Oxford University Press.

Laroche, L. & Rutherford, D. (2007). *Recruiting, retaining and promoting culturally different employees.* Amsterdam: The Netherlands: Elsivier.

Lao Tzu. (1999) *Tao Te Ching.* Translated by Arthur Waley. Beijing, China: Foreign Language Teaching and Research Press.

Lederer, R. (1996). *Crazy English: The ultimate joy ride through our language.* New York, NY: Pocket Books.

Levett, M. (2010: March 20). www.thirdculturestories.com .

Lewin, T. (2010: November 15). China surges past India as top home of foreign students. *New York Times.*

Liang, S. (2008). *The whole essence of Chinese culture.* Shanghai, China: Shanghai People's Publishing House.

Lin, Y. T. (2004). *My country and my people.* Beijing, China: Foreign Language Teaching and Research Press.

Lin, Y. T. (2005). The importance of living. Beijing, China: Foreign Language Teaching and Research Press.

Lindner, E. (2010). *Gender, humiliation, and global security: Dignifying relationships from love, sex and parenthood to world affairs.* Contemporary Psychology Series. Santa Barbara, CA: Praeger Security International.

Locke, J. (1690, 2005). *An essay concerning humane understanding.* Encyclopedia Encarta Online.

Lu, X., Jia, W., & Heisey, D. R. (Eds.) (2002). *Chinese communication studies: Contexts and Comparisons.* Stamford, CT: Ablex.

Lustgarten, A. (2008). *China's great train: Beijing's drive west and the campaign to remake Tibet.* New York, NY: Henry Holt and Co.

Lustig, M. W. & Koester, J. (2007). *Intercultural competence: Interpersonal commuinication across cultures. 5th edition.* Shanghai, China: Shanghai Foreign Language Education Press.

MA, Doctoral and post doctoral theses from the People's Republic of China (annual).

Ma, R. (2002).The interface between culture and technology in Chinese communication. In Jia, W., Lu, X, and Heisey, D. R. (2002), *Chinese Communication and Research.* Westport, CT: Ablex.

Ma, Y. Y. (2010, March 6). *BBC World Wide Television.*

Mandela, N. R. (1994). *The long road to freedom.The authobiography of Nelson Mandela.* London, England: Abacus.

Marchette, G., Feng, P. X., & Tan, S.-K. (2009). *Chinese connections: Critical perspectives on film identity and disapora.* Singapore: John Wiley and Sons.

Markus, H. R. & Kitayama, S. (1991). Culture and the self: Implications for cognition, emotion, and motivation. *Psychological Review, 20,* 568–579.

Martin, J. (2002). *Organizational culture: Mapping the terrain.* Thousand Oaks, CA: Sage.

Martinez, A. (2010: March 22). The next American century: Don't believe the prophets of doom. *Time.*

Martinez, W. (2008). The challenges of a pioneer: Tim Asch, otherness, and film reception. Visual Anthropology Review 1 (1): 53–82.

Mathews, G. and White, B. (2006). *Japan's changing generations: Are young people creating a new society?* London: : Routledge: Japan Anthropology Workshop.

Mavides, G. & Hayes, K. (2007). *Foreign teachers' guide to living and working in China.* [city, publisher not identified].

McKay, S. L. & Bokhorse-Heng, W.D. (2008). International English in its sociolinguistic contexts: Towards a socially sensitive EIL pedagogy. New York, NY: ESL and Applied Linguistics Professional Series.

McLuhan, H. M. (1964). *Understanding media: The extensions of man.* New York, NY: New American Library.

McLuhan, H. M. (1970). *Culture is our business.* New York, NY: New American Library.

McPhail, T. L. (2010). *Global communication: Theories, stakeholders, and trend (3rd edition).* Malden, MA: Wiley-Blackwell.

Mead, M. (1970). *Culture and commitment.* Garden City, NY: Doubleday.

Merrill, J. C. (1989). Global commonalities for journalistic ethics: Idle dreams or realistic goal. In T. W. Cooper (Ed.), *Communication Ethics and Global Change.* 284–290. White Plains, NY: Longman.

Milyukova, I. (2002). The political future of Russia through the eyes of young students. *Young, 10,* 3/4, 12–25

Montagu, A. (1971). *Touching: The human significance of the skin.* New York, NY: Columbia.

Moore, M. (2010: April 16). Nanjing: A journey to hell!" *TheTelegraph.*

Mumford, L. (1962). *Technics and civilization.* New York, NY: Harcourt, Brace & World.

Murdoch, G. (1945). Common denominator of cultures. In R. Linton (Ed.), *Science of Man in the World Crises.* New York, NY: Columbia University Press.

Nanda, R. T. (1997). *Contemporary approaches to value education in India.* Washington, D.C.: Regency.

Networked Digital Library of Theses and Dissertations (DLTD). (annual).

Nocotera, A. M. (2009). Conflict communication theories. In S. W. Littlejohn and K. A. Foss (Eds.), *Encyclopedia of Communication Theories 1.* Los Angeles, CA: Sage.

Nieburg, H. L. (1973). *Culture storm: Politics and the world order.* New York, NY: St. Martin.

[No author] (2003: December 26). *Li Yang a crazy talker.* www.cityweekend.com.

[No author] (2003).*What is public diplomacy? Washington,* DC: US Information Agency Alumni Association

[No author] (2010). Best Chinese writers. My Top Dozen.

[No author]. (2010). Chinese radio. Wikipedia.

[No author] (2010: November China Central TV (CCTV). Wikipedia.

[No author] (2010: June 30) Chinese internet. Statistical Survey Report.

O'Connor, P. T. (2005). *Woe is I: The grammaphobe's guide to better English in plain English.* New York, NY: Penguin.

Oliver, R. T. (1971). *Communication and culture in ancient India and China.* Syracuse, NY: Syracuse University Press.

Obama, B. H. (2008). *Audacity of hope: Reclaiming the American dream.* New York, NY: Crown.

Osgood, C. E., May, W. H. & Miron, M. S. (1975). *Cross-cultural universals of affective meaning.* Urbana, IL: University of Illinois.

Pan, F. & Wen, S. X. (2004). *The Analects of Confucius.* [Chinese-English Bilingual Edition]. Jinan, China: Qilu Press.

Pant, S. (2009). International development theories. In S. W. Littlejohn and K. A. Foss (Eds.), *Encyclopedia of Communication Theory 1.* Los Angeles, CA: Sage.

Pautova, L. (2009, December). *iX izuchaet Y i vospityvaet Z. Russki reportyor.* Retrieved 20, 2010, from www.rusrep.ru/2010/12/sociologi_o_pokolenii

Pautova, L. & Lebedev, P. (2008). *Molodyozh kak tselevaya auitoriya v internete: Segmenty i podxody k nim.* Retrieved May 20, 2010, from http://bd.fom.ru/report/map/pokolenie21/pr_r210410np

Pearce, K. J. (2009). Media and mass communication theories. In S. W. Littlejohn and K. A. Foss (Eds.), *Encyclopedia of Communication Theory 2.* Los Angeles, CA: Sage.

Pease, B. E. (2005). *The definitive book of body language.* New York, NY: Bantam Dell.

People's Daily Online (2009: December 4). America becoming isolationist.

People's Daily Online (2009: December 4). Wordsmith [Han Han] is feeling misunderstood. *China Daily.*

People's Daily Online (2010: January 22). Chorus of Approval for Han Han. *China Daily.*

People's Daily Online (2010: April 7). Han Han makes Time magazine top 100. *China Daily.*

Pollock, D. C. & Van Reken, R. E. (2005). *Third culture kids: growing up among worlds.* New York, NY: Nicholas Brealey.

Powers, J. H. & Kluver, R. (1999). Introduction: Civic discourse and civil society in Chinese communities. In R. Kluver and J. H. Powers. (Eds.), *Civic Discourse, Civil Societies, and Chinese Communities.* Stamford, CT: Ablex.

Pribram, K. (1949). *Conflicting patterns of thought.* Washington, DC: Public Affairs Press.

Prosser, M. E. (2008). *Excuse me, your God is waiting.* Charlottesville, VA: Hampton Roads Publishing Co

Prosser, M. H. (1970). *Sow the wind, reap the whirlwind: Heads of state address the United Nations (two volumes).* New York, NY: William Morrow.

Prosser, M. H. (Ed.) (1973). *Intercommunication among nations and peoples.* New York, NY: Harper and Row.

Prosser, M. H. (1978, 1985, 1989). *The cultural dialogue: An introduction to intercultural communication.* Boston: Houghton Mifflin; Washington, D.C.: SIETAR International. Trans. into Japanese by R. Okabe. Tokyo: Toko University Press.

Prosser, M. H. (2003–2011). www.michaelprosser.com.

Prosser, M. H. (2007: April). China: Selected books in English. *Review of Communication [online]. 7*(2) 135–179.

Prosser, M. H. (2007). One world, one dream: Harmonizing society through intercultural communication: A prelude to China intercultural communication studies.In S. J. Kulich and M. H. Prosser (Eds.), *Intercultural Perspectives on Chinese Communication.* Shanghai, China: Shanghai Foreign Language Education Press.

Prosser, M. H. (2009). Cross-cultural communication. In S. W. Littlejohn and K. A. Foss (Eds.), *Encyclopedia of Communication 1.* Thousand Oaks, CA: Sage.

Prosser, M. H. (2009). Media diplomacy. In S. W. Littlejohn and K. A. Foss (Eds.), *Encyclopedia of Communication 2.* Thousand Oaks, CA: Sage.

Prosser, M. H. (2009: September). Obama's culturally transformational identities and accommodations toward the Middle East and Islam. *Journal of the Middle Eastern and Islamic Studies (in Asia) 3*(3).

Prosser, M. H. (2010). Barack Obama: Culturally transformational identities and accommodations. In S. D. Dai, and S. J. Kulich (Eds.), *Identity and Intercultural Communication I: Theoretical and Contextual Construction.* Intercultural Research. 2. Shanghai, China: Shanghai Foreign Language Education Press.

Prosser, M. H. (2010). Contemporary Chinese youth: Language and culture. In O. Leontovich (Ed.), *Chinese Linguoculture in the Modern Global World.* Volgograd, Russia: Peremena Press.

Prosser, M. H. (2011). Universal human rights as universal rights. In S. J. Kulich and M. H. Prosser (Eds.), *Value Frameworks at the Theoretical Crossroads of Culture: Intercultural Research*, 3. Shanghai, Chinai: Shanghai Foreign Language Education Press.

Prosser, M. H. & Sitaram, K. S. (Eds) (1999). *Civic discourse: Intercultural, international and global media.* Westport, CT: Ablex.

Pryor, J. H. et al. (2009: Fall). *The American freshman national norms fall 2009.* www.heri.ucla.edu .

Raghatta, C. (2008: July). Bollywood in Hollywood. *The Times of India.*

Raj A. (2007). Indian cinema and Indian disapora. In D. Dicispora and S. Steinberg (Eds.), *Media Literacy: A Reader.* New York, NY: Peter Lang.

Random House Webster's Dictionary (1991).

Reich, C. A. (1971: March 8). Beyond consciousness. *The New York Times,* 311.

Reynolds, M. M. (1985). *Guide to theses and dissertations: An international bibliography of bibliographies, Revised and enlarged.* Phoenix, AZ: Oryx.

Rich, F. (2010: March 27). The rage is not about health care. *The New York Times.*

Ritzer, G. (1996). *The McDonaldization of Society. An Investigation into the Changing Character of Contemporary Social Life, revised edition.* Thousand Oaks, CA: Pine Forge Press.

Ross, R. B. & Faulkner, S. L.(1998). Hofstede's dimensions: An examination and critical analysis. In K. S.Sitaram and M. H. Prosser (Eds.), *Civic Discourse: Multiculturalism, Cultural Diversity, and Global Communication.* Stamford, CT: Ablex.

Rubin, B. D. (1922). *Communication and human behavior, 3rd edition.* Englewood Cliffs, NJ: Prentice-Hall.

Russell, B. (1959). *My philosophical development.* New York, NY: Simon and Schuster.

Salam, R. (2010: March 22, 46–47). The dropout economy: The future of work looks a lot like unemployment. *Time.*

Samovar, L. A. & Porter, R. E. (2004). *Intercultural communication: A reader.* Belmont, CA: Wadsworth.

Samovar, L. A. & Porter, R. E. (2004). *Communication between Cultures, fifth edition.* Beijing: Peking University Press.

Samovar, L. A., Porter, R.E., & McDaniel, E. R. (2008). *Intercultural communication: A reader. 12th edition.* Belmont, CA: Wadsworth.

Samovar, L. A., Porter, R. E. & McDaniel, E. R. (2009). *Communication between cultures. sixth edition.* Beijing, China: Peking University Press.

Shanahan, J (2009). Broadcasting theory. In S. W. Littlejohn and K. A. Foss (Eds.), *The Encyclopedia of Communication Theory. 1.* Los Angeles, CA: Sage.

Shanahan, J. & Morgan, M. (1999). T*elevision and its viewers: Cultivation theory and research.* London, England: Cambridge University Press.

Shiemke, A. et al. (2006). Japanese communication practices website.

Shine from Yahoo. (2010: December 1). Ten things your teenager won't tell you.

Singer, P. W. (2009). *Wired for war: The robotics revolution and conflict in the 21st century.* New York, NY: Penguin Books.

Sitaram, K. S. (1995). *Communication and culture: A world view.* New York, NY: McGraw Hill.

Sitaram, K. S. & Cogdell, R. (1976). *Foundations of intercultural communication.* Columbus, OH: Merrill.

Sitaram, K. S. & Prosser, M. H. (Eds.) (1998). *Civic discourse: Multiculturalism, cultural diversity, and global communication.* Westport, CT. Ablex.

Skinner, B. F. (1971). *Beyond freedom and control.* New York, NY: Knopf.

Slomanson, W. R. (2010). *Fundamental perspectives on international law.* London, England: West Group Publishers.

Spurlock, M. (2004). *Super Size Me: A film of epic portions. Feature documentary movie.* Kathbur Pictures, Inc.

State Commission for Population and Family Planning (2007: January 18). Labor surplus of 150–170 million in country side. *China Daily.*

Statistical survey report on Internet development in China (2010: June 30). China Internet Network Information Center.

Steven, J. (2010: January 12). China's migrant workers. www.libcom.org .

Stevenson, R. L. (1994). *Global communication in the twenty-first century.* White Plains, NY: Longmans.

Stewart, E. C. (1971). *American cultural patterns: A cross-cultural perspective.* Washington, DC: SIETAR International.

Stewart, E. C. (1984). Outline of intercultural communication. In F. Casmir (Ed.), *International and Intercultural communication.* Washington, DC: University Press.

Strunk, W., Jr., White, E. B. & Angell, R. (2000). *Elements of Style. Fourth Edition.* New York, NY: Longman.

Sun, K.-I. & Owen, S. (Eds.). *The Cambridge history of Chinese literature. 2 vols.* Cambridge, England: Cambridge University Press.

Swerdlow, A., Bridenthal, R., Kelly, J. & Vine, P. (1989). *Families in flux.* New York, NY: Feminist Press.

Tan, Y. (2011). *Chinnovation: How Chinese innovators are changing the world.* Singapore: John Wiley & Sons.

The value of perspective (2010). *Beliefs and Values: Understanding the global implications of human nature.* New York, NY: Springer.

Thomas, C., Cooper, P. J., & Blake, C. (1999). *Intercultural communication: Roots and routes.* Boston, MA: Allyn and Bacon, Co.

Thomas, D. C. & Inkson, K. (2004). *Cultural intelligence: People skills for global business.* San Francisco, CA: Berrett-Koehler.

Thomson, A. (2010: January 6). Post to festivals, games, documentaries. Blog.

Ting-Toomey, S. (1999). *Communicating across cultures.* Shanghai, China: Shanghai Foreign Language Education Press.

Ting-Toomey, S. (2007). *Communicating across cultures.* New York, NY: The Guilford Press.

Top 10 English newspapers in the world. www.mapsoftheworld.com (2010: December 6).

Top 10 online newspapers. www.virotourist.com (2010).

Toyomasu, K. G. (Ed.) (2001: January 10). *Haiku for people.* www.toyomasu.dot.com

Tracy, S. J. (2009). Organizational culture. In S. W. Littlejohn and K. A. Foss (Eds.), *The Encyclopedia of Communication Theory 2.* Los Angeles, CA: Sage.

Trompenaars, F. (1993). *Riding the waves of culture: Understanding cultural diversity in business.* London, England: Nicholas Brealey.

Trudgill, P. & Nahan, J. (2008). *International English: A guide to the varieties of standard English, Fifth Edition.* London, England: Hachette UK Co.

Tsai, C. C. (2005). *Confucius speaks.* Beijing, China: Modern Press.

Tsai, C. C. (2005). *Mencius speaks.* Beijing, China: Modern Press.

Tsai C. C. (2005) *Zhuang Zi speaks I: The music of nature.* Beijing, China: Modern Press.

Turdi, D. (2007). *Bilingual education and intercultural communication among Uyghurs in Xinjiang* [Abstract]. Unpublished MA thesis. Shanghai, China: Shanghai International Studies University.

United Nations Charter (1945). New York, NY: United Nations.

United Nations (2009). UN Human Development Report. New York, NY: United Nations.

Universal Declaration of Human Rights (1948). New York, NY: United Nations.

US Census Bureau (2000). List of United States cities by population. Washington, DC. US Census Bureau.

Useem, R. (1993: January). Third culture kids: Focus of major study—TCK "mother" pens history of field. *Newslinks—the Newspaper of International Schools Services.Vol. xii*(3). Princeton, N.J.

Useem, R. (1999). *Third culture kids biography: Studies in third cultures.* London, England: Academic Press.

Varis, T. (1998). Foreword. In K. S. Sitaram and M. H. Prosser (Eds.), *Civic Discourse: Multiculturalism, Cultural Diversity and Global Communication.* Stamford, CT: Ablex.

Views of Indian Youth (2006: January 25). *Hindustan Times.*

Walsh, J. E. (1974). *Intercultural education in the community of man.* Honolulu, HA: East-West Center Press.

Walsh, W. (2004). *The elephants of style: A trunkload of tips on the big issues and greay areas of contemporary American English.* New York, NY: McGraw Hill.

Wang, H. (2010: December 8). The Chinese dream: The rise of the world's largest middle class and what It means to you. *Forbes Magazine.*

Wardhaugh, R. (1998). *An introduction to sociolinguistics.* London, England: Blackwell Publishers Ltd.

Wasserstrom, J. (2010). *China in the 21st century: What everyone needs to know.* Palo Alto, CA: Stanford University Press.

Weiss, E. H. (2005). *The elements of international English style: A guide to writing correspondence, reports, technical documents and Internet pages for a global audience.* Armonk, NY: Sharpe.

Weng, L P. (2007). *Revisiting Chinese values through self-generated proverbs and sayings.* Unpublished MA thesis. Shanghai: China: Shanghai International Studies University.

Werder, O. H. (2009), Advertising theories. In S. W. Littlejohn and K. A. Foss (Eds.), *The Encycopedia of Communication Theory 1*. Los Angeles, CA: Sage.

Wikipedia (2010). Chinese literature. www.wikipedia.com.

Wildasky, B. (2010). *The great brain race: How global universities are reshaping the world*. Princeton, NJ: Princeton University Press.

Williams, A. F. & Monge, P. R. (2001). *Reasoning with statistics: How to read quantitative research*. New York, NY: Hartcourt College Publishers.

Williams, R. (2003). *Television, technology and cultural form (3rd ed.)*. New York, NY: Routledge.

Williams, T. & Myers, A. M.(2004: August). *Evaluation of search for common ground activities in Sierra Leone*. http://www.sfcg.org/programmes/westafrica/youth.pdf

Wong, E. (2009: May 23). The Saturday profile: A glimmer of humanity amid the atrocities of war. *New York Times*.

World press trends (2008). World Association of Newspapers and Journalists.

World Radio Online (2010). FREE Internet radio stations and online television TV Tuner with World TVRT.

Wu, T. (2010: March 22). Bandwidth is the new black gold: And it's a scarce resource. *Time*.

Xu, G.G. (2007). *Sinacape: Contemporary Chinese cinema*. Oxford, England: Rowman and Litchfield.

Yang, X. (2007). Integrating experiential learning techniques into intercultural communication courses. Unpublished MA thesis [Abstract]. Shanghai, China: Shanghai International Studies University.

Yu, W. (2009). Chinese Students' Acculturation in the U.K. and Their Use of Xiaonei. Unpublished MA thesis [Abstract]. Shanghai, China: Shanghai International Studies University.

Zhang, L. (2009). *Investigations into the influence of an intercultural communication founder—Michael H. Prosser, and his contemporary scholars*. Unpublished MA thesis, Shanghai, China: Shanghai International Studies University. [This thesis is located on www.michaelprosser.com.]

Zhang, R. (2007). *Multiple modernities: A comparative study on styles of managing interpersonal conflicts between American and Chinese university students*. Unpublished Master's thesis. Shanghai, China: Shanghai International Studies University.

Zhang, S. Y. (2009). *USCC's cognition on China and its influence on Sino-US relations.* Unpublished MA thesis. Shanghai, China: Shanghai International Studies University.

Zhang, S. Y. & Prosser, M. H. (2010: Autumn). G2 languages: Chinese and English. *Intercultural Communication Research.*

Zhang, S. Y. & Prosser, M. H. (2011: April). A comparative review of three current books on China. *China Media Reports.*

Zhang, Y. (2008). Reconsidering Schwartz's 10 basic human value types and locating young people. Unpublished MA thesis [Abstract]. Shanghai, China: Shanghai International Studies University.

Zhang, Y. & Goza, F. W. (2006). Who will care for the elderly in China? A review of the problems caused by China's one-child policy and their potential solutions. *Journal of Aging Studies. 20,* 2.

Zhao, X. (2010). *The new Chinese America: Class, economy, and social hierarchy.* Piscataway, NJ: Rutgers University Press.

Zhou, J. (2006). *Higher education in China.* Singapore: Thomson.

Zhou, M. (2009). *Contemporary Chinese: Immigration, ethnicity and community transformation.* Philadelphia, PA: Temple University Press.

Zhou, S. L., Prosser, M. H. & Lu, J. (2003). *Sino-American compositions of shared topics.* Zheng Zhou, China: The Heinan People's Press.

Zhu, W. (2007: September). Dialogue among civilizations: A close look at the Greater Middle East reform. *Journal of Middle Eastern and Islamic Studies in Asia. 1*(1).

Zhu Y. (2005). *Written communication across cultures, xxx.* John Benjamins Publishing Co.

Zoreda, M. L. (2006). Intercultural moments in teaching English through film. *Reencuentro 47,* 64–71.

Academic Biographies of Li Mengyu and Michael H. Prosser

Li **Mengyu** (Ph.D., Shandong Normal University), a Professor at Ocean University of China, has been a visiting scholar in the Institute for Intercultural Com-munication at the University of Louisville and the Center for Faulkner Studies at Southeast Missouri State University. She was a visiting scholar in the English Faculty at Cambridge University in 2013. She is a member of the International Association for Intercultural Communication Studies as well as of the China Association for Intercultural Communication. Her major academic interests include intercultural communication and comparative literature in the study of Shen Congwen and William Faulkner.

She is the author or coauthor of five books. Her book *The Comparative Study of Shen Congwen and Faulkner's Novels in Multidimensional Perspectives* was the first monograph dedicated to both the comprehensive and in-depth comparative study of the Chinese writer Shen Congwen's and American writer William Faulkners' novels. She has published thirty academic papers

The Authors of the Textbook at the 9th CAFIC Conference, Fuzhou, China

in Chinese authoritative and core journals such as *Literary Review*, *Chinese Comparative Literature*, Foreign Literature Studies, the international *Intercultural Communication Studies* and *China Media Research* (published simultaneously in mainland China and the United States).

She has been the First Prize Winner of the Qingdao Social Science Research Award and the Second Prize Winner of Shandong Social Science Research Award as well as other academic prizes. In addition, she has also undertaken many research projects, such as "The Intercultural Communication Study on the Chinese and Western Cultures (a key project approved by the Department of Culture of Shandong Province in 2009), "Intercultural Communication Textbook project "(a supporting project by "Textbook Construction Project Fund of Ocean University of China," 2006) and "Bilingual Teaching Innovation System Analysis" project (a supporting project by the "Undergraduate Teaching Research Project Fund of Ocean University of China", 2007).

She has been invited to attend many international and national conferences. She chaired the session on "Culture and Communication" in the 14th IAICS conference held in the United States and was a chair of the session on "Nonverbal Communication" at the 15th IAICS Conference held in Kumamoto, Japan, and a discussant in the 2008 Macau Conference on Linguistic and Intercultural Communication. She was a participant at the International Communication Association Conference in Singapore in 2010.

In her twenty years of university teaching, Li Mengyu has taught more than 3,000 students and has given independent lectures on intercultural communication, foreign literature, comparative literature, appreciation of English poetry, and English. Her "Intercultural Communication" course taught bilingually (English and Chinese) was rated as an "Excellent Course" by Ocean University of China in 2007.

She also serves as the tutor for a large number of students' research projects as well as for field trips to CCTV-9 television station, Qingdao television station, *Qingdao Morning Newspaper*, and ZhaoYuan television station.

Michael H. Prosser (Ph.D., University of Illinois), a founder of the academic field of intercultural communication, has been Professor Emeritus of the University of Virginia (1972–2001); Fulbright Professor at the University of Swaziland (1990–1991); the former William A. Kern and Distinguished Professor of the Rochester Institute of Technology (1994–2001); Professor at Yangzhou University (2001–2002); Distinguished Professor at Beijing Language and Culture University (2002-2005); Distinguished Professor at the Shanghai International Studies University (2005–2009); and Distinguished Professor at Ocean University of China (spring, 2011). He is chair of the International Advisory Board and Senior Co-editor of Intercultural Research of SISU Intercultural Institute at Shanghai International Studies University.

He is editor or author of fifteen books, including most recently as coeditor with Steve J. Kulich: *Intercultural Perspectives on Chinese Communication* (2007); *Values at the Theoretical Crossroads of Culture* (2011); and *Values: Dynamic Dimensions across Cultures* (2011). He was the series editor for "Civic Discourse for the Third Millennium" with eighteen books published by Ablex/Praeger, and Greenwood Publishers in the United States, 1998–2004.

He has taught 8,800 students in North America and more than 2,300 Chinese university students in four Chinese universities.

He has been a keynoter at thirteen Chinese communication conferences, and has given independent lectures to more than 8,000 secondary and university students in Cambodia, Canada, China, India, Japan, Russia, Singapore and Republic of Korea on topics such as intercultural and international communication and media, civic and rhetorical discourse, globalism and globalization, and the United Nations. He has been a frequent interviewee on CCTV 9 International's *Dialogue*, Shanghai International Channel, and China Radio International and was featured in *China Talent Semimonthly Magazine* in 2005 (in Chinese). Former President of the International Society for Intercultural Education, Training and Research, he received the first special award for contributions to intercultural communication in China by the China Association for Intercultural Communication in 2009. He is listed in the *Marquis Who's Who in American Education, Who's Who in America, Who's Who in Asia*, and *Who's Who in the World*. He is a Fellow of the International Academy of Intercultural Researchers.

ACKNOWLEDGMENT

Permission to reprint the following material is gratefully acknowledged:

Bob Gibson. Making the World Your Classroom. *Daily Progress*. 2010: April 10.

Richard Lederer (2010). *English Is a Crazy Language.*

Michael H. Prosser (2009). "Cross-Cultural Communication." *Encyclopedia of Communication Theory I*. Co-edited by Stephen W. Littlejohn and Karen A. Foss, Los Angeles: Sage Publications, Inc. 247–251.

Michael H. Prosser (2009). Media Diplomacy. *Encyclopedia of Communication Theory 2*. Co-edited by Stephen W. Littlejohn and Karen A. Foss. Los Angeles: Sage Publications, Inc. 627–612.

Li Mengyu and Michael H. Prosser express their gratitude to Dr. Uli Spalthoff of Dignity Press and Sun Yunpeng of Higher Education Press for their tireless efforts to bring this North American edition to publication.

With permission of Higher Education Press, this North American edition has added "Chinese" to the original edition title,, and has deleted the suggested readings and references in Chinese published originally by Higher Education Press (ISBN 978-7040345308).

INTERCULTURAL COMMUNICATION
MORE BOOKS FROM DIGNITY PRESS

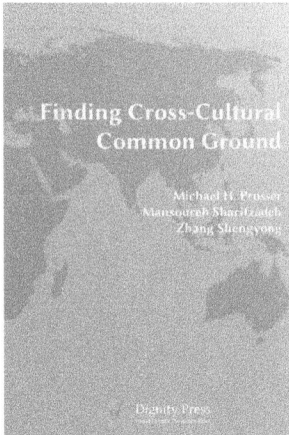

Michael H. Prosser, Mansoureh Sharifzadeh, Zhang Shengyong
Finding Cross-Cultural Common Ground

March 2013, 511 pages, softcover

ISBN 978-1-937570-25-5

www.dignitypress.org/fcccg

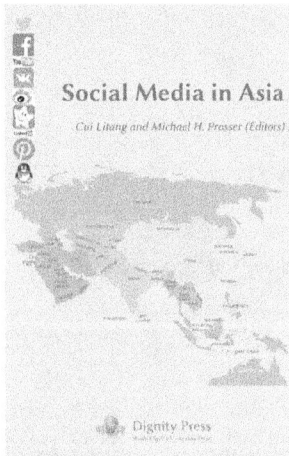

Cui Litang, Michael H. Prosser
Social Media in Asia

February 2014, 686 pages, softcover

ISBN 978-1-937570-36-1

www.dignitypress.org/social-media-in-asia

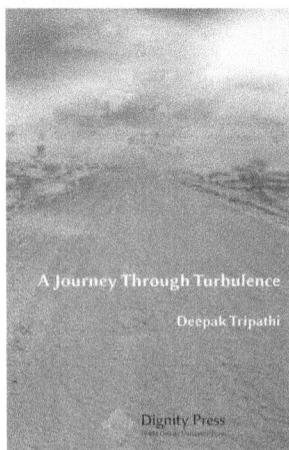

Deepak Tripathi
A Journey Through Turbulence

March 2013, 255 pages, softcover

ISBN 978-1-937570-32-3

www.dignitypress.org/turbulence

Dignity Press
World Dignity University Press

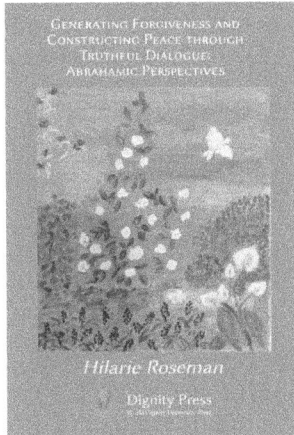

Hilarie Roseman

Generating Forgiveness and Constructing Peace through Truthful Dialogue: Abrahamic Perspectives

April 2014, xvi + 413 pages, softcover

ISBN 978-1-937570-48-4

www.dignitypress.org/forgiveness

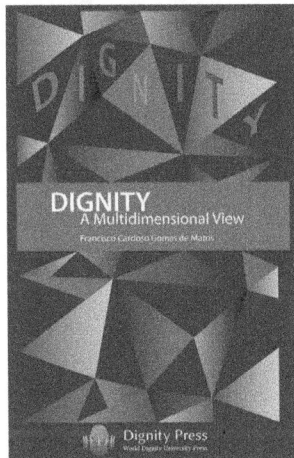

Francisco Cardoso Gomes de Matos

Dignity - A Multidimensional View

September 2013, 143 pages, hardcover

ISBN 978-1-937570-37-8

www.dignitypress.org/dignity-multidimensional

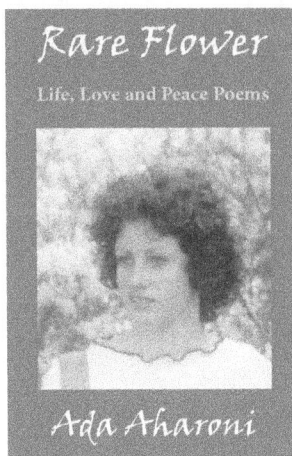

Ada Aharoni

Rare Flower – Life, Love and Peace Poems

November 2012, 324 pages, hardcover

ISBN 978-1-937570-10-1

www.dignitypress.org/rare-flower

Dignity Press
World Dignity University Press

www.ingramcontent.com/pod-product-compliance
Lightning Source LLC
Chambersburg PA
CBHW080604270326
41928CB00016B/2920